THE COMEBACK

Also by Daniel de Visé

I Forgot to Remember:
A Memoir of Amnesia (with Su Meck)

Andy and Don:
The Making of a Friendship and a Classic American TV Show

THE COMEBACK

Greg LeMond, the True King of American Cycling, and a Legendary Tour de France

DANIEL DE VISÉ

Atlantic Monthly Press

New York

FIRST EDITION

Published simultaneously in Canada
Printed in the United States of America

Text designer: Norman E. Tuttle at Alpha Design & Composition
This book was set in ITC New Baskerville
by Alpha Design & Composition of Pittsfield, NH

First Grove Atlantic hardcover edition: June 2018

Library of Congress Cataloguing-in-Publication data is available for this title.

ISBN 978-0-8021-2794-5
eISBN 978-0-8021-6579-4

Atlantic Monthly Press
an imprint of Grove Atlantic
154 West 14th Street
New York, NY 10011

Distributed by Publishers Group West

groveatlantic.com

18 19 20 21 10 9 8 7 6 5 4 3 2 1

To Pop

"It never gets easier, you just get faster."
—Greg LeMond

CONTENTS

THE COMEBACK

PROLOGUE

O N A SMALL PATCH OF BLACKTOP in a crowded plaza near the grand palace of Versailles, two riders pedaled bicycles in a warm-up exercise around a tiny oval, riding counterclockwise at opposite poles, like horses on a carousel. Their eyes never met. The two figures were almost mirror images—blond-haired, muscular, and taut.

After twenty days and three thousand kilometers of racing, Greg LeMond and Laurent Fignon sat fifty seconds apart in the standings of the 1989 Tour de France. They had traded savage attacks over the three previous weeks, neither man ever leading the other by more than mere seconds. The lead had changed hands three times. Greg had worn the *maillot jaune*, the race leader's yellow jersey, for seven days; Laurent had worn it for nine. Now, the jersey hung on Laurent's back, and Greg was in second place. By day's end, the Tour would be decided. And no matter who won, this would likely be the closest finish in the seventy-six-year history of *le Tour*.

On this July afternoon, the circling cyclists readied for a final twenty-five-kilometer dash downhill from the royal château to the finish line on the Champs-Élysées in Paris. They would ride at the end of a sporadic procession of 138 cyclists, starting a minute or two apart, each man racing alone as the clock ticked. This was the time trial, cycling's Race of Truth, in French the *contre la montre*—literally, "against the watch."

Savvy observers had surveyed the course and reckoned a middling rider could complete it in about twenty-nine minutes. A great one might win it in twenty-eight.

Greg needed to reclaim those fifty seconds from his French rival on this final day of racing—to pull back two seconds for every kilometer raced—in order to win the Tour.

For most of the three weeks prior, Laurent had pedaled within the protective cocoon of a great cycling team, Super U, a nine-man squad with talent and depth. Greg, by contrast, rode for the pitiful ADR team, a motley crew of sprinters and second-raters. Yet, in this final contest, teams wouldn't matter. Each cyclist would ride alone. And Greg was better at time trials than Laurent. In previous matchups, Greg had pedaled more swiftly than Laurent by a margin of roughly one second per kilometer of racing. That meant he could expect to beat the Frenchman by perhaps twenty-five seconds today.

But twenty-five seconds would not be enough. To most observers, Laurent had already won the Tour. His lead felt insurmountable.

Both Greg and Laurent were men of twenty-eight—young adults in the broad scheme of life, yet aging journeymen in the brief and brutal career of cycling. Each had conquered *le Tour* before, Laurent in 1983 and 1984, Greg in 1986, each, in turn, enjoying a brief reign atop the precarious pecking order of professional cycling. Then each cyclist had abruptly lost his "form," a term invoked by cycling writers to describe a rider at his peak. Both had dwelled for years in cycling's wilderness, missing races, abandoning them, or finishing at the back of the pack. Now, at the signature event of the 1989 cycling season, each rider had miraculously recovered his form. Greg and Laurent were back on top—both of them, at exactly the same time, a most inconvenient coincidence. Neither knew how long the second wind might last. If there was to be another victory at the Tour for either man, the time was now.

As the clock wound down to Greg's 4:12 p.m. start, television commentators interviewed cycling experts and one another, all asking the same question: Could LeMond catch Fignon?

"It will be close," predicted Paul Sherwen, a former professional cyclist turned broadcaster, speaking on the Channel 4 transmission in Britain. "But I think, logically, it's got to be Fignon."

Phil Liggett, Sherwen's broadcasting partner, weighed in: "LeMond is a very determined competitor, and he will not give up the fight for this final yellow jersey. One thing I'm very confident about, and that is this Tour de France will be the closest finish in the history of the race.

It could be decided, you know, by five or six seconds, and that would be absolutely unbelievable."[1]

At 4:11 p.m., Greg rolled to the starter's gate, a structure that resembled a backyard shed. He wore a streamlined teardrop-shaped helmet of his own design. A pair of odd-looking, U-shaped handlebars jutted out from the front of his candy-apple-red Bottecchia time-trial bicycle. The "tri-bars" set Greg apart; none of the European teams used them.

A man in a pink sports shirt held Greg's bicycle atop the starting ramp as another man counted down seconds on his fingers. Greg reached down to check that his shoes were locked into his pedals. In those last seconds, thoughts swirled through his head: *I don't like doing time trials. I don't know if I can do this again. I've got to push myself to the limit for the next thirty minutes. Oh, my God.*[2]

And then Greg was off, rolling down the ramp, out of his saddle, pushing his pedals with the full weight of his body until he reached a cadence of one hundred revolutions per minute along the Avenue de Paris.

Greg lowered his torso and stretched out his arms along the aerodynamic bars. He rode on a 54×12 gear: fifty-four teeth on the bigger front gear, twelve teeth on the smaller rear sprocket, a huge ratio that pushed the bicycle more than three meters for every turn of the pedals. Greg's gear, one of the largest on the road that day, allowed him to accelerate past fifty kilometers per hour without spinning his legs at an uncomfortable speed.

An ungainly cyclist, Greg bobbed up and down as he sped forward, periodically raising and lowering his head, almost as if he were swimming the crawl.

"I wonder what on earth he's thinking about, now, every time he looks down," Phil Liggett mused on British television, pondering Greg's odd cadence.[3]

Greg wasn't thinking. He was tucking his head down to create the maximum aerodynamic advantage, then raising it just long enough to follow the white line on the road and keep his bicycle pointed in the right direction—exactly as if he were swimming the crawl.

A minute later, Laurent strode up to the starter's shed. He looked proud and Parisian. But he felt sore, tired, and fretful, and he endured a silent scream of agony as he mounted the saddle of his bicycle. Unbeknownst to competitors and fans, Laurent was suffering from a saddle sore, a raw welt of flesh just where his left buttock met the seat of his bicycle. Doping rules precluded proper painkillers. So he swallowed the pain, as cyclists always did, exhaling slowly and deliberately as he prepared to ride forth.

Laurent had chosen to forgo an aerodynamic helmet, liberating his trademark blond ponytail to flap in the breeze, a concession to vanity as he greeted the Parisian throngs. He rode with two disc wheels; Greg had elected for just one. Cyclists replaced spokes with these solid sheets of carbon to minimize wind resistance in a time trial, but the wheels also caught the full force of any crosswind, and this was a windy day. Laurent rode on a traditional time-trial bicycle with lateral, upturned handlebars. That handlebar choice, so seemingly trivial at the time, would loom large in Laurent's thoughts by day's end.

At 4:14 p.m., Laurent pushed off from the gate. As he began to pedal, a fierce pain shot up from his saddle through his body. Cyclists are professional masochists, expert at sublimating pain. Yet Laurent could not ignore this one: "It was like being stabbed with a knife; every part of my body felt it, even my brain."[4]

In the broadcast booth, Paul Sherwen said, "It's a pity we can't get inside Fignon's mind to see what's going through it."

Phil Liggett replied, "Pain, I would think, Paul. Nothing more than that right now. He's shutting out everything else."[5]

Laurent tried to think past the pain to the moment when the torture would end, half an hour later, at the finish, and his victory at the Tour de France would be secured.

Up ahead, Greg, too, focused on the finish. His mind would admit nothing else: not victory, nor defeat, nor the series of events, fortunate, misfortunate, and miraculous, that lay behind him.

THE GIFT

GREG LEMOND'S FATHER, Bob, was born in December 1939 on Long Island, New York, where his own father worked for the Armour meatpacking company. Eight years later, the family relocated to California, chasing the postwar suburban dream.

The LeMonds bought one of the first houses in Lakewood, a vast planned community rising up in the industrial underbelly of Los Angeles County, replacing rows of closely spaced lima bean plants with rows of closely spaced homes. One of the earliest and largest postwar suburbs, Lakewood offered working-class families the promise of a two-bedroom home for fifty dollars a month, lifting the LeMonds to the lower rungs of the middle class.

Though he brimmed with energy, Bob had no time for sports; he was too busy making money. In junior high school, Bob took on a paper route and launched a brisk lawn-mowing service. At eighteen, he married his high school sweetheart, Bertha. With luminous green eyes and a beaming smile, Bertha was the daughter of a longshoreman. Her own mother had married at thirteen.

When Bob finished high school, he expanded his lawn-mowing franchise into a full-time business with fifty customers. He earned enough money to move east to Cypress, another new development that was replacing old dairy farms in Orange County. There the couple welcomed their first child, Kathy, in 1959. Greg, a tow-headed whirlwind, arrived two years later.

The LeMond children—three in all, including younger sister Karen—spent many idle hours in downtown Long Beach, where Bob's grandparents ran a motel along U.S. 101, some blocks from the ocean. The kids played among the pine trees in the grassy median of the coastal highway while their father tended lawns. On weekends, Bob would shepherd the children to Seal Beach while Bertha cleaned the family home. The motel business also offered a steady supply of coupons for discounted admission to Disneyland.

Bob was no outdoorsman, but Bertha's parents were avid campers, and they inspired Bob and Bertha to go on fishing expeditions at Lakes Arrowhead and Big Bear. Browsing at the drugstore one day, Bob happened upon a book about trapshooting, a competitive form of target practice designed to simulate a pigeon shoot. He bought the book, read it, and immediately resolved to adopt trapshooting as a hobby. Though he had never competed, Bob was naturally competitive, and soon both he and Bertha were seeking out regional shooting contests. In 1963, Bob traveled with his grandfather to an event in Nevada's Washoe Valley. There, as he gazed out at a John Wayne movie set come to life, Bob said to himself, *I want to live here.*[1]

Bob returned to California and studied real estate, acquiring a license in 1965. Three years later, the LeMonds left Orange County for Lake Tahoe, on the Nevada-California border. The family made its home in Incline Village, a settlement named for a cable railway that had once hauled timber up the mountain slope. They moved into a three-bedroom home; Greg, age seven, got his own room.

Hemmed in by the freeways and malls of southern California, Greg and his siblings had only dabbled in outdoor life. Now, with water to the south and mountains to the north, Greg often vanished into the Nevada wilderness. The boy adopted an outdoorsman's routine, "skiing in the winter and fishing in the summer," his father recalled.[2] Greg's hands were so quick he could catch fish without a pole.

The LeMond children roamed free. In winter, the three would hike up Incline Mountain unaccompanied and ski back down. In summer, they would barbecue food on the beach, with nine-year-old Kathy supervising the grill. Once, Bertha drove her children twenty-five miles across the mountains to Carson City and dropped them with their bicycles to pedal twenty more miles to their grandmother's house. "I don't remember us taking a bottle of water," sister Kathy said.[3]

Though Greg's father lacked a college education, he found he was exceedingly good at selling real estate; he was blessed with piercing blue eyes, a politician's good looks, boundless energy, and a fierce competitive streak. And the Nevada of 1970 was much like the southern California of 1950: real estate was booming. Bob went to work selling lots for Boise Cascade, the lumber conglomerate that had developed Incline Village. His income swelled. Bob rewarded himself with a yellow Cadillac.

Within three years, Bob had amassed enough money to purchase a five-acre spread in the Washoe Valley, a remote expanse east of Lake Tahoe and south of Reno along the shores of Washoe Lake. The family settled into a four-bedroom, four-bathroom house of four thousand square feet, on a property nearly fifty times the size of the Lakewood lot Bob's own parents had called home.

Washoe Valley was ranch country. Settlers baked in summer, froze in winter, and shivered in icy rain in fall and spring. The LeMonds endured winds that could overturn a tractor trailer on the interstate. A Washoe wind, Mark Twain once wrote, "is by no means a trifling matter."[4]

Young Greg would come to know every inch of that windswept valley. On top of skiing and fishing, Greg now took up hiking and trapshooting, all before he had entered his teens. He was a natural athlete, competitive, driven, and utterly tireless. His sky-blue eyes and sunny smile radiated a disarming sweetness and a puppy-dog zeal for life.

The LeMond family lived several miles from the nearest school, so perhaps it was inevitable that Greg would choose solitary pursuits and outings with his family over team sports and gatherings with other boys. He savored the freedom of the outdoors; he suffocated within the stale confines of a gymnasium. Throughout his childhood, Greg would favor sports in which, he recalled, "I could accomplish something myself without having to depend on others."[5] The choice reflected both his isolation and, in time, his ambition.

Greg's ample bedroom became a shrine to his many hobbies, holding an exhaustive collection of fur and feathers for fly-fishing and a vast bookcase filled with volumes on fishing, hiking, and hunting. Greg backpacked in the woods. He angled for brook trout in the stream behind his house. Around age twelve, he inherited a hand-me-down horse named Big Red.

When those pursuits failed to slake his competitive thirst, Greg became obsessed with freestyle skiing, a sport of aerial acrobatics that he chose over downhill skiing because, he recalled, "I wanted something more challenging than going up a ski lift and whizzing back down."[6]

As he entered sixth grade at Pleasant Valley Elementary School, Greg struck up a friendship with a classmate, Frank Kratzer, who was two years younger. Frank had skipped a grade in school, while Greg had been held back in the transition from California to Nevada.

Though clearly intelligent, Greg found it hard to focus on one thought for very long, a trait that did not serve him well in the classroom. Many of his misadventures ended in the principal's office; some of his teachers assumed he would end up in prison. In class, Frank and Greg cultivated a reputation as hyperkinetic class clowns. "I think we fed off of each other," Frank recalled.[7] Frank lived directly across from the school, while Greg lived eleven miles away. After school, they would play football at Frank's house. On ski days, someone's parents would shuttle the boys back and forth to the slopes.

Following his father's example, Greg spent many free hours working, mowing lawns and lifting hay to earn extra money. At thirteen, Greg apportioned $130 from those earnings to purchase his first ten-speed bicycle, a Raleigh Grand Prix, purely as a means of transit to the many remote locales on his weekly itinerary. Sturdy but clunky, the Raleigh was not even a proper touring bike, let alone a racing bike; it came with wheels too fat for serious riding and with pedals that lacked toe clips for continuous propulsion.

These were prosperous years for the elder LeMond, who was buying up ranch land and subdividing it into smaller parcels for homes. He made periodic dates to go trapshooting with his son. He sometimes pulled the children from school on weekdays for skiing excursions, but he had little time for recreation on weekends.

Greg's father had never regarded himself as particularly athletic. He had stopped smoking with the birth of his younger daughter, but he still drank, and as he neared his mid-thirties, Bob was hardly in peak condition. Greg described him as "a six-pack-a-day man."[8] Worse, the workaholic schedule strained his marriage to Bertha. Though Bob provided admirably for his wife and children, there were times when he barely saw them.

Greg needed a father figure. He soon found one.

In 1968, when Greg was seven, his parents befriended a Tahoe neighbor named Ron.[9] Ron became part of a larger group of friends that joined the LeMonds on occasional ski trips. Over time, Ron earned the confidence of Greg's parents and took an ever-fonder interest in their son. As Greg reached puberty, Ron began to broach sexual topics. "He talked about *Playboy*, girls," Greg recalled. One night, on a ski trip in Sun Valley, Idaho, Greg and another boy sat in thrall as Ron talked. Then, in one swift maneuver, Ron was on top of Greg, performing oral sex on a victim too shocked and confused to resist.

After that, Ron began paying regular visits to the LeMond home, preying on the inattention of a family distracted by a steady stream of overnight guests. Once everyone was asleep, "he'd slip into my room," Greg recalled. This happened "maybe three times, maybe five times," over a span of several months. Greg felt trapped. "The fact is, it feels good," he said. "But it's so shaming. You're confused. And you don't tell your parents, because you're ashamed."[10]

The abuse ended in the spring of 1975, shortly before Greg's fourteenth birthday. Greg's mother had tired of houseguests and declared Ron "a deadbeat friend," banishing him from the household. Overwhelmed with shame and fear, Greg told no one what Ron had done.

Bob gave Greg a lavish birthday present that summer, sending him to an elite freestyle ski camp at Whistler Mountain, outside Vancouver, British Columbia. Greg had never actually competed against other boys on skis, and he wanted to learn the acrobatics that distinguished a champion from an amateur.

A few days before Greg departed for ski camp, the championship road race of the Northern California Nevada Cycling Association rolled past his home. Greg and Bob walked down to the road to watch. As the blur of men and wheels blew past, Greg found himself deeply moved— by the swiftness of the race, the spectacle of competition, and the sheer athleticism of the colorful riders on their bicycles.

In the decade since Greg's birth, recreational cycling in the United States had transcended its roots as a means of transit into a form of exercise, part of a larger embrace of physical fitness that swept the nation in the first half of the 1970s. Heavy, Pee-wee Herman–style cruisers with foot-pedal brakes gave way to nimble road bicycles fitted with curved "drop" handlebars, with two gear wheels in front and five in back, allowing the rider to choose among ten "speeds," selected with the tug of a lever. Serious riders sometimes went further, eschewing fat American tires for narrower, lighter designs from Europe. Racers favored the "sew-up," an ultralight European tire stitched around an enclosed tube, over the American "clincher," a heavier ring of rubber fitted over a separate tube. The best frames and parts bore continental names: Campagnolo. Gitane. Jeunet. Bianchi. Peugeot.

Greg knew nothing of this burgeoning bicycle culture. But he was about to learn.

Greg injured his back shortly after arriving at the hotdog ski camp and failed to learn a single flip. But the sessions included ample instruction on other skills, and one particular piece of advice caught Greg's ear. A coach told the boys to avoid running, because the stress of pounding the pavement would hurt their legs. Instead, he said, try cycling.

Greg returned to Nevada and beheld his bicycle with new eyes: "It was the first time that I thought about my bike as anything but a form of transportation," he told journalist Samuel Abt.[11]

The LeMonds learned that the national amateur men's cycling team was training for the Pan American Games near Squaw Valley, California, an old Olympic facility tucked into the Sierra Nevada just an hour from Reno. Bob and Greg drove out one weekend to watch a training race. By the time of their return, father and son were hooked. Bob had never tested the limits of his own athletic ability. Now he resolved to scale back his drinking and shed some pounds. He quickly dropped the extra paunch and found, to his surprise, that he could keep up with his teenage son on the hills of Washoe Valley.

"Up until then, he'd tell you that he worked seven days a week, fourteen hours a day," Greg told journalist Richard Moore. "He had been drinking beer, putting on weight, and all of a sudden, he just stopped."[12]

Bob and Greg began to stretch their rides from twenty miles to forty and sixty, and to cross the steep mountain passes that flanked their home. One October day, Greg joined his father on an arduous ride up Spooner Pass to Incline Village, their old home, after a morning spent on a deer hunt. A mile from the finish, Greg "bonked"—cycling jargon for hitting a physiological wall, a condition of utter exhaustion reached when the body has consumed all of its stored glucose, leaving the rider weak, shaky, and disoriented.

"I was so tired I could barely walk my bike," Greg recalled. "I was close to tears."[13] The episode gave Greg fresh respect for an activity that he had not even considered a sport.

For Greg, cycling became something more than a sport, something akin to a drug. He would ride himself to exhaustion. His body would reward his efforts by releasing endorphins, the natural opiates produced by the pituitary gland during exercise, and adrenaline, nature's amphetamine. Greg desperately needed both. For all his considerable native intelligence, he was cursed with the attention span of a gnat, and he surely would have been diagnosed with attention deficit disorder in a modern public school. The focused concentration required by cycling "took a fog off my brain," he recalled.[14]

Great cyclists are said to be great masochists, driven by dark inner demons. Greg found, in cycling, the ultimate distraction from his own demons, the pain of guilt and sorrow and humiliation that still roiled his brain from the months of sexual abuse. The sport brought Greg such a powerful kick of pain and pleasure and heart-pounding excitement that it shut out everything else, leaving no margin for Greg's busy mind to focus on anything but the road beneath him.

That winter, Greg planned a return to skiing, his first love. But the winter of 1975–76 brought little snow, so Greg and Bob remained on their bicycles. Both LeMonds were amazed at how rapidly they improved. Come spring, skiing, like winter, would be forgotten.

One January day, Bob dropped his son at Rick's Bike Shop in Reno. Greg was perusing a display of leather helmets when an older boy approached. He asked whether Greg was interested in racing. The older boy introduced himself as Cliff Young. The son of a prominent Reno politician, Cliff was a few years older than Greg and had been racing on bicycles since age twelve. Yes, Greg replied, he did want to race.[15]

Cliff told Greg about the Reno Wheelmen, an amateur cycling club founded in 1896. Not long after their meeting, Bob and Greg happened upon a group of Wheelmen. These were seasoned riders, some of them racers, out on a brisk ride across the valley. One of them, Roland Della Santa, recognized Bob, who had purchased Greg's Raleigh at the shop where Roland worked. The grandson of Italian immigrants, Roland had discovered cycling in his teens and built a collection of cycling books and magazines from Europe. By the time he met Greg, Roland was both an amateur racer and a bicycle craftsman, building custom frames with skills he had learned in high school shop class. He was a true cycling aficionado and had an eye for talent.

Roland quickly sized up Bob's teenage son, who was riding in a mesh tank top and sneakers among men attired in cycling jerseys and cleats. "Greg had borrowed a racing bike, and it was too big for him," Roland recalled. "And, God, this guy was strong."[16]

It is customary in training rides for cyclists to take turns "pulling," riding at the front of the group and bearing the brunt of the wind. After a brief, exhausting spell in front, the rider slips to the back of the pack to recover. Greg was an inelegant cyclist, rocking back and forth atop a frame so large that his feet barely reached the pedals. Yet, he seemed indifferent to wind and immune to exhaustion.

"He would go to the front and do a pull and pretty much ride everybody off his wheel," setting a pace that the seasoned cyclists behind him could not match, Roland said. "Then, he would go to the back and recover almost immediately."[17]

In February 1976, the Reno Wheelmen persuaded Greg to enter his first race. It was an informal club contest, pitting the fourteen-year old against some of the most serious amateur racers in Nevada. Greg turned up in his tank top, jogging shorts, and tennis shoes, a curious sight in midwinter. Greg had a new bike: a Centurion Le Mans, a mid-priced model from Japan, with toe clips for proper pedaling and lighter, thinner tires than the Raleigh Grand Prix, but still a far cry from a proper racing bike. Like other American bicycles of its day, the Le Mans was named for an auto race.

The race comprised four laps around a seven-mile loop that passed right by the LeMond home, twenty-eight miles in all. At the finish, Greg had taken second place.

"You got a lot of talent, guy," Roland said to Greg afterward. "But you should get a real racing bike."[18]

That performance, and Roland's advice, moved Bob to buy yet another bicycle for his son: a $900, canary-yellow Cinelli, from Milan. The bicycle was two sizes too big, but Greg would grow. He selected an ensemble of woolen cycling gear, topped off with a bright yellow jersey that matched the bike. Garish? Yes. But now Greg felt sure he would be noticed the next time he entered a race. He was not yet aware that yellow was the color of the *maillot jaune*, the jersey won by the leader of the Tour de France.

The LeMonds now took regular rides with the Reno Wheelmen. One weekend the group traversed Ebbetts Pass, which crosses the Sierra Nevada at an elevation of eighty-seven hundred feet. On the final climb, Roland decided to test the LeMond boy: "I did everything I could to drop Greg, and I just couldn't do it." Roland finally gave up, and Greg sprinted off up the mountainside.[19]

Greg continued to train with his father and added a new partner, Cliff Young. After school, Greg would travel to Cliff's house. The two boys would ride for hours. Then Bob would appear in Cliff's driveway in his restored '48 Ford Woody station wagon, perfect for transporting bicycles. Bob was building a modest car collection with his real-estate earnings.

Greg proved an eager pupil. He told Cliff, again and again, "I want to be as good as you someday."[20] He had a lot to learn. On one of his first visits to Cliff's home, Greg couldn't free his sneaker from the toe clip that bound it to the pedal. He toppled over, bicycle and all, onto the pavement.

Cliff taught Greg the fundamentals of bicycle racing: how to pedal with a steady cadence; how to dress on a windy day; and when, exactly, to launch a final sprint to the finish. On gusty afternoons, the boys would flee into the protective cover of the hills. "I had ridden with a number of prospective racers," Cliff said, "but there was something special about Greg's enthusiasm."[21] Greg reminded Cliff of himself, a few years earlier—the overeager novice. Cliff also liked the way Greg's father would pick up the tab whenever they dined out.

Greg became a frequent visitor to Roland's bicycle workshop. There Roland would reel off stories about the great European stars, Eddy Merckx and Lucien Van Impe of Belgium and Jacques Anquetil and Raymond Poulidor of France, and he would recount for Greg the forgotten history of bicycle racing in America.

THE WHEELMEN

ONE NIGHT IN THE WINTER OF 1927, fabled boxing promoter Tex Rickard gathered the nation's most celebrated athletes for a banquet at a New York hotel, where the Kings of Sport could hobnob and sign autographs for an audience of Coolidge-era millionaires. A portrait from that event captures the faces of the era's greatest competitors: baseball home-run king Babe Ruth, world heavyweight boxing champion Gene Tunney, Olympic gold-medal swimmer (and future Tarzan) Johnny Weissmuller, hockey superstar Bill Cook, six-time U.S. Open tennis champion Bill Tilden, and golf legend Bobby Jones. Joining them, at the bottom right of the frame, were two luminaries of American cycling, Fred Spencer and Charley Winter.

At the dawn of the twentieth century, bicycle racing was America's favorite sport. New York alone was home to twelve hundred bicycle builders; eighty-three bicycle shops huddled within a one-mile radius. Top-drawer cycling events routinely drew twenty thousand patrons, many times the number who turned out for a baseball game. The racing season started in May in the Northeast and migrated west across a national circuit of tracks, through Toledo, Fort Wayne, Des Moines, Saint Louis, Denver, and Salt Lake City, and then on to San Francisco and Los Angeles, where the season would conclude in late fall. Children collected trading cards adorned with star cyclists, who reaped both fortune and fame. In 1901, the *New York Times* wrote roughly sixty-five articles about the greatest American men's cyclist, Frank Kramer, but only eight about Napoleon Lajoie, who led professional baseball that year in batting average, runs, and hits. In 1911, as Detroit Tiger Ty Cobb held out for a salary increase to $10,000, Kramer earned more than $20,000.

The bicycle had entered American popular culture after the Civil War. It started as a novelty according to historian Peter Nye, but by the 1880s cycling was a national hobby and by the 1890s a craze. The first bicycles carried their passengers two or three times the speed they could travel on foot. Some of the nation's greatest inventors tinkered with bicycles, sometimes in the same workshops that crafted prototypes of the automobile and airplane, presaging a coming revolution in human transportation. Orville and Wilbur Wright built bicycles. Henry Ford repaired them.

The quest for speed led inevitably to the question of who was fastest. The first recorded bicycle race in the United States was held on May 24, 1878, in Boston's Beacon Park. The winner, a Harvard student named C. A. Parker, covered three miles in twelve minutes and twenty-seven seconds. The first national championship was awarded four years later to George Hendee, a boy of sixteen descended from a founding father of Vermont. Hendee forsook Yale to race bicycles. He won four more national championships and became a local legend, his name branded on hats and cigars.

In 1893, the United States hosted the first world championship of cycling, a sport of surging popularity in Canada and Britain and across central Europe. Held in Chicago, the event showcased the next American superstar of men's cycling, August Zimmerman. "Zimmy" raced throughout Europe and became the first American athlete to attain international stardom. Bicycle racing made him a wealthy man; in the 1892 season, Zimmerman's winnings included fifteen diamonds, fifteen rings, fifteen bicycles, fourteen medals, nine pieces of silverware, eight watches, seven shirt studs, six clocks, two cups, two bronze sculptures, two wagons, one parcel of real estate, and one piano.

The next great American cycling star would dominate his sport like few athletes before or since; he also happened to be black. Marshall Walter "Major" Taylor was the son of a Civil War veteran. He grew up in the home of a wealthy, white Indianapolis family that employed his father as a coachman. Taylor would be the first African-American to claim a significant championship in professional sports.

By age thirteen, Taylor worked in a bicycle shop, where he drew in customers by performing tricks on his bicycle while wearing a military jacket, inspiring the "Major" moniker. Within a year, Taylor entered and won his first race. At fifteen, he raced at the Capitol City Velodrome in Indianapolis and broke the track record. He was promptly banned from the course.

Black cyclists were forbidden to join the League of American Wheelmen, the U.S. amateur cycling organization, in every state but Massachusetts, where Major Taylor eventually settled. Blacks were technically free to enter white cycling events, but few did. Taylor resolved to conquer the sport and to cross the color line. Working in a friend's shop, Taylor designed a metal extension that set the handlebars several inches in front of the frame, allowing him to stretch his back and assume a more streamlined stance on the bicycle, a position now universal in competitive cycling.

Taylor turned professional in 1896. Now he could earn up to $850 in a day, more than double what his father earned in a year. Future president Theodore Roosevelt became a fan. In the final years of the century, Taylor set seven world records on distances ranging from one-quarter mile to two miles. In 1899, on a track in Montreal, Taylor won the men's world cycling championship. The Canadian crowd greeted Taylor's triumph with rapture.

On American tracks, Taylor suffered grave injustices. After one victory, a white competitor lunged at Taylor and began to choke him. Rather than disqualify Taylor's attacker, race judges determined that the two men should ride the race again; owing to his injuries, Taylor could not. Officials routinely awarded Taylor second place in races he had clearly won.

The hostility extended to Europe. In 1901, Taylor paired off against the reigning men's world champion, Edmund Jacquelin, for a best-of-three sprint contest in Paris. Taylor won easily. The race director punished him by paying out the entire purse of $7,500 in ten-centime pieces. Taylor had to hire a wheelbarrow to collect it.

The event that would set competitive cycling forever apart was the six-day bicycle race, an exercise in sadism, superhuman exertion, and shock theater, whose spirit would ultimately spawn the Tour de France. The first six-day contest was waged in London in 1878, when a professional cyclist bet that he could ride one thousand miles in six successive days. He did, and the event caught on, fed by a nineteenth-century fascination with ultra-endurance freak shows. Some of the first American six-days were held at the old Madison Square Garden, in 1891, the year after it opened. The contests delivered just what their name implied: six-day marathons of pedaling, each rider completing as many laps as he could in a span of 144 hours. The racers were free to sleep when they wished. But as crowds swelled and prize money amassed, racers took to riding without sleep, employing "seconds," as a boxer might, to help them stay awake. These helpers would ply the racer with meat and grain, water, caffeine, cocaine, strychnine—anything that might keep him upright.

This peculiar species of trainer would be forever known by the French term *soigneur*, which translates roughly as "caregiver." The riders in their care would scream and cry, hallucinate and collapse—just what the crowd had come to see. An account of an 1896 contest described the winner, one Teddy Hale, as "a ghost, his face as white as a corpse, his eyes no longer visible because they'd retreated into his skull."[1] For his efforts, Teddy collected $5,000.

At the turn of the century, race officials introduced a sensible rule: no competitive cyclist could pedal for more than twelve hours in a day. Six-day racers now collaborated on two-person teams, one riding while the other rested. Races drew riders from around the globe; some would travel twenty days by sea and three more by rail to reach New York and earn as much as $1,000 for a day of racing. "Sixes" attracted sellout crowds and celebrity guests, including Douglas Fairbanks and John Barrymore.

The most celebrated American cyclist of the sport's golden era was Frank Kramer. Born in Indiana, Kramer turned to cycling when his parents feared he had contracted tuberculosis and sought to build his lung capacity. Big-boned, barrel-chested, and nearly six feet tall, Kramer won his first amateur national championship in 1898, at seventeen. Major Taylor convinced Kramer to turn pro. In 1901, Kramer edged Taylor for his first professional championship; he would hold the national title for the next sixteen years. He won his last championship in 1921, after his fortieth birthday. Upon his retirement in the summer of 1922, at age forty-one, Kramer was thought to be both America's oldest and highest-paid celebrity athlete. The *New York Times* ran stories for three days leading up to his final ride, on July 26, in Newark, New Jersey, a bold assault on the world record for the length of one-sixth mile. A crowd of twenty thousand held its breath as Kramer crossed the line. He hadn't broken the record of 15.4 seconds, but he had equaled it.

It is a measure of cycling's subsequent fortunes that Frank Kramer's name was almost never mentioned in the *Times* again. The arrival of the low-cost automobile in the 1910s filled the nation's roads and gradually pushed bicycle races indoors. Demand for bicycles plummeted, and production of frames and parts migrated to Europe. Then the economic collapse of 1929 decimated the indoor sport; two of the nation's premier tracks, in New York City and Newark, closed in 1930. By 1940, the Depression and changing tastes had wiped out professional cycling in the United States. A decade or two later, most Americans had forgotten the cycling sport ever existed. Competitive cycling endured as a niche activity among immigrants from central Europe, where the sport still flourished. Races were banished to unsung velodromes and remote highways and mostly ignored by the broader public. When, in 1969, a southern Californian named Audrey McElmury became the first American to win a world cycling championship in fifty-seven years, her nation took little note. Cycling had been exiled from the American public consciousness.

LEMONSTER

AMERICAN BICYCLE RACES OF THE 1970s resembled Grateful Dead concerts, albeit on a smaller stage. A fleet of station wagons and Econoline vans would arrive in some remote locale by dead of night. As dawn broke, the vans would disgorge their contents, and the lot would fill with frames, wheels, pumps, coolers, and lawn chairs, with riders, parents, siblings, and fans.

Decades earlier, bicycle races could bring entire cities to a halt. Now they existed at society's fringe, relegated to empty industrial parks and shuttered downtowns and underused recreation areas on sleepy Sunday mornings. Race organizers often lacked permits, and the highway patrol would occasionally sweep in to shut them down.

"It was kind of an underground sport," Roland Della Santa recalled. "It was totally off the grid."[1]

In March 1976, Cliff Young invited Greg to journey to California and enter a real bicycle race. The LeMonds piled into Bob's forest-green Volkswagen bus and drove two hours to Sacramento, where, on March 6, at age fourteen, Greg rode in his first amateur cycling contest, the William Land Park Criterium.

As a Nevadan, Greg would race in an amateur circuit that encompassed both his state and northern California. That would prove both a blessing and a curse; most races lay hundreds of miles away, but Greg would face some of the best cyclists in the nation.

American amateur cyclists raced in age categories. Preteens rode as "midgets." Greg, a relative latecomer, rode as an intermediate, with other boys of thirteen, fourteen and fifteen. His first race spanned ten miles. At the starting gun, Greg shot forth from the pack, leaving most of the other boys far behind. Soon, only three others remained in the lead group. Though Greg had never really raced before, he immediately asserted himself as the leader, "barking commands at us to rotate through and keep the speed up," one of the startled teens recounted.[2] Greg easily took the final sprint. He had won his first race. Greg was overjoyed.

The LeMonds drove another hundred miles to Dublin, east of San Francisco. There, on March 7, Greg entered his second cycling contest, the Tassajara Road Race. On this day Greg's father would race as well, riding as a senior; it was the first of many times father and son would compete on the same course. One can only imagine the looks that greeted the elder LeMond, riding his first race at thirty-six in a field of college-age men. Incredibly, Bob managed to keep up.

Greg's race, a course of twenty-five miles, pitted him against several other boys of various shapes and sizes. One was another fourteen-year-old, Kent Gordis. Like Greg, Kent was new to bicycle racing. Unlike Greg, Kent had trained with the great George Mount.

Born one day before Greg, Kent had grown up in Switzerland, where his father worked on one of the first corporate computer systems. When Kent's parents divorced, his mother decamped to Berkeley. Kent joined the Velo Club Berkeley, one of the nation's preeminent amateur clubs, founded in the 1950s. Its star was George Mount, a powerful cyclist who would place a remarkable sixth in the 1976 Olympic road race in Montreal. The club hosted weekly training rides; when Kent would reach the top of a particularly grueling climb, he sometimes found himself alone with George.

That spring weekend in Tassajara, Kent had entered his first race, emboldened by his training rides. Surely, he thought, no one in this ragtag bunch could beat him, least of all the kid in the Big Bird outfit. Greg's unruly golden locks spilled out from beneath a thick black leather Kucharik helmet, an apparatus whose curved temple protectors made the young cyclist look like an old-time football player. "And he had this goofy, goofy smile on his face," Kent recalled.[3]

But then the gun sounded, and Greg was gone, a canary-yellow blur receding into the distance. Kent could barely hold his wheel. At the end of the twenty-five miles, Greg held the lead, and Kent sat several lengths behind him, huffing and puffing in second place. The third-place finisher was ten minutes down the road.

Wiping the sweat from his brow, Kent asked the canary boy, "What's your name?"

"Greg. Greg LeMond."

"Hmm," Kent panted. "Well, you're not bad."[4]

Kent began to visit Greg at his Nevada home, and Greg visited Kent in Berkeley, and together they made pilgrimages to the French bookstore in San Francisco. Though he was no older than Greg, Kent possessed vital knowledge on the alien universe of professional cycling. Kent knew some French, and he would translate for Greg as they paged through yellowing copies of imported cycling magazines.

Greg and his father adopted a new diet, modeled on the hippie-era ethos of clean living that had spawned a new generation of health-food stores and jogging suits in American cities. Restaurant outings became scavenger hunts for root vegetables and unrefined sugars. After about a year of this, a hungry Greg succumbed to his weakness for Dunkin' Donuts. Thereafter, he would subsist on a perplexing blend of healthful fare and junk food.

Around his fifteenth birthday, Greg qualified for the national cycling championships with a victory in San José, California. He was one of four men and boys from Reno to earn a spot in the nationals. The others included Cliff Young—and Greg's father, who had very nearly won the senior men's road race. There could be no further doubt about the source of Greg's gift.

The relationship between a precocious child athlete and the child's parents can be complex. Parents sacrifice weekends and evenings to shuttle their children to events and practices. They live vicariously through the child's feats. Sometimes, the child's career becomes the parent's life.

It was not so for the LeMonds, because Bob raced right alongside his son. On the Nevada-California cycling circuit, many racers knew of Bob's exploits before they became aware of Greg. Within a year after he started cycling, Bob raced as a Category I senior, "competitive on a national level, which is unheard-of," Roland Della Santa recalled. In 1978, at thirty-eight, Bob would take fifth place in the Red Zinger Bicycle Classic, the nation's premier multistage men's bicycle race. Bob coached his son, but Greg also coached his father, dispensing endless advice on the topography of the course and the strengths and weaknesses of his rivals as the elder LeMond prepared for a race.

Greg had inherited his mighty heart from his father—and from his mother. At the cellular level, Greg's cardiovascular power came from his mitochondria, the tiny furnaces that convert oxygen and nutrients into energy. Mitochondria concentrate in skeletal muscle and in the heart, making up about one-third of its volume. They adapt and multiply to meet the body's needs. Thus, through genetics or conditioning or both, elite athletes have more mitochondria, and more productive mitochondria, than other people. Greg, who could consume more oxygen for energy than any other cyclist on the West Coast, had more mitochondria—or "better" mitochondria—than other elite athletes. And mitochondria are passed down by the mother.

Bertha LeMond also bequeathed to Greg her toughness; she removed cookie sheets from the oven with her bare hands. Greg received those considerable assets along with some liabilities, including chronic allergies and feet of such divergent sizes that he often purchased unmatched shoes. Greg also had a bad kidney; it failed following a severe infection at age eleven, costing Greg months of missed school, his only real health scare in childhood.

For all his promise, Greg was not generally regarded as the most gifted athlete in the LeMond family. That distinction went to Karen, his younger sister. Karen LeMond took ballet and dance classes from first grade and soon became deeply immersed in gymnastics. Throughout their teen years, Karen and Greg would crisscross the nation from one competition to the next. Their parents secured permission for both children to leave school early every day to train. At the dinner table, the two siblings would argue about whose sport was harder.

"It was my life for . . . it felt like my whole childhood," Karen recalled. "I got out of school at noon. Someone would come and pick me up. [We] would go over to the gym, and I would work out until my parents picked me up at seven."

Bertha generally traveled with Karen, Bob with Greg, until the children were old enough to drive themselves. While they offered full-throated encouragement and endless support, Bob and Bertha were not the stereotypically overbearing sports parents. The obsessive drive that compelled Greg and Karen to spend hours a day in training and competition seemed to have arisen spontaneously in the LeMond children.

"I loved it. I loved it," Karen remembered. "I kept getting injured, and I would still go to the gym, six, seven hours. I had a brace on my knee for almost a year. And I went to the gym every day. My parents begged me to quit, because they knew I was injured. But it just wasn't in me."[5]

Karen competed for five years, won an amateur national championship and enjoyed a growing reputation until 1980, when an accumulation of injuries forced her to stop.

With three LeMonds engaged in a more-or-less daily regimen of training and competition, older sister Kathy and mother Bertha were compelled to take up equally strenuous supporting roles. The family often traveled to weekend competitions together. Bertha preferred to dwell in the background, doing whatever was asked of her, never complaining.

"My dad, he's a hiker," Kathy explained. "My mom would sit for two or three days in a trailer park and read while my dad went hiking. She would sit and wait for him."[6]

When Greg grew inquisitive about cycling attire and equipment, his older sister shepherded him to fabric stores, helped him pick out thin nylon material, and stitched together custom jerseys for her brother. She learned to sew hook-and-loop fabric around Greg's shoes so that he could strap them more tightly to his pedals. She sewed padding into his cycling shorts.

In the spring of 1976, Greg won several more races on the intermediate circuit. He won so easily now that victory itself began to feel hollow. Though he was fourteen, Greg petitioned racing officials to allow him to ride with the juniors, boys of sixteen through eighteen. Such permission was rarely granted; among teens, even a single year of maturity could confer an overwhelming advantage in size and strength. Yet the officials approved, bowing to Greg's undeniable results. Now, he would face a much larger field of bigger, stronger boys, many of whom had been winning races for years.

A week before his fifteenth birthday, Greg entered the Nevada City Father's Day Classic as a junior. This was one of the largest and oldest cycling events in the nation, drawing ten thousand spectators. Greg's prior races had played out before thin crowds of parents and siblings. Now, as he glimpsed the vast throng in Nevada City, Greg imagined what it must be like to race in Europe.

The Nevada City course was a one-mile loop that featured a short but steep ascent, a good setting for Greg to exploit his talents for aggressive climbing and swift recovery. But Greg was still an intermediate, and the rules confined him to relatively small gears compared to those of the older juniors, a measure meant to protect young legs from injury. Out on the course, the gear restriction hindered Greg's speed on the descents—he could not turn his pedals fast enough to keep up. Still, at the end of the race, Greg stood in second place. "It was then," he recalled, "that I realized I could compete with some of the best American riders."[7]

The Sierra Nevada Sportswriter and Broadcaster Association named Greg athlete of the month. An interviewer asked him to quantify his ambitions.

"I'd like to turn professional and try to win the Tour de France, [and] the world professional championship," Greg replied. "That's the hardest kind of racing. I would like to win the Olympic gold medal in road racing—really, any medal."[8]

They were bold words. No American had taken any sort of medal in an Olympic cycling event since 1912. No American had ever won the men's world-championship road race. No American had even entered the Tour de France.

That summer in Nevada, Greg happened upon Noël Dejonckheere, a native of cycling-mad Belgium, who was touring the United States and entering races. Noël was riding behind a pace car, his speed approaching forty miles per hour, when "this little kid" suddenly appeared alongside him. Noël invited Greg to join him on training rides. "He dropped me very easily," Noël recalled, invoking cycling parlance for the act of riding away from one's competitor. When Noël returned home, he told his family he might have met the next Eddy Merckx. Merckx was the world's greatest male cyclist.[9]

By the end of the 1976 racing season, for all his efforts, Greg had not won a single trophy; cycling remained a woefully low-budget sport, and race winners generally collected a meager bounty of medals, tires, and trinkets. Cliff Young found an old bowling trophy at the dump and presented it to Greg, with a bicycle replacing the bowler, above a new inscription that read "Reno Wheelman Rider of the Year, 1976."

That fall, Greg enrolled at Wooster High School in central Reno. His arrival occasioned a reunion with Frank Kratzer, who had spent the prior two years at a different middle school. Once the pleasantries were past, Greg told Frank, "You've got to get a bike." Frank traded his skateboard to a classmate for a bicycle. He presented it to Greg, who cried, "Let's ride to my house!" Frank gamely joined him for the ninety-minute ride.

"Halfway there," he recalled, "I was just dying."[10]

Gradually, Frank supplanted Cliff Young as Greg's primary training partner, a role he played in a sort of tag team with Greg's father. Greg became the mentor, Frank the student. Greg enlisted Frank in an ambitious weekly regimen inspired by his father's exuberant work ethic, by his own burning ambition, and by the counsel of Noël Dejonckheere, who was now writing regularly from Belgium with advice.

Noël told Greg that races in Europe were twice the length of the thirty- and forty-mile contests staged for junior cyclists in the United States. He urged Greg to enter the longer races held for American seniors, and to ride hundreds of miles a week on his own, if he wished to become a professional one day.

Now Greg and Frank trained as hard as anyone in the Nevada-California racing circuit. Their week began on Tuesday with a ride of twenty to thirty-five miles, punctuated with a series of sprints.

Wednesdays brought a longer ride, of fifty or sixty miles. Thursdays brought "intervals," a punishing exercise in which Greg and Frank attacked a climb at top speed in a painfully large gear, pushing each boy's heart rate to the peak for thirty or sixty seconds at a time. The boys would unwind on Fridays with a lighter ride of twenty miles. Saturdays and Sundays were for racing.

Greg and Frank spent idle hours in Greg's room, listening to records and fantasizing about becoming rock stars. Greg "always had the best stereo," Frank recalled, just as he had the best fishing pole and the best bicycle.[11] His room was a Sharper Image catalog come to life.

The 1977 racing season dawned with Greg as the unrivaled star of the Reno Wheelmen. Greg strutted around the campus of Wooster High School asking befuddled classmates to place bets on his future prospects. "I'm gonna win the Tour, and I'll bet you a hundred bucks," he would say. No one would take the bet; perhaps they weren't quite sure which "Tour" he meant.[12]

Now Roland Della Santa stepped forward to take an active role in Greg's career. He took over sponsorship of the Reno Wheelmen, printing up Della Santa jerseys and building custom Della Santa bicycles for Greg and his team. Roland's invisible partner in this arrangement was Greg's father, who, unlike Roland, had the money to sponsor a bicycle team.

"I controlled the equipment, and Bob controlled the cash," Roland explained.[13] The team's annual budget for its star rider came to $5,000.

That spring, at the Santa Clara Criterium, Greg humiliated a reigning junior national cycling champion by "lapping" him, riding so far ahead of the field that he circled the course and caught him from behind. In months to come, Greg would lap the nation's top cyclists two or three times in a single race. The ease of his victories spawned an absurd rumor, fed in equal parts by television's *Six Million Dollar Man* and by an old scar on the back of a calf, that Greg's leg muscles had been transplanted from a kangaroo.

Racing officials now gave fifteen-year-old Greg permission to ride among seniors, the adults of bicycle racing. His first chance to challenge the cycling elite came in the three-day Tour of Fresno, a stage race modeled on the multiday races of Europe. This was a top-drawer contest, and it attracted members of the powerful Exxon cycling team. Their leader was John Howard, dean of American cyclists, four-time national champion and three-time Olympian.

In two days of intense racing, Howard and his Exxon team rode Greg to a stalemate. The contest came down to a final, ten-mile time trial, each cyclist riding alone against the clock. Now Howard was isolated from his team. In the first part of the course, riders rode into a head-wind, and Greg amassed a ten-second advantage over Howard. Then the course turned, and the riders picked up a tailwind. That was disastrous for Greg. He still rode with smaller, age-restricted gears, and now he could no longer pedal fast enough to match Howard's pace. The older rider pulled back the lost time and seized victory by a margin of six seconds.

Knowledgeable observers instantly recognized that the Reno teen-ager would have beaten the four-time American champion had he only pedaled a comparable bicycle. The LeMond legend was born.

With fame came nicknames: the Carson City Comet; the Reno Rocket; LeMonster. To Greg, nothing now seemed beyond reach.

Greg traveled to Princeton, New Jersey, in the summer of 1977 for a series of races that served as tryouts for the junior world cycling champi-onships in Venezuela. He won two of the three races, obliterating a field of older, larger boys. But they were hollow victories. Greg was barely sixteen, a year too young to actually compete in Venezuela.

Summer brought the junior nationals in Seattle. Greg crashed twice over the course of the seventy-one-mile race. But he dominated the field, and the contest climaxed in a final sprint between Greg and Jeff Bradley, an Iowa cyclist who was widely regarded as the nation's finest young sprinter. No one was more surprised than Bradley when Greg shot past him to the finish line.

Greg returned to Squaw Valley, the old Olympic training ground, for an intense summer training camp. He was one of the youngest in a group that contained some of the most promising talent in cycling. The camp was led by a man known as Eddie B. He spoke almost no English.

* * *

The broader cycling world still considered the United States a backwa-
ter, but the resurgence of American recreational cycling in the 1970s led
the nation's cycling establishment to seek out someone who might set
things right. Eddie Borysewicz, a Polish champion cyclist turned coach,
had traveled to the United States in 1976 and found work as the first
coach of the newly minted U.S. Cycling Federation. American cyclists
had trouble pronouncing his name, so he would forever be known as
Eddie B.

Eddie B. personified the Soviet work ethic. He derided American
cyclists as "fat guys with mustaches.[14] He urged riders to eat freshly hunted
venison and undercooked beef, and chastised them with warnings to
avoid beer and women, his advice rendered in a thick Belarusian accent
that only burnished his image among the mustachioed Americans.

Eddie surmised that most American riders sat either too high or too
low on the saddle, and that few of them knew how to pedal properly: to
pull, as well as push, using different muscle groups in the legs, to effect
a powerful, fluid, circular stroke. When Greg and the others arrived at
Squaw Valley, Eddie B. set about schooling them with a regimen that
surpassed anything Greg had gleaned from the cycling magazines in
Roland Della Santa's workshop. It felt like boot camp: wake-up call at
seven, lights-out at ten. Eddie taught the boys how to pedal with maximum efficiency, accelerating and decelerating only when necessary; how
to build muscle mass through weightlifting and running in the winter
months (time most American cyclists spent lifting beer mugs); how to
use abdominal muscles to balance on the bicycle; and how to keep a
diary to chart the body's response to all the new training.

"These guys go to bed, maybe eleven, maybe twelve, playing guitar,"
Eddie recalled. "I tell them one thing: 'You follow my way, or I leave this
place tomorrow.'"[15]

A few of the boys left an enduring impression on Eddie B. One was
Greg. Eddie marveled at how he flew up mountain slopes and at the
pain the boy would endure to sustain his velocity, all that effort etched
into the deep lines that already scored his young face. Greg's pedaling

technique was wrong: all pushing, no pulling. He was pigeon-toed. And Eddie gasped at his bizarre diet. Greg would binge on Taco Bell burritos or devour an entire tub of ice cream, and then climb on his bicycle and obliterate his rivals in a race.

But Greg was eminently coachable. "He asked me for everything," Eddie said.[16] When the camp was over, Eddie kept careful tabs on the boy, dispatching training plans to the LeMond home and refining them as he learned more about Greg's remarkable cardiopulmonary engine.

Greg now prepared for the 1978 junior world championships, which were being held that summer in Washington, D.C., the first such contest ever staged on American soil. In June, Greg traveled to Colorado Springs for a series of races that would select the members of the U.S. Junior Cycling Team, a winnowing process carried out under the unblinking eyes of Eddie B.

The week in Colorado Springs concluded a six-month campaign of attrition that had opened with dozens of riders at a winter training camp. Eddie had gradually thinned the herd until only the most promising juniors remained. Greg easily made the final ten-man team. The others were mostly his friends and adversaries, including Jeff Bradley, Greg's rival at the junior nationals in Seattle; a pair of exceptional riders from La Crosse, Wisconsin, Greg Demgen and Mark Frise; and Ron Kiefel, a shy but powerful cyclist from Denver.

The marquee event at the world championships was the road race, a swift, grueling, and unpredictable dash that generally climaxed in a mass sprint to the finish. Eddie B. was more interested in the time trial, a race against the clock among four-man teams. In contrast to the chaotic road race, the time trial was an exercise in athletic precision, very winnable with the right regimen and the right coach.

Eddie B. focused on the time trial obsessively. He taught Greg and the others how to "pull" at the front of a four-man team, setting the pace and bearing the brunt of the wind; and how to "swing off" to the back just as one's body reached the edge of exhaustion. He taught them to ride in such a tight formation that one rider's elbow would graze another's hip as he retreated to the back of the line. He informed them that every time a cyclist swung off, the team lost roughly eight feet of ground—more than the length of a bicycle.

Twenty-five thousand spectators turned out in Washington, D.C., on June 25, 1978, for the first world-championship cycling event staged on American roads since 1912. The seventy-six-mile road race through Rock Creek Park was largely flat, a design that frustrated breakaways and left the pack bunched in a white-knuckled frenzy as it neared the finish. None of the Americans had witnessed such aggressive racing; the Russians and East Germans seemed ready to risk lives for a win.

With just under a half-mile to go, the race leaders lined up across the road, with three Americans near the front. Ron Kiefel watched the Italian beside him crash to the pavement; somehow, Ron remained upright. The pack hurtled into a mass sprint at forty miles per hour along the park's wooded Beach Drive, packed so tight that the first fourteen finishers were awarded the same time. A Russian took the victory. Greg came in ninth, Jeff sixteenth, Ron nineteenth, all spaced a few feet apart. The three boys were the best-placed Americans in the history of the event. Afterward, Jeff told a reporter he had never been so frightened.

Three days later, on June 28, the four best young cyclists in the United States lined up for the climactic team time trial along the George Washington Parkway. At the gun, Greg set a blistering pace. Jeff Bradley, nearly as strong, easily matched it. The real surprise was the performance of the other two, Kiefel and Greg Demgen, one of the Wisconsin boys. Both cyclists managed to hold the wheel of their team leader, who was out to make a statement.

"[Greg] was the motor," Demgen explained, "and we three just kept tempo as best we could. We all had a good day, no weak links, and we surprised the world."[17]

The two Gregs led the team in a final lap, pulling back a seven-second deficit on the fading Italians and finally passing them in total elapsed time. The Americans would finish third, behind the East Germans and the Russians, to claim the nation's first medal in the modern era of world championship men's cycling.

That night, the boys snuck into a D.C. nightclub. They drank and danced until last call.

THE PILGRIMAGE

SHORTLY AFTER the triumphal Washington, D.C., trip, Greg boarded an airplane to Europe, accompanied by Kent Gordis, his buddy from Berkeley, whose father lived in Switzerland and hosted his son in summer. Greg and Kent had spent many weekends in the San Francisco bookstore worshipping at the altar of European cycling. Now, stepping forth from the airplane in Geneva, Greg beheld a three-dimensional landscape populated with the pictures he had studied in cycling magazines.

In Switzerland and France, Greg entered a slate of races against European juniors, boys from France and Belgium and Italy who were as good as the best American seniors. But Greg was better than any American senior, and he won every race he entered. Now, finally, Greg had an answer to the question that had haunted him since his first victory, two years earlier. He knew he was as good as any young cyclist in the world.

On July 18, Greg rode his bicycle up the Col de Joux Plane in the Alps, along with ski legend Jean-Claude Killy, a hero from Greg's skiing days, and a few dozen members of a Swiss cycling club. They arrived at Killy's wooden-beamed chalet and settled in to watch the Tour de France, which was due to roll past his property that day.

Greg was transfixed: "I had never seen so many people—it was just ten people thick, all the way down. . . . The noise, the cars, the spectators, and the mountains."[1]

As Greg absorbed the spectacle he thought, *That's what I want. That's it. I want to win the Tour.*[2]

Greg flew back to Milwaukee in July for the junior national championships, where he would finish second behind Jeff Bradley. One night during the week he spent in Wisconsin, Greg went on a double date with teammate Greg Demgen and two girls from Demgen's hometown of La Crosse. Demgen's date was Kathy Morris, the daughter of a prominent physician, a spritely, smiling girl standing five foot four, who hid sparkling blue eyes behind an enormous pair of glasses. Greg, romantically unattached, squired Kathy's younger sister, Lisa. It was a curious evening. Greg and Lisa danced and laughed, while Kathy sat politely with her date. Demgen had been Kathy's first kiss, back in ninth grade. Three years later, his affection had waxed, while hers had waned. Greg respected Demgen's romantic claim, but he found himself drawn to the lovely La Crosse girl.

Greg flew back to Europe, rejoined the Gordis family, and traveled to Belgium, the spiritual capital of the cycling world: no nation could claim more ardent fans. Over the next three weeks, Greg entered five races and won three. Junior bicycle races in Belgium spanned one hundred kilometers, twice the length of their American counterparts, and Greg found himself careening along repurposed cow paths. (European road races are generally measured in kilometers, American races in miles; 1.0 kilometers make a mile.) The visit provided Greg with a crash course in bicycle handling: how to race against the wind and over cobblestones, how to negotiate narrow roads built for hooves rather than tires, and how to avoid catching a handlebar on a spectator's purse. Returning home at summer's end, Greg was resolved: "Europe was where I wanted to be."[3]

The cycling season over, Greg returned to Wooster High School to begin his junior year. That fall, he penned a list of goals for his nascent cycling career. Such was the scale of his ambition that none of them had been met by an American male.

1. 1979—Win Jr. World Championship Road Race
2. 1980—Win Olympic Road Race
3. By age 22—Win Pro. World Champ. Road Race
4. By age 25—Win Tour de France

Now Greg bade a reluctant farewell to Roland Della Santa, the craftsman and enthusiast who had sponsored him for the previous two years.

He accepted a new amateur sponsorship from Avocet, a manufacturer of cycling components. The deal would net him $25,000 that season, good pay for a boy not yet turned eighteen.

Greg wasn't motivated merely to win races; from the start, he was equally driven by the unapologetic quest for compensation. As the 1979 racing season approached, Greg clipped some dollar-bill signs from a newspaper ad and pasted them to the handlebar stem of his bicycle, only partly in jest. In a business class at Wooster High School, the teacher assigned students to calculate profit-and-loss statements for the year. The exercise revealed that Greg was earning more than his teacher. Greg's new green BMW raised eyebrows in the student parking lot.

In June, Greg celebrated his eighteenth birthday. The next month, he journeyed to Colorado for the Red Zinger Bicycle Classic, which was now drawing talented professionals from Europe. It was a brutal field, and Greg finished in fourth place.

For Greg, the highlight of the week was not the race itself but the nightly outings that followed each stage. Greg had been joined by Greg Demgen, his Wisconsin buddy, who had again persuaded Kathy Morris to join him. In Demgen's mind, he and Kathy were still dating; Kathy did not agree. She was standing at the student union of a local college when she felt a pair of hands close around her eyes from behind and heard a familiar voice: "Guess who?" She turned around and beheld Greg LeMond. She was instantly smitten.[4]

Kathy dutifully paired off with Demgen for nightly double dates and assigned a hometown friend to mind Greg. While Greg respected his friend's claim on Kathy, his own feelings were growing, setting the stage for romantic conflict.

Kathy had grown up in West Salem, a town set along Wisconsin's La Crosse River. Her father, David Morris, was a local doctor who had pioneered a method of treating allergies without injections. By the time of Kathy's childhood, he had built a bustling practice and become one of the wealthiest men in La Crosse, the sort of breadwinner who could fly his entire family to France in the summer. Kathy's mother, Sacia, traced her own roots to the *Mayflower*.

Greg and his friends next traveled to La Crosse, where some of them lived, to train for the national road race championship. The big event in La Crosse that week was a concert by new-wave sensations the Cars, attended by nearly every able-bodied teen in town. Greg went with his friends, Kathy with hers. He spotted her through the crowd and cried, "You're here!"

Greg sat down. Kathy sat on his lap. The contact ripped a scab the size of a bacon strip from Greg's thigh where it had collided with pavement in Colorado. Soon, both parties were covered in his blood, but neither one seemed to mind.[5]

That night, Ric Ocasek and company serenaded the young couple with an intoxicating barrage of meditations on teenage love and adolescent angst, songs with such titles as "You're All I've Got Tonight" and "My Best Friend's Girl."

Greg hitched a ride with Kathy and her friends to Milwaukee, site of the impending championship. He impressed the girls by pulling out a hundred-dollar bill to cover gas—and by winning the race.

As he lingered in Wisconsin that month, Greg's growing infatuation with Kathy gradually overwhelmed any lingering twinges of loyalty to Demgen, his romantic rival. Unlike Kathy, Greg had barely dated. Almost from the start of adolescence, he had spent every weekend off at bicycle races, missing countless parties and potential date nights. Now he was hopelessly enthralled. Though Kathy came from Wisconsin, Greg found her positively exotic—this doctor's daughter, older than Greg and better educated, a girl who could date any boy she liked. She was funny and sociable and mature beyond her years; with her deep blue eyes, high cheekbones, and ivory skin, she was irresistible. Greg pined for her at night, moaning to Frank Kratzer about how he liked her and how he missed her.

Though Kathy could indeed have her pick of the boys in La Crosse, the boy she wanted was Greg. She loved his irrepressible glee and the way his cobalt eyes burned even brighter when the sun bronzed his face. She loved that he was the alpha male in the small society of cyclists in which she dwelled. She found his powerful athleticism sexy, along with his easy smile and the golden hair that spilled out beneath his helmet.

When the two briefly found themselves alone in a car while on an outing for ice cream, Greg turned to Kathy and asked, "Would you ever go out with me?"

"Yes!" she cried.[6]

Their first date was a roller-skating outing; the next, a midnight excursion to Bradford Beach, a long crescent of sand on Lake Michigan. When the rejected Demgen returned to La Crosse a few weeks later and beheld Greg and Kathy at the airport, standing so close to each other that they were clearly a couple, he collapsed onto the pavement in tears.[7]

Greg LeMond left Wisconsin without his cycling tool bag, which he had "forgotten" in the car that belonged to Kathy's friend. Now he had an excuse to write Kathy a letter, asking politely if he could come and retrieve the bag. Then Greg departed again for Colorado Springs to train for the world championships, which were to be staged in Buenos Aires. He and Kathy wrote to each other daily and spoke every night on the phone. Greg amassed hundreds of dollars in bills for the long-distance calls.

As usual, Greg both trained and caroused in Colorado Springs. When he returned to Wisconsin to meet Kathy's parents, he arrived at their home with a bandaged hand. Kathy's physician father leaned in to shake it; Greg recoiled. Dr. Morris inspected the hand, which was broken, infected, and swollen, and declared, "Ooh, looks like you have a problem there."

Greg replied, "Yeah, I hit a wall."

Dr. Morris looked a bit more closely and observed, "Those look like teeth marks!" The teeth had belonged to a boy Greg had punched in the mouth during a nocturnal adventure in Colorado.[8]

Greg's relationship with his future father-in-law was off to an inauspicious start. Two days later, David Morris ushered his daughter into a closed-door meeting in their suburban home. He asked, "Exactly what are your intentions with this young man?" Morris had watched his daughter run through one boyfriend after another. This one had an annoying habit of planting an endless barrage of kisses on her cheek. Kathy replied that she and Greg were serious. Her father advised her that he did not want the boy kissing her cheek in his presence. [9]

Kathy was due to start her sophomore year at Gustavus Adolphus College, an affiliate of the Evangelical Lutheran Church, in Minnesota. She was a year older than Greg and two years ahead of him in school; she studiously avoided revealing to her college friends that she was dating a high school student. Greg found a race to enter in the Twin Cities and traveled there in late August, affording the couple one last visit before the world championships.

The American team's surprise bronze medal at the 1978 worlds had left the riders with high hopes for 1979. Greg was now a favorite to win a medal in Buenos Aires. His teammate and rival Jeff Bradley was also riding at world-class speeds. For the team time trial, they would be joined by a newcomer, Andy Hampsten, a seventeen-year-old from North Dakota with a slender frame and prominent front teeth that would later inspire the nickname *le Petit Lapin*, the little rabbit.

Buenos Aires was like nothing the boys had seen. The team was housed in an Olympic training center tucked beneath a freeway along an airport flight path. At mealtime, the Americans beheld a cockroach the size of a matchbox. A police escort led the team bus into competition.

Eddie B., the sage American coach, sensed that he commanded the strongest rider in Buenos Aires. On a hunch, he entered Greg in an event he had ridden just once before, a three-thousand-meter pursuit race on a track. This, for Greg, was alien territory. The pursuit format placed single riders at opposite sides of a velodrome. The riders raced in circles, each trying to catch the other. Greg hadn't raced on a track all year; track racing and road racing were almost different sports. In his thickly accented English, Eddie assured Greg the contest would offer "very good training to you."[10]

The morning of the first pursuit, Greg jogged down to the track with a borrowed track bicycle. A coach taught him a few tactics. That evening, Greg rode his first heat. Not quite sure how to proceed, Greg pedaled the nine laps at a steady pace, never really pushing himself.

He finished within a few seconds of the American record. He cruised through the next round and into the quarterfinals, where he completed the course in three minutes and forty seconds, breaking the record.

In the semifinals, riding against a swift Frenchman, Greg led for two laps. When the Frenchman moved ahead, Greg lifted his pace. As the bell rang for the ninth and final lap, Greg had nearly pulled even with his foe, drawing deafening cheers from the crowd. Greg continued to accelerate; the Frenchman could not. Greg won by two seconds, securing the silver medal for himself and his country. Greg lost in the finals to a Russian pursuit specialist. Yet, by the next morning, the LeMond name was circulating far and wide in Buenos Aires.

Eddie B. and his riders had spent much of the year training for the October 11 team time trial, hoping to improve upon their performance of 1978. The American team that had won the bronze that year had been relatively balanced. A year later, it was lopsided, with Greg and Jeff Bradley riding at a considerably faster clip than the others.

Even so, the Americans managed to finish in third place, forty-three seconds behind the Russians, for another bronze medal. The outcome pleased everyone but Greg, who knew that four riders as strong as he would have taken the gold.

Now thoughts turned to the world championship road race, the week's signature event. The fifteen-kilometer course chosen for the October 13 contest was flat, a layout that presaged a chaotic mass sprint at the end. Race organizers placed the final four kilometers of the course within the packed Autódromo, home to the Argentine Grand Prix automobile race.

Few in the stands expected a breakaway. The crowd exhaled a collective gasp when, in the seventh of eight laps, two riders burst into the autodrome well ahead of the pack. One was Greg; the other was Kenny DeMarteleire, an elite Belgian who had raced against Greg in Europe. Greg had managed to escape the peloton. (French for "platoon," *peloton* describes the core group of cyclists in a race, the "pack" from which breakaways escape and laggards are dropped.) DeMarteleire had latched onto his wheel, and now the two riders held a twenty-second advantage on everyone else. The cyclists circled the track and rode off into the streets of Buenos Aires to complete the final lap. Spectators assumed the peloton would soon chase the pair down.

Out on the course, the Belgian was saving his energy, riding behind Greg, forcing him to battle alone against the wind. "Come on, Greg, you can do it, you can win," he told the American, over and over, in accented English. But DeMarteleire would not help him.[11]

Behind them, leading the chase, were the Russians—the same men who had just beaten the Americans in the time trial. Five of them had swept to the front of the peloton, lining up in the same mechanized formation that had delivered them the gold two days earlier. Greg would surely be caught.

Yet, when the race reached the gates of the Autódromo for the final kilometers, Greg remained in the lead. He had somehow retained most of his twenty-second advantage, single-handedly riding the Russians to impasse. DeMarteleire, the cagey Belgian, remained on Greg's wheel, holding out for the final sprint.

In a contest between two riders and a vast peloton, simple physics dictate that the peloton will usually win. But Greg had something to prove. The Russians ate into Greg's lead. Twenty seconds dwindled to fifteen, and then to twelve. Greg motored on. The Belgian held his wheel. Greg took stock. If the Russians caught him, Greg wouldn't just lose first place, he would be utterly annihilated; dozens of fresher riders would surge past him. It was first place or nothing. Greg tucked his head down and rode as hard as he ever had. Another kilometer passed, and then two, and suddenly the Russians realized that they would not close the gap. Greg, riding alone, had beaten them all.

With three hundred meters to go, Greg slowed, forcing the Belgian to pass him, a tactical move that put Greg in the superior position of drafting behind his foe as the line neared. Greg picked the perfect moment to explode in a slingshot burst past the Belgian. It was a textbook maneuver. Greg was going to win, and the Belgian knew it. In desperation, DeMarteleire swerved, pushing Greg and his bicycle into a row of tires that defined the final meters of the course. This was a dastardly tactic known to cyclists as a hook. Greg hit a tire and rode straight over it, a blow that snapped several spokes on his front wheel. Somehow, threading his way among the tires, Greg remained upright. The crowd roared its approval. An onlooker rushed forth and tugged a tire away so Greg could regain the course, surging back to the Belgian's side. The Belgian lunged again, sending Greg back into the tires. Greg had nowhere to go, so he rode straight into the tires, six in a row, snapping more spokes. Greg was still pedaling, but now DeMarteleire was ahead, and Greg's front wheel was no longer round. He wobbled to the finish, a bike length or two behind the Belgian, in second place.

Greg leapt from his bike and charged DeMarteleire; spectators intervened and separated the two riders. The Belgian was disqualified, and Greg was awarded the gold.

After the race, Greg told his astonished teammates that DeMarteleire had offered to let him win if Greg would give him $500. The deal had been proffered on the road, and Greg hadn't responded. He had heard about this sort of chicanery in European races, but this was the first time he had witnessed it firsthand.

Back home, Greg's fans couldn't help but compare the story of the Belgian and his tactics to a poignant scene from the hit movie *Breaking Away*, released just three months earlier. In the film, wide-eyed, blond-haired American racer Dave Stoller is betrayed by the Italian riders he adores, when one of them jams a pump into his spokes. Greg's friends must have thought the film was about him, though it wasn't. Yet the story uncannily captured his sweet and trusting nature, his manic enthusiasm, his adoration of all things European, and his yearning to race there. The movie won an Oscar and helped expand the growing community of amateur American cyclists.

For the airplane ride home, Greg and his teammates wore their team U.S.A. jerseys and dreamed of the throng that would await them on the tarmac. When they landed at Kennedy Airport, they found no one: no fans, no journalists, not even a representative of the U.S. Cycling

Federation, the group that had sent them to Buenos Aires. Greg had little use for his country's cycling establishment, and it seemed to have little use for him.

Upon Greg's return, he and Kathy ping-ponged across the Continental Divide to grab precious weekends together. They were falling in love. Kathy flew to Colorado for a three-day track event, surreptitiously staying in Greg's hotel room, although she and Greg remained in separate beds. (Kathy had promised her parents she wouldn't do "that" until they were engaged.) Then, back in Nevada, Greg resumed his senior year of high school.

Kathy flew to Reno for Thanksgiving. She walked into the LeMond family's living room to find Bob lying on the floor with his arm cradling the head of his daughter Karen as they watched TV, a striking contrast to her own father's Upper Midwestern reserve. She was immediately struck by the considerable mettle of Greg's mother, Bertha, the prize-winning trapshooter and championship bowler who kept no oven mitts in her kitchen.

Bob and Bertha lent their Mercedes to Greg and Kathy for a trip to San Francisco. There, with customary humility, Greg asked, "Would you ever marry me?"

"Yes!" Kathy gushed.[12]

Greg returned to Minneapolis. There, at a jewelry store on Nicollet Mall, he depleted his savings on a $2,000 diamond engagement ring. Kathy and Greg returned to their respective homes for Christmas with plans to break the news to their parents.

Greg was eighteen, Kathy nineteen. The thought of their engagement was just fine with Bob and Bertha. "The thing was, my wife and I didn't go to college, and we got married at eighteen," Bob said. "I was mowing lawns. I did OK, and I wouldn't change anything."[13]

Kathy's meeting did not go so well.

"How is he ever going to support you?" Dr. Morris asked. The notion that this high school kid could somehow support a doctor's daughter by racing bicycles—in Europe, no less—sounded patently absurd.

Kathy assured her father that the couple had a plan. If racing bicycles in Europe didn't work out, they would return to the States, and Greg would get a job. But David Morris expected all of his children to complete college, and the prospect of a looming marriage and an eventual move overseas imperiled that plan.

"You've had everything you ever wanted," he told his daughter, "and this is one thing you're never going to get."

Kathy knew in her heart that Greg was everything she wanted. She replied, "You're going to lose me before you stop me."

Kathy's mother greeted the news with a cooler head. "He already gave you a ring, didn't he?" she sighed. "Put it on."[14]

Tempers eased, and Kathy promised her parents that she would finish college. She would later regret the pledge—but not the decision to put her love for Greg first.

Greg had now met the first goal on his impossibly ambitious list. As 1980 dawned, he turned to the second: a gold medal in Olympic cycling.

The quest ended abruptly in March, when President Jimmy Carter announced that the United States would boycott the summer Olympics in Moscow over the Soviet Union's refusal to withdraw troops from Afghanistan. The turn of events was pure heartbreak for American coach Eddie B., who had spent four years preparing himself and his young team for the Moscow contest—and who had, in Greg, the world's greatest amateur cyclist at his disposal.

Losing the opportunity to compete in the Olympics was also a massive disappointment to Greg's American teammates, whose amateur careers now seemed destined to end in anticlimax. Perhaps the only cyclist who felt otherwise was Greg. "In my mind, the Olympics were just a stepping stone," he recalled. "I didn't care."[15]

The team had already scheduled a program of amateur racing in Europe to prepare for the summer games. Eddie B. proceeded with the April journey, though it now seemed pointless; no American rider had ever won a major European stage race, amateur or professional.

The first event was Circuit des Ardennes, a five-day contest held in the French mountain range. Greg entered as an unknown rider from an undistinguished nation. At the finish, he stood in third place, having won one of the five stages. To celebrate, Greg and Jeff Bradley absconded with a team car, broke into the velodrome where Greg had won the stage, and screeched around the track at ninety kilometers per hour.

The next event was Circuit de la Sarthe, a Loire Valley stage race that shared a name with a Le Mans car-racing course. More prestigious than the Ardennes contest, the Sarthe had recently been won by Bernard Hinault, the greatest men's cyclist in France, in consecutive years. This time, the surprise winner was Greg. His watershed victory drew a hearty round of international press, although almost none in the United States.

"He killed some decent pros there, and beat them badly," Jeff Bradley said. "And he did it without a team."[16]

By the time Greg entered the third race, the Ruban Granitier in Brittany, a crowd of scouts from professional cycling teams had gathered to watch the American boy in the rainbow jersey that designated the reigning junior world champion. Greg rode well in Brittany. On the final day of racing, he stood five minutes ahead of the main pack, chasing three Russians—always Russians—who had mounted a breakaway. Greg was ten seconds behind and closing fast when he heard a pop—a tire puncture.

At such moments, it is the job of the team mechanic to sweep up behind the crippled rider and deliver a new bicycle with the alacrity of a pit crew in an auto race. The transfer is supposed to happen in less than a minute. Alas, Greg rode for a team of amateur Americans, and the French mechanic charged with its care had fallen asleep in his car. By the time he reached Greg, the Russians were gone.

Greg was heartbroken. The unapologetic mechanic cajoled him to rejoin the race, for the "good name" of his team. This was more than Greg could bear. He picked up his bicycle and hurled it against the mechanic's car.[17]

The story of Greg's antics reached Cyrille Guimard, *directeur sportif* of the Renault professional cycling team, the best in Europe. Guimard was there to see Greg. Now, as he absorbed the story, a colleague asked, "Do you want a racer like that?"

Guimard did. "He's got character," he said.[18]

Guimard had been a great cyclist, winning nearly one hundred races in the 1960s and early 1970s. Chronic knee pain finally ended his cycling career, and Guimard moved into management. As team manager, Guimard quickly developed a reputation for two inestimable skills: a knack for predicting how the day's race would unfold, and a talent for telling a cyclist the right thing at the right time. By 1980, Guimard had guided fellow Frenchman Bernard Hinault to two victories at the Tour de France.

After the Brittany race, Guimard approached Greg and said, "You have the fire to be a great champion."[19] He told the American he had followed his career with great interest. Now Guimard wanted to offer Greg a spot on the Renault team. It was an offer no amateur cyclist could refuse, not even Greg, who was being courted like no American cyclist before.

A week later, Greg met with Guimard in Paris. He was now fielding offers from other teams, whose managers had noticed both Greg's results and Guimard's interest. Greg played the suitors off each other as best he could, but it was a bluff. He never seriously considered the other offers; he knew what Guimard had done for Hinault.

Guimard told Greg, "You're the biggest talent I've ever seen."[20] Greg told Guimard he would sign a contract with Renault after the Olympics, whether or not he rode in Moscow.

After the meeting, Greg related the offer to Kathy. "I think I've got to take it," he said, "but I won't take it if you don't come."[21]

The Morris and LeMond families conferred, and a deal was brokered. Greg and Kathy would travel to Europe for a month, in the summer break between Kathy's sophomore and junior college years, to sample the cyclist's life—and life as a couple, a state of existence they had experienced only briefly to that point.

"I wanted her with me," Greg told reporter Samuel Abt, "because we needed to get to know each other."[22] He already knew he had never felt for anyone what he felt for Kathy.

Greg returned to the United States for the Olympic trials, an exercise now shrouded in sad irony. He won the capstone road race and was named, at eighteen, the youngest captain of a U.S. Olympic cycling team. The team lacked only an Olympics.

Though Greg had reached a verbal agreement to join the Renault team, leaders of rival Peugeot kept at him with increasingly tantalizing counteroffers: first 10,000 francs a month, then 15,000, more than double the offer from Renault.

The Peugeot officials had misread Greg. Yes, his cycling career was about making money, but his overarching goal was to win races, and Greg thought no one would guide him to victory more adeptly than Cyrille Guimard. He had also heard whispers that the Peugeot team tolerated doping—and, whatever that was, Greg wanted no part of it.

Greg and his father tendered a reply to Peugeot: the team would have to offer 25,000 francs a month for Greg to even consider leaving Guimard. It was a sum "so outlandish," Greg recalled, "that I was sure they'd leave me alone."[23]

The tactic backfired. Greg's outrageous offer offended the Peugeot leaders, who leaked it far and wide, sparking outrage and envy among underpaid cyclists everywhere. Greg wasn't even a professional yet, and already he had acquired a reputation as an arrogant American money-grubber. The LeMond family business had stumbled, and not for the last time.

Greg and Kathy flew to Paris in July. Greg had a short-term contract to race with a French amateur team, confusingly named U.S. Créteil (*U.S.* stood for *Union Sportive*). Greg wanted another crash course in European cycling before he joined Guimard and Renault. His sponsor had promised 4,000 francs a month, a furnished apartment, and a car. But the car never arrived, and the promised apartment turned out to be a single room in an apartment already occupied by another family. The couple's begrudging hosts put them in a twin bed and telegraphed their displeasure.

"They served us a pig's ear with the hair still on it, and a bottle of vinaigrette," Kathy recalled.[24] The couple politely decamped to a succession of cheap hotels.

Greg was scheduled to meet with Guimard to sign his contract on the afternoon of July 20, the final day of that year's Tour de France. Signing Greg would be sweet consolation to Guimard, whose star, Hinault, had been forced to abandon his lead in the Tour because of tendinitis in the left knee.

Greg had just turned nineteen. The day of the fateful meeting found him in the home of Noël Dejonckheere, across the border in Belgium. For all his childhood ambition, Greg now faced a very adult decision, and he was waffling. The morning ticked away as Greg equivocated, seemingly waiting for someone else to tell him what to do.

Finally, Kathy looked deeply into Greg's eyes and said, "It's a two-and-a-half-hour drive to Paris. Your appointment starts in three hours. You jump in the car, or you don't."[25]

Greg and Guimard met in the prestigious Renault Club, gathering in a cramped room above the tour festivities on the Champs-Élysées. The negotiations dragged on for six hours; Greg swallowed his fear, read and reread every line in the contract, pausing repeatedly to telephone his father back in Reno for advice.

Greg's starting salary, tendered in francs, was worth about $18,000— less money than he had earned as an amateur cyclist in the previous year. Even that modest sum was more than Guimard had initially offered, and more than rookie professional cyclists typically earned.

After the signing, Greg and Kathy abandoned the amateur team, reneging on Greg's three-month contract, and flew home. They arrived with a nickel in their collective pockets.

Kathy returned to college that fall. Greg paid an extended visit to the Morris home, hoping his native charm might sway her parents to his side. He played tennis daily with Sacia, Kathy's mother. He tortured her, too. Greg would head out on a training ride and then telephone from some remote pay phone, claiming to be a policeman who had taken him into custody. He would brace himself between two walls and climb to the ceiling to hang like Spiderman and drop on poor Mrs. Morris when she passed by with a load of laundry. By the end of the visit, she adored him. Dr. Morris was less amused.

Cyrille Guimard wanted Greg on his team more than his paltry starting salary would suggest. In November, the Renault manager flew to the United States in the company of Bernard Hinault, the unrivaled star of European cycling, to visit the American at his family's ranch in Reno. The LeMonds and their French guests rode horses, visited a casino, and posed for pictures in Western boots and cowboy hats. Greg took Hinault on a quail hunt; Hinault, unfamiliar with firearms, accidentally shot into the ground, and a pellet ricocheted into Greg's eye, an oddly prophetic episode. Greg clutched the wounded socket and cried, "*Je suis blind,*" unsure how to finish the sentence in French.[26] In fact, the pellet had only scratched his eyelid.

The sight of LeMond and Hinault, "walking side by side across the prairie, guns beneath their arms, invoked a symbolic image of a sporting alliance between Old World and New, the reigning champion and the newcomer," a visiting journalist observed in the French cycling magazine *Vélo*.[27]

The group traveled to New York, rode bicycles in Central Park, and held a ceremonial signing with the American cyclist, mostly for the benefit of the European press; there is no record of the event in the *New York Times*. The entourage created a stir when it entered a Manhattan restaurant favored by actual French people, prompting muted gasps of "Hinault!"

"Greg is a simple, healthy boy, and I'm sure he will be welcomed into the team," Hinault told the French journalists. "He must only make the effort to learn the language and lifestyle of the French. But this will not be an insurmountable obstacle. I myself am ready to help."[28]

Greg was due in Europe after the first of the year for a few months of conditioning before his professional debut. He would need it. During the lengthy downtime in La Crosse, Greg had repeatedly sampled the wares of the hometown G. Heileman Brewing Company and had gained fifteen pounds. Friends had counseled him to have some fun before he turned pro, because, they said, he would never have fun again.

Greg would not go to Europe without Kathy, so their wedding was hastily arranged. It was a measure of Kathy's upper-crust milieu that she would be the first of her siblings or close friends to marry; Kathy had never even attended a wedding. Greg, a boy of decidedly working-class origins, had parents and grandparents who had married in their teens.

Kathy's mother had embraced Greg, but her father remained inconsolable. The couple vowed to return from Europe in four years, when Greg was twenty-three, if he hadn't found success in professional cycling. Kathy left college eight credits shy of a business degree. Greg would earn his high school diploma via a correspondence course.

The ceremony was set for December 21 in La Crosse, where the temperature hovered below twenty. Bob and Bertha, unaccustomed to the local weather, arrived without coats. Bob had sold one of his beloved cars so that he could fly his entire extended family to Wisconsin for the ceremony.

Greg and Kathy had endured a long-distance relationship. From the day of their meeting until the day of their engagement, they had seen each other exactly sixteen times. Their feelings, however, were timeless.

Greg and his friends spent the weekend "walking from bar to bar and drinking these sloe gin fizz things" in a futile effort to stay warm, recalled Frank Kratzer, who served as best man.[29] Also there was Kent Gordis, Greg's Berkeley friend, who had given up bicycle racing and enrolled at Yale. Kent's suitcase never arrived, so he attended the ceremony dressed in a uniform borrowed from a Radisson hotel bellhop.

As a practical joke, Greg's buddies procured a beat-up car in which to chauffeur the couple when they emerged from the church, "with some beer cans that we'd emptied ourselves tied to the back," Frank recalled.[30] The pranksters unwittingly struck at the heart of the conflict between Greg and his new father-in-law, who still could not fathom how this overly affectionate teenager was going to earn a living in Europe.

At the ceremony, David Morris cried.

Meanwhile, in a suburb of Paris, another promising young athlete contemplated how he might earn his keep racing bicycles in Europe.

LE PARISIEN

LAURENT PATRICK FIGNON was born on August 12, 1960, in the waning summer of France's postwar baby boom. He arrived a month early, in the maternity ward of the Hospital Bretonneau, tucked beneath the white-domed Sacré-Cœur basilica, at the foot of the Parisian historical district of Montmartre. He came home to a ground-floor apartment in the seventeenth arrondissement, an address at the very heart of French civilization, a dwelling populated with Parisian rats that would occasionally make off with his pacifier. Laurent celebrated his first birthday and took his first steps on the beaches at Pénestin, on the coast of Brittany. He was an energetic child. "As soon as you could stand," his parents later told him, "you didn't just walk, you ran."[1]

When Laurent was three, his family moved thirty-five kilometers east of the capital to Tournan-en-Brie, a town at the terminus of a suburban commuter rail line. The family was expecting a second child and sought escape from the cramped confines of an urban apartment. Today the town sits within a growing sprawl of Parisian suburbia; fifty-five years ago it was farmland and forest.

"All I had to do was go down the stairs to be in the middle of the wilds," Laurent wrote of the new home in his memoir. "My friends and I built huts, knocked them down and built them up again. The days seemed to last forever."[2]

Like Greg, young Laurent craved the adventure and independence afforded by the outdoors, where he would act out elaborate Tarzan fantasies with his friends. At dinnertime, his mother would open a window, shout his name, and wait. Sometimes Laurent would appear with singed clothing, the smoking evidence of a forest bonfire gone awry.

Laurent was born into the working class. While Bob LeMond would rise above his class and provide for his family in relative splendor, Jacques Fignon would remain a blue-collar man to the end. Jacques worked as a foreman in a metalworks factory, driven by "a strong work ethic, a sense of self-denial, and a bit of a hard attitude towards himself and other people," his son recalled.[3] He left for work at six in the morning and returned most evenings at eight.

Father and son coexisted in more or less perpetual conflict. Laurent was "wild and hyperactive," and his father could not mete out enough spankings to keep pace with the child's tireless pranks: "One day, he decided to punish me for a week and whacked my backside the minute he got in, every evening. I gritted my teeth. I didn't make a sound. When he stopped, I looked him in the eye and said, 'Is that it?' Then I pulled my pants up in silence. No tears. Not a drop of sweat on my face." Well before his cycling years, Laurent knew how to suffer.[4]

Laurent's mother, Marthe, was a housewife, always with a book in her hands. His younger brother, Didier, was exceedingly quiet and shy, even by comparison to Laurent, who was an introvert. The Fignons lived in a small, white, two-story dwelling with a lovely garden, tastefully decorated inside and out. The family kept a small collection of parrots and parakeets that forever serenaded their guests; Laurent loved birds.

The confines of the public-school classroom posed a formidable challenge for Laurent. Like Greg, he simply could not sit still. "The mere idea of doing nothing left me in hysterics," he recalled. "I was afraid of inactivity, afraid of the emptiness." Laurent's teachers could not handle the fidgety child, so "they just shouted at me all the time." He acquired a reputation for disassembling toys and fighting with classmates.[5]

Laurent's temperament proved similarly ill suited to the family's weekly tradition of leisurely Sunday luncheons in the cramped Parisian apartment of his grandmother. He came to dread all family gatherings.

At age six, Laurent was prescribed a pair of wire-rimmed glasses. Laurent was always losing them in the woods, prompting his father to set out on bitter nocturnal excursions with a flashlight.

The glasses gave Laurent the visage of an intellectual, a pretense not entirely unearned. For all his struggles to sit still in a classroom, Laurent loved school. He discovered a zest for reading and devoured boys' magazines. Reading became another escape, just as inviting as the woods behind his home. His grades were good enough for the honor roll; on a sixth-grade report card, teachers praised both his industry and his businesslike demeanor.

Laurent's first sport was soccer, and he played it with passion, both at school and in the fields around his home. He excelled at left wing, a position that relied more on speed than ball control. Teammates marveled at how Laurent never seemed to run out of breath.

Riding in the car with his parents one day in July 1969, Laurent became transfixed by the voice crackling out of the radio speaker, shouting the praises of some "phenomenal Belgian" riding across the mountains of the Pyrenees. Laurent was hearing a live account of the birth of a cycling legend. It was the seventeenth stage of the Tour de France, and Eddy Merckx, age twenty-four, led the race by an insurmountable margin of eight minutes. He had only to keep pace with the other favorites to claim his first victory in cycling's preeminent race. Instead, Merckx broke away from the peloton that day and rode alone over mountain passes for 140 kilometers, attacking the field with a naked aggression seldom witnessed in the modern Tour. By day's end, he stood sixteen minutes ahead in the standings.

Absorbing the frenetic commentary on the radio, Laurent could not quite grasp what all the fuss was about. But he would never forget the sound of that announcer's voice.

By age twelve, Laurent had fallen in with a tight group of schoolmates who spent nearly every waking hour together. They were already besotted with cycling; Laurent was not. By age fifteen, in fact, Laurent had never seriously considered climbing onto a bicycle for any purpose other than transportation, a bias he shared with the young Greg. But for a young Parisian to take so little interest in cycling was positively perverse.

Bit by bit, Laurent's friends persuaded him to take a closer look at his father's old *biclou*, an ancient Vigneron bicycle that had transported the

elder Fignon to work. Prompted by Laurent's interest, Jacques painstak-
ingly restored the vintage frame.

Laurent's first excursion on his father's antique bicycle was a revelation: "It wasn't just that I loved it straightaway, but from the word go—to
my great surprise and the amazement of everyone else—I was able to
keep up with the others. [6] Awkward and off-kilter, Laurent could barely
stay upright on the saddle. Nonetheless, he promptly discovered that in
cycling, just as in soccer, he never seemed to tire.

Circumstances permitted Laurent to ride his bicycle only one day
a week, on Thursdays; at this stage in his life, Laurent was boarding a
school bus at seven every morning, and his parents forbade him to ride
after dark. Laurent made the most of the weekly sessions. On the streets
around Tournan-en-Brie, he and his friends practiced the "attack," a
sudden acceleration to propel a cyclist away from the pack, and the
"counterattack," a similar burst of speed timed to carry a cyclist past
a competitor who has just attacked. One day, the other boys decided
to test Laurent's seemingly inexhaustible stamina. They rode at top
speed, accelerating again and again; try as they might, they could not
drop him. In informal races, Laurent soon found that he could beat his
friends to the line with relative ease.

Amateur cycling clubs crisscrossed France in the 1970s, forming a
vast network and talent pipeline not unlike America's youth baseball
infrastructure. "At the height of racing season," Laurent wrote, "France
was like one big bike race."[7] Many boys started racing at twelve or thirteen, and some of Laurent's teenage peers already had dozens of races
behind them. Rosario Scolaro, one of the more serious riders in Laurent's entourage, wore the green, yellow, and white jersey of a prominent
local club, Le Pédale of Combs-la-Ville, a regional powerhouse based
in a village twenty kilometers southwest of Laurent's home. Amateur
cyclists could not race without a license, so, in 1976, Rosario persuaded
Laurent to get one.

Greg's parents had wholeheartedly encouraged his cycling career, so
much so that his father stepped forward to race alongside him. Laurent,
however, found his parents decidedly unsupportive of his own cycling
pursuits—an odd contrast, considering the relative gravitas with which

cycling was regarded in France. Their opposition likely stemmed from their class. Cycling is a stereotypically blue-collar sport in Europe, and the Fignon parents harbored middle-class ambitions for their elder son. They prized his schoolwork above all else, and they deemed cycling a needless distraction from their Sunday family luncheons in the city.

Rosario's father was friends with Jacques Fignon and persuaded him to let Laurent join the cycling club, offering to chaperone both boys to training rides. One winter morning in 1976, Laurent arrived with Rosario and his father at a local cafe to meet with a club official.

"This kid breathed cycling," the official remembered. He warned Laurent, "This is a hard sport. You have to be serious. The fun and games are over."[8] Besides, Laurent was already fifteen, old for a rookie cyclist. Such talk only emboldened Laurent. Now he had something to prove.

The club approved Laurent's license and presented him with the team jersey. Laurent gazed at it with joy. Laurent's parents still opposed his cycling ambitions, so he went behind their backs to secure rides to the races with friends' parents. The rides arranged, Laurent's parents would reluctantly accede, knowing that once their headstrong son had resolved to act, there was little they could do to stop him.

Laurent's first race arrived a few weeks later: the Grand Prix de la Tapisserie Mathieu, a contest for young "cadets" of ages fourteen and fifteen, which spanned fifty kilometers around a small course in the town of Vigneux-sur-Seine, south of Paris. Out on the course, tucked within a pack of fifty-two riders, Laurent soon learned that the race had no more structure than the anarchic rides through the village with his friends. The pace would rise and fall, seemingly at random.

In the final laps, Laurent found himself in a breakaway, joined by two of his cycling buddies. With the same mindless abandon of the neighborhood rides, Laurent attacked, hard, just to see what would happen. After a time, he turned his head and found himself alone. "I looked back in amazement, once, twice," he recollected. "Then I decided to keep going, without thinking anymore."

When he crossed the line, forty-five seconds ahead of everyone else, Laurent didn't bother to raise his arms in triumph. He assumed he had done something wrong. As the team coach approached, he braced for a tongue lashing. Instead, the coach offered congratulations. Still baffled, Laurent asked, "Was it okay for me to win?" The coach just smiled.[9]

Laurent would win three more races in 1976. At the Fignon home, Laurent's second-floor room soon grew cluttered with trophies and medals. Down in the gravel-floored basement, Laurent and Rosario would "spend entire days disassembling and reassembling our bicycles," Rosario recalled.[10]

Laurent's second season, riding with sixteen- and seventeen-year-old juniors, should have delivered another string of victories. Instead, Laurent's nascent cycling career went disastrously off course. He became embroiled in a childish contest with Rosario to see who could turn up on race day with the cleanest, shiniest bike. Laurent was taking apart his bicycle every Saturday, piece by piece, and cleaning and polishing each component before reassembling it. But he was no mechanic, and in every Sunday race, something on Laurent's bicycle would inevitably break down or fall off. He lost ten races to various mechanical malfunctions. Finally, Laurent's father stepped in, forbidding any further repairs. Laurent won the next race he entered. It was his only win of 1977.

Laurent's early success had made believers of his parents. Henceforth, there would be no more Sunday family luncheons.

"They were quickly drawn into the cycling world," Laurent would write. "Meeting other parents, the smell of muscle cream on chilly mornings as early risers looked on with haggard faces, the smell of hot coffee, cars with cycling gear strewn everywhere in a chaotic mess; the whole Bohemian side of parking lots frequented by young bike riders."[11] The Fignons became immersed in the same Deadhead-like subculture that had embraced the LeMond family across the Atlantic.

Unlike Greg, Laurent showed no early faculty for cycling tactics. He rode on pure power, always pedaling near the front of the peloton and always attacking. He drew motivation from the possibility of victory; to ride at the rear of the pack made no sense to him. Laurent never knew what was coming around the next bend, could never predict how a race might unfold. Yet, whenever he paid attention, he seemed to reach the finish line ahead of everyone else.

The next year, 1978, Laurent entered more than three dozen races and won eighteen, guided by a one-word strategy: *attack*. "I won in sprint finishes, on my own, on the flats, in the hills. However the race panned out, I attacked, and I won."

One day, after a string of five consecutive victories, a trainer turned to Laurent and muttered, "You have a gift."[12]

That summer, Laurent made his boldest statement yet in the regional championships of l'Île-de-France, the district that encompasses Paris and its suburbs. Riding in a team time trial, Laurent proved so much stronger than his teammates that he led the group for thirty-five of the forty-two kilometers raced.

In the championship road race, Laurent maneuvered himself into a group chasing a breakaway. The lead group included a boy named Pascal Jules, a fellow junior with a strong reputation in the region. Tired of chasing, Laurent broke free of the chase group, easily caught the leaders and then surged past them at the finish, stunning Pascal and the others.

After the race, at a village pub, Laurent spotted Pascal and his father. Laurent avoided Pascal's gaze, and something about the bespectacled Laurent struck the other boy as supremely arrogant.

A new Laurent Fignon was taking shape. "From the introverted boy there began to emerge a strong character, someone decidedly sure of himself," Rosario Scolaro recalled. "Laurent was normal, as a boy and as a man, but when he got on the bicycle, then he was not normal, he possessed something more, and anyone who saw him there would have no doubt that this man on the bicycle was a champion. All of his character, his strength, his will, came pouring out."[13]

Some in the Parisian cycling community read Laurent's self-confidence as conceit and misread his native shyness as studied aloofness. The less flattering traits seemed to wax when he won. Victory went to his head like cheap champagne. Now, when Laurent and Rosario would roll up to the club headquarters to check the weekly schedule, Laurent would lounge in the car with his feet on the dashboard while Rosario shuffled inside to see where his friend would be racing on Sunday.

From the start of his career, Laurent struggled to handle both success and failure. Hard luck would leave him sullen and withdrawn, while good fortune would transform him into an insufferable brag-gart. There was no in-between. Laurent's shyness only amplified these mood swings, complicating the task of expressing himself to the out-side world. Only close friends seemed to understand him, and Laurent had few of those.

Just as young Greg had pored over French cycling magazines in the Nevada workshop of Roland Della Santa, Laurent, too, became immersed in the European cycling press. He read *L'Équipe* every morn-ing, and he devoured every new copy of the glossy magazines *Miroir du Cyclisme* and *Vélo*. "I learned that the Tour de France was related to the history of France itself in the twentieth century," he recalled. "The sto-ries of the nation and its bike race were intertwined."[14]

Laurent pursued his scholastic studies with considerably less ardor. At age seventeen, he sat for the *baccalauréat*, a series of exams that largely determine whether a student will proceed to college. Laurent had ignored his studies in favor of cycling, and he assumed he would fail the exams. But he managed to pass, and in the fall of 1978 he enrolled at a university in the Parisian suburb of Villetaneuse, seeking a degree in structural and material science. His grades hadn't been high enough to pursue his first career choice, veterinarian.

The trek from Tournan-en-Brie to Villetaneuse took two hours each way. Often Laurent arrived to find that lessons had been canceled amid an ongoing faculty labor protest. Eventually he stopped showing up, and no one at the university seemed to care.

Up to this point, Laurent had never considered cycling as a career. Now, his studies abandoned, Laurent found his thoughts increasingly dominated by his bicycle. One Saturday, a group of kids went to fetch Laurent from his home for a nocturnal outing. Laurent demurred. He had to train the next day. "For him," Rosario said, "cycling was already that important."[15]

Laurent envisioned a new future for himself. One day, he made a bold pronouncement to Rosario: "I am going to be a champion, and sooner or later I will win the Tour de France."[16]

Laurent summoned the courage to confront his parents. He told them he was through with school, and he pledged that he would enter his obligatory twelve months of military service at year's end. After a heated argument, they relented. "All right," Jacques Fignon said to his son. "But if you don't go to the army for any reason, you go to work."[17]

Laurent applied to the Bataillon de Joinville, an elite French military unit that catered to aspiring athletes. France's greatest male cyclist, Jacques Anquetil, had passed through its ranks. Laurent had amassed nearly thirty victories as an amateur racer. Yet, for all his outward arrogance and easy command of the sport, Laurent still lacked self-confidence and underrated his own abilities. He expressed genuine surprise when the battalion accepted his application.

Laurent's military service began in October 1979. At Joinville, Laurent was back in the welcome company of cyclists he had faced in past races. As a military unit, the *bataillon* proved surprisingly lax. Laurent was free to go home on weekends to race, and when the men weren't actively training, they were left largely unsupervised: "As soon as our superior officers had their backs turned—which was pretty much every day—we would disappear, and stroll around Paris."[18]

On his bicycle, Laurent still raced with wild abandon. But at Joinville, he gradually began to learn the workings of a cycling team, and to appreciate the transcendent joy that came of collaborating with teammates to win a race. The apex of his military service was a three-man team time trial at the Isle of Man. "We worked together, in complete youthful harmony," Laurent would write. "We won, but you could see something else in our eyes besides mere delight at the victory. Try and explain that to people who haven't done sports."[19]

When Laurent returned home from the Bataillon de Joinville, his parents promptly posed the question that had hung in the air during the year of his absence: What was he going to do with his life? Laurent was ready with a reply: "I'm going to ride my bike. I've decided, and that's all there is to it."

"Okay," his father said. "But you have to go to work."[20]

Laurent had won more than three dozen races with his amateur club in the Paris suburbs. His name was spreading around the cycling world, and he had little trouble finding a home in one of the region's top amateur clubs, Union Sportive Créteil—a few scant months after Greg LeMond's ill-starred run with the team.

Laurent's tenure with U.S. Créteil would prove more lasting. Rather than pay him outright, the club assigned Laurent to spend weekday mornings at the town hall in Créteil, working a job of vaguely defined duties for a monthly salary of 1,000 francs. Laurent passed most of the time flirting with secretaries. Blond-haired, blue-eyed, and sculpted like a statue, Laurent was a distraction. Soon he was reassigned to a new sinecure, traveling around the network of Parisian sports clubs to collect seemingly meaningless measurements, such as exact counts of lockers and "bounciness" ratings for gymnasium mats.

At the start of the 1981 season, Laurent, aged twenty, was drafted onto the French national cycling team. Greg, by contrast, had made the U.S. national team at sixteen. But the French national team was considerably harder to crack. In five years, Laurent had compiled a cycling résumé to rival the résumés of the best young cyclists in France—but he had not yet ridden away from them.

Though hardly a social butterfly, Laurent had friends, and two of them would loom large in the years to come. The first was Pascal Jules, the fellow Parisian whom Laurent had upstaged at the regional championships in 1978. After the first tense standoff in the village pub, Laurent and Pascal had ridden under separate banners until 1981, when they came together on the national team. The union was inevitable, as both men showed vast promise. Pascal's background was even more deeply blue-collar than Laurent's. But they shared "an outrageous, voracious appetite for life," Laurent wrote. "Together, we could whip up storms."[21]

Alain Gallopin was three years older than Laurent and hailed from a family of cyclists in the Loire Valley. Alain had first glimpsed Laurent in 1979 at the multistage Tour de Seine-et-Marne. On the final day, Laurent had launched a suicidal attack with one hundred kilometers yet to race, and he had somehow held off the peloton to the final kilometer. "There was a steep climb at the finish, and we caught him there," Alain recounted. "Without the steep climb, he would have won." Alain was impressed.[22]

The two men met the next year at Joinville, where Alain was on his second tour of duty as Laurent completed his first. Laurent remembered Alain as "unbelievably talented."[23] They raced together in 1980 and 1981, and Alain sometimes stayed in the Fignon home. He was a frequent passenger in the family car, heading to some weekend race, Laurent and his father in front and Alain in the back with Laurent's mother. Laurent and Jacques "were always arguing, all the time, over small things," Alain recalled. "Me and the mother, we wouldn't say a thing."[24]

Laurent and his fellow recruits were about to glimpse the broader cycling world. After a brief training camp at La Londe-les-Maures, in southern France, the national team prepared for the 1981 Tour de Corse, a major international stage race in Corsica that allowed amateurs to compete alongside professionals. The prerace favorite was none other than Bernard Hinault, two-time Tour de France winner and reigning world champion, the man they called *le Blaireau*—the Badger—for his tenacity.

"He didn't say much," Laurent said of Hinault, and "he didn't show off. He just showed the power in his jutting chin. Everything about him breathed confidence. His whole being expressed a single thought: 'I know who I am.'"[25]

Surely no one in Corsica regarded Laurent as a potential heir to Hinault, least of all Laurent himself, who had not even expected a spot on the national team. Yet, when the race started, Laurent affixed himself to Hinault's wheel and remained there, fighting doggedly back into his slipstream whenever the ebb and flow of the peloton pulled them apart.

After a time, Hinault eased back beside Laurent, turned his head, and grumbled, "What are you doing stuck to my backside?"

Laurent replied, "I've never ridden my bike behind a world champion, and I wanted to see how it felt."[26]

Laurent had to prove himself among the professionals if he was to impress the cycling world. When the race reached the mountains, the lesser pros and most of the amateurs fell away, leaving the elite riders at the front. And there was Laurent, riding among them.

"My technique left much to be desired," he recalled. "I thought I was going to die on every hairpin." Yet, Laurent finished seventh in the stage, a remarkable placing for an amateur in the mountains.[27]

Laurent's performance drew the attention of Cyrille Guimard, *directeur sportif* of the great Renault team, the man who had just signed Greg LeMond. Guimard had followed Laurent's career. "I knew that he had a lot of potential, a lot of talent," he recounted. "Also, like Greg, he had a strong personality, lots of character."[28]

On the final day of racing, Guimard called a meeting with Laurent and Pascal Jules, who had also been riding well. "Do you want me to keep an eye on you this year . . . ," he asked the young riders. He paused, leaving the two cyclists hanging onto his words: ". . . with an eye to having you as pros one day?"

Turning professional with the vaunted Renault team was the dream of every cyclist in France. Guimard's words were as good as a contract. "It was now up to us," Laurent recalled, "to prove that he had not made a mistake."[29]

L'AMÉRICAIN

O N JANUARY 9, 1981, newlyweds Greg and Kathy LeMond arrived in Paris. There to meet them at Orly Airport was Bernard Hinault, the most famous cyclist in France. This was hardly a customary welcome for a rookie earning $1,500 a month. Then again, Greg was no ordinary cyclist. He was an American, with an American wife and American tastes and a *nouveau riche* upbringing. Who could say whether Greg and Kathy would survive the transition to France? Cyrille Guimard and his Renault team were making a long-term investment in Greg, and they wanted to make a strong first impression.

Hinault steered his Renault sedan onto the *autoroute* and accelerated to 100 kilometers per hour, then 150, then 200, talking nonstop all the while, though neither Greg nor Kathy understood a word he said.

"And the highway was parting for him," Kathy recalled. Motorists making way for the speeding sedan would peer into its windows and spot the great Hinault at the wheel. Their reaction suggested they had seen God; Hinault's young passengers feared they might soon meet him.[1]

Hinault proceeded not to the hotel where Greg and Kathy would be staying but to a bicycle race in which he would be riding. There, the LeMonds sat in a jetlagged stupor and watched the Badger compete.

The next evening, Hinault chauffeured Greg and Kathy to the apartment of a Renault executive for a formal dinner. A butler answered the door and led the couple into an elegant parlor, where they were greeted by a beautiful woman in a Chanel suit, who introduced herself as the executive's wife. The butler departed and then returned, wheeling in an enormous bottle of cognac. He solemnly handed Hinault a hammer to break the wax seal. The cognac was poured, and a glass was offered to Kathy, who demurred.

"I don't drink."

The room fell silent; this was an unthinkable breach of etiquette.[2]

By the next day, the Parisian honeymoon was over. Greg's sponsor delivered the automobile that he and Kathy had been promised, a vehicle decidedly more sedate than Hinault's. It arrived with a flat tire. Greg, for all his skills, had never changed a car tire. Once again, the Badger swept in, rolling up his sleeves and replacing the tire himself. When the couple climbed into the vehicle, they discovered that the windshield was warped, giving the Gallic landscape a psychedelic hue. Undeterred, they set out from Paris to Brittany, where Cyrille Guimard had offered to set them up in Nantes, near his own home.

However, the LeMonds arrived to find their dwelling was not ready. They wound up in a hotel room above a store, at their own expense. They lived there for a month, with toilets and showers down the hall, recovering from a crippling bout of food poisoning, as they peered out the windows at a ceaseless rain. They were grateful to have each other.

And then Greg was gone, off to southern France for a six-week training camp to prepare for the racing season.

At the Renault camp, the weather was dreadful. Greg found himself riding only one hundred kilometers a day, four days a week, lighter than his usual regimen. Rather than riding himself into shape, Greg was falling out of it.

Greg was naturally sociable, but he did not yet speak French well enough to converse with his new teammates. So Greg sat alone through the team's multicourse, two-hour luncheons, reading Robert Ludlum thrillers while his teammates dined and chatted. Reading at dinner was another horrific offense against Gallic sensibilities.

Back in Nantes, Kathy, too, sat alone and read. She missed Greg, just as he missed her. And she was strapped for cash. After a month in France, Greg had yet to be paid. The couple spent their wedding money to cover Kathy's lodging. When it ran out, team officials suggested she move into the rented house, with the ominous caveat that it was still not "ready." Kathy arrived to find the three-bedroom residence had no heat, no hot water, and no furniture; the prior residents had even removed the appliances and cabinets, per local custom.

"It had a toilet and a bathtub, and that's it," Kathy recalled.[3]

Concerned that the despairing Kathy might bolt, the LeMond family dispatched Bertha, Greg's rugged mother, to stay with his young wife. They purchased hot plates to cook on. Kathy began drinking coffee simply to keep warm. She and her mother-in-law slept on foldout cots flanked by mousetraps. Every three days, Kathy would stake out a pay phone and await a call from Greg, who was growing increasingly concerned about her plight. Guimard was off with the team, so Kathy telephoned and visited Guimard's wife repeatedly, asking when the furniture would show up. Madame Guimard would coolly reply, "The furniture is on the way," before shooing her out the door. She counseled Kathy to remain at home in case the truck should arrive; after that, Kathy and Bertha never left the dwelling together.[4]

Whatever his failings as host, Cyrille Guimard truly believed he was looking out for his new rider. He went so far as to recruit the other American racing prominently in Europe, and offer him a spot on the Renault team.

Jonathan "Jock" Boyer was a Europhile from California who had traveled to Europe in 1973, just after high school, and raced with ragtag amateur teams for four years before turning professional in 1977. Jock was not just the only other American in the peloton but very nearly the only other native English speaker, along with hard-boiled Irish sprinter Sean Kelly and a few others. Guimard hired Jock to mentor Greg, a plan that sounded sensible. Greg had always admired Jock as an American pioneer of European cycling. But when Jock arrived on the Renault team, their relationship immediately soured.

Jock chastised Greg for his failure to adopt French customs, which Jock himself had embraced, along with the French language, to an extent that struck some American cyclists as delusional. In that regard, Jock might have been a closer match to Dave Stoller, the Midwesterner in *Breaking Away* who fancied himself Italian. Jock lectured Greg about his many gaffes in the dining room.

If Greg was slow to embrace French culture, he was quick to conquer French cycling. Jock surely resented Greg's success and envied his celebrity. Already Greg's teammates referred to the nineteen-year-old Nevadan as *l'Américain*, as if he were the only one. With Jock on the team, Greg could interact with his French-speaking teammates and with the press, using Jock as interpreter. But this arrangement soon backfired. Greg began to suspect Jock of twisting his words in translation to make the young star sound arrogant and self-important. (Jock denied this, suggesting instead that perhaps French reporters twisted Jock's translations.)

In a February 1981 interview in *Miroir du Cyclisme*, some of his first comments to the French press, Greg announced, through his envious interpreter, his displeasure with French cuisine, housing, recreation, and overall culture. "Almost everything repelled me," he said, his words printed beneath an ironic photograph of *l'Américain* wearing a beret and holding a baguette, a French newspaper, and a glass of *vin rouge*.[5]

Such comments cemented Greg's image as an American ingrate. It would remain thus until he had learned enough French to speak for himself.

For the elite men of cycling in the 1980s, the season effectively began in March with Paris–Nice, one of the oldest and toughest stage races in Europe. Next came Milan–San Remo, at nearly three hundred kilometers one of the longest single-day events in cycling; and then Paris–Roubaix, a grubby contest famous for its bone-rattling cobblestones. April brought the Vuelta a España, the first of the trio of three-week races known as the Grand Tours, and Liège–Bastogne–Liège, the oldest of the five epic single-day Monuments of European cycling. May brought the Giro d'Italia, the second Grand Tour, followed in June by two races that served as warm-ups for the third, the Tour de France: the Critérium du Dauphiné Libéré, in France, and the Tour de Suisse, in Switzerland. *Le Tour* and its attendant festivities occupied most of July and August. The season's symbolic close came in October with the Giro di Lombardia, the Classic of the Falling Leaves.

In the old days of professional cycling, racers entered races more or less indiscriminately, riding for as many victories as they could seize. Eddy Merckx stands today as the greatest male cyclist of them all for the sheer number and variety of races he conquered in the 1960s and 1970s: five Tours de France, five Giri d'Italia, one Vuelta a España, and three world championships, along with seven victories in Milan–San Remo, five in Liège–Bastogne–Liège, three each in Paris–Roubaix and Paris–Nice, and two each in the Giro di Lombardia and Tour of Flanders, among many others.

Greg and his generation arrived in the peloton just as those barnstorming days were drawing to an end. Cyclists prepared more methodically, ate more carefully, trained more scientifically, and earned more money for their efforts. The Tour de France loomed ever larger as the ultimate prize—indeed, the only prize—for those few men with a real chance to claim it.

Greg's first professional race would be the Étoile de Bessèges, held in February, 1981, in the Languedoc-Roussillon region of southern France. The team bus departed in the afternoon, two days before the race. Arrival was scheduled for the following morning, which struck Greg as curious; the trip covered only five hundred kilometers. But this was France. The coach had traveled only a fraction of the route when it pulled off the road for a languorous dinner. The bus proceeded for another hour and then stopped for the night. The team set out late the next morning and spent another full day on the road. On arrival in Bessèges at seven that evening, having lost two full days of training, Greg was exhausted and carsick.

From the start of his inaugural race, Greg struggled. "I just couldn't believe how fast they were going," he recalled. "I was in shock." Greg was dropped. After a time, Guimard drove up in his team car and helpfully instructed his young charge: "You've got to lose some of that weight."[6]

When the stage was over, Greg went off and rode another fifty kilometers on his own. The next day, he was dropped again. He rode another sixty kilometers that afternoon. He proceeded in that fashion until, after six weeks, he had shed the extra pounds and was finally in racing form.

In April, Kathy's parents came to visit. Two months had passed since their daughter's arrival in Nantes. Yet the flat remained empty and cold—and felt especially so when Greg was on the road. And Greg had returned from training camp looking, Kathy recalled, "like a POW."[7] Upon witnessing their plight, Kathy's mother burst into tears.

On April 9, Kathy's birthday, the refrigerator and stove finally appeared. The rest of the furnishings soon followed. That weekend, Kathy and her parents watched Greg guide Hinault to victory at Paris–Roubaix, cycling's Hell of the North, the one-day classic with its infamous cobblestones. Before Kathy's parents returned home, David Morris made peace with his daughter. "Now, I get it," he told Kathy. "He really is one in a million."[8]

Greg's contract included several round-trip airplane tickets to the United States, a perk that probably rivaled his cash salary in value, for Cyrille Guimard knew his young star would grow homesick. After all Greg's hard work in the spring of 1981, Guimard rewarded Greg and Kathy with a trip home to visit family. They returned to France in May, fresh and confident, and Greg journeyed to another epic stage race, the Tour de l'Oise. This time Greg rode well, and one stage found him nearing the finish in a breakaway. The group rounded the last turn, and Greg shot forth to victory, claiming his first stage win as a professional. He crossed the line with a joyful, cathartic cowboy cry—*YEEE-HAAAA!* No French cyclist had heard the like.

Ten days later, Greg rode the Dauphiné Libéré, a weeklong contest that covered much of the same Alpine terrain as *le Tour* itself. The Dauphiné had been conquered by the greats—Anquetil, Merckx, Hinault. The mountainous course yielded a great sorting, weeding out the sprinters and the time-trial specialists and leaving a handful of climbers who could challenge for victory in the great tours to follow.

Greg didn't win the Dauphiné, but he proved himself the equal of the great climbers. Riding alongside Hinault and shepherding him to victory, Greg finished in fourth place. Two weeks later, the man who had finished in front of him, French star Pascal Simon, was penalized for doping. He was not disqualified, merely reprimanded, and an extra ten minutes were added to his time. Such was the lenience with which French racing officials regarded doping in that day. The dustup elevated Greg to third place, his most remarkable showing since his victory at Circuit de la Sarthe as an amateur the previous spring. It was not the most inspiring way to earn one of three steps on the victory podium; nonetheless, the result showed to the broader cycling world that Greg had the tools to win a Grand Tour one day—if he lasted that long. Guimard raised Greg's annual salary to $25,000.

Greg did not yet speak French well enough to feel comfortable joining his teammates in the dining room. Worse, he made few concessions to the ancient traditions of French cycling; he recognized most of them for what they were, prescientific superstitions. French cyclists welcomed cheese but eschewed ice cream, which they deemed harmful to the liver. They approved yogurt, and of course wine, but not salad, which was said to induce lethargy.

Greg ate what he liked. He devoured entire tubs of ice cream, sometimes in front of his teammates. He scoured France for Tex-Mex cuisine, and he seized every opportunity to grill a cheeseburger. He sometimes golfed on off days, breaking another cardinal rule of cycling that prescribed bed rest for idle racers.

The French riders kept their hotel rooms sealed like tombs, for fear that a stray draft might give them pneumonia; Greg liked fresh air. Accustomed to chilly Nevada nights, Greg often found himself hot. He once removed his shirt at the team dinner table—a sin far worse than opening a Robert Ludlum book. One night when he could not get to sleep in a Provence hotel room, Greg dragged the mattress outdoors, plopped it down in the dirt, and promptly fell asleep, only to awaken the next morning within a throng of French families, naked but for a bedsheet.

French cyclists forswore sex on a race day. Greg did not. He and Kathy burned with such passion that they made love nearly every time they saw each other, and Kathy often traveled with Greg in racing season. Sometimes Guimard followed them to Greg's room, laboring in vain to keep them apart. French cycling tradition dictated that sex—especially "emotional" sex, intertwined with love—dampened the competitive spirit. Sean Kelly, the great Irish cyclist, was said to abstain from marital relations for weeks before a major race.

"It's all right if they pick up a groupie, but keep them away from the wives," Kathy told *Winning* magazine, explaining the tradition in a feature on the wives of English speaking cyclists. "It's antiquated."[9]

When Greg and Kathy were apart, Greg would line up at a pay phone every evening to call her. Sometimes loneliness overcame him, and Kathy would drive through the night to join him. In time, Greg's handlers realized it was best to keep them together.

In late June 1981, Greg returned to the United States to ride in the Coors Classic. Inaugurated in 1975 as the Red Zinger Bicycle Classic, the Coors had evolved into the premier event in American cycling, rivaling European stage races with its program of brutal mountains and scorching heat. This year, organizers planned an unofficial makeup event for the boycotted 1980 Olympics and extended an invitation to the feared Russian national cycling team. Most observers assumed a Russian would win.

Instead, Greg won. Victory brought his first feature in *Sports Illustrated,* which named Greg "the world's next great spoke hero."[10]

As the 1981 season drew to a close, Greg's name began to surface in discussions of a new and potentially historic cycling trend. Some termed it the Anglo-Saxon invasion.

At that point in the history of men's cycling, no one from an English-speaking nation had ever won the Tour de France, the Giro d'Italia, or the Vuelta a España. Until 1950, in fact, only four nations had produced Tour winners: France, Italy, Belgium, and tiny Luxembourg. Spanish and Swiss riders conquered the Tour in the 1950s, and a Dutchman followed in the 1960s. The Spanish and Italian contests remained truly provincial affairs; in the Giro, it was not uncommon for Italian riders to work together—sometimes in cahoots with fans, motorists, and even helicopter pilots—to spoil the chances of outsiders.

English-speaking nations produced only a handful of professional riders. Over time, a few of them had shown sufficient talent to earn spots on European teams, which, to satisfy partisan sponsors and fans, seldom employed foreigners. Englishman Tom Simpson joined a French team in 1959, after winning a medal at the 1956 Olympics; in 1962 he briefly led the Tour de France, becoming the first British rider to wear the yellow jersey for a day, and finished the race in sixth place.

The 1980s brought a new generation of young cyclists from English-speaking nations with real prospects for victory in the Grand Tours. Irish sprinter Sean Kelly won two stages in the 1979 Vuelta a España and two more in the 1980 Tour de France. Australian Phil Anderson couldn't sprint like Kelly but climbed well enough to finish tenth in the 1981 Tour. Irishman Stephen Roche, barely twenty, looked capable of outdueling both Kelly and Anderson in the Tour one day.

Greg entered the 1982 cycling season with a similar aura of promise. There was talk that he might already be regarded as leader-in-reserve on his elite Renault team. Greg brushed it off modestly.

"This seems a little premature, especially as there are very good riders on our team, even if they are young," he told the French journal *Sprint International*. "I do not want to name names," he added, "but I'm not the only one."[11] He referred, of course, to Laurent Fignon.

April found Greg riding in the prestigious Liège–Bastogne–Liège. The press and public expected great things; on the very first kilometer, a photographer called out to Greg, asking *l'Américain* to turn his head for a shot. As Greg did, he squeezed his brake to slow down. It was a cold day, and his brakes had iced up. He rolled straight into another rider and went down hard. The impact fractured his right collarbone. And, just like that, the first half of Greg's racing season was over.

The broken bone was a major setback; as a rule of thumb, a cyclist loses two or three weeks of training for every week spent recovering from injury or illness; in cycling, one's form can be lost far more quickly than it is gained.

Greg's professional season would stagnate until August, when he traveled to southeastern England for the world championship road race. He trained tirelessly for the marathon contest. Then he fell ill with food poisoning—a setback, once again, of exponential proportions. Greg thought of dropping out but decided against it. His and Kathy's parents were traveling from the United States to watch him race, and their tickets were not refundable.

The world championship would put Greg back in contact with Jock Boyer, George Mount, and the other top American riders, and it would present an ethical dilemma: whether to race for himself, for his fellow Americans, or for his French cycling team. As Greg saw it, American cycling officials voiced faint enthusiasm for his victories and discounted his role in popularizing American cycling. Greg felt he knew more than they about how to win in Europe.

The Americans were accustomed to racing against each other at the worlds. The best-placed American earned the right to wear the stars-and-stripes jersey of national champion in the following year. For anyone but Greg that was a big deal. Greg urged the Americans to ride as a team. The great cycling nations rode as teams in the worlds, racing to elevate one of their own to victory. But the Americans voted to ride for themselves. The decision would prove fateful.

The world championship race, staged on September 5, covered eighteen laps around a 15.3-kilometer course that ended with a short, steep climb. Over the first dozen laps, a powerful Italian team controlled the race and thinned the herd, until only a few dozen of the strongest riders remained. Their goal was to launch the nation's great sprinter, Giuseppe Saronni, to victory.

As the finish neared, both Greg and Jock Boyer remained in the lead group. Jock, a weak sprinter, knew his only chance for victory lay in launching an attack at the foot of the steep hill, before the Italians had loosed their sprinter. Jock accelerated out of the peloton, putting a small stretch of daylight between himself and the others.

For a time, none of the favorites reacted to Jock's move. Then, in the final kilometer, Greg shot forth from the pack and began closing the gap. Greg knew that his own best chance to win was to surge forward and drop Saronni.

The sight of an American cyclist reeling in his countryman was more than some racing fans could bear. On British television, commentator Phil Liggett cried, "Now, really, LeMond should not be doing this."[12] Liggett was honoring the code of European cycling, which, on that day, the Americans had elected not to follow. In truth, there was little chance Jock could have held off the fearsome power of the peloton to win the race. But that, for cycling purists, was beside the point: Greg had spoiled the chances of a fellow American.

In the end, this would not be Greg's day or Jock's. Saronni clung tenaciously to Greg's wheel. When Greg caught Jock, Saronni flew past them. It was a perfect move; Greg would sprint for second place. He crossed the line five seconds behind Saronni. Jock limped home in tenth.

Jock was crushed. Greg's purported betrayal would fuel the first real scandal in the modern history of American cycling.

Greg's motives were complicated. In racing for himself, Greg was doing just as his American team had instructed. With his performance in England, Greg simultaneously defeated a rider he disliked, seeded chaos in a national team he had disavowed—and rode to the highest finish ever posted by an American man.

Three days later, Greg entered the Tour de l'Avenir, the Tour of the Future, a ten-day stage race put on by the organization that ran the Tour de France and following a similar course. A showcase for rising stars, excluding only seasoned pros, l'Avenir pitted young professionals against the best of the amateurs.

The race opened with a series of flat stages, and a group of East Germans took an early lead. Then the peloton hit the mountains, and Greg exploded, taking first place in a twenty-two-kilometer mountain time trial. The next day, he escaped on a long Alpine stage, finishing five minutes ahead of everyone else. At day's end, Cyrille Guimard climbed out of his car and told an elated Kathy, "I've never seen anyone as strong as Greg was today."[13]

Greg extended his lead by winning another time trial. At the end of the race, his victory margin was more than ten minutes, the most commanding performance in the history of l'Avenir. Greg had never dominated a race so completely. His feat startled the European cycling press, even after all the months of hype about l'Américain.

It did not surprise Bernard Hinault. The Badger told the New York Times, "I consider him my successor."[14] Hinault had won both the Tour de France and the Giro d'Italia that year, claiming the two greatest events in cycling. Yet Greg's victory in l'Avenir somehow carried equal gravitas.

The only one who didn't seem impressed was Greg. "I have merely taken a step," he said, "in the path that leads to the goal I set for myself: to be a champion."[15]

Bit by bit, the French were falling for *l'Américain*. The initial culture shock of his arrival in France was now a distant memory. Greg had learned to speak a sort of pidgin French, to the immense satisfaction of his Gallic hosts. He could now convey his essential sweetness to the French public and press.

"It can be said that Greg LeMond is a teenager pushed too quickly to seed," the *Miroir du Cyclisme* observed. "The body is that of an adult male, while the face beneath the downy blond hair retains the cheeky humor of childhood. With one of those smiles that some would call naïve, but which nevertheless betrays nothing but confidence. Confidence in himself, and in others, and in the future, plain and simple."[16]

At the close of the 1982 season, Greg signed a new three-year contract with Guimard and his Renault team, ending months of rumor and gossip. Greg had fielded offers from several other teams, his stock soaring after his triumph at l'Avenir. *L'Américain* now earned $100,000 a year. David Morris could stop worrying about how Greg would support his daughter.

That fall, the LeMonds traveled to Belgium to house hunt. A few months earlier, while Greg recovered from the broken collarbone, he and Kathy had spent some time in a Belgian hotel. There the LeMonds had discovered an Anglophiliac treasure trove: BBC television. English-language movies. Cheddar cheese. There were even American riches: Cap'n Crunch. Peanut butter. All of these things Greg had been denied in France, a society that fastidiously filtered out nearly every speck of English or American culture.

Belgium had another thing that France lacked: Phil Anderson.

Philip Grant Anderson had grown up in Melbourne, Australia, and distinguished himself as a top amateur. He turned pro in 1980, a year before Greg, and rode for the Peugeot team, archrival to Renault. He entered the Tour de France in 1981 and briefly led it, becoming the first cyclist from another continent to wear the *maillot jaune*. In 1982 he led the Tour again—this time for nine full days—and finished in fifth place, among the cycling elite.

Phil and Greg had met at the Red Zinger Classic in 1979 and quickly become friends. When Greg arrived in Europe, they became best friends. Phil had an American wife who had grown as close to Kathy as Phil had to Greg. The Andersons were living in the Belgian town of Waregem, where cycling was a religion and English a near-universal second language.

"We'd see each other at races, and I was telling him how great it is up there," Phil recalled. "He really missed America. There was no English spoken where he was. All he'd do is complain about how alien he felt. And I was just raving about how great Belgium was. The next time I saw him, he said, 'I'm making the move.'"[17]

The LeMonds moved into a gray-brick two-story house in Kortrijk, a Belgian city near the French border—and not far from Waregem. Greg quickly discovered that the Belgians worshipped cycling possibly even more than the French. And the Belgians were a gregarious lot. Here, if Greg lacked a couch, neighbors would offer to lend him their own.

The Belgians hosted bicycling races daily. For training rides, Greg could choose his backdrop, "from the windswept coast of the North Sea to the steep hills of the Flemish countryside."[18] Greg and Kathy finally felt at home.

Greg's 1983 season began in February at a Parisian restaurant where the Renault cycling team revealed its riders to the press. This was a team of unrivaled depth; yet its unchallenged leader was Hinault. To drive home that point, team organizers had all the cyclists walk on stage wearing papier-mâché Hinault masks.

One by one, the announcer called each rider's name and listed his feats as the cyclist lifted his mask. Soon it was Greg's turn: "*Le vanqueur de le Tour d'Avenir, l'Américain . . .*" Greg didn't move. His French wasn't good enough; he'd missed his cue. Hinault strolled over, flipped up Greg's mask, and smiled at his potential successor. Greg just blinked.[19]

By 1983, the Badger was a four-time winner of the Tour de France and, at twenty-eight, threatening to eclipse the other greats of his sport with a fifth and even a sixth victory in the years to come. Hinault had tagged Greg as his protégé; as the French magazine *Vélo* observed, "only the moment of succession is yet to be determined."[20] Yet, in 1983, Hinault was still *le patron*, not just of his team but of the entire peloton.

Greg would ride now as one of Hinault's top lieutenants, an exalted role—but a supporting one. Great deeds lay ahead for Greg, but for now, he and his team would serve the Badger, for that was their job.

Greg telegraphed to the cycling world that he was in no hurry. "I enjoy the advantage of age," he told *Miroir du Cyclisme*. "I am seven years younger than Bernard, and when I am at my peak, he will be retired."[21]

Indeed, the great Hinault had broadcast his intention to retire upon his thirtieth birthday.

In a time before the science of doping could restrain the ravages of time, a professional cyclist could reasonably expect a career peak of perhaps five years. Tour de France winners had ranged in age from nineteen to thirty-six, but those results were outliers; most Tour champions were men between the ages of twenty-five and thirty. Older riders lacked the necessary power to win decisive stages; younger men lacked the stamina to endure three full weeks of breakneck racing. Jacques Anquetil had won his first Tour at twenty-three and his last at thirty. Eddy Merckx had claimed his first victory at twenty-four, his fifth at twenty-nine.

If Hinault was the Renault team's unquestioned leader, Greg fell more into the role of team diplomat: affable, cooperative, and conflict-averse. "He was a very, very happy person," Cyrille Guimard recalled. "He always wanted us to have a relationship based on harmony and peace."[22]

That season Greg had a new roommate, Vincent Barteau, a young Frenchman from Normandy, just turned professional. Vince was assigned to room with Greg when no one else would have him.

Off his bicycle, Greg could be a scatterbrain and a slob. On social outings, he would become too deeply immersed in conversation to keep track of his wallet. When he checked out of a hotel after a race, someone would be sent back to fetch the jerseys and shoes that he had invariably left behind.

"There was stuff everywhere," Vince recalled of their shared room. "The two of us got along, because I'm also very messy." At season's end, each man would return home with several pairs of his roommate's underwear.[23]

Vince immediately saw that Greg was lonely. Though he had learned some French, Greg was not yet fully conversant with his teammates.

"I noticed that Greg wasn't eating the food we were serving," Vince recalled. "No one else noticed that he was not eating well, or if they noticed, they didn't say anything. Bernard Hinault and the others probably thought it was a good thing," he joked, "because the next day they would be stronger than him.

"So I asked Greg, 'What would you like to eat?'"[24]

Greg wanted Chinese food. He and Vince found a Chinese restaurant and stayed out till five in the morning. After that, the two made regular nocturnal excursions in the team car. Vince helped Greg polish his French.

"Everybody else was in bed at ten and lived like a monk," Greg told Irish journalist Paul Kimmage. "I didn't want to go to bed at ten."[25] Neither did Vince; they would stay up together past midnight, chatting and reading in their messy room.

That spring Greg entered his first Grand Tour, the Vuelta a España, a race quite similar to *le Tour* in format and length but beneath it in prestige. Racing in cold, rainy weather, Greg fell ill with bronchitis, a common affliction among cyclists. He struggled on, recovered sufficiently to aid his team captain, and gracefully retired a few days before the finish, when Hinault's victory was assured. But Greg would never ride *la Vuelta* again.

Greg's ailments left him despondent. He missed Kathy, and between injury and illness, his professional career seemed like a parade of false starts. One night, after a particularly disappointing ride, Greg came home so tired and depressed that he drank five beers and fell into a stupor on the couch. He thought of taking an extended break from cycling.

But Greg was scheduled to ride that June in the Dauphiné Libéré stage race. Remembering his third-place finish at the Dauphiné two years earlier, one of his most celebrated results to date, Greg managed to snap out of his funk. He rode the Dauphiné with dominance, seizing victory on the opening road stage with a solo breakaway. Greg won a second stage a few days later, which placed him in second overall. The race leader was Pascal Simon of rival Peugeot, the man who had bested Greg at the same race in 1981, only to be penalized for doping.

The 1983 Dauphiné would be decided on stage six, a torturous climb up Mont Ventoux. Greg rode up the mountain in the lead group, along with Simon and two others. Then, four kilometers from the top, Greg "cracked."

In the colorful vernacular of cycling, *crack* and *bonk* are subtly different. A cyclist who bonks hits a physiological wall at a random moment and for the sole reason that he has failed to consume enough carbohydrates. A cyclist who cracks hits the same wall not for want of nutrition but because his competitors have exhausted him, usually on a mountainside.

On this day, Simon had cracked Greg. "I couldn't believe how fast Simon was riding," Greg recalled.[26] Simon sped away and won the stage and the leader's jersey. Greg recovered to win the final time trial, but it was not enough. Simon edged him out to win the overall race.

Two weeks later, their fortunes reversed. Simon had been caught using a respiratory stimulant called Micorene. This time Simon's ten-minute penalty—a punishment, again, rather than a disqualification—would deliver the race to Greg. Yet the victory, the biggest to date in Greg's career, was bittersweet.

Doping is a tradition as old as bicycle racing itself.

In the glory years of six-day racing, riders staved off exhaustion with help from the *soigneur,* whose care extended well beyond kneading tired legs. Treatments included nitroglycerin, a drug used to stir the heart after cardiac arrest; and strychnine, a toxic compound that could tense tired muscles. Such substances were not banned; indeed, they were deemed necessary to any rider who hoped to complete a 144-hour bicycle race.

Competitors in early Tours de France took whatever substance might help them endure. Cyclists drank alcohol to blunt pain and wore ether-soaked handkerchiefs to soothe burning lungs. Early Tour rules stipulated only that race organizers would not provide the drugs themselves.

The 1924 newspaper exposé "Les Forçats de la Route," or "Convicts of the Road," portrayed the professional cyclist as a rolling apothecary. "Do you want to see how we cope?" snapped Henri Pélissier, winner of the 1923 Tour. "Look." He began to pull items from his bag. "Cocaine for the eyes, and chloroform for the gums."[27]

"And there are pills," another cyclist offered. "Do you want to see pills?"

For many years, neither participants nor fans seemed particularly concerned that chemical enhancements might harm the cyclists who took them; those risks paled next to the perils posed by the race itself. Attitudes changed, somewhat, in 1955, when a group of Tour favorites fell collectively ill on the summit of Mont Ventoux, seemingly stricken by a "preparation" of the same batch. The cycling establishment feigned shock at the public discovery that some of its riders were doping. Tour organizers politely advised that team leaders "oppose the use of certain products." The sports paper L'Équipe promptly pronounced, "The fight against doping seems to have been won." Le Tour had narrowly averted disaster.[28]

Amphetamines and painkillers circulated freely in Grand Tours of the postwar 1950s. In 1960, cyclist Roger Rivière flew off a mountain into a ravine and broke his back; he had ingested so much of the opioid Palfium that he could no longer operate his brakes.

Clearly, the fight against doping had not been won. "Doping is now in the arsenal of the champion, and the lesser rider," L'Équipe opined following the Rivière affair. "They dope to finish twentieth, they dope for the time-trials, they dope to climb a mountain, they dope to overcome their nerves. Then they dope to get to sleep at night."[29]

One morning in 1962, a dozen Tour riders abandoned the race, claiming food poisoning from bad fish. But then—sacrebleu!—the Tour doctor discovered that some of the stricken riders hadn't eaten fish. An oblique communiqué instructed riders that Tour officials could "only draw their attention to the dangers of certain types of care and preparation," advice apparently not limited to fish.[30]

France passed its first anti-doping law in 1965. Anyone caught taking or supplying drugs in any sport would be fined between 500 and 5,000 francs. But Tour officials were timid in enforcing the new rule for fear of what they might find. Most of the Italians boycotted the next year's Tour in protest. Anquetil, the great French champion, led a riders' strike. He told an interviewer that only a fool would think it possible to ride from Bordeaux to Paris on water alone. "Leave me in peace," he said. "Everybody dopes."[31]

One scorching day in July 1967, the Tour set out to scale Mont Ventoux in hundred-degree heat. The race doctor told a journalist, "If the boys stick their nose in a 'topette' today, we could have a death on our hands."[32] He alluded to sacks filled with drugs carried by cyclists. Near the summit, British rider Tom Simpson began to lose command of his bicycle, weaving across the tarmac. A kilometer from the top, he collapsed. Simpson ordered his mechanic to help him back on his bike. He pedaled another half kilometer, and then he began to wobble once more. Spectators held him erect, but Simpson was already unconscious.

Tom Simpson had been the first man from an English-speaking nation to wear the *maillot jaune*; now, he was the first man to die at the Tour for reasons other than injury. An autopsy found amphetamines and alcohol in his system, and very little water. Tour organizers responded by declaring the 1968 edition the Tour of Good Health and starting the race in the mineral-water mecca of Vittel.

Such gestures notwithstanding, cyclists still did not complete the Tour on water alone. The great Eddy Merckx was caught using amphetamines in the 1970s. Two-time Tour winner Bernard Thévenet confessed to using cortisone in that decade, the dawn of the steroid era. As cycling entered the 1980s, cyclists routinely ingested cortisone and testosterone to ease pain and speed recovery, and amphetamines to boost energy, always striving to stay a step ahead of the drug testers.

By the time of Greg's arrival in the peloton, doping was rampant, but doping science remained crude. Both testosterone and cortisone occur naturally in the body, complicating the task of detection. Amphetamines were easily detected—so cyclists ingested them only in races where they would not be tested. Within the peloton, it was widely agreed that while drugs could bestow a small advantage, they could not elevate an average rider into a winner—yet.

In Greg's first year as a professional cyclist, Kathy had found herself seated at a table with the wife of Jock Boyer at the formal presentation of the Renault team. Kathy later recounted this exchange:

During a lull, Boyer's wife turned to Kathy and said, "Well, now that Greg's pro, he's going to have to take drugs."

Kathy replied, "We agreed that Greg isn't going to use drugs. He'll ride until he is twenty-three, and if he can't make it, we'll go home."

At this rebuke, Jock's spouse rose from the table and stalked off, muttering that Kathy was "fucking naïve."[33]

Greg had known of cycling's doping culture since his arrival in Europe, though he had never seen men dope; cyclists generally performed such rituals in private. Greg was steered by a confidence born of unbridled success. Up to that point in his career, Greg had beaten nearly every challenger, met every goal. His performance continued to improve from one season to the next, while the abilities of other men leveled off. Greg believed he was the most gifted cyclist in the peloton; there was no need for further enhancement.

Besides, he hated needles.

Dope was as common as massage oil in the stale hotel rooms of professional cycling, but cyclists who spoke out against doping were swiftly branded as traitors. It was treasonous even to publicly acknowledge the doping culture.

By 1983, attitudes toward doping remained so ambivalent that a world-class cyclist such as Pascal Simon could risk doping in a major race, not once but twice, firm in the knowledge that he would not be disqualified from the event, let alone banned from cycling, if he were caught. The coaches, the executives, and the press all fell into line. Thus, in discussing the turn of events that stripped Simon of victory at the Dauphiné, *Vélo* magazine proclaimed that he had "suffered the wrath of anti-doping."[34]

In that context, Greg's response to the Simon affair was revealing. Greg set himself apart from the dope and the doper, telling one interviewer he had no problem winning a race through Simon's penalization: "It's a victory clear and simple," he said, "because the guy who beat you probably wouldn't have been able to do it if he hadn't been taking illegal substances."[35]

Greg's comments were not quite heretical enough to draw censure from the cycling community; instead, they functioned as a sort of subliminal message to his peloton colleagues: Greg did not dope.

Greg passed a quiet summer in 1983, riding lesser races and preparing for the world championship. His training partner was Phil Anderson. When Greg was not on a bicycle, he was disheveled and undisciplined. Phil would arrive for a morning ride and find him still in bed.

"You'd get round there to his place, and he wouldn't have unpacked his bloody suitcase from the last race," Phil recalled. "And there'd be shit everywhere in his house. . . . We'd make plans to leave his place at nine, but by the time he bloody got ready and got organized, and found his helmet and shoes, it'd be nine-thirty or ten. Then, yeah, he could train hard."[36]

Heart rate monitors and other physiological gadgetry had not yet taken hold, Phil recalled, so "a lot of the training was just on how you felt. A lot of it was on quantity rather than quality."[37] On some days, Greg and Phil would ride for six hours straight. Sometimes Greg would break up the rides with stops for junk food.

Phil was an elite cyclist. Yet, as the world championship approached, Greg found that he could drop Phil—outpace him on a climb—at will. He had never felt stronger.

The race was to be held in Switzerland. Greg took up residence in a five-star chalet on a Swiss lake with Kathy and her parents, an arrangement that drew snickers from the cycling press; professional cyclists generally lodged in threadbare hotels and laundered their own jerseys. Greg acted on the advice of his old coach, Eddie B., who had advised him, "Before big race you must stay in good hotel and eat well."[38]

The world championship road race spanned eighteen laps on a fifteen-kilometer circuit, or 270 kilometers in all. To prepare, Greg and Phil followed a training plan scripted by Cyrille Guimard and employing the strategy of overcompensation. On the Wednesday before the Sunday race, they spent seven and a half hours in the saddle, pushing beyond the physical demands of the actual race. On Thursday, they rode seven more hours. On Friday and Saturday, they eased their effort. By race day, in theory, their bodies would have recovered and been ready for a mammoth effort.

On Saturday night, the chalet staff presented Greg with a cake for good luck. Greg waved it off, saying, "We'll eat it as a victory cake tomorrow."[39]

In the crucial hours before the race, Greg could not sleep. He tossed and turned, summoned room service, wolfed down some food, and then vomited it back up. By morning, he had slept only a few hours.

Greg reported his rough night to Guimard. Ever the psychologist, Guimard replied, "Greg, you're going to do really well today. Before their best days, all great champions have a sleepless night, because they know they can win." It was exactly what Greg needed to hear.[40]

The racecourse along Lake Constance featured two climbs, one a quick, steep ascent into a Swiss village, the other a three-kilometer rise followed by a long descent. Over eighteen laps, the cyclists would climb the equivalent of halfway up Mount Everest.

From the start, the Italians maneuvered to control the race, fielding a thirteen-man team in support of two stars, defending champion Giuseppe Saronni and national road-racing champion Moreno Argentin. Greg had no real team, but he did have a friend in the peloton. Before the race, Greg and Phil reached an agreement: They would ride as if they *were* teammates, neither man attacking the other, each vowing to help the other in a pinch.

On the eleventh of eighteen laps, seven men broke free, and Phil sat among them. The group built a three-minute lead on the peloton. Greg's informal alliance with Phil freed him from chasing the breakaway, which would have exhausted him. If it happened to succeed, then Phil stood a good chance to win the race with his strong sprint. If it failed, then Greg could duke it out with the Italians back in the peloton. Eventually, the breakaway folded back into the field, leaving a lone Swiss rider out front. As the peloton wilted around him, Greg waited for the right moment to mount his own attack.

When the contest entered its final three laps, the Italians lined up at the front, a show of force meant to intimidate fellow cyclists and to launch one of their own to victory, just as in the previous year.

But Greg was becoming a specialist in the counterattack, chasing down a rider who has broken away and then using him as a springboard to launch a new attack. With thirty-eight kilometers to go, Scottish climber Robert Millar broke through the gauntlet of Italians. This was Greg's moment. He gave chase, caught Millar, shot past him, and was off. Two other riders came along: Argentin, the Italian favorite, and Faustino Rupérez, a strong but spent Spaniard.

With an Italian now sharing the lead, the rest of the Italian national team eased off, a stratagem that would soon backfire horribly. The three-man breakaway pushed ahead and caught the lone Swiss survivor of the earlier break. On the seventeenth of eighteen laps, the Swiss cyclist faded. Then Argentin cracked, throwing the race into turmoil, as he had been favored to win.

Greg now sat in a two-man breakaway, dragging along a weaker rider. Cyclists chased furiously behind with the inevitable momentum of a vast pack pursuing two men, but Greg would not be reeled in. He was riding a time trial now, putting precious seconds between himself and everyone else. At the start of the last fifteen-kilometer lap, Greg and the Spaniard had a full minute on their pursuers.

When the race reached the final incline, Greg accelerated slightly to test the strength of his sole remaining adversary. Rupérez immediately fell back. He was finished. At the summit, Greg rode alone.

Greg reached the finish line seventy-one seconds ahead of the peloton. He had obliterated the best cyclists in the world. Among the witnesses was Eddy Merckx, who famously looked up from his watch and observed, "Never did I win a world championship by so much."[41]

Greg was the first American world champion of modern men's cycling, and the youngest winner in more than a decade. His friend Phil crossed the line in ninth place, at the head of the peloton. All told, four bannermen of the so-called Anglo-Saxon invasion had finished in the top ten, with Irish cyclist Stephen Roche in third, Sean Kelly eighth.

Greg climbed off his bike into a mob of cheering fans. Frantic hands tore at his jersey and hair. When the peloton finally arrived, riders crashed into the mob. Greg's mother, celebrating with her son, was almost knocked to the ground. Surveying the throng, Greg's father observed, "Now I know what it's like to be a rock star."[42]

Greg's win would dominate news coverage in Europe. He returned to Kortrijk to find its town square filled with revelers, a sight he had never beheld in America. Others waited outside Greg's Belgian home, where fans had camped out for two days, painting ecstatic greetings on the windows and hanging bicycle wheels over the front door.

For most American athletes, this would be a moment for flag-waving patriotism. American readers, unaware of Greg's ongoing feud with his nation's cycling establishment, were probably startled by his wounded words the next day.

"People have said that my victory is a victory for American cycling, but that's far from the truth," he said. "I fashioned this win in my own way, and the title belongs to nobody but me."[43]

In the United States, Greg's victory would merit only a modest squib on an inside page of the sports section. He dreamed of the day when his feats could no longer be ignored.

LE TOUR

THE TOUR DE FRANCE began life as a marketing gimmick. Henri Desgrange edited a daily sports newspaper called *L'Auto*, its title reflecting the French public's infatuation with automobile racing. Desgrange also covered cycling, and in 1902, an employee suggested he stage a bicycle race around France.

The first Tour was advertised as a twenty-four-hundred-kilometer marathon of cycling, the distance to be covered in six stages of indeterminate length over a span of thirty-five days. Desgrange conceived *le Tour* in the spirit of the six-day bicycle race, less an athletic contest than an experiment in testing the grotesque limits of human endurance. In his newspaper, Desgrange promised "the steepest mountains, the coldest and blackest nights, the sharpest and most violent winds, constant and unjust setbacks, the most difficult routes, never-ending slopes and roads that go on and on."[1]

Only fifteen riders entered. Desgrange responded by shortening the duration of the race (but not its length), lowering the entry fee, and offering riders a tiny per diem. The pool of entrants swelled, and the race was on.

Sixty riders started the inaugural Tour on July 1, 1903. Twenty-one men finished it. The winner, a Frenchman named Maurice Garin, completed the course clad in a white blazer and full-length black pants tucked into woolen socks. For ninety-three hours of cycling, Garin earned 6,000 francs. The last rider arrived at the finish line sixty-four hours later.

Early Tours were brutal, lonely slogs around France. Team cars were unknown, and riders carried spare tires and medical supplies on their backs. Cyclists generally rode alone and unobserved. Almost immediately, *le Tour* became rife with corruption.

By the second year of racing, 1904, the Tour had devolved into slapstick. One cyclist cheated by drafting behind a car. Another hitched a ride inside one. Fans of one entrant beat his rivals with sticks. Riders barricaded the road to thwart one another's progress. The four top finishers were eventually disqualified.

In 1905, fans carpeted the course with nails to puncture the tires of the competition. In 1906, three riders covered part of the route by train.

Yet the dual promise of heroism and human suffering drew spectators to the course, and the Tour gained a following. Desgrange responded by pushing the race ever higher into mountains, across unpaved roads that were alternatively buried in snow or liquefied into mud. As the eventual winner of the 1910 Tour passed race officials atop the Pyrenean pass Col d'Aubisque, he hissed, "*Murderers.*"[2]

In the early years of the Tour, even the French struggled with the notion that the man leading the peloton on a particular day was not, in most cases, leading the race. Cyclists started each stage together, regardless of their individual standings. Desgrange might have simplified matters by having them set out each morning according to their relative times the previous night; but that arrangement would have left riders strung out along many kilometers of road, sapping the race of its drama.

When Tour competition resumed after the First World War, a shortage of dye transformed the peloton into a sea of gray wool, seeding further confusion over the identity of the race leader. Desgrange resolved to clothe him in yellow. The *maillot jaune* was born.

The Tour tested both endurance and mechanical fortune. Riders who suffered a tire puncture or a crash had no recourse to team vehicles or even spare parts. One cyclist in the 1919 contest, after breaking the fork that held one of his wheels, trudged thirteen kilometers to a forge and fashioned a new one. Such imponderables could propel the Tour winner an hour or two ahead of his nearest rival in overall time.

The race changed dramatically in 1925, when Desgrange ruled that riders could exchange equipment and food and even pace a fallen comrade back to the peloton. The Tour now became a team event suffused with an Old World class system. Each team employed several vassals whose sole purpose was to ride in service of their leader. The vassals were called *domestiques*—literally, "servants."

The sheer brutality of the contest still made for unpredictable results. One year's winner might crash out of the next year's race, or be sidelined by bronchitis or tendinitis or saddle sores. In 1935, Spanish rider Francisco Cepeda fell on a breakneck descent from the Col du Galibier in the Alps. He died five days later, the Tour's first casualty.

The next year, Henri Desgrange retired. New race director Jacques Goddet promised that the Tour would retain its many inhuman qualities: "Excess is necessary."[3]

Le Tour could also seed joy and peace. In the summer of 1948, a would-be assassin gravely wounded Palmiro Togliatti, leader of Italy's powerful Communist Party. Workers called a general strike, pushing the nation to the brink of civil war. That evening, the Italian president telephoned Gino Bartali, his nation's greatest hope in that year's Tour, who sat many minutes behind in the standings. The president pleaded, "Do you think you can still win the Tour? It could make a difference, and not just for you." The next day, Bartali launched a heroic mountain attack, regaining eighteen minutes of his deficit. The next day, he attacked again and seized the *maillot jaune*. All of Italy sat mesmerized. The Communists called off the strike. Bartali won the Tour.[4]

By the close of the 1950s, after improvements in both medical and mechanical support, great riders stood a reasonable chance of at least finishing the race year after year.

Over the next quarter century, the Tour would pass through three distinct eras, each dominated by a single man. Jacques Anquetil, an aloof and elegant Frenchman, claimed five victories in the 1950s and 1960s. Belgian Eddy Merckx, nicknamed the Cannibal for the way he devoured races, won the Tour five times between 1969 and 1974. Bernard Hinault, the Badger, led the peloton into the 1980s.

The United States loves champions; France loves to hate them. Anquetil, Merckx, and Hinault struggled for acceptance by French racing fans. All three were vilified by the public and the press for the very qualities that made them champions: controlling the race from start to finish with an icy grip of inevitability; attacking according to strategy, rather than impulse or whim; and never betraying a whiff of human fallibility. Then again, none of them seemed to care whether the public liked him or not.

Though all three bore endless Gallic antipathy, Merckx, the Belgian, fared the worst. He stood on the brink of winning a record-breaking sixth Tour in 1975, when a French fan leapt forth from the crowd on a mountain slope and punched him in the back. He never fully recovered.

It is telling that perhaps the most beloved of all French cyclists is Raymond Poulidor, the Eternal Second, a man who rode the Tour fourteen times but never won—and never donned the *maillot jaune* for so much as a single day. Instead, "Pou-Pou" finished the race three times in second place, and five times in third. Poulidor's greatest battle with Anquetil, in 1964, ended with Anquetil prevailing by a mere fifty-five seconds after a cruel battle through the mountains. For French cycling buffs of a certain age, there was no greater Tour.

By the time of Greg LeMond's arrival in France, the Tour had evolved into a bewildering ballet of team tactics and stratagems, a contest filled with negotiation and backroom deals, some of them brokered at forty kilometers per hour.

In the modern Tour, nine-man teams race for one golden boy, laboring and sacrificing in service to the man most likely to win. In football or basketball or soccer, great teams work together as one. In cycling, great teams work together *for* one. The design generally favors the strongest riders, boosting their chances for victory, but it can also have the opposite effect, holding back a cyclist who is strong enough to win.

Teams generally ride under a manager, who hires riders, pays salaries and shapes the broad goals of the team. Second in command is the *directeur sportif,* who travels to races and dictates strategy on the road, often trailing riders inside a team car. (On some teams, such as the Renault of Guimard's era, those roles were combined.) Back in the hotel, a cyclist's best friend is his *soigneur,* who feeds, clothes, and massages a rider. Behind closed doors, the *soigneur* sometimes provides further care of a more pharmaceutical sort.

During the three weeks of the Tour, the peloton puts forth an effort of exertion and endurance that few athletes in other modern sports would contemplate.

Riding the Tour is somewhat akin to running a marathon every day for three weeks. A Tour contender rides his bicycle flat out, pedaling as fast as his heart will allow, for some two hundred kilometers over five hours of cycling, daily. On each racing day, he burns six thousand calories, the equivalent of five pounds of steak, more than a runner consumes in a marathon. A soccer player, by contrast, might burn twelve hundred calories in a two-hour match, and a basketball player might consume a thousand calories from buzzer to buzzer. To fuel the daily effort, a Tour competitor might start the day with a full breakfast of pancakes, muesli, and eggs, followed by two heaping plates of pasta for lunch, chased with a steady stream of energy bars, rice cakes, and electrolyte drinks on the road. The next day, the rider gets back on the bicycle and does it all again, and again, twenty more times. The cruel routine is broken up by perhaps two days of rest, a reprieve so brief that it serves mostly to disrupt the cyclist's rhythm of serial suffering.

Cyclists eat, drink, urinate, and occasionally defecate on moving bicycles; padded cycling shorts can double as adult diapers. Their daily caloric intake yields so much gastric distress and gassy waste as to render the peloton a rolling cloud of flatulence. Riders pedal up alpine passes with air so oxygen-thin that sedentary spectators faint from altitude sickness. While climbing, the cyclists' bodies generate power at a rate exceeding four hundred watts, an output a recreational athlete might endure for a single minute. Over time, the effort suppresses the immune system, leaving riders more susceptible to illness. Tour contenders routinely suffer through extended bouts of flu, sinusitis, and bronchitis, all the while producing a cardiovascular effort no weekend athlete could sustain.

No longer are Tour riders beaten up by rival fans. But cyclists still face any number of hazards and indignities on the road. Controversial riders are periodically doused with vinegar, urine, and spit. Riders suffer horrific injuries in a seemingly endless cascade of crashes. Some injured cyclists abandon the race, but a great many remount the bicycle with a cracked collarbone or a dislocated pelvis and ride on toward Paris.

Each of the Tour's more than twenty daily stages yields a winner, but overall victory goes to the man with the shortest cumulative time at the end of the race. This arrangement still confounds viewers, who might tune in to a television broadcast of a Tour stage and watch an unknown French *domestique* win the day's race, only to learn that the man stands in eighty-eighth place overall and that an entirely different man is leading the Tour. A caravan of timekeepers precedes the peloton from stage to stage, collecting results with cameras at the finish (and, more recently, with transponders mounted on race bicycles) and feeding them to officials, teams, and the press.

For much of its duration, the Tour amounts to a long, tedious, and ultimately indecisive road race. The peloton hurtles around France, a relentless, rainbow-hued freight train. Ahead and behind it rolls an entourage of police, promotional vehicles, journalists, masseurs, doctors, referees, mechanics, and cooks—a vast, mobile carnival that rivals a modern American presidential campaign.

Riders periodically dart forth from the pack, only to be reeled slowly back into the amorphous blob of the peloton. Within the pulsing spearhead of cyclists at the front, riders claw for position like crabs in a barrel.

"Guys push on both sides of you so hard that if you don't keep your speed up, you get squeezed back between them like a watermelon seed," one rider told *Rolling Stone* in the 1980s. "If I stop pedaling for one second, thirty guys will pass me. If I stop pedaling for ten seconds, I'll be the last guy in the race."[5]

The Tour is a race of attrition, a gradual thinning of the peloton herd through illness, injury, and exhaustion. For those who remain, the race is decided on a handful of select stages set in the Alps and Pyrenees, and in the time trials. In most years, the contest is settled and the winner identified several days before riders coast into Paris. Once in a very long while, the standings are so close that the Tour is decided on the final day.

LE GRAND BLOND

IN FRANCE, as in the United States, the stories of the bicycle and the automobile are intertwined. In 1898, a young Parisian engineer named Louis Renault designed an automobile fitted with a three-speed gearbox. He bet some friends that his car could beat their car, which employed a bicycle-style chain drive, up the slope of Rue Lepic in Montmartre. Louis's car won, and the Renault automobile company was born.

Renault grew and prospered until the Second World War, when Louis collaborated with the Nazis rather than see his operation move to Germany. By war's end, Louis was dead and his company seized by the French government. A decade later, Renault was the largest nationalized company in France.

By the time Laurent Fignon joined the Renault cycling team, in 1982, its sponsor was widely known as simply *la Régie*, the company. "*La Régie*," Laurent noted in his memoir, "was part of the flesh and blood of French life."[1] The team's distinctive black-and-yellow wasp-striped jerseys inspired awe.

The man who led the Renault team was another French institution. By the start of the 1982 cycling season, Bernard Hinault had entered four Tours de France and won three. Yet, the man who arrived at the Renault training camp that winter to lead his team barely resembled the great champion of the previous fall.

The men of professional cycling exist on the brink.

During racing season, a rider sheds pounds and builds strength, honing his body into a finely calibrated machine that is lightweight and powerful, much like the bicycle beneath him. Relentless training carves deep lines into his face and sculpts his legs into taut sticks of muscle and vein. He trims his quotient of body fat to 4 or 5 percent, less than half that of a baseball or football player. Deathly thin and perpetually exhausted, the champion cyclist is a fragile creature, dwelling at the edge of illness and collapse. A *directeur sportif* once said, "*Un homme en forme est un homme en malade.*" A cyclist in form is a sick man.[2]

Every rider awaits the end of racing season, when he can spend perhaps a month doing all the things other people do: vacation, eat and drink with abandon, and sleep. By the end of that hiatus, muscle has softened and stubble has returned to the legs (shaved clean in racing season, largely to ward off infection from road rash).

The season commences with a two-month recovery period of reintroducing rider to bike. The cyclist gradually regains the muscle and form of a professional, spending many hours in the saddle and rebuilding the cardiopulmonary machine. He will ride up icy mountain passes and pedal a stationary bicycle for hours at a time, keeping a constant heart rate of 180 beats per minute. The routine might top out at twenty-five hours and several hundred kilometers a week on a bicycle.

The cyclist works his heart while systematically building up the muscle groups responsible for turning the pedals. Picture the front gear wheel as a clock. A professional cyclist generates most of his power between the twelve o'clock and five o'clock positions, pushing the pedal forward and downward. The muscles in play, in the buttocks, at the front of the thighs, and in the calves, give the cyclist's body its distinctive shape: enormous thighs, ham-hock calves, and a sculpted posterior. From the six o'clock to twelve o'clock position, the knees flex and the thighs tense to pull the pedal up with one leg as the other leg bears down. To build those muscles, a cyclist might complete sixty leg curls, sixty lunges, two hundred abdominal crunches, and one hundred repetitions of a jump-rope-style shuffle in a day of training.

Elite cyclists finally turn their focus to "threshold power," pushing the limit of exertion the rider can sustain for mountain climbs or time trials. Great cyclists can ride almost indefinitely at a pace that would destroy the typical young, healthy male in a few minutes.

The cycling year begins in the waning frost of spring and runs through fall, three seasons of racing. A single crash or illness can undo the work of an entire year.

Bernard Hinault would hang up his bicycle in the winter for a month or two of gluttony, like many professional cyclists of his day. He turned up at camp in 1982 looking, Laurent recalled, "as if he had been inflated." When training commenced, Hinault adopted the visage he wore on his worst days in competition, a mask of pure agony. He sweated, he swore, and he suffered. Noting the surprise on the faces of his teammates, Hinault taunted, "All right, smart guys. You'll see how good you are in a few months."[3]

The ribbing would continue into the dinner hour, when inseparable teammates Laurent and Pascal Jules would tease and tweak the Badger to the very limits of propriety, until the stoic veterans on the Renault squad burned with shame. But Hinault took the cracks in stride, answering their barbs with, "Well, guys, just remind me how many races you've won."[4]

Laurent was, by his own account, a promising rookie, but nothing more—until he began to win.

Hinault's pursuit of Grand Tours and other top-drawer races left Laurent and his unsung teammates free to vie for victory in lesser events; *domestiques* subsisted on such scraps. In one early-season contest called La Flèche Azuréenne, Laurent pedaled near the front of the pack when four riders launched a breakaway, one after the next. Laurent hesitated. A veteran rider from a rival team goaded the young Parisian: "Come on, Fignon, you star. Now is the time to move."[5] Laurent wasn't sure whether this was encouragement or mockery, but the words lit a fire. Laurent stood up on his pedals and took off.

Five kilometers from the finish, Laurent rode among the race leaders. Two were Renault teammates. Given the pecking order in professional cycling, Laurent expected Cyrille Guimard to order him to work in support of one of his teammates. But when Guimard pulled up alongside the cyclists in his car, he instructed the others to work for Laurent.

Guimard had called the bluff of his impertinent rookie, and Laurent was stricken with fear. He turned to the director and pleaded, "*Non, Monsieur Guimard.*" But Guimard's mind was made up. The two teammates surged forward, and Laurent fell in behind, conserving his energy for a final sprint.

"I was shivering with fright," Laurent recalled, "literally wobbling with the weight of responsibility."[6]

One kilometer from the end, Laurent felt the strength leave his legs; it was as if they had died from stress. This was an entirely new feeling. At that very moment, the other riders launched their sprint. The man to beat was Pascal Simon, who had vexed Greg at the Dauphiné.

As Laurent watched Simon ride away, he felt yet another novel sensation. He stamped on the pedals and found that his strength had miraculously returned. The panic was past. He easily bridged the gap to Simon, and then rode right past him, moving so swiftly that it looked as if the Peugeot star were standing still. Laurent sat twenty meters ahead when he crossed the line.

In that moment, Laurent had discovered how to harness the stress of competition and distill it into energy. After the race, rather than offer congratulation, Guimard dispassionately explained to his young rider that he had made the correct decision, as he always did, in selecting Laurent for the win.

In March, the Renault team traveled to Hinault's native Brittany for a stage race. One afternoon, when the team had finished its daily labors on the road, Hinault stole away to his home and returned with a case of wine under each arm. The Badger and a few teammates emptied a dozen bottles. Then they staggered up to their rooms, where they found a sleeping teammate in bandages, head to toe, covering road rash from a fall. They lifted his bed and stood it on its end. "He screamed like a stuck pig," Laurent recalled.[7]

They caroused until dawn, waking riders from the other teams. When racing resumed, the sleep-deprived rivals conspired to set a blistering pace, and the Renault men paid dearly for their indulgence. Still, they did their job, and Hinault won the race.

At month's end, Hinault returned the favor by helping Laurent win the prestigious multistage Critérium International, an unofficial national championship of France, Laurent's most impressive laurel to date.

With that win, Laurent began to advance within the hierarchy of the Renault team. In May he commenced his first Grand Tour, riding as an elite lieutenant to Hinault in the epic Giro d'Italia, the second-greatest contest in men's cycling.

For all its depth, the Renault team that entered the 1982 Giro was widely dismissed as weak. Laurent was an anonymous rookie. Greg, his ascendant teammate, was off his bicycle recovering from a broken collarbone. At pivotal moments, Hinault found himself alone, while riders from the powerful Italian Bianchi team remained in force, telltale measures of each team's relative strength. But the Badger held on to win his second Giro. Laurent finished the race in fifteenth place, a performance befitting a super-*domestique*, who had sacrificed his own chances to elevate a teammate to victory.

When the race was over, Guimard announced to the press that Laurent would be "a very good stage-race rider for the future." Laurent believed the future was now. Shortly before the Giro's finish, he told an interviewer, "Hinault's lucky. If I hadn't been in his team, I'd have just kept attacking him."[8]

The Parisian said exactly what he thought, which was just what professional athletes were instructed not to do. From that day forward, Laurent's words would often leave an even deeper impression than his deeds on the professional cycling community.

The criterium, a fast-paced exhibition race staged around a small circuit ringed with inebriated fans, was the WrestleMania of 1980s cycling. The term derives from *criterion*, which suggests the contest sets a standard against which cyclists might be judged. Nothing could be further from the truth. Organizers staged dozens of criteriums every summer in towns scattered around Europe. "Stage" is the operative word: the outcomes were generally fixed, the winners predetermined, the prize money divided before the racers mounted their bicycles.

The criterium circuit functioned as a sort of touring company for professional cycling, offering thousands of fans a chance to see their heroes perform—if not actually compete—in the flesh. Races were held on closed courses, where spectators could watch their idols whir past over and over while draining steins of beer. This was an antidote to the Grand Tours, which stretched across thousands of kilometers, a design that left fans little hope of glimpsing their heroes up close for more than a few blurry moments. The busiest season for criteriums followed the Tour de France. In August and September, the Tour winner and his rivals could collect thousands in fees for riding in post-Tour "crits."

Many races followed a predictable script. In the early laps, a local favorite would break away, circling the track in glory as the peloton struggled in mock duress to reel him back. Eventually, the local boy would be caught, the pack would regroup, and the anointed favorites would ride forth to victory.

Laurent entered the criterium circuit in 1982, and his temperament immediately clashed with its conventions. By the time the entourage reached Laurent's home turf for a race near Paris, Laurent was tired of allowing undeserving rivals to garner all the glory. In the customary prerace negotiations, a senior Renault rider asserted his right to take the victory. Laurent protested: "It's my turn." The older rider exploded: "Don't fuck with me." It should have fallen to Bernard Hinault, as team leader, to settle the dispute. But the Badger refused to step in, leaving Laurent free to challenge his elder.

"My rival was raging mad," Laurent recalled. "All through the race he kept furiously doing deals left, right, and center to convince most of the big names to ride with him." Finally, the rival came up alongside Laurent and announced, "I'm winning."

Laurent replied, "No, you're not."

Laurent rode away. Then he slowed, taunting his older teammate from a safe distance, so Laurent could watch his rival's face as he crossed the line in victory. By upending the race, Laurent had defied cycling custom and shown up a senior rider, not to mention stirring trouble for Hinault, who was expected to keep his team in line. In professional cycling, such things simply were not done.

"My reputation," Laurent recalled, "was established for good."[9]

Laurent finished the 1982 season by riding in his first cycling classic, one in a series of elite, single-day road races that drew the sport's top riders. The Blois Chaville race stretched 250 kilometers, from the Loire Valley to the outskirts of Paris. Hinault was taking the day off, so on the morning of the race, Laurent stood up and informed his teammates that he wanted to be the leader. They smiled mockingly.

Yet, fifteen kilometers from the finish, Laurent rode alone, forty-five seconds ahead of the pack, buoyed by a tailwind that would all but assure his victory—when he suddenly crashed to earth. An axle on his bicycle had cracked. His race was over.

It was the first great misfortune in a career that would be defined by them.

One evening at the start of the 1983 racing season, Bernard Hinault sat at the dinner table, lambasting his teammates for riding too hard in a team time trial. The Badger had returned to training camp overweight again, and he was struggling to keep up. The team endured Hinault's barbs in silence—until Laurent spoke up. "All you have to do is train," he said. "You'll find it a lot easier."[10]

A chill descended upon the table. No one spoke to Hinault that way. Laurent, startled at his own insolence, braced for reprisal. But Hinault only stared at his dinner plate.

Around the table that night sat perhaps the greatest professional cycling team ever assembled. And therein lay the problem: no cycling team could suffer two leaders, let alone three. Hinault, LeMond, or Fignon—sooner or later, one of them would have to go. Even without Laurent's impudent jabs, the tension around the table was palpable.

Though they pedaled on the same team, Greg and Laurent were barely teammates. "They were not friends at all," said Vince Barteau, the only Renault cyclist who endured Greg's French.[11] Greg and Laurent were natural rivals—either a potential future heir to Hinault—and rivalry sparked envy.

Greg had emerged, after his humbling struggle with the French language, as a darling of the French press. By 1983, he could charm the French with his open heart and kind nature. He also knew how to wield his linguistic limitations to his advantage. Now he could deflect an unwanted question by replying, with deepest apologies, that he didn't quite understand it. Laurent, by contrast, had already acquired a reputation as temperamental, impatient, and blunt. It upset him that Greg could play the press so well.

In April 1983, the three Renault stars rode together for the first time in a Grand Tour. Hinault coasted into the Vuelta a España as the favorite, a *patron* at the height of his powers, flanked by two elite lieutenants (although one of them, Greg, would abandon the race with bronchitis). Spanish fans spat and hurled stones at Hinault. The Badger claimed the race lead in the fifth stage but lost it the next day to a Spaniard. The leader's jersey passed from Spaniard to Spaniard then, as an epic battle raged between the Spanish cyclists and the Renault men. In years past, Hinault would have obliterated these rivals. Something was not right with the Badger.

Patellar tendinitis, inflammation in the tendon that links kneecap to shinbone, is the cyclist's Achilles' heel—although injuries to the actual Achilles tendon seem to run a close second. The patellar tendon sits below the kneecap, working in tandem with the rider's mighty quadriceps to straighten the knee as he pushes down on the pedal. Extreme overwork—thousands of pedal strokes on a large gear—can inflame the tendon and seed small tears.

Hinault's right knee had troubled him from the dawn of his career. Tendinitis had driven him from the 1980 Tour while he held the *maillot jaune*. Three summers later, it was back.

"Victory seemed to be slipping away," Laurent recalled. "But our Hinault was clinging on through the pain, scraping down his last bits of strength to the very bone, every day."[12]

With three stages remaining and time running out, Cyrille Guimard plotted a desperate final assault on a day when the peloton would cross four mountain passes on the road from Salamanca to Ávila. On the third ascent, Guimard deployed Laurent as a rocket to propel Hinault to victory, instructing the Parisian to climb with abandon, towing the Badger along. Laurent's acceleration was a revelation; the Spaniards wilted behind him. Hinault managed to hang on, driven by pure force of will, the grinding pain of his injured knee momentarily forgotten. He reclaimed the race lead.

Overnight, the knee swelled. Hinault held on to the finish in Madrid, cocooned within his team. But when he dismounted his bicycle for the last time, he found that he could barely walk. His season was finished.

And suddenly the Renault team was without a leader.

Guimard had left Greg off the roster for the 1983 Tour on the pretext that he was too young for cycling's grandest race. True, Greg had ridden most of the Vuelta, a contest of comparable length, but the peloton regarded the Tour as an entirely different beast.

"Put the Tour of Spain out of your minds," Guimard barked at his young riders. "The Tour de France is ten times more difficult. . . . The course is harder, the pace is higher, the pressure is greater. Everything is multiplied."[13]

With Hinault out of the running, Guimard asked Greg if he wished to ride the Tour. Greg politely declined. His entire season was focused on the upcoming world championships, where he would triumph.

That left Laurent as the only logical choice to lead the Renault team. Yet, when *L'Équipe* named sixteen men who might claim the *maillot jaune* in Hinault's stead, it did not name Laurent. Even the brilliant Guimard seemed to underestimate the Parisian; without Hinault, he harbored no hope of victory.

Laurent's own goals were, for him, modest: a stage win, a top-ten finish, and perhaps the white jersey of best young rider, a sort of rookie-of-the-year award for professional cyclists at the Tour. Yet Laurent already held himself in sufficient regard that he neither envied nor feared the other men who were now considered favorites.

The Tour commenced on July 1. To Laurent, the race seemed over almost before it had really begun. For the second of twenty-two daily stages, organizers staged a hundred-kilometer team time trial, a test that effectively measured each team's performance on the pace of its weakest riders. Twenty kilometers in, Laurent bonked, his ravenous cardiopulmonary furnace having consumed the last of its energy stores. "I was barely moving," he would recall.[14]

From his car, Guimard ordered the rest of the team to slow down. A teammate gave Laurent all the food he had in his own pockets, and Laurent gradually recovered. By the end of the course, the teammate had bonked, sacrificing himself for his leader. Laurent and his team finished a respectable seventh.

Stage 3 took the peloton across some of the famed cobblestones of the Paris–Roubaix road race. No one had taught Laurent how to ride on cobblestones. A cyclist's natural impulse was to grip the handlebars tightly along the bumpy roadway; the trick was to handle them loosely, to minimize damage to the skin. Laurent held on for dear life. By day's end, he could barely flex his blistered hands. The next day's stage brought three hundred kilometers of racing and more cobblestones. "It was purgatory," Laurent remembered. "I couldn't bend my fingers, and it was all I could do to put my hands on the bars."[15]

During Stage 5, Laurent contracted a brutal case of conjunctivitis, a virulent eye infection that was sweeping the peloton. He pedaled for days with one eye shut. Such were the torments of the Tour.

Stage 10, a two-hundred-kilometer roller-coaster ride through the Pyrenees, would sort climbers from sprinters and yield some long-awaited answers about who could win this Tour. Guimard sensed Laurent might have a good day. He advised his new captain not to chase the climbers up the mountains: "You'll get them back on the descents." Bide your time, Guimard counseled, and try to sneak into a decisive breakaway in the valleys.[16]

Laurent followed the counsel to the letter. He rode smartly, latching onto a promising breakaway on the descent of the Col d'Aubisque. When the climbers accelerated again, Laurent eased off, saving his energy. Just then, Pascal Simon of the rival Peugeot team shot past him without a backward glance.

Simon was exploiting the misfortune of a teammate. Phil Anderson, the cyclist with whom Simon shared leadership on Peugeot, had crashed on the Aubisque. Then Phil had lost precious minutes struggling to undo the knot on a shoe, which had fallen off. None of this should have posed a problem. At the moment of the crash, Phil was the "virtual" *maillot jaune*, the man with the fastest overall time in the Tour. Race etiquette dictated that Phil's teammates gather round and pace him back into contention. (Even his opponents were theoretically bound by cycling's odd chivalry, which prescribes a cessation of hostilities when a contender—especially the *maillot jaune*—has crashed, gotten a flat, or paused to eat or to empty his bowels.) Yet Phil's Peugeot teammates, most of them French, refused to help. Instead, one of them attacked. Simon launched an inspired ride across the final fifty kilometers, wresting the yellow jersey from Phil's shoulders onto his own. A Frenchman in the *maillot jaune* was, after all, exactly what the French public wanted.

Laurent held on to finish a few minutes behind Simon; he had not set the mountains ablaze, but neither had he cracked. Cyclists who hit a wall, who reached the limit of their endurance on a mountain slope, could lose minutes by the dozens.

The stage appeared to deliver the race to Simon, who now sat several minutes ahead of the other favorites. Only now did the pundits finally notice the exploits of Laurent, the non-favorite who had finished the day in second place, four and a half minutes behind his countryman.

This would be a Tour of misfortune—or, from Phil Anderson's perspective, poetic justice. Forty kilometers into the eleventh stage, Simon crashed, coming down hard on his left side. His shoulder blade had cracked.

Guimard counseled Laurent to bide his time. "If this injury of his is as bad as they say," he told him, "the *maillot jaune* will come to you sooner or later. Then there will be a lot of work to be done."[17]

Laurent became convinced he was going to win the Tour. The circumstances, he noted, "suited me perfectly": all the media attention was going to Simon, and all the cameras were trained on his shoulder. Simon clung bravely to the yellow jersey as the Tour passed through the Massif Central, a mountain range in central France. His exertion elevated him overnight into a national hero. The peloton sat mostly quiet; one did not attack a national hero. Laurent fixed his own gaze on the remaining so-called favorites—men who, he perceived, "clearly were under the illusion that they had the race in their pockets before we had even reached the Alps."[18]

Shoulder injuries are routine in cycling, and riders can endure them for days on the saddle in a Grand Tour. The act of cycling exerts no direct stress on the bone of the shoulder blade, so long as the rider remains in the saddle. But when the cyclist rises from the seat to pump the pedals for rapid acceleration, the up-and-down motion becomes an exercise in agony.

For Stage 15, the cyclists climbed sixteen kilometers up the dormant volcano Puy de Dôme in an individual time trial. The effort cost Simon dearly, as he could not rise out of his bicycle seat to accelerate up the final slope. By day's end, Laurent had narrowed his time deficit to fifty-two seconds. But other men were also closing in.

Laurent grew increasingly frustrated with Guimard, who kept cautioning him not to attack for fear he might tire. It seemed the coach was the only man on the Renault team who did not recognize that Laurent was now its leader. The Parisian competed on aggression and pride; it was his nature to attack. Guimard's restraint drove him mad. In those tense days, Laurent came close to abandoning the race. Pascal Jules, his loyal teammate and confidant, talked him out of it.

On Stage 17, Simon finally retired, and the *maillot jaune* passed to Laurent. He now held a lead of barely a minute over his closest rival, a talented young Spaniard named Pedro Delgado. "I felt a weight on my shoulders that was new to me," Laurent recalled, "a responsibility that seemed to extend deep into the mists of time."[19]

The cycling press treated Laurent's lead as ephemeral; no one expected him to hold it. The London *Times* looked right through him as it mused, "Who will win the Tour de France? This is a question no closer to an answer [than] it was 17 days ago."[20]

Indeed, Laurent's first day in the jersey was almost his last.

Stage 18 offered a 247-kilometer battle across five summits. A Dutch cyclist launched a brutal attack, opening a four-minute gap on Laurent, who now stood to lose his lead. Laurent panicked. Guimard rode up alongside him. "Calm down, Laurent," he counseled. "Calm down. Just keep riding, breathe deeply, it'll be OK."[21]

Teammates helped Laurent give chase, but when they reached the punishing Col de la Colombière, they could not keep up, and Laurent was alone. "I knew this was a turning point, and I felt every last detail of it intensely," he recalled. "I was looking into a void; if I didn't pull through, I would be sent back where I had come from and there would be no second chance."[00]

With his last drops of strength, Laurent managed to catch the Dutchman. Delgado, the Spaniard, had faded, leaving Laurent with a reasonably comfortable three-minute lead in the Tour. Laurent's performance could no longer be ignored. The *Irish Times* reported that the "bespectacled newcomer" had displayed "untapped and unsuspected powers over the toughest of mountain climbs."[23]

Other commentators began to term the 1983 contest a *Tour à la Walko*. They alluded to Roger Walkowiak, a Franco-Polish nobody who had won the Tour in 1956 after a breakaway placed him nearly twenty minutes ahead of the favorites. Walkowiak would retire from professional cycling in 1960 with no other major win to his credit, history's least-celebrated Tour champion.

By the final days of the 1983 Tour, Laurent led the race but had failed to win a single stage, a badge of ignominy for anyone wearing the *maillot jaune*. There remained one more stage that mattered, a fifty-kilometer time trial through the wooded hills of Burgundy on July 23.

After twenty stages of racing, most of the peloton was spent, but Laurent felt stronger than ever. As the race leader, he started last, three minutes behind the man in second place. Five kilometers in, Guimard pulled up in his team car and shouted, "Relax, you're in front." It was a lie. Laurent was steadily losing time. But Laurent relaxed, as instructed, saving his energy for the kilometers to come. At the halfway point, Guimard yelled, "Go for it, Laurent!" Laurent attacked with everything he had.[24]

In the final twenty-five kilometers, Laurent rode faster than anyone who had ridden before him. Guimard didn't tell him that, but his occasional shouts of encouragement told Laurent he remained in control. When Laurent crossed the finish line, he raised his arms skyward in victory. He had won the time trial, and the Tour de France.

Laurent's achievement drew swift praise from men who had preceded him in victory. "His coolness and mastery astonished me," Jacques
Anquetil told the *New York Times*. "He's going to be a super-champion."[25]
Not yet adapted to the role of superstar, Laurent sounded genuinely surprised at his victory, as indeed he was. "The yellow jersey did things for
me," he told a reporter. "Everybody was astonished by my performance
in the mountains; well, so was I."[26]

The modesty was genuine; it would also be short-lived.

Much of the cycling press remained dissatisfied. The London *Times*
declared the outcome "A Victory for Caution," reasoning that Laurent
hadn't really won the race—his rivals had lost it.[27] This was the voice of
a cycling establishment not entirely comfortable with an unsung cyclist
winning the great Tour.

The night of Laurent's victory on the Champs-Élysées was a baccha-
nal of drink, dance, and song. Laurent and his teammates "did everything we needed to ensure we didn't slow down before bedtime."[28]

From his earliest days on the team, Laurent had wondered at the private
rituals of the older riders who sometimes shut the neophytes out of their
rooms. He would catch fragments of mysterious conversation, wisps of
guarded talk about "preparation." When Laurent and his young friend
Pascal Jules would ask the elders about their training methods, the veterans would politely demur.

"Preparation" had a broad definition in that era. It meant training, diet, and rest, Laurent recalled; it also meant dope. Doping was
"unproven and primitive" in the 1980s, in Laurent's account.[29] He
admitted that he and many of his peers used amphetamines, particularly in races with no drug tests, such as the cyclo-tainment spectacle
of criteriums. Cyclists took more speed to fuel nightclub excursions in
criterium season, Laurent recalled, suggesting that riders spent the final
weeks of the season in a more or less perpetual amphetamine haze.

Anabolic steroids were barely used, Laurent said, because they were
too easily detected; other forms of doping, including growth hor-
mones and the magical elixir known as EPO (erythropoietin), had
yet to appear. The drug of choice for Laurent and his teammates was

cortisone, a steroid that functioned much like aspirin, offering swift relief and recovery to riders vexed by inflammation and pain. Cortisone did not grant a rider supernatural abilities, but it could soften the agony of an ultra-endurance event such as the Tour. "Everyone did it," he said.

Laurent doped infrequently: "I always hated medicine of any kind, and my body didn't accept it." For some of his peers, dope was a way of life, "totally assimilated" into their training regimens. "And most of the time, it was not viewed as cheating, which must now seem completely incredible."[30]

With the help of some postrace "preparation," Laurent and his teammates now found themselves dancing on a pleasure boat in the Seine hours after they had finished riding nearly four thousand kilometers on their bicycles. This was Laurent's first taste of celebrity. A press photographer caught him at the party's peak, drunk and dancing with an attractive young woman. The next day's papers pictured the happy couple with the caption, "The winner of the Tour de France relaxes with his fiancée."[31]

Laurent indeed had a fiancée, but she was not in the photo.

Nathalie Rambault de Barallon was born in Paris and raised in Normandy. She was the very antithesis of the professional cyclist: patrician, pampered, and proud. She passed her first twelve years at Château des Genêts, a towering, cathedral-like brick mansion, surrounded by horses, dogs, and greensward. Her father was a chemical engineer, her mother a proper French homemaker.

"I had a very strict upbringing," she recalled, "very aristocratic, very principled." She called her parents *Père* and *Mère* (Father and Mother). She rode horseback, learned to fence, and passed her time with "many other activities very unlike cycling." *Le Tour* was never spoken of.[32]

When she entered adulthood, Nathalie traveled to Paris and took a job at Radio France. In 1982, a cycling journalist invited her to attend the Giro d'Italia as his assistant. She had nothing but disdain for the sport—until she met the cyclists, a gaggle of tanned, fresh-faced, intelligent, funny young men whom she could not help but admire. One June day, her team set out to cover an epic mountain stage that crossed 254 kilometers from Cuneo to Pinerolo. As she watched the cyclists pedal past, Nathalie glimpsed their haggard faces, which seemed to have aged ten years. She started to cry. Nathalie had fallen in love with cycling.

The Giro ended the next day, and Nathalie joined the victorious Renault team at dinner. She was the lone woman at the table, seated next to one of the team's rising stars, Laurent Fignon. She had never heard of him.

"During this dinner, we discussed everything: music, sports, litera-ture, cinema," she recalled. Afterward, they decamped to a cabaret, where Nathalie danced with the great Hinault. Then she danced with Laurent. A month later, Nathalie traveled to a French hotel to interview Hinault. In a hallway she happened upon Laurent. They exchanged pleasantries and then phone numbers. "Two days later," she remem-bered, "Laurent called me, and our love story began."[33]

By the summer of 1983, Laurent and Nathalie were engaged, but they kept their relationship secret to avoid a conflict at her job. Thus she did not join Laurent at the party on the pleasure boat the night of his triumph in Paris. The next day she awakened him with a phone call, demanding, "Who was that tart?" Laurent barely remembered the dance, or the woman. Nathalie eventually forgave him.[34]

It seemed to Laurent that the celebration would never end. The next month brought a criterium nearly every day, and a party every night, a routine almost more exhausting than the Tour itself.

This was Laurent's first taste of global celebrity. He became insuffer-able: "I put ridiculous demands on people, said things I shouldn't have said. I thought the world revolved around me." Men envied him; women wanted him. One Belgian fan offered Laurent his wife. In truth, Lau-rent acknowledged, "I was never the center of the world, but at most— and only for a few days—the center of the cycling world." After a month or so, Laurent emerged from the reverie into a woozy hangover of self-awareness. "The whole thing horrified me. I felt truly pathetic."[35]

That is not to say Laurent became a model celebrity. To fans and autograph seekers, he would remain impassive and aloof. Greg, a born people pleaser, would reflexively sign anything that was handed to him, once even scribbling his name on a reporter's notebook by mistake. Laurent was another sort.

"He took on all the bad habits of Hinault," recalled Alain Gallopin, his friend. "Not being nice to people, not signing autographs. If you win the Tour every year, you don't have to be nice."[36]

According to Samuel Abt, the longtime cycling correspondent for the *New York Times*, most French cyclists of Laurent's era were "well-mannered and soft-spoken, uncomplaining and accommodating."[37] But Laurent was not French; he was Parisian, and he greeted the world with the surly indifference of a *bistrot* waiter. His disposition, along with his spectacles and abortive college education—both novelties in professional cycling—spawned a nickname that would endure to the end of his career: *le Professeur.*

Greg watched his Parisian teammate ride to victory in Paris with mounting horror. Hinault's exit had left a void. Laurent had filled it. Greg wondered what might have happened if he had entered the race. Summing up the episode years later, Greg said, "All you need's a couple of good guys out of the Tour, and you can win it." Laurent had.[38]

Laurent's Tour victory had anointed him as, if not the future of cycling, at least the future of the Renault team—until Greg's world championship, on September 4. Now, the Renault team had two young champions, and little use for an old one. On September 6, team officials announced the dismissal of Bernard Hinault. The Badger had gone to the corporate headquarters and offered management a choice: himself or Guimard. Doing the math, the company brass apparently reasoned that a coach who might deliver any number of future Tour victories was a safer bet than a rider who had already claimed four; no one had ever won more than five.

By month's end, Hinault had a new team. Bernard Tapie, a flamboyant French entrepreneur, placed him at the center of a new cycling organization that would ride under the banner of La Vie Claire (The

Clean Life), a chain of health-food stores Tapie owned. He pledged to invest 10 million francs.

Hinault's exit scarcely improved matters for Greg. He had started the 1983 season following one presumptive leader, and he ended it following another. Whatever their relative merits as cyclists, Laurent had now won the Tour, and Greg had not.

Greg "was in a difficult position," Laurent recalled, "and didn't keep quiet about it."[39] After his world championship win, Greg approached Guimard for a fat new contract. Guimard refused him. The rivalry with Laurent had seeded frustration; Guimard's parsimony amplified it.

The only beneficiary of the failed negotiation was Laurent. Renault leaders now feared that he, too, would demand an impossible sum. So when Laurent asked for a million francs a year, the Renault negotiator assented. Laurent immediately wished he had asked for more.

Laurent had earned 12,000 francs a month in 1982, about $20,000 a year. After his Tour win in 1983, he had earned 50,000 francs a month. Now, he would earn nearly twice that.

Mike Schmidt, home-run king of the Philadelphia Phillies baseball team, earned about $2 million dollars in 1984. Earvin "Magic" Johnson, the superstar basketball player, earned $2.5 million. Bernard Hinault, considered the world's greatest cyclist, earned about $150,000. Greg, cycling's world champion, earned $125,000—roughly the same pay allotted to Laurent.

Much of Greg's material comfort depended upon not salary but perks: eight round-trip plane tickets per year to the States, a credit card for free gasoline anywhere in France, the rental house in Belgium, a pair of company cars, and a $25,000 bonus for each major win, up to three a year. Toss in appearance fees for criteriums, and twenty-three-year-old Greg would earn about $350,000 in 1984.

The 1984 season started sluggishly for Laurent. Cold, rainy weather vexed him, and he contracted a nasty case of sinusitis. He skipped or abandoned several early races, prompting fresh talk that he might not, in fact, be one of the greats. "I was the only person," he remembered, "who felt that my results from the previous year and my freshly found confidence were more than just a front."[40]

Laurent trained harder than ever. He also played hard. One night, after an exhausting race and lengthy party, Laurent and five teammates returned to the training camp in a caravan of three Renault team cars, each carrying two cyclists. They careened across France at two hundred kilometers per hour, spaced a bike's length apart, their drivers behaving very much like automobile racers, whose skill set the cyclists seemed to think they shared.

At such moments, Laurent found himself guided by a sort of internal circuit breaker, a little voice that told him to halt a risky endeavor just as it became truly dangerous. "I so loved racing," he explained, "that anything that might compromise it seemed puerile."[41]

That night, cyclist Vince Barteau fell asleep at the wheel at top speed and crashed his car. Miraculously, he escaped with a broken hand.

Laurent wondered how long their collective luck would hold.

At a spring race in Colombia, Laurent watched riders line up for a man who was selling cocaine for ten dollars a kilo out of the trunk of his car. Out of childlike curiosity, he and a few teammates resolved to buy some. "Nobody even knew what cocaine was," recalled Greg, whose own experience with recreational drugs had been limited to sampling pot with friends at sixteen.[42] Laurent shared a room with Greg and kept urging his roommate to try the mysterious powder, pleading, "Oh, come on, just a pinch," Greg recalled. Finally, Greg did. The rush that followed was energizing and empowering but also frightening; Greg knew that dabbling in drugs could destroy his career.

On the night before the final stage of the race, Laurent and three other teammates gathered in a hotel room with four grams of coke and divided a gram among themselves.

Nothing happened. "Can you feel anything?" Laurent asked a teammate. "No." They pulled out another gram, divided it, and tried again. Still nothing. Unsure what to do, they apportioned the two remaining grams and inhaled them. Impatience had betrayed them. "My head turned inside out," Laurent recounted. "It was an indescribable feeling, a total loss of mental control; my feet left the ground. I felt as if I was producing ideas so fast that my mind couldn't keep track of them. I had no idea who I was."[43]

Suddenly restless, the cyclists wandered out into the night. Eventually they stumbled across Guimard in a bar. "Don't mess around, get to bed," he barked. The riders ignored him. He herded them back to their hotel. Safely ensconced, they talked until dawn. The next day, sleepless but curiously vibrant, Laurent flew across the finish in first place. Only when he was told to report to medical control did he realize his error. As the stage winner, he would be tested for drugs.

"In a fraction of a second, I saw my whole career run past me," he recalled. His mind burned with self-recrimination. Then Laurent thought about where he was and what he had seen. Colombians had won most of the stages, and they seemed to be powered entirely by cocaine. Surely someone was turning a blind eye. He peed into the bottle, and— ¡Milagro!—the test came back negative.

As in prior years, Guimard assigned his star riders to careful scripts in the 1984 season. Young cyclists who attempted too much were prone to burnout, rather like young pitchers in baseball. Laurent, who had already ridden the Tour to victory, would defend his maillot jaune while also leading a team to Italy to ride in the Giro. The ultimate prize, of course, would be to win both. Greg, who had never entered the Tour, would ride a more cautious season, working his way up to that race.

Greg's season began just as slowly as Laurent's. If Laurent's weakness was susceptibility to the cold, Greg's was to food. Once again, he turned up at training camp carrying too much weight, and he suffered in early races.

Greg had always competed under lofty expectations, but this year was different. He was now a Tour favorite—even though he had never ridden the Tour, and one of his teammates was defending champion. L'Américain was a darling of the European press, who had hyped his career since his arrival. Some of this acclaim came at the expense of Laurent, whom the cycling community seemed to habitually underrate.

Laurent was now de facto team leader, and Greg his henchman; yet the French public tended to appraise the two in reverse roles.

In May the Renault team traveled to Italy, minus Greg, to ride the Giro, landing the Frenchmen in hostile terrain. Italian entrants were not above conspiring with fans and officials to deliver an Italian victor. For the 1984 contest, organizers had plotted a comparatively flat course, which would avail the Italian favorite, Francesco Moser. A time-trial specialist who held the world record for an hour's travel on a bicycle, Moser would never make much of an impression on the mountainous terrain of the Tour, but he had sufficient skill and partisan support to dominate the flatter Giro.

The chosen route encompassed few epic climbs, most notably, the 2,750-meter-high Stelvio Pass in the Eastern Alps. Prerace prognosticators speculated that Laurent could beat Moser only with a truly inspired ride over its top.[44]

Laurent expected to lose three minutes to Moser in two lengthy time trials the organizers had helpfully inserted near the end of the race, and in the first contest he lost a minute and a half. He plotted to get back the lost time with an attack on the slope of the Stelvio, where he would be strong and Moser weak. Then, at the last moment, race officials announced that the Stelvio was impassable. They warned of avalanches. Photos suggested otherwise, but the race was rerouted, the Stelvio erased, and Laurent's advantage melted away.

Together, Laurent and Guimard mapped out another attack a few days later, on a stage that included five climbs. Laurent attacked furiously in the cold and fog, weather he hated, and managed to drop Moser. Seeing the Italian champion on the ropes, all of Italy responded. Spectators and fellow riders offered hands to push the struggling Italian up the slopes. Moser was even allowed to draft behind moving cars. At day's end, Laurent had still managed to improve his position by more than two minutes. Instead of penalizing the Italian for his many alleged infractions, race leaders docked Laurent twenty seconds for the modest sin of accepting food outside the designated feeding zone.

Laurent now led the Giro by ninety-one seconds. There remained one more individual time trial, stretching forty-two kilometers from Soave to the Shakespearian mecca of Verona. The stage was perfectly flat and suited Moser, who executed the ride of his life, pedaling at an average speed of nearly fifty-one kilometers an hour, a new record. Laurent, defending his pink jersey as race leader, rocked back and forth behind Moser, weaving across the blacktop, wind whipping through his spokes and his long blond hair. Once more, Laurent felt that he was riding against an entire nation. The race helicopter flew in dangerously close behind him, "almost mowing the number off my back," creating turbulence and slowing him down.[45]

By the end of the course, Moser had gained nearly two and a half minutes on Laurent, retaking the race lead and sealing his triumph at the Giro. Laurent seethed with righteous anger at having been robbed of victory.

The press and public billed the 1984 Tour de France as a generational showdown, with Bernard Hinault, aged twenty-nine, representing the old, and Laurent and Greg, both twenty-three, the new. All three were deemed favorites.

No cyclist could win the Tour without two skills: mountain climbing and time trialing. By the summer of 1984, Greg ranked among the best climbers in the world. He also commanded immense time-trial skills, amply demonstrated in his two world championship rides. Yet he was not quite the equal of the greatest time-trial specialists, such as Moser and Hinault. Greg knew only how to ride like a locomotive from one end of a course to the other. The specialists knew how to find the shortest distance from start to finish, cutting every corner at a precise angle to shave meters off the course and seconds off their time, drawing upon an internal sense of geometry acquired over years of training. Guimard felt that Greg could trim vital seconds if he could learn to take the shortest route. Greg would spend the next two summers perfecting his technique.

As Greg prepared for the 1984 Tour, the mainstream American press finally seemed to notice him. The *New York Times* declared him "almost certainly the greatest bicycle racer in American history," a burst of hyperbole that ignored the forgotten labors of Major Taylor and Frank Kramer.[46] Press accounts celebrated the boyish family man; Greg and Kathy had welcomed their first child, Geoffrey, in February. In his first year of life, Geoffrey would spend a hundred nights in hotels, following his father and his father's bicycle around Europe. Greg rode faster with his wife and child in tow.

"I want to do the best that's possible," Greg told the *Times*. "If I don't succeed this year, I've got five or six more tries." At the time, his reasoning sounded almost conservative.[47]

Laurent now led the Renault team. He was no *patron*, and his leadership was not absolute; yet, if both he and Greg rode well at the Tour, there seemed little doubt which man their French coach and French teammates would follow.

Hinault swiftly put his stamp on the 1984 Tour by winning the short time-trial prologue that opened it. Laurent finished in second place, just three seconds behind him. Greg betrayed his first-time jitters by forgetting to sign in for the prologue. Race officials had to summon him from the crowd, and he barely had time to tighten his toe straps before he left the starter's tent. He would finish twelve seconds back, still among the contenders.

Stage 3, a team time trial, revealed an advantage that should have elevated Laurent to race favorite. His Renault team was the strongest at the Tour, one of the deepest squads ever assembled for a bicycle race, a quality that would aid its leader at every stage. Renault won the time trial; Hinault's La Vie Claire team finished seventh, nearly a minute behind Renault.

On Stage 7, a sixty-seven-kilometer individual time trial, a new Laurent seemed to emerge, an indomitable cyclist of frightful power. He won the contest, beating Hinault by forty-nine seconds and Greg by more than two minutes. Laurent had obliterated his rivals, and Hinault would spend the rest of the Tour on the defensive. Greg had fallen ill, contracting a case of bronchitis that left him answering reporters' questions in a wheezy rasp. His hopes for a podium finish were fading.

The next day, Pascal Jules, Laurent's dearest friend, won a sprint into Nantes. Guimard's Renault team had now claimed four of eight race stages; the team had the *maillot jaune* and, given the way Laurent was riding, wasn't likely to lose it. "Our celebrations that night were joyful and noisy," Laurent would recall. "These were evenings of fraternal warmth and expansive friendship: If you weren't there, you would struggle to understand what shared happiness is."[48]

The generational rivals now drifted in opposite tactical directions. Hinault, facing a superior cyclist for the first time in his Tour career, rode ever more aggressively, fighting for bonus seconds awarded for winning intermediate sprints sprinkled along the route. Laurent rode more conservatively, at the urging of Guimard, who knew the Tour was his to lose. Whenever Laurent strained against the leash, Guimard would bring him to heel, beseeching the impatient rider to "keep calm" and "hang on."[49]

Laurent felt that he could attack, and win, at any time. Yet in the pivotal eleventh stage, through the Pyrenees, Guimard had him hold off his attack until three kilometers from the mountaintop finish, a stratagem that would allow Laurent to gain only a minute or so on Hinault— but would leave the Badger no chance to make it up. The tactic worked, and Laurent ended the day two full minutes ahead.

Greg felt as if he were riding with his brakes on. He could barely breathe. Each time the course went uphill, he would fall a minute or two behind the other climbers. Guimard, eternally patient, would dispatch lesser teammates back to help him rejoin the leaders. He would pull up alongside Greg and tell him, "Take your time. Take your time." Guimard's roadside psychology would keep Greg in the race.[50]

In Stage 16, Laurent won the Tour's second individual time trial, gaining another half minute on Hinault and two minutes on Greg, now suffering from both bronchitis and blistered feet, inflamed by the heat of the asphalt. "His youthful features were hardening," a reporter from *Bicycling* magazine wrote of Greg. "His bright eyes were drawn; his short, blond hair looked lank and limp." Such were the tortures of the Tour.[51]

Greg now stood in eighth place overall. "Fignon is above the rest of us," he conceded.[52]

The next stage would finish atop the legendary Alpe d'Huez, a climb with twenty-one switchbacks. This was an ideal spot for a decisive battle. Along the 150-five-kilometer route, Hinault launched an attack. Laurent and his Renault team pulled him back. Then Hinault attacked again, and again—five times in all, on the ascent of the penultimate climb, the Laffrey. Each time, Laurent reeled him back, although the attacks splintered the Renault team and left Laurent alone among a handful of climbers.

Hinault was accustomed to terrorizing his adversaries. Yet on Laurent, the attacks seemed to have no effect. Laurent felt oddly detached, viewing the battle as from a distance. He was still steered by an essential frivolity. "I didn't feel I was taking part in the making of cycling history," he recounted. "If I won, I won. If I lost, I lost." The great Hinault did not intimidate him, nor did the Tour and all its gravitas.[53]

At the foot of l'Alpe d'Huez, Hinault attacked yet again. Behind him on the road, Laurent began to laugh. "Not in my head," he recalled, "but for real, physically, there on my bike."[54] Even as he tore off up the road, Hinault was beaten. His attack, meant to instill fear, had instead inspired mirth.

Laurent caught Hinault and passed him. The Badger had never known such defeat. The sight of his young protégé gliding past him threw the French spectators into apoplexy. Shirtless old men screamed at Hinault, scampered alongside him, shaking their water bottles and begging him to give chase. His shoulders heaved, his face contorted in agony. Suddenly, Hinault seemed transformed into a tragic figure.

Laurent's impulse was to drive on, leaving the Badger far behind, but Guimard instructed him to wait, to hover just ahead of Hinault on the road, within sight of his prey. "Guimard wanted to crack Hinault completely," Laurent recalled.[55] It worked: Hinault pedaled ever more slowly, until lesser cyclists were passing him. At the stage finish, Hinault had lost three more minutes to Laurent.

"We witnessed yesterday one of the great stages in Tour de France history," the London *Times* observed.[56]

With the eyes of the cycling world upon him, Laurent appraised the day's events with anything but magnanimity. "Am I becoming 'one of the greats'? I have no idea," he mused. "But what I do know is that all good things come to an end. Look at Hinault."[57]

Hinault was now a national hero, and Laurent seemed to be mocking him. In truth, the two men understood each other perfectly, and Hinault knew that Laurent bore him no ill will. This was a good, clean fight, and Laurent had proven the better man; that was all. But the French public had no time for such nuance. Laurent's reputation as *l'enfant terrible* of French cycling was secured.

The next day brought perhaps the most difficult stage of the 1984 Tour. Every climb in the race is rated with a number, one through four, that corresponds to its gradient and overall difficulty. The lower the number, the steeper the climb. Truly epic climbs are rated *hors catégorie*, beyond categorization, a bit of hyperbole in keeping with the Tour's extreme-sport origins. Stage 18 featured three *hors catégorie* climbs. Laurent dominated the race all day, and on the final climb, to the Alpine resort La Plagne, he launched an attack that none of his rivals could answer. Laurent muscled up the mountainside in a huge gear, "shoulders rocking gently from side to side, his lips pursing as he gulped in great chunks of air," putting on a display of "animal strength and incredible vitality," one reporter observed.[58] Laurent broke into a huge grin at the finish—having gouged another three minutes out of Hinault—and downed a can of Pepsi. He seemed unstoppable.

The day's other revelation was Greg. Finally recovered from his many maladies, he flew up the mountainside and decimated his rivals, an effort that left him in third place, on the stage and in the Tour.

Laurent won another mountain stage two days later. Then he won another time trial. He rode into Paris to chants of *feen-YON, feen-YON,* his straw-blond hair, yellow-and-black headband, and granny glasses plastered across the media landscape. American youths donned headbands to emulate tennis bad-boy John McEnroe; French and British youths wore them to honor cycling bad-boy Laurent Fignon, *le Grand Blond.*

Greg's third-place finish marked the first podium appearance by an American in the annals of the Tour. He had proven himself the greatest American male cyclist of his era, and of every era since the forgotten heyday of American cycling. Kathy was overjoyed. And yet, the performance left Greg himself feeling underwhelmed: "I'd half-expected to win the thing."[59]

Laurent had won his second Tour, and his victory evoked the most dominant wins of Hinault and Merckx. Pressed by reporters again and again to predict just how far he might go, the brash young Parisian finally rewarded them: "I'll win five or six, and then I'll stop."[60]

THE DEAL

ONE NIGHT during the 1984 Tour de France, atop the cycling shrine of l'Alpe d'Huez, Greg was approached by a glamorous young woman in black leather.

"Monsieur LeMond," she said, "Monsieur Tapie would like to speak to you."

Greg climbed onto the back of her motorcycle, and his hands found uneasy purchase around his escort's waist as the motorbike sped off toward an Alpine hotel. There the woman led him to a room, where Greg beheld the face of an old teammate. It was Bernard Hinault, and with him was Bernard Tapie, the entrepreneur who ran Hinault's new cycling team.

Tapie asked Greg, "How would you like to make more money than you ever imagined?"[1]

Born in 1943, Bernard Tapie started out selling cars. Then he sold television sets door to door, and he revealed such a talent for sales that he eventually bought the store that employed him. He learned how to revive bankrupt businesses. Flamboyant, self-promotional, and handsome, Tapie evolved into an entrepreneurial celebrity. He dabbled in singing, acting, and television hosting.

As creator and chief executive of La Vie Claire, Tapie emerged as one of the more colorful characters in the cycling community. The Vie Claire jerseys, designed by the Italian clothing company Benetton, framed the team colors of red, yellow, blue, and gray within a sea of floating rectangles, inspired by the geometrical artwork of Dutch painter Piet Mondrian. By investing in Hinault, Tapie seemed just as interested in the Badger's promotional currency—he was, at the time, the most famous competitive cyclist—as in his diminished prospects for victory at the Tour.

But Tapie wanted victory as well. And when Hinault fell to Fignon in the Tour of 1984, Tapie set his sights on the aging champion's protégés.

"Bernard Hinault was already starting into decline," recalled Maurice Le Guilloux, a veteran rider turned assistant director on La Vie Claire. "On the Renault team, two great racers remained, Fignon and LeMond. . . . [Tapie] wanted both of them."

Laurent and Greg rode under multiyear contracts with Renault. Cyrille Guimard surely wouldn't release both of his stars, but he might part with one. Tapie would have to choose. "And the answer," Le Guilloux continued, "was Greg LeMond."[2]

Greg was not, apparently, Tapie's first choice. According to the cycling journal *Vélo*, the Vie Claire boss first approached Laurent, who looked indomitable after the 1984 Tour. Laurent declined, citing his commitments to Renault. Thus rebuffed, Tapie turned to Greg. After the clandestine mountaintop summit, Tapie and Hinault met with Greg and his father on the final day of the Tour at Tapie's office, off the Champs-Élysées, to discuss terms. Greg was earning $125,000 a year with Renault. Tapie was ready to hire Greg at a base salary of $225,000. A brisk negotiation ensued.

Greg told Guimard, "I want to stay with you, but I can't ignore this kind of money."[3] Guimard refused to match Tapie's offer, or even to split the difference with a $60,000 raise. Bob LeMond traveled to the Renault factory for an in-person meeting, but company officials refused to receive him without his son.

A few weeks later Tapie announced that he had signed the world's first million-dollar cyclist. He was stirring the pot. Greg had not, in fact, signed a new contract. Tapie was pressuring him to make a decision.

Greg was torn. Guimard was a tactical genius; yet, as 1984 drew to a close, there seemed little chance the coach would leverage that genius to generate victory for Greg in the Tour. Greg was a foreigner riding for that most French of French teams, *La Régie*, led by a Frenchman who was now a two-time Tour winner.

In the end, Greg defected to La Vie Claire. The contractual drama played out just as Tapie had envisioned—and largely at the expense of Greg, already professional cycling's living symbol of American greed. On its October 1984 cover, *Vélo* pictured a smiling Greg and an American flag against a backdrop of paper currency, beneath the headline "Attack of the Dollars."[4]

The contract Greg signed that winter promised $225,000 in 1985, $260,000 in 1986, and $300,000 in 1987. At the time, the average professional cyclist pulled in perhaps $15,000 a year; even the great Hinault took home only $150,000.

Tapie brought a fresh perspective to the peloton. Like Guimard, he played to win; but unlike the Renault bosses, he didn't seem to care whether the man who won for him was French.

"We wanted only to build the best team in the world," Tapie recalled to journalist Samuel Abt. "If the best had been French, we'd have had an all-French team. . . . If we needed to recruit a Martian to win, I'd have done so. Greg cost a lot, but he was the best available."

Tapie also grumbled to the press that "there would have been a zero less" on the contract, were Greg not American.[5] He alluded to the hardball tactics of Greg's father, who still ran the family cycling business. Greg and Bob had determined, like the families of football and baseball players before them, that a professional cyclist's salary should reflect the brevity of his career—generally a decade or less.

A comparatively unaccomplished American now earned more than Hinault. But Hinault remained the unrivaled leader of La Vie Claire, and Greg's presence at his side would make him the favorite to win a fifth Tour in 1985. Hinault viewed the looming contest as a battle of wits against his old coach. In that spirit, he had hired a new coach, a man who had been Guimard's mentor.

Paul Köchli had turned to coaching in his mid-twenties after a brief career as a professional cyclist in Switzerland in the late 1960s. He studied at the Swiss national sports school, and he became one of the first cycling coaches to develop a truly scientific approach to training. He filled binders with data on the intensity and duration of pedaling sessions, and took careful measurements of weight and heart rate.

By the time he started work with La Vie Claire in 1984, Köchli had taught his training program to a number of other coaches, including Guimard.

"He wanted to put together the best possible team by cherry-picking from all over the world," Hinault told journalist Richard Moore. "He knew who was the best Australian, the best Canadian, and so on and so on. When he came into the sport, the other *directeurs sportifs* were mocking him, saying, 'The computer can't sit on the bike and turn the pedals.'"[6]

While other coaches built ethnocentric teams around provincial stars, Köchli found himself relatively free to build La Vie Claire as a team of cycling all-stars. In addition to Hinault and Greg, he recruited Steve Bauer, the finest men's cyclist from Canada; and top young riders from Switzerland and Denmark—seven non-Frenchmen in all by 1985.

Before Greg departed for La Vie Claire, he had a final conversation with Guimard. Renault had Greg under contract for another year, but cycling teams didn't generally fight to keep a rider who wanted out. "If you leave me and the team," the jilted coach predicted, "you'll never win the Tour."[7]

Laurent entered the 1985 racing season in "dazzling form," he recalled in his memoir, wearing the tricolor jersey of French national champion along with "what amounted to a massive sign on my back," denoting his status as the new master of *le Tour*. But after the very first race, he felt a twinge in his left heel. It began with a simple knock from a bicycle pedal. "It came and went, but sometimes became unbearable when I had to press suddenly on the pedals." After a few more races, he said, the pain was "like being stabbed with a knife."[8] A doctor diagnosed inflammation in the sheath of the Achilles tendon. Tiny ruptures in the tendon had spawned scar tissue. The tendon would have to be opened, and the scar tissue removed.

Laurent's racing season was over.

The mighty Renault cycling team was without a leader.

And Greg found himself, once again, cast onto the wrong team.

* * *

Greg had ostensibly been hired as joint leader of the Vie Claire team. Yet, it seemed clear that his immediate role was to help Bernard Hinault win a fifth Tour de France. The top earner in professional cycling would be paid to ride for second. To the more cynical of Greg's American fans, Hinault had employed the American to neutralize him, for no one posed a greater threat to the Badger's chances for a fifth victory.

For the 1985 season, Hinault declared that his goal, and his team's, was to win both the Giro d'Italia and *le Tour*. "After that," he said, "I am at Greg's service."[9] It was a credible narrative. Hinault had already announced he would retire after the 1986 Tour; he had stated repeatedly that he hoped to spend his waning years grooming a successor; and he had identified that successor as Greg.

Paul Köchli had built his Vie Claire team with an international roster for the explicit purpose of muting partisan nationalism, which he viewed as weakness. Though he commanded, in Hinault, the most dominant personality in the peloton, Köchli rejected the concept of team leader; this, too, he saw as weakness. He realized that every rider should sacrifice himself for the greater good of the team. In a given race, the team would ultimately work for one of its own—but that man's identity would not be known until after the race began. It remained to be seen how Köchli's cool Swiss neutrality would play out on the roads of France.

The new Vie Claire announced itself in May 1985 at the Giro d'Italia. Hinault outmaneuvered both Italian favorite Francesco Moser and a meddlesome race organization—the one that had vexed Laurent Fignon in the previous year—to seize the pink jersey of victory. Greg proved himself a most capable lieutenant by finishing just behind Moser, in third.

The 1985 Tour de France began on June 28 with a seven-kilometer time trial, a brief prologue to set the tone for the weeks to come. Greg was near the finish and flying down the road when his chain became stuck in a single gear. Rattled by the mishap and afraid to shift again, Greg lost precious seconds pedaling in the wrong gear. The mishap plunged him from a possible first-place finish to fifth, twenty-one seconds behind the eventual winner—Hinault.

In a crowing postrace press conference, Hinault ignored the inconvenient fact of Greg's misfortune. The French public, too, seemed relieved; *L'Équipe* declared that Hinault's victory, in this briefest of contests, proved that the Badger was still "master of the peloton . . . and his team."[10]

Stage 8, on July 6, offered a seventy-five kilometer individual time trial, the longest such exercise written into the Tour in a generation. Greg's supporters wondered if the ride had been inserted to favor Hinault; the time trial was his strong suit. The timing, too, was advantageous. The mature Hinault was prone to weaken over the course of the Tour, and this contest came near the beginning.

Hinault utterly dominated the day, completing the course more than two minutes faster than anyone else. Greg, looking young and undisciplined, lost two minutes and thirty-four seconds to his teammate, a result that left him in second place overall.

Now holding a comfortable lead of two and a half minutes, Hinault reprised the role of *patron*, marking his territory with the oratorical flair of a rapper. "When you are the strongest, you make the law," he announced. "Let the others suffer."[11] If Hinault's rivals—including Greg—harbored any remaining hope to reel him in, they would have to act quickly once the race hit the mountains, where the Badger had proven vulnerable in the previous year.

On the first mountain stage, La Vie Claire plotted to extinguish that hope. Hinault attacked on the very first climb, breaking away with a Colombian climber. All of Hinault's rivals were free to counterattack— except Greg, his teammate, who was forbidden by age-old Tour custom to make any move that might aid the Badger's rivals. But on that day, no one else could summon the strength to respond. Finally, a pair of climbers broke free and bridged some of the gap, and Greg followed. But it was too late. Greg had lost another minute and a half on Hinault. The gap between them now stood at four minutes.

A few days later, Greg surrendered more time to Hinault in another time trial, afflicted with both fatigue and fluky mechanical problems of the sort that always seemed to beset him in the Race of Truth. That evening, Kathy sneaked into the team hotel to comfort him.

The next day, Hinault sauntered into a press conference forty minutes late. Asked if he feared the mountain stages yet to come, he replied, "I'm never afraid of anything."[12]

The race approached the Pyrenees, and Vie Claire coach Köchli finally let Greg off the leash. Greg now trailed Hinault by more than five minutes, and other men lay within a minute or two of Greg's second place. Köchli didn't want the American to slip to third.

A Colombian climber attacked on the day's major climb. Behind him, Greg launched a counterattack, joined by two fellow climbers who posed no threat to Hinault's lead. The play worked brilliantly, bringing Greg to the finish minutes ahead of the men in third and fourth place, firming La Vie Claire's hold on the two top places on the podium.

Behind him, Hinault played the role normally assigned to Greg, blocking the other favorites from breaking free to catch Greg. Four hundred meters from the finish, he became ensnared in a suicidal mass sprint. The jostling brought one rider down, and then another, six men in all, hurtling to the pavement at fifty kilometers per hour. One of them was Hinault.

The *maillot jaune* sat on a curb, stunned and bleeding, for several minutes; race rules dictated that he would not be penalized for a crash so close to the finish. Finally, he staggered to his feet, remounted his bicycle and pedaled limply to the line, blood dripping from his bowed head.

Hinault would blame the crash on Phil Anderson of the Panasonic team, Greg's closest friend in the peloton, whose body and bicycle had brought the Badger down; Hinault suspected Phil had taken a spill to improve Greg's chances. Phil blamed Steve Bauer, Greg's Canadian training partner, saying Bauer's back wheel had slipped on a plastic reflector in the road.

The impact had driven Hinault's Ray-Bans into his nose, breaking it. A pedal had clipped his head. Yet, after a visit to the hospital and a few stitches, the Badger looked no worse for wear. Television cameras pictured him cavorting with his young children later that day, images meant to relieve the French public and to intimidate his rivals.

"Any other racer would have abandoned," recalled Maurice Le Guilloux, the assistant team director. "But against medical advice, and against everyone's recommendations, Hinault was there the next morning."[13]

The injuries gradually took their toll. The broken nose forced Hinault to breathe through his mouth; this, in turn, brought on bronchitis. Hinault limped into the Tour's seventeenth and most difficult stage, two hundred kilometers over a pair of climbs so steep they were rated *hors catégorie*, beyond categorization.

On the slope of the Tourmalet, the highest Pyrenean pass, Hinault began to falter. He was dropped by a group containing Irishman Stephen Roche, who stood in third place overall. Greg was riding with Roche and, according to team etiquette, was permitted, even compelled, to follow him, provided he didn't help Roche. Follow Greg did, and suddenly the time gap that separated him from Hinault in the race standings began to dwindle.

This was before the era when cyclists wore earpieces for constant contact with their teams. From the moment he slipped ahead of Hinault, Greg never knew precisely where his teammate sat on the road behind him. He knew nothing at all, in fact, until he and Roche approached the final ascent, up Luz Ardiden, and a passing television crew told Greg that Hinault sat several minutes behind.

Roche turned to Greg. "I'll take the stage," he proposed, "and you'll take the yellow jersey."[14]

For the first time in his life, Greg stood poised to claim the *maillot jaune* and the lead in the Tour de France. He had started the day roughly three and a half minutes behind his team leader. Now he sat ahead of him. If he were allowed to attack, he might easily take the race lead. Of course, that triumph would come at Hinault's expense.

Greg was expected to follow Roche to the finish, an unfortunate but necessary hedge, lest the Irishman ride away with the race. But he was not permitted to help Roche, to take turns setting the pace and blunting the wind as they crawled up the mountainside. If Greg and Roche worked together, both men would reach the summit that much more quickly; but then Roche might end the day in second place, ahead of Hinault.

Shortly after Greg's exchange with the television crew about Hinault's whereabouts, and the subsequent invitation from Roche, a Vie Claire team car rolled up behind them. Greg drifted back for a talk with Maurice Le Guilloux. Greg had two questions: "Where's Hinault?" and "Can I ride with Roche?"[15]

Le Guilloux relayed Greg's queries by walkie-talkie to Köchli, who sat in another team car behind Hinault. Le Guilloux conveyed Köchli's reply: "You can't ride with Roche. Hinault's coming up. You need to wait for him." Köchli envisioned La Vie Claire claiming first and second places at the Tour; he would not risk aiding the interloper Roche.

Video footage did not betray the content of the conversation that followed, only that the perpetually sunny Greg LeMond had finally lost his temper. He waved his arm angrily; he shouted at his coach; he wore a visage of righteous outrage. Greg pressed Le Guilloux: Exactly how far back was Hinault? About forty-five seconds, Le Guilloux replied.

Greg and Roche rode together; but in a tactical sense, they rode apart. Roche was setting the pace, slogging up the mountainside and into the wind, while Greg rode beside him, matching his pace but never lifting it, never aiding him. Roche was conserving his strength, lest Greg should launch his own attack.

The two men had ridden themselves into a stalemate. As Greg awaited a resolution to his argument with his coaches, other riders loomed ever closer behind.

Le Guilloux pressed Köchli: "Greg is telling me he wants to ride. He's asking to ride." Greg wanted permission to go all out, to collaborate with the Irishman for joint victory or to break away and win the stage alone. Thus pressed, Köchli reluctantly relented: l'Américain could attack. "But you tell Greg, he attacks once, full gas, and drops Roche. And then he can go and win the Tour."

It was ambiguous counsel from a coach trapped between competing priorities. His job—indeed his governing philosophy—was to seek victory for the team, not for any one cyclist. Yet this was a French team, and the French public demanded a fifth Tour victory for Hinault. Allowing Greg to seize the race lead would serve the first agenda but not the second.

The element of surprise is key to any attack in a bicycle race. Alas, the man Greg had been instructed to attack had heard the instruction, broadcast over a loudspeaker mounted inside the team car. Greg made a few tentative jabs, accelerating away from Roche. The Irishman patiently reeled him back.

"Stop this," Roche pleaded. "You can ride with me."

Finally Greg gave up, fell back, and let Roche set the pace. Roche limited his own efforts, still fearing Greg might sprint away from him. Pedaling side by side, the two looked as if they were out on a recreational club ride.

Before long, a swifter group containing several race favorites came up to join them. To Greg's surprise, Hinault was not among them. Clearly the gap that had separated the two Vie Claire stars was greater than forty-five seconds. As Greg and Roche bided their time, a Spaniard and two Colombians sprinted off up the slope. Greg was not allowed to bridge the gap and join them, because it was Roche, not they, who posed a threat to Hinault.

Greg finally rolled across the line with Roche and most of the other contenders, nearly three minutes behind the eventual stage winner, Pedro Delgado, the ascendant Spaniard. A minute or so after that, Hinault rolled in, a wounded hero, breathing through clenched teeth. An indulgent Bernard Tapie draped a jacket over the Badger's shoulders. Greg's slowed pace had allowed Hinault to regain much of the lost time. Greg now stood two minutes and twenty-five seconds behind in the standings.

Hinault had lost time, but Greg had lost so much more. Had he been permitted to ride his own race that day, "Greg would have won the Tour, easily," Le Guilloux conceded. American television crews, covering *le Tour* for the first time as legitimate news, awaited Greg at the finish; they found him before his Vie Claire handlers could intervene. "I had my chance to win today," Greg despaired. "My team stopped me."

Later, a camera caught an anguished Greg bickering with Köchli. "All I have to say is, if Hinault was in my place, he would not have waited," Greg said, as the cameras closed in. "That's all I have to say." Then, his frustration boiling over, he turned to an intruding reporter and cried, "Do you want me to punch you in the face? Get outta here."

When the dust had cleared, a CBS television interviewer asked Greg, "Still think you have a chance to win?"

A dejected Greg replied, "It's over now."[16]

That night Greg was ready to quit. His father, who had just arrived in France, stepped in, cooled his temper, and helped to reconcile the wounded parties. Köchli swore to Greg that he hadn't intentionally misled him about Hinault's position on the road. Greg remained certain he had been deceived.

Apologies weren't enough. Greg wanted assurances. That night, Hinault and Tapie offered him a deal. If the American continued to work for Hinault in this Tour, then Hinault would work for Greg in the next one. Greg agreed. He emerged from the meeting contrite.

When Roche attacked hard again the next day, Greg did not follow. Instead, he rededicated himself to the role of lieutenant, literally pushing an exhausted Hinault up parts of the towering Col d'Aubisque. Greg had forsaken yet another chance at the *maillot jaune*. He had been neutralized.

In Paris, hundreds of thousands gathered to await Hinault, whose fifth Tour victory was now all but assured. "We'll accept him in our club with pleasure," Jacques Anquetil told the *New York Times*.[17] Hinault would be the third man, after Anquetil and Merckx, to win five Tours. Nobody had won more.

There was one final test, a forty-six-kilometer time trial. This was Hinault's specialty, and he rode with panache. But Greg was the stronger rider, and for once—perhaps because the Tour's outcome was decided and the pressure was off—he completed the course without a mishap. At day's end, Greg was the winner, the first American to claim a stage in the Tour. Television cameras captured Hinault embracing Greg at the finish as he exclaimed, "Beautiful."[18]

Greg was already looking to next year. When reporters asked *l'Américain* for a comment, he replied, "Now I know I can beat Hinault."[19] The larger question was whether Greg would be allowed to beat him.

As the Tour rolled into Paris, it appeared that he would. On the victory podium, Hinault turned to Greg and said, "Next year, it's you."[20] That night, Greg and Kathy went out with Hinault and Tapie and their wives. At the proper moment, Hinault stood.

"Thank you, Greg, for allowing me to win my fifth Tour," he said.
"And I, in 1986, will do everything I can to make you a winner."[21]

Greg and Kathy hoped they could trust him.

In May 1985, Laurent Fignon had checked into the Pitié-Salpêtrière
hospital in Paris for surgery on his left Achilles tendon, a minor operation had swelled into a major story for the French cycling press. Laurent
took every precaution to avoid being photographed limping into the
hospital. *Vélo* magazine caught him on the way out, a grainy photograph
published beneath the pronouncement, "Laurent Fignon has traded
pedals for crutches."[22]

With the French public, Hinault's currency had risen and Laurent's
had fallen apace. Hinault's crushing defeat at Laurent's hands in 1984
had revealed the Badger to be human and vulnerable, qualities that had
finally endeared him to Gallic fans, a constituency that always favored a
lovable loser over an aloof champion. Laurent's stock had tumbled further when he mocked Hinault's heroics in the mountains. In one final
affront, Laurent had sold the luxurious Renault automobile awarded
him by *la Régie* after his Tour triumph and purchased a Ferrari, a slap
in the face of French industry.

Old-timers dismissed Laurent as a playboy. Laurent was engaged;
yet he had been spotted, at the victory party after his second Tour
triumph, dancing with English actress Jane Seymour. One writer con-
trasted Laurent's lifestyle to that of his American rival: "He is unmar-
ried and has a reputation as a partygoer who loves the company of
young women. Sounds like the typical American-about-town. LeMond,
at just 23, is married with a young baby boy, and lives in an unos-
tentatious home in the suburbs. Sounds like a typical, conservative
Frenchman."[23]

Other, darker rumors swirled around Laurent's hospital stay. Whispers of doping nipped at the pedals of every great champion in cycling,
driven by the irresistible logic of Jacques Anquetil: one did not win a
Grand Tour on water alone. Anquetil himself had implied something
unseemly in Laurent's utter dominance of the 1984 Tour, when he said,
"Nothing explains Fignon's progress in the last twelve months."[24]

Doubters noted that Laurent hadn't lit the world on fire in the years before his first Tour victory. Then again, just like Anquetil and Merckx, Laurent had won the first Tour he entered. The skeptics seized on Laurent's tendinitis as proof he had doped. Doping allowed cyclists to perform beyond their natural limits, putting excess wear on the joints.

The drug *du jour* was cortisone. And when Laurent's team finally answered the rumors, no one bothered to deny *le Grand Blond* had taken it. Instead, the team doctor reasoned that cortisone could not lie at the root of what was, after all, an inflammatory injury. "Cortisone is primarily an anti-inflammatory," he wrote. The naysayers might just as well have blamed Laurent's swollen ankle on Advil.[25]

The operation went well. But before the wound could heal, it became infected, prompting a second operation. Laurent languished through months of rehabilitation. The long layoff prompted fresh rumors, and Laurent's stock began to sink anew. Journalists asked what the cyclist would do if he never fully recovered. He laughed them off.

Just as Laurent was learning to walk again, Cyrille Guimard dealt his psyche another blow. He announced that Renault was folding up its cycling team. *La Régie* was, in fact, ending all sports sponsorship.

"It was a national trauma," Laurent recalled.[26] And a personal one.

Under the conventions of the day, a professional cycling team was utterly dependent on its sponsor. An executive from Renault had wielded complete authority over the team and supplied its cash—a relationship that had worked just fine until the sponsor pulled out, leaving coaches and cyclists in disarray.

Guimard invited Laurent into the negotiations for a new sponsor, hoping his name and pedigree might sweeten the deal. Laurent had other ideas. After a few days of thought, he asked himself, *What if we owned the team?*[27]

He thus proposed a new business model. He and Guimard would create a company whose product was advertising space on the jerseys of a professional cycling team. The two friends would run the team. The sponsor would pay the bills. It was a radical idea, from a cyclist with little regard for the staid traditions of his sport.

"You're crazy," Guimard replied when he heard it. "No one will buy into it."[28]

But Guimard had underestimated the two men's currency. He was the most successful cycling coach of his era; Laurent was two-time Tour champion. In any case, Laurent had made up his mind. Together they created two companies, a sports club and a promotional firm, jointly run by Laurent and his coach. They were free men. The next time a sponsor pulled out, they would simply find another. In time, many other teams would adopt the Guimard-Fignon model.

It didn't take long for the two cyclists-cum-businessmen to attract a sponsor—Système U, a supermarket chain whose chief executive wanted no part of hiring employees and dispensing salaries on a cycling team but was happy to sponsor one. The company pledged 45 million francs, roughly five million American dollars, over three years.

Laurent designed the jerseys, which featured the same yellow, white, and black colors of Renault and were liberally festooned with the sponsor's ubiquitous trademark, a giant red *U*.

At the end of June, just as the 1985 Tour de France was setting forth from Brittany without him, Laurent climbed back onto his own bicycle for the first time since his injury. Was he drawing inspiration from the Tour, or torturing himself by juxtaposing the elite pedal strokes of Greg and Hinault against his own pitiful efforts?

Laurent pedaled for twenty kilometers, feeling very much a mere mortal. "It was hell," he would recall. "My legs didn't work. I had no muscles. I was just a dismembered carcass sitting on a machine that wouldn't move forward."

After the ride, Laurent inspected the spot where the doctors had operated. "Where the scar was, I felt a kind of water-filled ball. When I put my finger on it, the muscle did nothing."[29]

He wondered whether his career was over.

Laurent traveled south to sunny Nîmes, near the Mediterranean Sea, to search for his lost strength. Recreational cyclists would speed past him on the road, unaware that the man creeping along the pavement was *le Grand Blond*. Each day, he rode a little farther. He walked daily in a swimming pool to regain strength and flexibility in the stricken ankle.

One day, Laurent took stock of his streamlined body and thought, *You are the man you were.*[30]

To the naked eye, Laurent may have resembled the athlete he had been, all his muscle mass restored along with most of his cardiopulmonary strength. But there was a problem: Laurent's left leg was no longer as strong as his right. His left ankle was permanently weakened, lacking both the flexibility and the power of its mate. Though he never acknowledged it publicly, Laurent would not be the same man again.

THE BETRAYAL

I N NOVEMBER 1985, the cyclists of La Vie Claire gathered at Brian-çon, an Alpine village that would host an epic stage in the 1986 Tour de France. They arrived at training camp as members of the greatest cycling team in the world—a distinction that had migrated to La Vie Claire from Renault.

Coach Paul Köchli continued to refine his cycling all-star team, now populated with talent from a half dozen nations. Most cycling coaches mixed and matched, supporting their stars with a few sprinters who couldn't climb, a few climbers who couldn't sprint, and one or two time trial experts who could neither sprint nor climb. Köchli, by contrast, hired all-rounders—cyclists who weren't the best at any one cycling discipline but were good at them all. In addition to Greg and Hinault, La Vie Claire now employed Jean-François Bernard, a young Frenchman viewed by many as the true heir to Hinault, Steve Bauer, the great Canadian; and new hire Andy Hampsten, the young North Dakotan who had ridden with Greg in Buenos Aires.

Greg would spend much of the 1986 racing season cocooned among his English-speaking friends, dwelling and dining and con-versing away from their French-speaking teammates. To the three North American invaders, there seemed little doubt who would lead the team in the 1986 Tour. Hinault had framed his final season as a victory lap. Out on the Alpine passes, training with his team, he dropped hints that seemed to reaffirm his promise to ride for *l'Américain*. "Greg will have the yellow jersey here," Hinault instructed Andy, one day in Briançon.[1]

But once the season got underway, Bernard Tapie began to spin an unflattering narrative about Greg, the man to whom he had pledged his team in the upcoming Tour. "[Greg] is among the five best cyclists in the world," Tapie told Samuel Abt. "But he is missing that little bit extra to make him number one. He has class, he has the will, the physical tools, the team, but he must take the initiative. As long as he doesn't, he will not be a leader."

Tapie's talking points conveniently ignored that Greg had *tried* to take the initiative in the prior year's Tour, only to be blocked by his own team. It was a clever tack. For all his talent, Greg had not, in fact, won an iconic race in either of the two previous seasons. His greatest victory to date remained the 1983 world championship, now three years past.

Greg had posted high finishes in both the Tour and the Giro, always in support of the eventual winner, always on the orders of Tapie or someone like him. Now Tapie twisted those acts of service into signs of weakness. "Second, third, second, third—his record is full of those finishes," Tapie scoffed. "Second place is the same as twenty-fifth place."[2]

Such thinking soon went viral. Laurent Fignon confided to a *Sports Illustrated* writer, "Greg LeMond has all the physical qualities needed to win the Tour. But he doesn't have the mind-set of a winner." His words set off a modest feud between the old rivals. When the writer asked Greg about Laurent, Greg sniffed, "He hasn't done anything in two years."[3]

While that was true enough, Greg knew better. Once, when Laurent's name came up in conversation with Andy Hampsten, Greg's eyes widened, and he grew serious: "If he ever comes back to the form he had in '84 and '83," Greg said, "we're finished."[4]

As the Tour drew near, the French cycling press suffered a bout of amnesia over the looming deal between Greg and Hinault. Prerace coverage proceeded almost as if Greg didn't exist. The June issue of *Miroir du Cyclisme* pictured Hinault on one side of its cover and Laurent on the other, framing breathless talk of a rematch.

On the day the Tour set forth, *L'Équipe* declared, "Hinault for the Tour record." Five-time winner Jacques Anquetil went on French television

and named Hinault and Fignon as the obvious favorites; he listed three
or four long-shot candidates for victory, none of them Greg. An entire
nation stood in denial of the arrangement their champion had reached
with the impetuous American.

Apart from Greg and his North American teammates, everyone in
France seemed intent on the Badger riding for a sixth victory. The
French president, François Mitterrand, telephoned Hinault and deliv-
ered the instruction, "Ride your own race."

Eventually, perhaps inevitably, Hinault began to waffle on his promises to Greg. On the eve of the race, he told *L'Équipe*, "The strongest
rider will win."[5]

The fabled Hinault-Fignon rematch was just that: a tall tale, laughable
to anyone who was tracking Laurent's progress in 1986. Laurent had
started the season in January by breaking his collarbone after winning
a pursuit race in Madrid, in a freak collision with a Spanish rider who
had ridden up to congratulate him. "It was a bizarre way to come back
to racing," Laurent recalled in his memoir.[6]

Optimists cheered the former champion wherever he rode, but Laurent knew he would not regain his former strength any time soon. He
had missed half a year of racing; full recovery would require one or even
two seasons of competition. "It's terrible," he told *Vélo*, "to feel tired after
twenty-five kilometers, to feel stuck at thirty kilometers an hour." His
face on the magazine's cover, hair disheveled, eyes bloodshot, seemed to
answer the question posed in the headline—"Fignon: Can he return?"[7]

Laurent's weakened body began to afflict his mind. At the Paris–
Camembert race in April, Laurent worked himself into a decisive breakaway with a Danish rider. A kilometer from the finish, Laurent stood
poised for victory. Then his mind began to wander. He imagined his
victory salute, replaying it over and over in his mind, euphoria washing
through his body. His reverie came to an abrupt halt as the Dane accelerated past him to victory. Laurent had forgotten he was there.

"I couldn't even call it a beginner's error," Laurent admitted, "because
not even a beginner forgets his opponent."[8]

Two weeks later, at the one-day classic Flèche Wallonne, Laurent found himself in another winning breakaway—joined, oddly enough, by the same Danish rider. This time Laurent paid attention, and he rode to an easy victory, his first major laurel since 1984. That evening, Laurent said to himself, *I'm back.*[9]

Laurent proceeded to the Vuelta a España. In the fourth stage, he crashed heavily to the pavement, cracking a rib and dislocating a bone in his chest. Rather than retire to France and recuperate, Laurent chose to go on. He stood high in the standings and had to keep racing if he hoped to regain his form. While he finished the Vuelta in seventh place, a show of strength to the cycling world, he returned to France "completely in pieces"; the decision to keep riding had been a grievous error. Laurent approached *le Tour* with dwindling hopes.[10]

La Vie Claire skipped the Vuelta to ride the Italian Giro, a race that began just as the Spanish contest was ending. Hinault sat it out, elevating Greg to team captain for three weeks. Slowed by a crash and other misfortunes, Greg nonetheless managed a fourth-place finish, buoying his own confidence as the Tour neared.

The 1986 Tour began, fittingly, on July 4. For the first time, the peloton positively buzzed with Americans—an entire team of them, riding under the banner of 7-Eleven. Their leader was Colorado native Alexi Grewal, who had edged Canadian rider Steve Bauer to claim America's first Olympic gold medal in men's road racing at the 1984 Olympics. Grewal's supporting cast included Ron Kiefel, Greg's old amateur teammate, and Eric Heiden, winner of five Olympic golds for speed skating, who had reinvented himself as a middling cyclist.

A brief prologue through the Paris suburbs seemed to affirm the prerace fantasies. Bernard Hinault finished within two seconds of the winner, a time-trial specialist. Laurent and Greg finished two seconds behind Hinault.

While all of France envisioned a battle between Laurent and Hinault, only Laurent seemed convinced it was not to be. Asked to name a favorite, he said, "Hinault, because he's won it five times. And because

LeMond hasn't fulfilled all the hopes placed in him."[11] Tapie's public-relations campaign had taken hold.

The next day further burnished the illusion that Laurent was back. His Système U team, still a strong squad performing under the baton of the estimable Guimard, obliterated the field in a fifty-six-kilometer team time trial, finishing nearly two minutes ahead of La Vie Claire and elevating Laurent and his teammates to the leader board.

Laurent knew the truth: "I was riding on natural talent and nothing else."[12]

Stage 9 brought the first real test of the 1986 Tour, a 61.5-kilometer individual time trial along the Loire River in Nantes. In this Race of Truth, the true contenders were revealed. First among them was Hinault, who claimed victory that day. Greg finished in second place, forty-four seconds behind his teammate. Once again, bad luck had betrayed Greg, in the form of a punctured tire seven kilometers from the finish. The seconds he lost in mounting a replacement bicycle had probably cost him the win. Hinault's victory, however flimsy, perfectly suited the narrative the Badger's team and fans were building around him. Hinault now stood as the best-placed cyclist on his team. The rest of La Vie Claire would ride for him.

Laurent finished the day's race in an abysmal thirty-second place, nearly four minutes behind Hinault, his frailty revealed. He would abandon the Tour soon after.

The next day, Greg put La Vie Claire's loyalties to the ultimate test.

"Pass me your hat," he called to a teammate as they raced toward the Futuroscope amusement park. Greg referred to the Italian *biretta* that covered most cyclists' heads in those days before mandatory helmets. Deeper than a baseball cap and fitted with a shorter bill, the *biretta* absorbed sweat and blocked the sun. Riders occasionally put it to other uses.

"What do you want my hat for?" the teammate replied.

"Please, just pass me the goddamn hat."[13]

The hat was passed. Greg shoved the garment down his shorts, positioned it beneath him, and emptied his bowels. Something—a bad peach, perhaps—had afflicted him with a violent bout of diarrhea. He removed the hat and tossed it to the roadside.

A phalanx of teammates escorted him back into the peloton. "God, the smell was terrible," recalled Irish journalist Paul Kimmage. "It was rolling down his legs."[14]

Greg finally reached the finish, dismounted his bicycle and pushed through the throng, searching for the Vie Claire motor home and a toilet. He found it, climbed inside, and tiptoed among the boxes to the bathroom. He opened the door. Inside, where once a toilet had been, there were now only boxes. He ripped one open. It was filled with hundreds of postcards, all emblazoned with the smiling visage of Bernard Hinault. Greg sat down and relieved himself on his teammate's face.

The course of the 1986 Tour had been rated the most grueling in a generation. July 15 brought the first of several stages in the high mountains, featuring four climbs. It was a hot day of aggressive racing, with attack following attack. Near the halfway point, Greg spotted Hinault at the front of the pack, setting a fierce tempo. He wondered what his teammate was up to. Greg lost track of Hinault for a time; then, on a lull between two peaks, he spotted a motorbike carrying a blackboard that showed the numbers of several riders who had broken away, a courtesy afforded the peloton in an era before wireless communication. His pulse quickened when he saw that one of the numbers on the board was 1. *That's Hinault*, he thought.[15]

The Badger had slipped away on a stretch of road between two French peaks, joined by two other top-drawer cyclists, Pedro Delgado of Spain and Jean-François Bernard of France. The latter was Hinault's teammate and heir apparent. Together, they were blowing the field apart.

Greg had pedaled for several kilometers, unaware of Hinault's attack; in pre-wireless days, riders shared race developments mostly by word of mouth, and Greg's teammates had said nothing. By the time Greg could react, the Badger commanded a two-minute lead, and several purported favorites were fading behind.

Now Greg found himself in a familiar bind. As teammate of Hinault, he could not give chase. All he could do was wait for another contender to counterattack. He eased back to his team car. As in the previous year, head coach Paul Köchli had been assigned to ride with Hinault, while his assistant, Maurice Le Guilloux, followed Greg.

Greg asked Le Guilloux, "Why is Hinault attacking?"[16] The coach was as surprised as he. Now the American began to suspect that Hinault and his French teammates had plotted the attack without him.

Greg accelerated up to the group that was chasing Hinault, and he began pleading with Hinault's other rivals to attack. But each of them refused. It was still early in the Tour; the cyclists riding around Greg were unsure of their own chances for victory in Paris; and none of them fancied pulling Greg up to his teammate, a maneuver that would only bolster La Vie Claire's lead. Greg was trapped.

Finally, ten kilometers from the finish, Greg launched a desperate attack and dropped his other rivals. But Hinault had put so much daylight between himself and his teammate that he finished the day four and a half minutes ahead.

Greg was stunned and hurt that Hinault had betrayed his promise. Yet, at the finish, it was Hinault who charged at the American, crying, "How dare you chase me down?"[17] Had other men not intervened, the altercation would have ended with fists. Since Greg's arrival in France, five years earlier, Hinault had acted, publicly and privately, like an older brother. To Greg, this sudden turn of events was more than betrayal—it was fratricide.

At day's end, La Vie Claire held first, second, sixth, and seventh places on the leader board. Greg trailed Hinault by a yawning margin of five minutes and twenty-five seconds. He telephoned Kathy that night and said, "I lost the Tour today." Kathy had never heard her husband sounding so distraught.[18]

The next day brought perhaps the most challenging stage in that year's Tour: four major climbs, including the legendary Tourmalet, the highest Pyrenean pass. Hinault attacked on the very first descent, riding off alone, with three mountain peaks ahead. For a group of riders to attack so early in such a grueling stage would be foolhardy; for a cyclist to attack alone was suicidal. Hinault's escape evoked memories of the great Eddy Merckx, who, at his peak, attacked alone on the Tourmalet and rode 140 kilometers to victory. That attack had seeded the Merckx legend precisely because it succeeded against impossible odds.

That was a young Eddy Merckx. This was an old Bernard Hinault. His move looked like raw hubris, a bid to seal his final victory—and to end the contest with Greg—with a flourish that would add yet another page to the record books. In truth, Hinault had little to lose. If his attack succeeded, he would cap his career with a performance so dominant that all talk of indebtedness to Greg would fall silent. If it failed, then Hinault could go to sleep that night with a clean conscience, having delivered the race to Greg, just as he had publicly promised.

Once again, Greg was powerless to give chase until Hinault's rivals tendered a response, which, this time, they did. On the penultimate climb, the other contenders began to narrow Hinault's lead. As the Badger crossed the Col de Peyresourde, riders appeared on the horizon behind him. Hinault was slowing. His deceleration was imperceptible at first, and then it was obvious. The exhausted cyclist wove and wobbled across the road. In his single-minded pursuit of victory, Hinault had neglected to eat. Now his body was drained. Hinault had bonked.

"And Hinault is cracking!" Phil Liggett cried on British television.[19]

In the brief lull between the descent of the Peyresourde and the day's final climb, to the Pyrenean resort of Superbagnères, Hinault's rivals caught him. As Greg rode past his spent leader, he asked how he was feeling. The Badger just grunted.

Greg sped toward the summit. The leash finally off, Greg was free to attack; indeed, he *had* to attack if he wished to close the gap that separated him from Hinault on the leader board. But something was holding him back. Greg was a fundamentally reactive rider. Other cyclists attacked; Greg preferred to counterattack. He needed a rabbit to chase.

Andy Hampsten, *le Petit Lapin*, would be the rabbit. Greg's faithful teammate chose a point where the road grew suddenly steeper, within the final ten kilometers. Then he took off alone, sweeping gracefully around a hairpin and up the mountainside, accelerating so effortlessly as to create the illusion that the other riders were slowing down. As he passed Greg, he gave him a look that said, "Follow me."

The other contenders took off after Andy, but it was a lackluster pursuit, and soon the group began to splinter. Greg's rivals were on the ropes. Suddenly Greg shot forth, lurching left and right, up and down on his bicycle, in his saddle and out of it, looking as if he and his bicycle couldn't quite come to terms, muscling forward with brute, clumsy strength. He caught Andy, who offered Greg a bottle and paced him for as long as his legs would hold. When the last of his power was gone, Andy faded, and Greg rode on alone. He pedaled forward on a huge gear, which combined with his awkward gait to create the impression he was struggling up the mountain. In fact, he was obliterating his rivals, climbing as he had never climbed before.

As Greg approached the finish, he raised his arms in victory almost as an afterthought, so focused was he on clawing every second out of his opponents, out of the Badger. Behind him, Hinault had replenished his blood sugar and staged a miraculous recovery. At the foot of the final climb, all his enemies had given him up for dead. But Hinault fought his way up the slope and lurched across the line in eleventh place, having lost nearly five minutes to Greg. At day's end, Hinault still held the yellow jersey, but by only forty seconds.

Hinault had started the day leading the Tour by a seemingly insurmountable margin; now, somehow, he had gambled it away. This looked to be the greatest victory of Greg's cycling career, although that distinction hinged on what he could make of it in the days to come.

At the finish, Hinault confessed that he had been riding to win, just as all of France had expected of him. Had he succeeded, he said, "I would have won the Tour, and everyone would have lavished praise on me. If I failed, I knew that Greg was behind me ready to counterattack, and that I was tiring his adversaries. It was a sound strategy."[20]

But it was not the deal Hinault had brokered with Greg. That night Greg confronted his teammate, as Tapie attempted to intervene. The trusting Greg was shaken to the core by his teammate's evident betrayal.

In his defense, Hinault cast himself as *agent provocateur*, weakening Greg's opponents to clear a path for his ultimate victory.

Hinault claimed to be looking after Greg, but as the Tour rolled on, he seemed more inclined to take care of himself. On Stage 16, a fast, windy road race, Hinault jumped into a breakaway, which quickly began gaining time on the peloton. The group included two other Vie Claire riders. It also contained Urs Zimmermann, a Swiss rider who stood in third place, just behind Greg.

In that scenario, race protocol dictated that Hinault and his teammates not cooperate with Zimmermann, who might pass Greg on the leader board if the group held on to win. But Hinault and his teammates ignored that rule, and soon the group had gained nearly a minute on everyone else.

This time Greg didn't wait for instructions from his team. He brokered a deal with Robert Millar, a Scottish rider in fourth place overall. "Robert," he beckoned, "I'm getting screwed here."[21] He asked Millar and his team to chase down Hinault. In exchange, Greg pledged he would help Millar win a mountain stage—Millar was a climber—if he was ever in a position to do it. Millar agreed, and his Panasonic team reeled in Hinault with Greg in tow. When the Badger was caught, Greg greeted him with an impolite gesture. Hinault replied in kind.

That evening, Tapie appeared on French television, claiming all was well between his two stars. "Perfect harmony," he said.

Greg, however, was devastated; on the way to the hotel, he threatened to quit. "Fuck it. I'm done. I'm going home," he told Tapie. "I'm not going to race against Hinault, against my teammate. I can't do it anymore."[22]

The Vie Claire owner swore he would speak to Hinault—and no doubt he did, probably telling each cyclist exactly what he wanted to hear. Nothing was settled.

The Vie Claire team was split in two. At the dinner table, Greg would sit at one end with his North American pals, Bauer and Hampsten. Hinault would sit at the other, with the other Frenchmen. Paul Köchli's Swiss contingent would sit in the middle, resolutely neutral.

No such rift divided the French public. Hinault was at that moment the most beloved cyclist in France, exalted as a champion and, more important, as an underdog. After each stage, the Badger would retreat into his personal camper, dubbed the Hinaultmobile, where he would shower, change into a crisp white *blouson* and emerge, one writer observed, "to bless the crowds with a pontifical wave."[23] His *suavité* cut a sharp contrast to the histrionics of his increasingly haggard and haunted American teammate.

A poll published in the French sports newspaper *L'Équipe* showed that four-fifths of the peloton favored Hinault to win. Greg began to wonder how far they might go to help him.

Kathy LeMond, whose constant presence at this Tour would revolutionize the role of cycling spouse, took a heartfelt appeal directly to French television in defense of her husband. "If Hinault's going to continue attacking Greg during the race, he should say so, instead of pretending they're teammates," she said. "If he's going to break his promise, at least admit it."[24]

Up to that point in the race, and for the entirety of the prior year's Tour, team tactics had hindered Greg from riding to victory. The next day, as the Tour reached the Alps, his fortunes would finally change. Stage 17 promised the Tour's highest-elevation finish, atop the 2,413-meter-high Col du Granon. Along the way, Hinault fiddled with the height of his bicycle seat. His leg was hurting, perhaps a flare-up of the old knee injury. His rivals sensed opportunity. On the descent of the Col d'Izoard, the second of three climbs, several riders broke free of the peloton. The group included Urs Zimmermann, in third place, and Greg, whose job was to shadow him.

Race etiquette did not permit Greg to pull the Swiss cyclist up the mountainside. He was, however, allowed to let Zimmermann pull him. The pair reorganized, and race cameras showed Zimmermann leading Greg up the final climb. Greg was following the rules of the game, which permitted him to "mark" Zimmermann to the finish, no matter how far that effort put him ahead of Hinault. The Badger was having a bad day, and Greg was finally having a good one.

As Zimmermann approached the summit, with Greg pedaling just behind him, French spectators on the roadside reacted with shock and polite applause; it was the *maillot jaune* of Hinault they had come to see.

On British television, Phil Liggett intoned, "There is no doubt now that Greg LeMond will take the yellow jersey for the first time in his career, and," as the feed cut to a camera lower down the mountain, "he'll take it from this man's shoulders, his friend and teammate, Bernard Hinault."[25]

Hinault finished more than three minutes behind Greg and his Swiss accomplice. Greg now led the Tour, the first American to don the *maillot jaune*. Yet, if the American public expected fist pumps and cowboy yelps, they would be disappointed; Greg's remarks to the press were guarded.

"The race isn't over yet," Greg told the *New York Times*, "and I won't really have the yellow jersey until I wear it on the victory podium when we finish in Paris."[26]

Hinault now trailed Greg in the standings by nearly three minutes and Urs Zimmermann by twenty-three seconds. Though no doubt horrified, Hinault spun the day's events into a collective victory. "I'm very pleased for Greg," he told the *Times*. "He rode perfectly for the team."[27]

That night, Hinault called a meeting of the Vie Claire team. He wanted to attack Zimmermann, the rider who now stood in second place, ahead of him in the standings. The strategy certainly suited Hinault—but not Greg. In less divisive circumstances, the team would have been instructed to forget Zimmermann and focus on protecting Greg and his *maillot jaune*.

The next morning Greg looked anxious, while Hinault glowed with ambition. The race route filled with French supporters cheering *hee-NOL, hee-NOL*. The day featured three epic climbs. As the peloton descended the first, the Col du Galibier, Hinault launched an attack, opening a gap on Greg, Zimmermann, and the others. For Hinault to attack his teammate in yellow was a breach of protocol; for Greg to chase him would have been equally unchivalrous. Greg waited to see whether Zimmermann would take off after Hinault, but the Swiss rider did not make a move. Terrified that the race was slipping away again, Greg eased back to Paul Köchli and asked what he should do.

The coach asked, "Do you want to win the Tour?" Yes, Greg replied. "So drop Zimmermann," Köchli instructed. "Catch Hinault."[28]

Somehow Greg had to bridge the distance to Hinault without towing along the man in second place. A long descent lay ahead. Greg hit it at full throttle, sweeping around hairpin bends at breakneck speed, opening an ever-wider gap between himself and Zimmermann. Greg was attacking, not counterattacking, emboldened by his *maillot jaune* and by his desperation. The Swiss cyclist, with weaker bike-handling skills and a fainter heart, could not keep up. Greg finally lost him and closed in on Hinault. When he caught him, Hinault's face registered surprise. "Come on, let's go," Greg said as he swept past.[29]

Hinault's final attack had failed. It had also succeeded—not at defeating Greg but at reclaiming second place from Zimmermann. United now against a common foe, Greg and Hinault rode forward, carving up the rest of the field. Their descent of the dizzying Croix de Fer would become the stuff of legend; they reached a speed of one hundred kilometers per hour, leaving Zimmermann minutes behind.

Greg and Hinault approached the foot of l'Alpe d'Huez, cycling's grand cathedral, with its twenty-one hairpin turns. Bernard Tapie approached the pair in his car and delivered instructions, as if he were choreographing a pageant. "Greg, you've won the Tour," he said. But this was Hinault's last Tour, and the French throngs would delight in watching their hero command the race one last time. "Let him lead up the climb," Tapie instructed, "and let him win the stage."[30]

The two cyclists proceeded into a narrow corridor between solid walls of people, most of them screaming for Hinault. Greg dutifully fell into line behind the Badger, calmed by Tapie's assurance that the Tour was his. Tapie had read the crowd correctly. Along the route, the two cyclists were met with a rapturous cheer from mollified fans: *le-MOND . . . hee-NOL . . . le-MOND . . . hee-NOL . . .*

As they arrived at the summit, Greg pulled up to Hinault and put his arm around his shoulder. They chatted briefly, like friends out on a weekend ride. Then they clasped arms in a joint victory salute, before

Hinault rode ahead to win the stage. In the team car behind them, Tapie beamed.

Greg rejoiced. The battle was finally over. He was naturally conflict-averse, an openhearted and trusting peacemaker; he had hated fighting Hinault, a man he had revered as a hero and mentor. But Greg's respite would be brief. In a joint appearance on live television a short while later, still atop the mountain summit, a French commentator asked Hinault to sum up his chances. "The Tour is not finished," he replied, as Greg's face sank.[31]

The image of Greg and Hinault with hands intertwined at the summit of l'Alpe d'Huez might have endured as one of the most iconic moments in sports, had it been genuine. In truth, it was more like a glorified handshake, sealing the deal the two cyclists had brokered with Tapie on the road. By day's end, that deal, too, would be off.

Gallic passions had been roused. "I am up against a terrible nationalism," a despairing Greg told reporters at the Alpine summit.[32] Henceforth, Greg would ride against all of France.

On Stage 19, the last in the mountains, Hinault launched another attack. This move breached at least two rules of cycling etiquette: He attacked a teammate wearing the *maillot jaune*. And he did it in the feed zone, where riders call off hostilities to eat and drink. Yet, no one other than Greg appeared to mind. The peloton now seemed to ease off whenever Hinault attacked, behaving much like the partisan Italians in their Giro.

With nowhere else to turn, Greg summoned his two loyal teammates, Andy Hampsten and Steve Bauer. Together, they caught the Badger.

"It's the only time I ever chased a teammate in my life," Hampsten recalled to journalist Richard Moore. "I felt sick doing it."[33]

In postrace interviews, Greg looked as if he had been crying, and he sounded like a man at his wits' end. "If they want to crash me, I'd rather they tell me now," he said. "I'd rather give the race to them."[34]

That night the Tour director, Jacques Goddet, walked up to Greg and his family at the dinner table. He congratulated Greg and said how happy he was to see an American win the Tour. Then his eyes darkened. "Be careful," he said. "There are many who do not want you to win."

Goddet told Greg he would do all he could to protect him; but he could do only so much. "Watch your bottles," he said. "Watch everything."[35]

Later that night Greg learned that a former teammate of Hinault's had tendered an offer to take Greg out—to cause him to crash. Hinault declined. That was not how he wanted to win the Tour. Kathy now feared for her husband's safety.

Greg's coaches were equally concerned. Paul Köchli and Maurice Le Guilloux faced a relentless barrage of intimidation and veiled threats, much of it coming from supposedly impartial observers. "They were telling me, 'Do everything you can: Hinault must win,'" Le Guilloux recalled. "It came from all the media, radio media, television media, and also from the directors of the Tour," he said, raising intriguing questions about Goddet and his offer of help. "They all wanted Hinault to win."[36]

Greg took to buying his own food, or grabbing someone else's *musette*—a meal in a bag—at the feed station. He feared someone might tamper with his daily urine sample, collected from the wearer of the *maillot jaune* after each stage. In the waning days of the Tour, he insisted on leaving a fingerprint in the wax that sealed the bottle containing the sample, and then he photographed the bottle.

The 1986 Tour would deliver just one more day of consequence: a fifty-eight-kilometer individual time trial at Saint-Étienne, in central France.

Though Hinault trailed Greg in the standings, he was winning the psychological battle for the fate of the Tour. Two years earlier, Laurent had laughed at the Badger and his bluster. But Greg was not Laurent. He was a wreck. He felt he could trust no one but Kathy and the rest of his family.

Thirty-seven kilometers into the time trial, Greg's nerves caught up with him, and he crashed. He leapt back onto his bike, and men stepped forth from the crowd to help him. He pedaled forward desperately, but something wasn't right. He summoned the team car. His front brake was rubbing against the wheel. He slowed to a stop and leapt onto a new bicycle, pried off a rooftop rack by Maurice Le Guilloux. All the while, precious seconds ticked away; the cumulative cost of the crash and bike change was at least half a minute. Had Hinault broken Greg's spirit at last?

Hinault had started the day two minutes and forty-three seconds behind Greg in the standings. He was a master of the time trial; he rode superbly, and he posted the fastest time of the day—two minutes faster than anyone else.

Behind him, Greg climbed back onto his bicycle, banished the Badger from his mind, and pedaled as he had never pedaled before. At the finish, he had lost just twenty-five seconds to Hinault. Kathy burst through the crowd to find him. They hugged and then kissed, as a swarm of reporters with cameras encircled them to capture their joy.

Greg had won the Tour. Yet he looked like a cornered animal. Kathy was close to tears as she spoke to a puzzled American crew. "He's just killing himself to win this thing by himself, with no help," she said. Then she broke down in sobs.[37]

Hinault knew he was finally beaten. "After today, we won't fight any more," he announced; this time he meant it.[38] On the final, largely ceremonial ride into Paris, Greg crashed again, landing deep beneath a pile of riders. He dug himself out, remounted his bicycle—and there was Hinault, waiting to pace him back into the peloton, a loyal teammate at last. Years would pass before Greg again regarded his erstwhile brother as his friend.

As the peloton arrived on the Champs-Élysées, the crowds greeted the cyclists with a new chant: *le-MOND, le-MOND, le-MOND.*

Atop the podium, Greg hoisted his two-year-old son Geoffrey onto his shoulder, as a French military band played "The Star-Spangled Banner." In his moment of triumph, Greg felt—not joy, exactly, but relief. His careworn face was not that of a champion but of a victim, a man who had survived three weeks of emotional torture. As hundreds of thousands of French cycling fans chanted his name, Greg's mind drifted back to another man who had tortured him, to Ron, his abuser. Greg wondered in horror if Ron was out there somewhere, watching him on television at that very moment.[39]

*   *   *

Race officials presented Greg with the *maillot jaune*, a bouquet of victory flowers, a blue ceramic Sèvres vase, and a trophy of silver and diamonds in the shape of the Tour map, the last item valued at $45,000. Then Greg pushed through the throng for his final daily drug test. A five-minute interview with CBS Sports followed, and then Greg traveled to city hall for a reception with Jacques Chirac, the mayor and future French president. Then came a steak dinner, champagne, and cabaret at a Parisian nightclub. The obligatory team celebration seemed to go on forever.

Finally, Greg and Kathy sneaked off and found a bar. As they settled in for a victory toast, a song came on the jukebox. It was Bruce Springsteen's bittersweet anthem "Born in the U.S.A."

TWENTY MINUTES

GREG AND KATHY RETURNED to their home, across the Belgian border in Kortrijk, at three thirty in the morning on July 29. There they found five hundred Belgians awaiting them on the sidewalk, holding balloons, flags, and signs. Someone had set up spotlights to illuminate the LeMond home. A local restaurateur sold beer and wine from a makeshift booth. A twenty-one-piece band was playing. Bottles of champagne flanked the front door. Someone had painted a yellow jersey onto the pavement; another illustration depicted Greg holding the severed head of Hinault under his arm. Clearly, Greg was no longer in France.

Thirty-five hours had passed since Greg's Tour victory, on Sunday, July 27. Greg and Kathy had awakened Monday morning to a press conference, a round of photos for American magazines, and a trip to the American embassy for a cocktail-and-canapé reception. After lunch, the couple had motored west in their white Mercedes for a race in Normandy, the first of four celebratory criteriums Greg was to ride over two and a half days, netting $10,000 per race. Then they had driven five hundred kilometers home, arriving before daybreak Tuesday.

After a few hours of sleep, the LeMonds emerged from their home, and an entourage escorted them to Kortrijk's city hall for another reception. That afternoon, Greg and Kathy drove to the Netherlands for an evening criterium. Wednesday brought the third and fourth races and a full-day interview with a Belgian newspaper. The couple arrived home at midnight. On Thursday, the LeMonds flew to Washington, D.C., where, on Friday morning, they met with President Ronald Reagan. Greg presented the president with a yellow jersey; Reagan reciprocated with a jar of jelly beans. When the president offered his hand to Geoffrey, the jet-lagged toddler pushed it aside.

Then the LeMonds returned to Reno for an old-fashioned homecoming parade. Ten thousand people turned out. Greg expected little from his compatriots, so he was genuinely surprised and deeply moved. "I never thought Americans would act this way," he told a UPI reporter.[1]

Greg had hardly been a household name in the United States. When a French television station queried a random sampling of pedestrians on the streets of New York City just before the historic victory, reporters were stunned that fewer than half could identify Greg LeMond. The victory put Greg on the covers of European cycling magazines, space he had occupied before. Back home, he finally made the front page of the *New York Times*. His triumph drew coverage in *Time* and *People* and lengthy features in *Sports Illustrated* and *Rolling Stone*.

Lacking a proper handler, Greg fumbled at times with his new celebrity. In an interview with the *Washington Post*, the Tour winner spoke a bit too plainly of his prospects, veering into the vainglorious rhetoric of Laurent Fignon. "I'll be a major force in cycling for the next five to six years," he said. "I see no American taking my place."[2]

By summer's end, Kathy was pregnant with a second child. Mindful of his growing family, and aware that his cycling fame might be fleeting, Greg set about parlaying his name into a brand and the brand into a business.

At the close of 1986, American interest in recreational cycling stood at a historic high, the apex of a two-decade trend, a movement of which Greg was both a cause and an effect.

Bicycle sales had exploded in the 1970s, driven by the national fitness boom. The gas crisis added further fuel, pushing sales to a record 15.2 million bicycles in 1973, up from 3.7 million thirteen years earlier. Competitive cycling rose apace. Membership in the Amateur Bicycle League surged from about 1,000 in 1960 to 8,600 in 1973.

The currency of cycling as an American sport had ascended gradually, beginning with George Mount's surprising sixth-place finish at the 1976 Olympics and Greg's early successes. In Greg's wake, a new generation of globally competitive Americans swept into the sport. At the 1984 Olympics in Los Angeles, four years after the Carter boycott, U.S. amateur men and women claimed nine cycling medals in a lopsided field, this time with the Soviets absent. Still, it was a breakthrough for the American cycling establishment.

The 1984 games also served up an ominous portent of cycling's future. A subsequent investigation found that several American cyclists had experimented with blood doping, a new and potentially transformational technique for enhancing performance on a bicycle, in which athletes received transfusions to boost the quotient of oxygen in their blood. Olympic officials promptly banned the practice, although they did not yet have the means to detect it.

Greg's 1986 Tour victory seeded another round of celebration, this time without the attendant scandal. A month later, the burgeoning cycling mecca of Colorado Springs hosted the world championships— an event that had begun in Chicago ninety-three years earlier and had not been staged in the United States since 1912. In the marquee road race, Greg finished seventh.

Amid Greg's first wave of real American publicity, in the summer of 1986, Bob LeMond walked into a Reno bicycle shop and approached its owner, Jeff Sanchez. "We're thinking of coming up with a Greg LeMond bicycle," Bob told Jeff, "and we're wondering if you have any connections to help us do this."[3]

Jeff would spend that fall and winter in an office at Bob's real-estate business, building Greg's enterprise, Team LeMond. It was a promising concept. American cycling lacked a branded celebrity—a Wilt Chamberlain or Jack Nicklaus or John McEnroe, someone whose name could boost the salability of a jersey or water bottle or cap. Greg seemed the perfect choice. Not only was he the first American cyclist of his era to attain worldwide celebrity, he was also a tireless student of innovation. Greg had been among the first in the peloton to experiment with the solid disc wheel, the aerodynamic helmet, and the strapless pedal; he would bring that spirit to Team LeMond, along with bib-style shorts and lightweight Campagnolo bicycle components from Italy, exotica unknown to most American recreational cyclists.

From his Reno office, Jeff Sanchez assembled a full line of LeMond cycling gear: bicycles, jerseys, shorts, gloves, shoes, socks, and such, all chosen from different manufacturers that met Greg's approval. He and Bob journeyed to Italy to ink contracts. The products would be stamped with the LeMond brand and sold at Team LeMond Pro Centers, boutiques set within existing bicycle stores. Roland Della Santa, the Reno craftsman, would design the $3,000 bicycles at the top of the line. The low-end bikes, priced at $600, would come from the Bottecchia factory in Italy.

Team LeMond rolled out in January 1987 at a trade show in Long Beach, California. Stores that agreed to carry the brand had to commit to the entire line, and to a sizable swath of floor space—a tall order. But the LeMond name was hot, and forty bicycle dealers immediately signed on. Thirty more joined the team at a show in New York the next month. "We had dealers fighting over the rights," Jeff recalled.[4] Production began in earnest.

Greg was now a champion cyclist, a millionaire and a successful businessman. As the LeMonds drove home one night that spring, Kathy turned to her husband and marveled, "You know, it's almost like we're too lucky. We have everything."[5]

Greg awoke before dawn on the morning of April 20, 1987. It was the day after Easter. He was about to return to Europe, to rejoin the peloton and resume preparations to defend his title in the Tour de France. In ordinary circumstances, Greg would have been in Europe already. But this morning found him at home, outside the California capital of Sacramento, convalescing. A month earlier, Greg had broken his hand in a crash at a race in Italy. Rather than recuperate in Belgium, Greg had returned to the United States, where he could be with Kathy at their lovely house in Rancho Murieta, a gated community built around a pair of golf courses. The dwelling lay two hours west of Greg's boyhood home, on land with milder winters and gentler winds. Greg was an odd sight, a man in his mid-twenties motoring off in a Mercedes past homes populated with graying executives—who probably assumed he was someone else's petulant child, until word of his Tour victory reached their ears.

The French cycling press, already indignant at Greg's defeat of their champion, loosed a fresh volley of criticism over his decision to flee the continent at the start of racing season. He was now the de facto leader of La Vie Claire; he belonged in France, with his team.

Greg wondered whether he would ever return. His experience in the Tour—the treachery of teammates, the savagery of fans—had left him disillusioned, his naïveté shattered. Greg had lived nearly half his life dreaming of winning the Tour; in its fulfillment, the dream had become a nightmare. "You try to do something that's your heart's desire, and you work hard for it, and you think it would give you a sense of accomplishment. And I don't have that at all," he had confided to loved ones in his California home. "If you ask me right now, I hate cycling. I hate everything about it."[6]

But eventually the darkness lifted, and Greg resolved to return to France when his hand healed. During six weeks of recovery, he had done little but train on his bicycle; the cast on his left hand precluded golfing and other cathartic pursuits.

Greg's uncle, Rod Barber, had repeatedly invited his nephew to drive out to his own property, a thirty-acre ranch on land more remote than Greg's. With the return to Europe looming, Greg had finally agreed to make the trip the Monday after Easter. He would join his uncle for a turkey hunt in the morning, pedal the forty miles home, and then visit his doctor in the afternoon to get the cast removed from his hand.

Greg packed his bicycle into his car and left at 6:30 a.m. for his uncle's home in the ranch community of Lincoln. He arrived an hour later, and uncle and nephew readied for the hunt. Joining them was a third man, Pat Blades, the husband of Greg's older sister, Kathy. Pat was a contractor, who had pledged to help Greg design and build a new, more spacious home in Rancho Murieta.

The three men set out on foot around eight o'clock across a dry riverbed, bound for a hill dotted with blackberry bushes and trees a few hundred yards from the house. The hunters slowed and split up, Greg's uncle heading off to the left, his brother-in-law to the right. Their plan was to pad haltingly across the prairie in pursuit of their quarry.

Greg was an experienced hunter; his brother-in-law was not. After a time, Pat became disoriented and began to whistle, hoping his fellow hunters would respond in kind, so that he could discern their location. All three men wore camouflage gear and nets covering their faces to conceal themselves from the skittish birds. Greg had settled into a suitable patch of cover among the berry bushes. He heard the whistling but did not respond; he assumed that if he could recognize Pat's whistle, then the birds would recognize his. Eventually, the whistling stopped. Now Greg wondered where the other men were hiding. He finally gathered himself up to stand.

At the moment he rose, Greg heard a shot. It was so loud, so close, that at first he thought his own gun had somehow discharged.

Greg sank back down into a crouch. After a moment of confusion, he glanced at his left hand and saw blood on the ring finger. Then he felt numbness wash over his body. He tried again to stand, and suddenly felt as if he were going to pass out. He sank down again. He tried to speak but found that he could only gurgle. Greg's lungs were flooding with blood, he could barely breathe.

Oh, my God, he thought. *I've been shot.*

Pat came running. "What happened?" he cried. "What happened?"

Greg's life—or, more precisely, its end—was flashing before his eyes. "I'm going to die," he gurgled. "My God, my life is going to end."[7]

Greg was in shock. Pat was calm—until he heard Greg's words, whereupon he became hysterical. Greg's uncle heard Pat's screams and ran over to join the younger men, prying the shotgun from the stunned shooter's hands. Soon both of Greg's hunting companions had succumbed to a muddled panic, yelling at each other and fumbling about with Greg, trying in vain to lift his wounded body.

Their hysteria calmed Greg, who had made a career of enduring pain. He turned to the two men and shouted back at them, "I'm going to die if you guys don't calm down."

His companions collected themselves. Greg's uncle Rod ran back to the house to call an ambulance, placing the call at 8:49 a.m. Then he returned to Greg. The two men again attempted to lift him, but Greg was now in too much pain to stand. Greg instructed Rod, "Back up your truck." Rod departed to get it.

Pat remained with Greg. "It doesn't look so bad," he said. "There's a little blood coming out, but it's going to be okay."

Rod returned with the truck; twenty minutes had now elapsed since the shooting. Greg felt his breath shortening and his body weakening. "Let's just try to get out of here," he instructed. The men helped Greg to his feet and led him to the truck, still a good distance away. Then the three of them awaited the ambulance. Five minutes stretched to ten, ten to twenty. Forty minutes had now passed since the shooting. Growing impatient, the men finally decided to steer the truck up to the main gate of the sprawling ranch. There they met an armada of rescuers who had arrived at the property to find the gate locked.

Paramedics laid Greg on a stretcher, took his blood pressure, inserted an intravenous tube, and cut open his shirt, trying to stabilize his body for the half-hour drive along bumpy roads to the provincial hospital. Greg found it progressively harder to draw air into his lungs.

I'm never going to make it, he thought.

Then he heard the whirring blades of a helicopter.

The California Highway Patrol chopper had departed McClellan Air Force Base in Sacramento bound for a traffic accident. En route, the pilot had learned two things: that the injured motorist was beyond help, and that a man had been shot on a remote ranch. The copter rerouted to the ranch, where the pilot found a clearing in which to land. He touched down at 9:40 a.m., an hour after the shooting.

A rescuer asked Greg his name and address. He told her, spelling it out, though he could barely speak for lack of breath. She asked him to repeat it three, four times, probably laboring to keep him conscious. Finally, affable Greg lost his patience: "Damn it! Greg LeMond, 745 Anillo Way, Rancho Murieta, California, 9-5-6-8-3, and don't ask me again."[8]

Greg was loaded onto the helicopter, which regained the air and flew twenty-five miles southwest to the University of California at Davis, whose Sacramento hospital specialized in traumatic injury. The flight took eleven minutes. As he arrived at the hospital, around 10:00 a.m.,

Greg felt relieved. *Maybe it's not so bad,* he thought. Then a doctor began to yell instructions, and hospital staff rushed Greg into the emergency room, and his fear returned.

The human body holds eight to twelve pints of blood. By the time Greg arrived at the hospital, he had lost between two and three pints. Much of the blood that remained had pooled into the pleural space that surrounded his lungs, causing them to collapse. Blood had also seeped into Greg's pericardium, the membrane that enclosed his heart. Shotgun pellets had perforated both organs.

Few other human beings would have survived an hour with those injuries. In the previous summer, Greg's massive cardiovascular engine had powered him to victory in the Tour. Today it would save his life. Rescuers loaded Greg onto a gurney, ripped open his shirt, delivered a local anesthetic and plunged a tube into his chest to drain the space around his lungs. He arched his back in agony. Hospital staff then rolled Greg into the prep room and sponged him down for surgery. Greg slipped into sleep and surgery commenced.

Kathy's morning began calmly enough with a telephone call from Paul Köchli, Greg's coach. He and Kathy spent some time discussing Greg's impending return to Europe and a looming race in the Netherlands. Neither party knew that the subject of their talk was fighting for his life.

A very pregnant Kathy was making pancakes for her son when the telephone rang again.

"It's UC Davis Medical Center," the voice said. "Your husband has been shot." As the weight of those words sank in, Kathy hurried into a bathroom and sat on the toilet to conceal her welling tears from three-year-old Geoffrey. "At this moment, he's alive. Get here as soon as possible," the voice instructed.[9] Kathy hung up the phone and sobbed. Then she collected herself and her child and drove to the hospital. She had forgotten all about the hunting trip. She wondered whether Greg had been caught in a holdup at a 7-Eleven. She thought, *Please let him live.*[10]

The emergency room staff, too, wondered whether the patient before them—pale, gaunt, oddly attired, and afflicted with gunshot wounds—had been ensnared in some random robbery. Someone had misspelled Greg's surname as Lemont, and the first caregivers to treat him that morning failed to recognize the reigning Tour de France champion.

Greg's life now passed into the hands of Sandra Beal, age thirty-three, the critical-care surgeon who happened to be there. Dr. Beal had been called in to treat a stabbing victim from nearby Folsom State Prison who was bleeding to death; her presence and immediate availability were part of a long chain of small miracles that availed Greg on his darkest day.

More than one hundred lead shotgun pellets had entered Greg's body. Dr. Beal knew that to remove them all would further harm his vital organs. The two pellets lodged in the lining of his heart could not be touched; there was too much risk. Most of the others had already done their damage; leaving them where they lay posed no immediate risk. The seven-person surgical team sealed two small holes in Greg's diaphragm and two more in the small intestine. Two additional holes in his liver were left to heal on their own.

When a terrified Kathy arrived at the hospital, doctors told her that Greg would be in surgery for two hours, and that doctors would do all they could. Kathy sat in shock and waited. Two hours stretched to three, and hospital staff told her nothing of Greg's condition. Reporters began to trickle in; the shooting victim had been identified at last, and word had leaked out. Some broadcasters in Europe interrupted their programming to announce that the great LeMond had been shot.

Kathy telephoned her mother, Sacia, in La Crosse. She told her it was bad. Sacia could hear panic in her daughter's voice. She also noticed that Kathy's speech was punctuated with little gasps, as if some silent pain were passing through her body every few minutes. She finally interrupted Kathy to ask, "Are you in labor?"[11]

Kathy was eight months pregnant; the due date was a few weeks away. The emotional force of the morning's events had propelled her body into premature labor. Now she had to choose between waiting for Greg to emerge from surgery and rushing off to admit herself as a patient in the maternity ward of a different hospital. She chose to stay.

Kathy pleaded with the staff to let her see her husband. Finally, at 2:30 p.m., she prevailed. Greg was sedated, but as Kathy walked into the room he moaned, as if he sensed her soothing presence.

Kathy wasn't quite prepared for the sight that greeted her. Her unheralded visit had surprised the workers who tended Greg. He was stripped naked, his body suspended above the bed by a harness so nurses could change the sheets, which were soaked crimson. Greg's body looked "like a colander," Kathy recalled, his skin a patchwork, dotted with sixty holes, each one dripping blood.[12]

She was overjoyed to see her husband alive but horrified at his grievous wounds. She turned to his caregivers and asked, "Are you sure he's going to be all right?"[13] Yes, they replied, Greg would probably live. Hearing that, Kathy leaned over, gently kissed Greg, and then reluctantly departed his hospital for her own, where doctors administered drugs to calm the contractions. Her own plight precluded a visit to yet another hospital, where her brother-in-law Pat Blades had been taken for observation. Unable to bear his role in the day's events, Pat had suffered a nervous collapse. When he spoke of ending his own life, police had had him admitted.

Greg had survived, barely. He had lost nearly half of the blood in his body. The perforations in his small intestine had leached waste into his body, inviting infection. Even greater, perhaps, was the danger to Greg's damaged kidney. Doctors learned, after admitting him, that it was Greg's only functioning kidney. The other had failed in childhood.

Greg had arrived at the hospital twenty minutes from death. Had a helicopter not magically appeared above his uncle's ranch, Greg almost surely would have bled out or suffocated on the half-hour drive to the local hospital. Had he survived the trip, he likely would have died in that hospital's emergency room, which lacked a surgeon with the expertise to save him.

Five shotgun pellets remained in Greg's heart, five in his liver, and two dozen more in his back, arms, and legs: more than thirty pellets in all, each one roughly half the size of a BB. The volley, blasted from a twelve-gauge shotgun, had broken two of Greg's ribs and shattered his left ring finger. Thirty more pellets had been removed from Greg's body, some of them preserved in a plastic specimen bottle, which was later presented to the patient and became a macabre memento in the LeMond home.

The shooting was news in the United States, but even bigger news abroad; journalists flew in from France. Dr. Beal spoke to the assembled media. "Because he's young and in very good condition, he'll recover," she said. "He'll probably lose about two months of training."[14]

Little in her remarks hinted at how close Greg had come to death. Greg's body was his livelihood; if anyone in the professional cycling community learned the full extent of his injuries, there was little chance he could return to La Vie Claire or any other team. Without telling any untruths, Greg's doctors and his loved ones did what they could to spin the narrative as a minor setback in his career.

In fact, for Greg, the most dangerous procedure still lay ahead. An unknown quantity of blood remained in his lungs, where it had clotted. The blood would have to be removed. The obvious solution was a thoracotomy, a procedure in which Dr. Beal would open Greg's chest cavity and remove the clotted blood. A thoracotomy had helped President Reagan recover from the damage inflicted by a would-be assassin's bullets six years earlier.

But a thoracotomy would cost Greg a portion—perhaps one-fifth—of his lung function. For a professional cyclist, that price was too steep.

Greg's family, close-knit but scattered, rushed to his side.

Bob LeMond had been on his bicycle, riding the twenty-five miles from his home to his office in Reno, when a pickup truck screeched to a halt across the road. At the wheel was Jeff Sanchez, the Team LeMond employee.

"Bob," he cried, "Greg's been shot."

"That son of a bitch Pat Blades," Bob cursed, as if he were psychic. "I bet Pat did it." Bob knew his son-in-law was no hunter.[15]

Bob and Bertha raced to Sacramento with Greg's sister Karen, driving at one hundred miles per hour, not knowing whether Greg would be alive when they arrived. Kathy's sister Mary flew in the next day. She was a newly minted doctor, running an urgent-care center in Milwaukee.

Mary found Greg in piteous shape—his body racked with spasms and seemingly endless coughing fits, his temperature erratic, his eyes red from tears, his skin paper-white beneath the *maillot-jaune*-colored sheets of his hospital bed.

Tubes protruded from Greg's chest. A cast still covered his arm; a catheter siphoned his urine. His back looked "like a target," Mary recalled, with a dense array of holes at the center and more widely spaced perforations at the outer edges.[16]

Doctors inserted an epidural into Greg's spine to deliver a steady morphine drip. He had spent the previous decade of his life training to endure ever-higher thresholds of pain; yet here was a pain even he could not bear. He would politely alert his nurse, "I don't believe this epidural is working." The nurse would ask, "Where is the pain between one and ten?" Greg would reply, "Twelve." The nurse would shake her head—"I know you're not in that much pain if you can joke with me"—and move on with her rounds.[17]

Mary quickly surmised something was not right; she would later learn that the tube meant to deliver the painkiller had kinked. Walking out into the hall, she noted that some other rooms had police posted outside the doors, guarding patients with rap sheets and drug dependencies. To these nurses, Mary concluded, Greg was another drug addict. Kathy's doctor sister worked around them, eventually persuading the hospital to install a new unit that allowed Greg to control the flow of morphine himself. Finally the pain became tolerable. The episode left Greg so frightened of his nurses that he asked Mary to spend the night at his side. "*They don't believe me*," he pleaded.[18]

Brighter days followed. Flowers from well-wishers began to arrive, and soon they filled Greg's room to overflowing, striking a colorful contrast to the austerity of the other rooms on the ward. Greg gleefully regifted the bouquets to nurses and patients, policemen and convicts. Kathy visited daily, staying until the raw emotion stirred by his plight would trigger a fresh onslaught of contractions; then Kathy would retreat to her own hospital.

The nurses kept prodding Greg to rise from his bed. They seemed not to grasp the severity of his injuries. Any movement triggered waves of pain so brutal it would reduce Greg to tears. Yet, these nurses seemed to think he was lazy—an amusing thought, given his profession, which was not, apparently, common knowledge on the ward. Finally, on the third or fourth day in the hospital, Greg eased himself up to a seated position, lowered his feet to the floor, and struggled to his feet.

"He stood up and walked maybe two steps," Mary Morris recalled, "and barely made it back to the bed. It took every ounce of energy he had."[19]

Geoffrey, Greg's three-year-old son, came to visit. It was a tender reunion—until Greg leaned forward, and his son saw the dozens of circular scabs that covered his back.

"Oh, Daddy," Geoffrey cried. "Why do you have spots?" That night, at the family home, Geoffrey asked his Aunt Mary if she would put spots on his back, too. She dotted Geoffrey's back with a felt-tip marker.[20]

On April 26, six days after the shooting, Greg went home. "It's my best day," he told reporters—and it was, provided one's memory reached back no further than six days.[21] Doctors had predicted a two-week hospital stay, so Greg's prompt release was a victory in itself, sufficient, perhaps, to quash the rumors that his cycling career was finished.

It was time, though, to face one cruel fact. "The Tour de France is out of the question," Bob LeMond told reporters in a press conference shortly before Greg's release.[22]

Greg returned to a home that now resembled a sick ward. Greg convalesced in one room, Kathy in another. Their mothers slept in cots in the living room. They and Kathy took turns sitting at Greg's bedside, so someone would be with him twenty-four hours a day. Whoever wasn't watching Greg would mind Geoffrey. One evening, as an exhausted Kathy and her equally spent mother trudged along a manicured street in the LeMond's gated community with Geoffrey in their pajamas, Sacia Morris thought, *My gosh, what has happened to us?*[23]

Get-well cards continued to roll in—along with a surprising amount of vitriol, much of it from Europeans, expressing bafflement at Greg's decision to hunt in the middle of bicycling season. To cycling traditionalists, Greg's sins were manifold. Why had the captain of La Vie Claire abandoned his team and flown home in midseason to recuperate from a comparatively minor injury? And why on earth had he interrupted that convalescence to hunt? Cycling custom dictated that racers, in racing season, belonged in two places: on their bicycles or in their beds. Greg mystified the French by golfing on rest days. The notion of a mid-April hunting expedition left them flabbergasted.

Greg's latest faux pas afforded the cycling press a chance to reflect on his fundamental ethnocentrism, on the many ways he had failed to adapt to his European workplace. Many in the peloton still could not bear the sight of Greg eating ice cream—right out in the open—at some Italian café on a race day, or the sight of Kathy glued to her husband's side. Worse, Greg had defied cycling's code of silence, speaking openly and disapprovingly of doping and shady deals in his sport.

"He is very much an American in Europe, who does not really understand how things operate over here," sniffed Sean Kelly, the great Irish sprinter, in *Bicycling* magazine.[24]

Apart from teammates, only one European cyclist sent Greg a kind note, Laurent Fignon. Laurent knew the purgatory that awaited Greg, for he still dwelt there. Three years removed from his last Tour victory, against ever-lengthening odds, Laurent was still clawing his way back. In the months to come, Laurent's struggles would inspire Greg.

Greg now found his world confined to the distance between a bed and a chair, where he would sit and shake, sweat and tears running down his face, never able to find a comfortable position. He was allowed pain medications every four hours; the fourth hour was torture.

Greg's body was covered with scars, which one visitor likened to "angry mosquito bites."[25] He walked with the stoop of an old man. The simple act of talking put so much exertion on his wounded diaphragm it would sap his strength. His lungs pumped at a fraction of their former capacity. X-rays showed the right one, more gravely damaged, now markedly smaller than the left. Like Laurent, Greg would never be quite the same cyclist again.

Dr. Beal still agonized over how to remove the syrupy blood that remained in Greg's lungs without opening his chest. "If we open your chest," she warned him, "your career is over."[26] Finally, she came to Greg and Kathy with an alternative. An experimental blood thinner could be injected into Greg's chest cavity to dissolve the grapefruit-sized clot. The liquefied blood could then be sucked out with tubes. The LeMonds agreed. Two weeks after the shooting, Dr. Beal performed the procedure, thinning and removing the clotted blood without further damage to Greg's priceless lungs.

Bit by bit, Greg improved. In week three, he summoned the strength to walk out his front door.

"He took a chair," recalled Sacia Morris, "and put it out on the lawn and just sat and looked out. He was very emotional. His career was gone."[27]

A month earlier Greg hadn't been sure he wanted to return to professional cycling. Now he feared the decision was no longer his.

On May 12, twenty-two days after the accident, Greg accompanied Kathy to the hospital for the birth of their second child, Scott. Though Greg was overjoyed, the journey proved too arduous; he wound up in a bed next to Kathy and their new baby.

Finally, the day arrived when Greg climbed back onto a bicycle. It wasn't a racing bike, just a fat-wheeled ten-speed with straightened handlebars and a baby seat fitted to the back. He rode it around the garage of his suburban home, his chest heaving from the effort. Soon Greg and his three-year-old son were riding together, Greg on his ten-speed, Geoffrey on his tricycle, wobbling down the street. Tears welled in Sacia Morris's eyes at the memory. "Greg could barely pedal, and Geoffrey would ride along with him."[28]

By the end of May, five weeks after the shooting, Greg found his body beginning to heal. The profound weariness that had gripped him was loosening, giving way to his native restlessness. And yet, Greg's celebrated cardiopulmonary engine lay in ruin. He had lost thirty of his 150 pounds. His wounded body, deprived of food, had sought protein in Greg's thigh and calf muscles, which had wasted away. His body fat, a measure of fitness, had swelled from 5 percent to 19 percent. Put together, those metrics suggested Greg had lost perhaps one-third of his muscle. The share of red blood cells circulating in his blood, vital in moving oxygen to body tissue, had dropped by more than half, from his normal 45 percent to 19 percent.

To seed his recovery, Greg turned to an activity both familiar and sedate: fly-fishing along the banks of a lake at his country club. At first even that meager effort left his back in a knot after fifteen minutes. Next Greg commenced daily three-mile bicycle rides around his gated community, enough to stretch shriveled muscles and stir his stricken heart. He gradually lengthened the sessions, riding on a mountain bike and studiously avoiding actual mountains. He set out on a forty-five-minute ride, and then another, his first proper exercise since returning home. He kept the rides low-key, and he felt fine afterward. The cycling would restore Greg's injured lungs. He began gingerly lifting weights to regain lost muscle mass, while still recovering from abdominal surgery.

Greg's injuries were not entirely physical. He and Kathy had endured profound emotional trauma. Greg was twenty-five, Kathy twenty-seven. They had a three-year-old son and an infant, two homes in two countries, a business to run, and a cycling career to manage. Over the previous two months, one of them had nearly died, the other had given birth, and their life's work had come crashing to earth.

Needing a vacation, they rented a motor home and took a two-week trip to Montana and Wyoming, touring Yellowstone National Park and hiding from the world. Greg breakfasted daily on bacon, eggs, and pancakes, lunched on bacon cheeseburgers, and dined on chicken-fried steak, all to gain weight. He spent most of his waking hours fly-fishing, a gentle activity that gradually built up his stamina and his muscles as it mended his psyche. Greg brought his mountain bike along, but it never left the motor home. He and Kathy savored the time together with their expanded family.

Greg returned to Rancho Murieta refreshed but facing mounting pressure to prove to the world that his cycling career was not over, a conclusion some of his peers had reached despite the rosy appraisals of his progress in the press. Leaders of Greg's Vie Claire team, whose sponsorship was now shared with the Japanese conglomerate Toshiba, quietly mapped out a plan for the remainder of the 1987 racing season that did not include him. A month after the shooting, a letter arrived from team boss Bernard Tapie, politely apprising Greg that he was fired.

The larger unknown, one columnist mused, was "whether LeMond will be able to return to winning form at any time in the future."[29]

On June 19, two months after the shooting, organizers of the Coors Classic announced that Greg would compete in the nation's premier bicycle race that August. Bob had negotiated Greg's return to cycling in his son's absence, not fully comprehending the depth of his injuries. Greg was incredulous, but he played along. He had mostly avoided reporters during his convalescence. Now, he threw open the doors and launched a PR campaign to announce his recovery.

"I feel normal," Greg told the *Chicago Tribune*. "I'm 100 percent recuperated."[30]

Normal was a relative term. Most of Greg's lost weight had returned, but much of it was fat. Greg was training for two hours a day, riding along back roads near his home. He had found an anonymous partner, a recreational cyclist whose path kept crossing his. Greg found that he could keep pace until the two cyclists reached steep climbs, when Greg—the reigning Tour de France champion—would be dropped.

Until, one day, Greg did the dropping.

"I started feeling like a normal bike racer," he recalled. "An out-of-shape bike racer, but not one with a disability."[31]

The 1987 Tour de France began on July 1. Greg watched it on television.

Laurent Fignon's progress since his consecutive Tour wins had followed a frustrating pattern. Laurent would spend months on end in the cycling wilderness, recovering from one malady or another, with the French press forever anticipating his return. Then he would post a remarkable result in a significant race, rekindling talk of a comeback. Then another setback would sideline him, and the cycle would begin anew.

At the close of the 1986 season, Laurent came tantalizingly close to victory in the Grand Prix des Nations, a contest against the clock, whose winner could claim the unofficial title of men's world time-trial champion. After crashing in the rain, Laurent finished just six seconds behind the winner, Sean Kelly. The result should have buoyed Laurent's spirits; instead, it fed his essential pessimism. By season's end, Laurent was close to abandoning the peloton.

"For the first time in my career," he recalled in his memoir, "I could feel true hatred, of myself, everyone else, and the whole world."[32]

The next year held little promise for Laurent or his team, Système U. Two or three years earlier, Laurent had been regarded—for a time—as the world's greatest cyclist, Cyrille Guimard as the sport's greatest coach, and Renault as its greatest team. Now, they were diminished men running a depleted team. Système U had not yet claimed a Grand Tour. Laurent hadn't won a major race since 1984. The litany of success had migrated with Hinault and LeMond over to Paul Köchli and his celebrated team, Vie Claire.

While Guimard remained a superb tactician, Laurent found him less adept at managing a cycling business. He was cutting corners, sending too few vehicles to races. "Sometimes we were left asking other teams to give us a lift back to our hotels," the cyclist recalled.[33] Laurent used his own funds to hire a new *soigneur*, someone to fill the critical role of masseur, trainer, and valet at races. He tapped an old friend.

Alain Gallopin had met Laurent in the military. They had raced together as amateurs and had turned professional together in 1982. Three months after Alain's professional debut, his own team director had accidentally run him over with a car. His skull was fractured. Alain recovered, but he would not race again. He returned to school to train in sports therapy; Laurent told him to telephone when he completed his degree. Alain "was many things at once" to Laurent. "a brother, a confidant, a masseur, a trainer, a shoulder to lean on."[34]

Alain's first project with his new employer was to work on Laurent's people skills. "He would go into the crowd and he would push people," Alain recalled. "He didn't like to be famous, Laurent."[35] Alain counseled his friend to lighten up, to indulge the occasional autograph seeker, theorizing that his public prickliness and private angst might be somehow linked. After attending to Laurent's image, Alain began to hunt for races the struggling star might conquer. It would take more than a year, but his efforts would eventually bear fruit.

In the spring of 1987, at the Vuelta a España, Laurent found himself riding in third place, his best showing in a Grand Tour since 1984. Yet, before the final day of racing, his Système U team accepted an offer of

30,000 francs per rider to ease up, an inducement paid by a rival team to protect its lead. Laurent took the money, but he immediately regretted it. He later claimed, "If we had wanted to take the initiative, we could have blown their scrawny carcasses to the four corners of Spain."[36] Laurent held on to third place; but another Grand Tour had slipped through his fingers. He failed to appear at the awards ceremony, leaving an empty step on the podium.

In late May, Laurent endured an episode that might be termed *Fignonian*, combining elements of triumph, misfortune, and petulance. First, he rode to victory at the one-day Grand Prix de Wallonie in Belgium. Then, a few days later, race officials announced that he had failed the postrace drug test. Laurent swore he was clean. Nonetheless, the finding sparked fresh rumors that Laurent was doping, plunging the cyclist into another trough of depression, irritability, and self-doubt. With the 1987 Tour looming, he recalled, "my morale was at a low ebb."[37]

With Hinault retired and Greg injured, the Tour stood wide open. Laurent was certainly a favorite, in many minds if not his own. So were Stephen Roche, the Irishman who had conquered the Giro d'Italia earlier that year, and Pedro Delgado, the Spaniard. Both of them revealed their form with good showings in the brief prologue time trial—which Laurent finished in seventy-second place. The race progressed through France "as if I wasn't there," Laurent recalled. "My body was pedaling but my mind was wandering."[38] This time there was a happy reason for his distraction. Laurent's fiancée, Nathalie, was about to give birth to their first child.

The tenth stage, an 87.5-kilometer individual time trial, brought the Tour's first real test, and Laurent did not pass. Stephen Roche came in first, while Laurent's teammate Charly Mottet finished second, and suddenly Laurent was reduced to a supporting role behind Mottet, who now held the race lead. Laurent found himself surprisingly content at the thought of riding for the team.

Laurent labored for Mottet and slipped ever further back in the standings. Stage 18 presented an individual time trial up the famed Mont Ventoux. "On this mountaintop, in front of a hysterical crowd, I had decided to give it my all, absolutely everything I had," Laurent recalled. "Unfortunately, nothing happened, nothing at all."[39] He finished in sixty-fourth place.

Laurent's first child, Jeremy, had been born on the previous day. On the climb, fans shouted, "Come on, Dad!" Alone in his hotel room, Laurent wept. "I had the very distinct impression that this was the end."[40]

Pride forbade him to quit. Two days later, on a climb to l'Alpe d'Huez, Laurent finally found his form and finished ahead of the other contenders, riding himself into the top ten at the Tour. He felt even stronger on the following stage, which ended at the Alpine resort of La Plagne. He rode to victory, his first stage win at the grand race in three years.

Laurent rode into Paris to finish the Tour in seventh place. He was grateful for the result, though he stood many minutes behind Stephen Roche, the eventual winner.

Laurent and other Frenchmen had won the Tour eight times between 1977 and 1985. Now, just two years later, the French cycling community lay in disarray. English speakers had won the Tour for a first time and then a second. With Hinault retired and Laurent flagging, Frenchmen occupied just three spots in the top twenty of the World Cycling Federation rankings. Of those three, only Laurent had won a Grand Tour. Oldtimers began to wonder whether the so-called Anglo-Saxon invasion was moving a bit too fast.

The LeMond family traveled to San Francisco on July 12, 1987, and dined in Chinatown. On the drive home, Greg became afflicted with the most severe pain he had ever felt, before the shooting or since. He returned to the emergency room at Davis, where doctors diagnosed an intestinal blockage, a kink that had formed at one of the scars where a shotgun pellet had been. They were forced to cut along the fresh surgical scar of the original abdominal incision.

Greg was due to resume his racing career in ten days. That was now out of the question. Desperate to quell further rumors of his professional demise, Greg concocted a cover story that contained just enough truth to be palatable. Greg asked the doctors to remove his appendix. When he emerged from surgery, he told reporters his appendix had been removed.

Not everyone was convinced. The next day, Bob LeMond telephoned Greg and asked, "What the hell's going on? Nobody wants you."[41] Greg's manager-father had been in denial about the gravity of his injuries. Now Bob was in Europe, negotiating with cycling teams.

Greg's tenure with La Vie Claire was over. Only two other teams expressed interest. One was Carrera, an Italian squad named for a jeans manufacturer, whose leader, Stephen Roche, was about to win the Tour. The other was PDM, a decidedly unromantic partnership between the Dutch electronics firm Philips and the DuPont chemical company. Greg's "appendectomy" thinned the field of bidders to one, and PDM officials told Bob they would employ his son only if he proved his fitness by returning to the peloton within two months.

La Vie Claire and its team captain publicly parted ways on July 21; news accounts hinted he was close to signing with PDM. Greg praised the Dutch for their "American attitude" and hinted at his hurt over being mistreated by Vie Claire. "You win the Tour de France," he told an interviewer, "you'd think you'd get a little more respect."[42]

The second surgery reset Greg's comeback schedule almost to day one. Greg could not lift weights to build muscle mass until the new abdominal incision healed. He quietly scuttled his summer racing schedule.

Behind the scenes, Team LeMond was in shambles. Within days of Greg's shooting, interest in the LeMond brand had evaporated. The telephones at Bob's office, which had rung two hundred times a week with calls for or about Greg, now lay silent. "It was almost like a death in the family. Everything just stopped," recalled Jeff Sanchez, the bike-shop owner turned Team LeMond employee. "We had hung our brand on a star, and the star had gone out."[43]

The shooting triggered a wave of cancellations from bicycle dealers across the nation. The business plan had called for Team LeMond Pro Centers in one hundred bicycle shops. By summer's end, only ten stores stocked the products.

Bob eventually found a distributor in Florida willing to purchase the Team LeMond inventory for pennies on the dollar. Maybe it was for the best. The $600 Bottecchia bicycles at the heart of the LeMond brand were "pretty crappy," Jeff Sanchez acknowledged. By the time Team LeMond folded, Roland Della Santa and his celebrated workshop had turned out perhaps two dozen handcrafted LeMond bicycles.

The gunshot blast had reverberated beyond Team LeMond. By 1987, Greg had attracted a handful of brand-name sponsors, including Puma shoes, Huffy bicycles, and Avocet saddles. His face was pasted across hundreds of ads in bicycle magazines, sometimes without his consent. Now some of those sponsors wanted out.

Within the close-knit community of riders, bicycle shops, and manufacturers, Jeff said, "We thought it was over."[44]

THE COMEBACK

G REG AND KATHY RETURNED to Europe on August 29, 1987, four months after the hunting accident. Greg's body was in no shape to enter a bicycle race, but he had little choice.

The contract with cycling team PDM, negotiated by his father on the day of Greg's emergency "appendectomy," required him to resume racing within two months. Greg fulfilled it by entering a ceremonial criterium in Belgium. At the gun, he set off with the pack, pedaling furiously to keep up. At the end of a single lap, he raised his hand and halted, signaling mechanical trouble. Then he reached down to the valve on his tire and surreptitiously drained the air. When race officials arrived, he said it had gone flat, which it had.[1] Greg abandoned the race.

Greg entered a few more short contests in September near his seasonal home in Belgium, keeping a low profile and speaking vaguely of his recovery, all part of a marketing campaign to persuade the peloton that he was back.

The first real test was the Tour of Ireland, a multiday stage race held in October. "It would be great just to finish," he told a reporter.[2] Expending every ounce of his strength, Greg managed to complete the race in forty-forth place, in the middle of a pack he usually led.

Rejoining the peloton put Greg's heretofore private plight on a public stage. On October 11, at the prestigious Créteil–Chaville race in the suburbs of Paris, fans and press watched the pack leave him behind, huffing and puffing up the modest Madeleine hill. By month's end, Greg had entered two dozen minor races in Europe and the States. Among those he had managed to finish, his best showing was seventeenth, at a contest in Nashville. Coaches from other teams would roll past Greg on the road, point at his struggling form, and snicker, telling each other he was finished.[3]

That fall the LeMonds sold their California home and moved into a five-bedroom, $725,000 mansion along Lake Minnetonka in Wayzata, Minnesota, a green, hilly suburb of Minneapolis. Their plan to build a dream home in Rancho Murieta had unraveled after the shooting. With all Greg and Kathy had suffered, the gated community evoked too many bad memories.

The move marked a subtle shift in allegiances. Before, the LeMonds had lived within a few hours' drive of Greg's parents. Now they would live within a short drive of Kathy's. Minneapolis lay 160 miles north and west of La Crosse, the Wisconsin brewing town where Kathy's father had built his allergy practice.

Greg and Kathy felt a bit like kids living in a grown-up's home. They had purchased the house, along with all the furnishings, from a contractor. The LeMonds imported few items of their own.

After a decade of competitive cycling, Greg struggled for the motivation to pedal a bicycle for hours a day in the off-season. Even before the shooting, he had veered perilously close to quitting. Now, in the snowbound Upper Midwest, Greg would hang up the bicycle at autumn's end and spend the winter cross-country skiing across frozen Lake Minnetonka.

Greg labored to spin the events of recent months into an inspirational tale of recovery and redemption. "There is always a time in your career when you need a break," he said. "I've been a professional for seven years and had never had one before. Maybe everything happened at the right time. . . . I still believe I'm better than ninety-nine percent of the other guys. My prime years are yet to come."[4]

The races told another story. In November, Greg entered the Tour of Mexico only to abandon the race when the grade grew too steep. In February 1988, at a minor Spanish race called Ruta del Sol, Greg's new PDM teammates had to push their leader to the finish line, literally—placing their hands on the small of his back and propelling his bicycle forward.

This was one of professional cycling's beloved rituals; when a cyclist cracked on a mountain pass, fans would line up along the road to form a chain of pushing hands. But the road where Greg had cracked was flat. Greg *looked* fit. Indeed, he looked stronger than ever. A winter of cross-country skiing had planted rippling muscles across his shoulders and arms. Most other cyclists looked, by contrast, like stick figures with enormous thighs. Yet, inside that body, Greg's remarkable cardiopulmonary machine was stricken.

At Greg's peak, his body could process more than ninety milliliters of oxygen per kilogram of body weight per minute. This volume of oxygen—or VO_2—rating was training-room shorthand for an endurance athlete's raw talent. A recreational cyclist might attain a VO_2 max of 50. A VO_2 peak around 70 was probably necessary, though surely not sufficient, to compete in the Tour de France. Elite cyclists sometimes boasted truly gaudy VO_2 numbers. Andy Hampsten, leader of the 7-Eleven squad, reported a VO_2 max of 79. Phil Anderson, leader of the Panasonic team, rated 82. Laurent Fignon topped out near 85. The great Hinault claimed a VO_2 max of 93.

Greg's VO_2 max had been measured as high as 93. Now, a year after the shooting, it had slipped to near 70: good enough for a *domestique*, he reasoned, but not for a team leader and certainly not for a Tour champion.

When Greg was fit, his blood could deliver enough oxygen to meet the energy demands of his muscles far beyond the limits of most other cyclists. Even among elite cyclists, Greg enjoyed an unusually high threshold for oxygen debt, that moment when the blood can no longer keep pace with the body's oxygen needs. Beyond that threshold the body turns to anaerobic respiration, producing energy without the aid of oxygen. This triggers a buildup of waste products in the muscles, leading to a gradual slowing of effort and a steady arc of pain. In his now-weakened state, Greg's body progressed quickly into oxygen debt. He could still turn the pedals, but with little of his former power.

At the moment of the shooting, Greg had ranked second, just behind road-race specialist Sean Kelly, among professional cyclists in the ordered list maintained by the Union Cycliste Internationale, cycling's governing organization. By the spring of 1988, Greg's ranking had slipped to sixty-ninth. By year's end, it would fall to 345th.

Greg pressed on, hewing to a brisk schedule of winter and spring races spread across three continents. Greg, like Laurent, had a new *soigneur*. And Otto Jácome, like Alain Gallopin, was an old friend. A competitive cyclist and champion weight lifter in his native Mexico, Otto immigrated north and settled in San José. He met Bob and Greg LeMond in 1976. Otto immediately recognized Greg's potential. He began to offer Greg the occasional tactical tip and to instruct Bertha LeMond on how to feed her son on race days.

At the start of the 1988 season, Otto left his family in California to join Greg in Belgium. The consummate *soigneur*, Otto would come to Greg and Kathy's home and help with the cooking. He set to work at rebuilding Greg's confidence, telling him, "It's just time that you need to come back to the top."[5]

Riding in the Tour of the Americas in February, just days after the Ruta del Sol humiliation, Greg found himself suddenly able to keep pace with his former peers in the peloton. At the close of a long and hilly road stage in Venezuela, Greg rode among the leaders, and he won the final sprint, his first victory of any stripe since the shooting.

"Today, for the first time in a year and a half, I felt like a bike rider," an elated Greg told *Winning* magazine.[6]

But then, at the Tirreno–Adriatico stage race in Italy, Greg faded back into the peloton, finishing in forty-fourth place. Worse, he suffered a rare attack of nerves during a boisterous sprint, slamming on his brakes when a notoriously reckless Belgian cut him off near the finish. When Greg crossed the line, he found he was still clutching the brake handles; he had never released them.

Two weeks later, at a minor race in Belgium, Greg crashed at fifty kilometers per hour, flipping end over end and sliding thirty meters on the pavement. A hard-shell helmet saved his head from serious injury. Nothing was broken, so Greg returned to racing. And then an ominous pain announced itself, just above the ankle in Greg's right leg.

Tendinitis had vanquished the greatest cyclists of Greg's era. It had sidelined Hinault after his fourth Tour victory in 1983, delivering the race to Laurent Fignon. Two years later, it had sidelined Laurent, delivering victory back to Hinault.

Greg took two weeks off to recover, which set him back a month or more in his training, according to the cruel calculus of conditioning. By the time he climbed back onto his bike, Greg was at roughly the same level of fitness he had attained at the season's start, when teammates had pushed him to the finish in Spain.

Desperate to catch up and yearning to enter the Tour, now two months away, Greg rejoined the peloton, but with steadily dwindling results. He regrouped and entered the multistage Tour de Romandie in western Switzerland. Each day the pain in his lower leg grew worse, until he could barely turn the pedals. Eleven kilometers from the finish of the final stage, Greg quietly dismounted his bicycle and retreated to Belgium.

Team doctors offered contradictory advice. Rest and anti-inflammatory shots didn't help. Frustrated, Greg returned to Minnesota, where surgeons performed a relatively minor procedure, cleaning out scar tissue that had formed in the sheath around the tendon, an operation not unlike the one performed on Laurent's Achilles tendon three years earlier.

The surgery took place on July 12, a day when most of Greg's rivals completed Stage 10 of the Tour de France. For a second consecutive year, Greg watched the Tour on television. He and Kathy wondered again whether his racing days were over.

If there was a precise moment when Laurent Fignon hit bottom, perhaps it was the day in the fall of 1987 when, just once, he tried a new drug.

Laurent didn't identify the substance in his memoir, but other cyclists were using it, and it was "supposed to be 'fantastic.'" Laurent tried it—and immediately contracted a splitting headache. So ended the experiment.

That Laurent had tried the drug at all revealed the depths of his desperation after three years of diminished performance. "I was vulnerable," he recalled, "at the mercy of any temptation."[7] The worst was yet to come. On October 25, Laurent's dearest friend, fellow cyclist Pascal Jules, fell asleep at the wheel and crashed his car. He was returning home from a charity soccer match, drunk and driving too fast, as cyclists often did. Cyrille Guimard awakened Laurent after midnight to tell him "Julot" had died.

The sudden and untimely death of his best friend gave Laurent a new appreciation for his own mortality. In the difficult days ahead, Laurent would confide in Alain Gallopin, his *soigneur*, "I'm not happy that I am not doing well; but look, Julot is dead. I can't complain."[8]

Laurent had concluded another frustrating cycling season with a poor finish at the Grand Prix des Nations, the unofficial time-trial championship of men's cycling. Victory had gone to his teammate Charly Mottet, a result that left Laurent effectively demoted to co-leader of his own team. On the advice of Guimard, Laurent took a two-month hiatus from his bicycle.

During the layoff, Laurent married his longtime fiancée, Nathalie, in a private ceremony on December 30 that was followed by a modest party at their home. He returned to his bicycle feeling renewed. "There was never a problem with my legs," Laurent told *Winning* magazine. "It was only a question of my head."[9]

Apart from his new wife, Laurent had few friends. With the loss of Pascal Jules, Laurent's relationship with Alain Gallopin moved to the center of his world. As the 1988 racing season dawned, Alain—Laurent's *soigneur*, former teammate, and now best friend—took on the additional role of coach, subtly shaping a strategy for his friend to reclaim his former glory.

Laurent's Tour wins were now four and five years past. Since then, he had logged only one major victory, at the 1986 edition of the one-day Belgian classic La Flèche Wallonne. Laurent needed more wins—even one or two, at major races, would restore his currency as a once and perhaps future champion.

Alain set his sights on one race: Milan–San Remo, the spring classic. Traditionally staged on the third Saturday in March, Milan–San Remo was a marathon of nearly three hundred kilometers, the longest single-day contest in modern professional cycling. Alain thought the race was perfect for Laurent: a course long enough to exploit his legendary stamina to full advantage, ending with a series of intense climbs—a perfect venue for Laurent to launch one of the long, sustained attacks that had defined his career. As they trained together, Alain kept repeating to Laurent, "That race is made for you."[10]

Laurent arrived in Milan sporting a new look, shoulder-length blond hair bound into a ponytail; an odd sight in the peloton, it drew taunts from fellow riders. The yellow-and-black headband was gone, along with some of the hair beneath it.

Le Professeur was the first racer to collect his jersey number—"because I'm going to win," he told officials.[11] He felt calm and supremely confident, the same mental state he had brought to the Tour in the years when he had won it.

Laurent's plan was to remain hidden within the peloton through much of the race, then work his way to the front of the pack as it approached the Poggio, a twisting climb that led to the finish. He would launch his attack on the section of hillside with the steepest grade, a stretch where his rivals might weaken. Sure enough, when the peloton reached the appointed spot, the rider at the front faltered ever so slightly. Laurent shot forth, pushing his pedals with "all the weight of all my time on the bike, and the anger I felt at all the sacrifices I'd made in the last few years."[12] A yawning gap opened. Only one other rider managed to bridge it, a young Italian star named Maurizio Fondriest. On the final descent, Laurent swung wide on the bends, deliberately slowing his pace so that the inexperienced Italian would be forced to pass him. Fondriest took the bait. Now he would lead Laurent toward the finish, giving the Frenchman the advantage. Laurent launched his marathon sprint. By the final hundred meters, the Italian could no longer keep pace. Laurent crossed the line alone, unleashing a primal yell, ponytail flapping in the wind.

Thus emboldened, Laurent approached the Tour with rising confidence—until he began to suffer bouts of inexplicable fatigue out on the road, and the old unease returned. Something was sapping his strength, but neither Laurent nor his team could discern what it was.

The 1988 Tour was easy to dismiss as a race of also-rans, much like the previous year's contest. Greg was out, Laurent erratic. The defending champion, Stephen Roche, was hobbled with knee injuries. That left Spaniard Pedro Delgado, who had lost to Roche in 1987 by a mere forty seconds, as the clear favorite.

Laurent would contend at the Tour for exactly two days. The second stage was a forty-eight-kilometer team time trial, and in the waning kilometers, Laurent's strength gave out. His Système U comrades slowed, allowing him to rejoin the group. When Laurent slipped off the back a second time, he instructed them to go on without him. The Système U leader would finish more than a minute behind his team. "I was wasted," he recalled, "and neither my doctors nor I had any idea why."[13]

A few days later, slipping ever further down the leader board, Laurent sat on the toilet and unclenched his bowels. What came out was slimy and long; it felt as if he were expelling his intestines. Too horrified to look, he summoned a teammate, who inspected the grisly scene and burst out laughing. It was a two-meter tapeworm. Laurent was shattered, physically and emotionally; he abandoned the Tour. Delgado, the prior year's runner-up, rode to victory in Paris.

An asterisk would soon be affixed to Delgado's triumph. On the day of Stage 13, a brutal mountain time trial that he would win, Delgado tested positive for probenecid. While not technically "dope," probenecid was popular among dopers as a masking agent, used to conceal the presence of steroids. Steroids were banned in professional cycling, but probenecid was not. Delgado hadn't been caught breaking any rules, yet his victory was tainted.

A Dutch cyclist, teammate to the absent Greg, tested positive for excess testosterone, a hormone that yields power and endurance. Testosterone *was* banned, and the Dutchman was fined the customary ten minutes, dropping several places in the standings.

These were the first major doping cases at the Tour since the start of the decade. Hindsight paints an even darker picture. Twenty-five years later, a Dutch newspaper would allege that seven of Greg's eight PDM teammates rode the 1988 Tour on banned substances, ranging from testosterone to cortisone to blood transfusions.[14]

*   *   *

Greg's Dutch team approached the science of "preparation" with an expansive philosophy. In 1988, early in Greg's brief tenure on the team, the PDM doctor approached him for a meeting to talk about "vitamins." Greg summoned Otto, his trainer, to accompany him.

"No," the doctor instructed, "only you."

Greg insisted. "Otto has to hear everything."

The meeting began, and, according to Otto, the doctor proceeded to trot out a parade of pills and offer them to Greg: "This one will kill the pain. This one will make your heart accelerate."

Greg replied, "I won't use your vitamins, doctor. I'll use my vitamins."[15]

The doctor insisted Greg accept his offering, a collection of little plastic bottles filled with "vitamins" to be taken at various times before a race. Greg never took them. After that, Greg grew fearful that someone from the team might sneak something into one of his drinks—an eerie reprise of the paranoia that had gripped him in the 1986 Tour. Greg's contract with PDM hedged against poor performance, paying him $350,000 in base salary and offering another $200,000 in bonuses for victories that never came. Still, by the close of the 1988 season, team officials were growing restless. They accused Greg of lacking dedication, implying that his failure to complete his comeback was his own fault. They invoked old canards about training and diet, although, by Otto's account, Greg's real sin lay in rejecting their program of preparation. They threatened to cut his pay.

In response, Greg sent his employers a card, telling them that they were wrong, and that he would prove it.

On the last day of 1988, Greg opted out of his contract with PDM and joined a new cycling team, ADR. These letters stood for the distinctly unglamorous All Drive Renting, a car-rental business. The team had been organized and financed as a pet project by Belgian entrepreneur François Lambert. Lambert was a sort of bargain-basement Bernard Tapie, his team a cut-rate La Vie Claire. The team had fared so poorly that Flemish cycling fans modified its name to *Al De Restjes*, "all the leftovers." They were the Bad News Bears of professional cycling.

ADR was a low-budget operation. The deal arranged by Bob LeMond called for a joint sponsorship with Coors, the Colorado brewer and

Marshall Walter "Major" Taylor, 1899 world cycling champion and the first African-American world champion of any significant professional sport.

Frank Kramer, eighteen-time American cycling champion between 1901 and 1921.

Greg LeMond 10/18/78

Cycling Goals

1. 1979 – Win Jr. World Championship Road Race

2. 1980 – Win Olympic Road Race

3. By Age 22 – Win Pro. World Champ. Road Race

4. By Age 25 – Win Tour De France

Greg's improbable cycling goals, fall 1978.

A young Greg LeMond pursuing his first athletic passion, freestyle skiing, in 1973.

Greg and Bob LeMond, father and son bicycle racers.

Greg in his Della Santa jersey,
collecting an early victory.

Eddie Borysewicz, "Eddie B,"
Greg's first real cycling coach.

Greg courting Kathy Morris
on his bicycle.

Greg and Kathy and their
parents. L-R: David Morris,
Greg, Kathy, Bob and Bertha
LeMond, Sacia Morris.

Bernard Hinault and Cyrille Guimard, then the world's greatest cyclist and cycling coach, visit the LeMond ranch, 1980.

Guimard with his protégé, 1981.

The greatest cycling team in the world, 1983.
Greg stands to the left; Laurent Fignon is third from the right.

Laurent leads, Greg follows, at the 1984 Tour de France.

Toasting Laurent's second Tour de France victory, 1984. L-R: Guimard, Fignon (on unknown teammate's shoulders), Vincent Barteau, LeMond.

Victory ceremony, 1985 Tour de France. LeMond sacrificed himself to help Hinault win. On this podium, Hinault promised to repay the favor. Irishman Sean Kelly sits to the right.

LeMond and Hinault join hands atop l'Alpe d'Huez
at the 1986 Tour de France, an iconic moment later unmasked as a fraud.

Hinault congratulates LeMond on his—and his nation's—first victory
at the Tour de France.

Greg and Kathy with Hinault and Vie Claire boss Bernard Tapie at the Tour de France victory dinner, 1986. Kathy's face reflects the mood.

Laurent caps his comeback with victory at the Giro d'Italia in 1989.

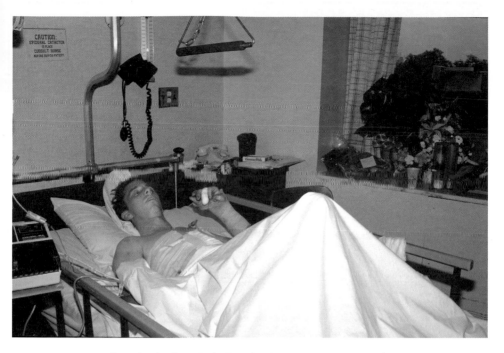

Greg in the hospital after the hunting accident, 1987.

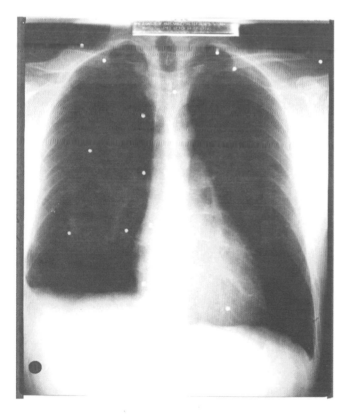

The X-ray of
Greg's torso.

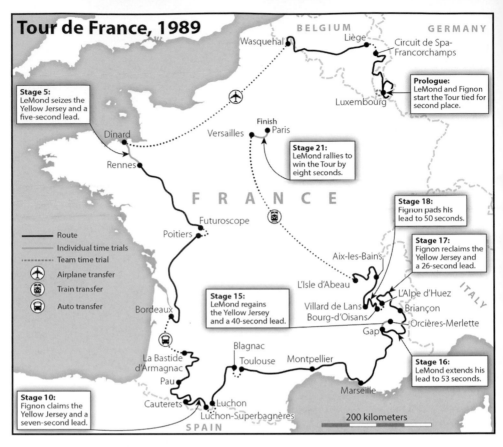

Tour de France, 1989

BELGIUM GERMANY

Wasquehal

Liège

Circuit de Spa-
Francorchamps

Prologue:
LeMond and Fignon
start the Tour tied for
second place.

Luxembourg

Stage 5:
LeMond seizes the
Yellow Jersey and a
five-second lead.

Dinard

Finish

Versailles

Paris

Stage 21:
LeMond rallies to
win the Tour by
eight seconds.

Rennes

F R A N C E

Stage 18:
Fignon pads his
lead to 50 seconds.

Futuroscope

Stage 17:
Fignon reclaims the
Yellow Jersey and
a 26-second lead.

Poitiers

Aix-les-Bains

L'Isle d'Abeau

ITALY

Route

L'Alpe d'Huez

Individual time trials

Villard de Lans

Briançon

Team time trial

Bourg-d'Oisans

Orcières-Merlette

Airplane transfer

Stage 15:
LeMond regains
the Yellow Jersey
and a 40-second lead.

Gap

Train transfer

Bordeaux

Auto transfer

Blagnac

Stage 16:
LeMond extends his
lead to 53 seconds.

La Bastide
d'Armagnac

Toulouse

Montpellier

Pau

Marseille

Stage 10:
Fignon claims the
Yellow Jersey and a
seven-second lead.

Cauterets

Luchon

Luchon-Superbagnères

200 kilometers

SPAIN

The route of the 1989 Tour de France.

Laurent and Greg exchange blows in the Alps on Stage 16
of the 1989 Tour de France.

Greg winning the final time trial in 1989 . . .

And Laurent losing it, three minutes later.

Greg at the moment of victory in Paris on July 23, 1989.

Laurent at the
moment of defeat.

Greg and Kathy embrace
after his victory.

Greg and Laurent on the victory podium, 1989.

Greg powers past Russian Dimitri Konyshev and Irishman Sean Kelly
to win the 1989 World Championship, raw emotions etched on every face:
the quintessential cycling photograph.

Greg logs his third Tour de France victory in 1990, finally leading a strong cycling team. Coach Roger Legeay stands to the right.

Greg dropping off the back on the Tourmalet at the 1991 Tour de France.

Greg chats with Lance Armstrong, cycling's new world champion,
at the end of his own career, 1994.

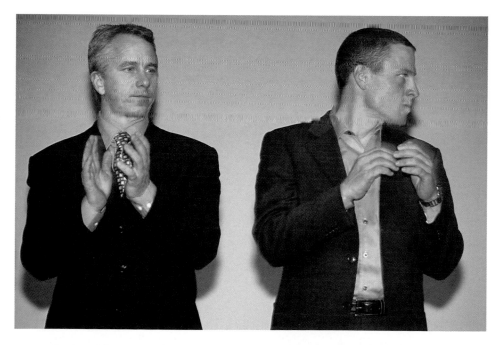

Greg and Lance at a 100th-anniversary Tour de France celebration in 2002,
looking none too pleased at their pairing.

Greg and Kathy exit a hearing room in 2007,
on the day he revealed his sexual abuse to the world.

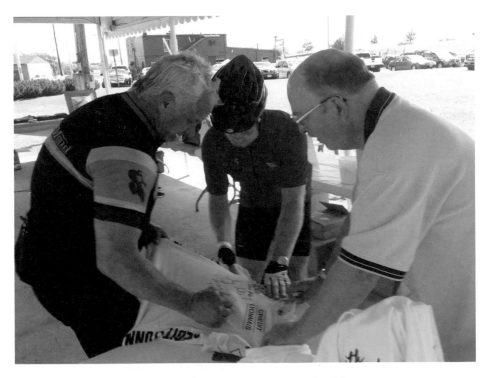

Greg signs a jersey at a 2016 charity ride.

bicycle-race sponsor; together the two companies could raise Greg's salary to $500,000 for the 1989 season. Greg would ride for ADR in Europe and for Coors in the States, partly fulfilling his oft-stated goal of leading his own American cycling team.

At the start of the 1989 cycling season, Greg LeMond and Laurent Fignon were diminished men. There was no longer much hope of either cyclist regaining the dominant form he had once enjoyed, Laurent in 1983 and 1984, Greg in 1985 and 1986.

Laurent's tendon injury had left one leg irreversibly stronger than the other. At his best, he could still eke out a victory; but Laurent was seldom at his best, owing to a seemingly endless cascade of medical setbacks and emotional troughs. Greg's hunting accident had permanently sapped his own uncanny strength, wreaking untold havoc on the heart and lungs that had powered his historic victories, and filling that stricken heart with despair. Greg still seemed capable of winning bicycle races, but he hadn't actually *won* a bicycle race since descending the steps of the podium in Paris three years earlier.

When Greg was on top, he would enter each cycling season with waxing momentum, riding listlessly in the early months and then steadily gaining speed and power until summer, when he would be unbeatable. Since the shooting, his seasons had played out in reverse. Greg would start strong, and as months passed and fatigue mounted, his results would dwindle. Laurent had followed a similar pattern in his recent career; he had won important races in the springs of 1986 and 1988, only to falter in summer and fall.

Worse, Greg's body now carried a toxic payload: three dozen pellets, all at inoperable loci in his body, each of which could leach lead into his bloodstream at any moment. Those pellets were a time bomb, and no one knew when the inhuman exertions of *le Tour* might set it off.

The 1989 season opened with a familiar whiff of promise. In early March, Greg finished sixth in the Tirreno–Adriatico stage race across Italy. A few days later, Laurent rode to victory at Milan–San Remo, claiming the peloton's longest single-day race for a second consecutive year. At month's end, Greg briefly led the Critérium International, the unofficial cycling championship of France, before fading to fourth on the final stage.

"I have never felt this strong at this point in the season," an exuberant Greg told the *Chicago Tribune*.[16]

The same could not be said for his team. By spring, Greg had not received any of the salary he was owed by François Lambert, and the ADR team was beginning to resemble a house of cards. Greg's impoverishment, in turn, strained his relationship with his father, who had shelved his real-estate career to devote himself fully to Team LeMond. Bob was struggling to sustain the remnants of the family business; he and Greg were still looking for ways to sell bicycles under the LeMond name, for such was the birthright of a Tour de France champion. Now, with cash flow depleted, Bob's calls to Greg grew increasingly dire. He seemed to be losing his grip.[17]

Kathy lovingly offered reassurance, telling Greg she would happily return with him to Minnesota and take a job in a grocery store if it meant reclaiming their peace of mind. One April night, desperate and drunk on port, Greg resolved to go on strike. When the ADR coach, José de Cauwer, appeared at his door the next day, Greg issued an ultimatum: "Fuck you. I'm not doing it. You guys have not paid me a dime. I am going home."[18]

The LeMonds returned to the States, where Greg could collect a portion of his salary from his American sponsor, Coors.

Greg was ready to quit. He refused to train, refused even to climb onto his bicycle. Kathy finally persuaded him to stick it out until the end of the season.

Once he had resolved to carry on, Greg became intrigued by the approaching start of a new and highly touted American race called the Tour de Trump. The contest was to begin on May 5 in upstate New York and to end 837 miles later in Atlantic City. Casino owners were approached for sponsorship. Developer Donald Trump emerged as lead sponsor and lent his name to the contest, theorizing—correctly, as it turned out—that the promotional power of his name would outweigh the inevitable ribbing from the press.

Greg entered the inaugural Tour de Trump utterly unprepared, having ignored his bicycle for the better part of a month. He fell ill, lagged far behind his lesser-known American peers, and limped to the finish in twenty-seventh place. Greg and his Coors teammates found themselves upstaged by other American riders on another American team, the ascendant 7-Eleven.

Ron Kiefel, Greg's friend and long-ago amateur teammate, won the final time trial for 7-Eleven on a bicycle fitted with a most unusual set of handlebars. He rode the course with his body extended forward along the front of his bicycle, arms bent at the elbows and resting on a pair of bars that stretched over the front wheel. They were called "tri-bars," because triathletes used them.

Over the previous century, the design of bicycle frames and handlebars had evolved steadily forward and downward, enabling cyclists to lower their bodies against the wind in an endless quest for aerodynamic perfection. Tri-bars signaled a breakthrough. Out on the course, Ron caught and passed three cyclists who had started before him. His peers in the peloton took careful note.

The latter half of May 1989 ushered in the glorious, two-month peak of the men's cycling season, beginning with three weeks of Giro d'Italia and ending with three weeks of *le Tour*.

Greg arrived at the Giro in low spirits. Andy Hampsten, who had won the Giro in the previous year, was generally regarded as the better cyclist, and Andy's 7-Eleven squad was surely a better team than Greg's laughable ADR.

Laurent came to Italy in a considerably brighter mood. He and Nathalie had just welcomed their second child, a daughter named Tiphaine, born April 26. His Système U team, rechristened Super U over the winter, looked stronger than ever. And the Giro's aging director, Vincenzo Torriani, had tendered a personal invitation to the race, promising Laurent a course that played to his strengths.

The second day of racing brought the first climb, up Sicily's famed Mount Etna. Laurent finished among the leaders, while Greg slipped eight minutes behind. Greg had never been dropped so easily, and so early, in a Grand Tour. His depression deepened. His ADR teammates now openly mocked their leader, perhaps to disguise their own unease over the plight of their franchise.[19]

Otto Jácome was growing concerned at Greg's pallor; his face now looked much as it had in the intensive care unit after the shooting. "Greg, look at yourself in the mirror," the *soigneur* told the cyclist. "You're white." Otto urged Greg to take an iron shot.

Greg bristled: "When do I take shots? I never take shots."[20] Greg hated shots. Besides, he had been eating red meat at every opportunity. Surely iron wasn't the problem.

Stage 10 brought an individual time trial. Laurent finished in eighth place. This wasn't quite the dominant Laurent of 1984; yet, in those five years, he hadn't ridden a better time trial at a Grand Tour. Three days later, Laurent was the second man across the summit of Tre Cime di Lavaredo, a trio of battlement-style peaks in the Italian Dolomites. He moved into second place in the standings.

"I felt five years younger," Laurent recalled.[21]

He knew that the following day, Stage 14, would be taxing. Icy rain would pummel the riders across five mountain peaks. As strong as he felt, Laurent had never ridden well in the cold. Alain Gallopin, Laurent's faithful *soigneur*, brokered a solution. He persuaded a reluctant Laurent to permit a rubdown with a cream that would warm his muscles. Laurent had sensitive skin and could barely handle the gentlest balm. Unbeknownst to Laurent, Alain had chosen a highly potent cream, and proceeded to apply it to every inch of his body. When the lotion kicked in, Laurent's body burned so badly that he leapt from the team car into the icy drizzle just to cool off.

Once the race started, Laurent forgave his impudent trainer. The bitter cold had no effect. Laurent rode among the leaders until the fifth and final summit, the Passo Campolongo. There he attacked, "countering the violence of the weather with violence of my own, as if the insanity of the elements was drawing the best out of me."[22] The effort put Laurent into the *maglia rosa*, the pink jersey worn by the Giro leader.

As Laurent's fortunes had risen, Greg's had plummeted. On the first day in the Dolomites, while Laurent pedaled among the leaders, Greg lost seventeen minutes. He was still shivering as he walked into the kitchen of the hotel opposite the finish, where riders were being offered basins of hot water. He didn't bother to remove his shoes before plunging his feet into the pot.

That night, on the telephone to Kathy, Greg burst into tears. It had been a rough month for the LeMonds, with Greg's struggles among myriad worries. A cousin of Kathy's had perished in a helicopter crash. And Kathy was pregnant with their third child, a girl, and a blood test raised fears—later allayed—that the baby might have Down syndrome.

"I can't do it," Greg sobbed into the telephone. "I've got to quit."

Kathy tried to console her husband by offering him an out: "If you want to quit, you can quit."

Greg had expected his wife to offer encouragement, even a gentle remonstrance, to carry on. Instead, she was telling him it was all right to give up.

"You know what?" Kathy reassured him. "If you're done, you're done. It's okay. We'll be fine." Kathy reminded her husband that she could get a job at the grocery store.

"Just make sure you gave it everything you could," Kathy said, "so you don't have regrets."

At her words, Greg felt a weight lift from his soul.[23]

Over the previous two years, Greg had become his own adversary. Whenever he raced, a voice in his head asked whether he would ever regain the form he had once enjoyed—whether he would ever equal the Greg LeMond who had won the Tour. Every day on a bicycle felt like Judgment Day.

Now Greg's wife, his soul mate, was allowing him to quit—to stop chasing his shadow. As she counseled him that night, Kathy knew the one thing her husband did not need was more pressure. She hoped her words would ease his mind. They did better than that: The pressure disappeared entirely. Greg felt released from a hopeless quest; he felt liberated. And he no longer wanted to quit.

Kathy flew to Italy. Greg acceded to Otto's pleas and submitted to a blood test. The results showed his iron stores were indeed utterly depleted. His body had not been absorbing iron from the food he ate. The team doctor prescribed a series of three iron shots. Greg agreed, though reluctantly. A shot of anything in the middle of a Grand Tour would raise eyebrows. The doctor administered the first shot two days after Greg and Kathy's fateful conversation, with Kathy now in attendance. Ever fearful of shots, Greg paced around the hotel room four times before he finally allowed the doctor to plant the needle into his posterior.

Stage 16, scheduled for the next day, was canceled amid worsening weather, giving Greg some badly needed rest. He walked up to Otto, gave him a soft punch in the arm, and said, "I'm feeling better now."[24] Already his body was responding to the infusion of iron.

A brief, eleven-kilometer time trial two days later delivered another respite. Greg took his second iron shot, and bit by bit he recovered. It was the iron shots, the rest—and also the rain, which calmed Greg's pollen allergies—and the soothing presence of Kathy. Greg's power was finally returning.

Laurent had gained the pink jersey of race leader in the cold; now he feared the cold would pry it from his back.

The cancellation of Stage 16, which had brought timely relief to Greg, felt like a karmic reward to Laurent, who felt certain he would have lost his lead in the icy mountains. In an ironic twist, Italian racing fans now turned on the race organizer, claiming he had annulled the stage to favor Laurent, just as he had scuttled a stage to aid Laurent's opponent five years earlier.

Stage 18, a short time trial, nearly cost Laurent the race. Struggling mightily in the cold, he lost dozens of valuable seconds to his rivals. A young Italian star named Flavio Giupponi now stood just seventy-five seconds behind him, and a resurgent Andy Hampsten was in third, a few seconds farther back.

Just as Laurent's lead looked doomed, the weather broke. No longer tormented by cold and rain, Laurent rallied to win a punishing mountain stage, fortifying his lead.

The race's final stage was a fifty-four-kilometer time trial. Unlike the Tour, the Giro did not conclude with a ceremonial ride into the capital, and organizers were free to insert one last drama. Laurent did not win the time trial, but he limited his losses, finishing in fifth place, a performance strong enough to seal his victory in the Giro. As he uncorked the champagne, Laurent paused to meditate on all he'd endured in the past five years: the setbacks, the letdowns, the humiliations.[25] His two Tour victories had cracked open the door to cycling immortality. Now the opening creaked a bit wider.

The next day, Cyrille Guimard, came to have a word with his team leader. He looked concerned. Guimard was already thinking about the Tour, and he wanted Laurent to know what was troubling him. He looked Laurent straight in the eye and said, "LeMond will be at the Tour."[26]

Two days earlier, Laurent would not have cared. Now, suddenly, he did.

L'Américain, a man most of the peloton had given up for dead, had somehow ridden himself to second place in the final time trial at the Giro, a minute or two ahead of Laurent and all the other favorites. It was his most commanding performance on a bicycle since the summer of 1986.

THE BATTLE

Luxembourg City, July 1

The 1989 Tour de France began with a curious omen.

On the first morning of July, 198 cyclists lined up in turn to ride a 7.8-kilometer time trial, a gentle prologue to loosen the legs and, perchance, to establish a rough pecking order for the days to come.

For just the tenth time in its history, the Tour de France did not start in France. It set out instead from tiny Luxembourg, 373 kilometers from Paris. *Le Tour* had a new director, Jean-Marie Leblanc, the former *Vélo* journalist who had accompanied Bernard Hinault and Cyrille Guimard to the LeMond ranch in Reno, Nevada, a decade earlier. Leblanc wanted to accelerate the globalization of *le Tour.* Already, the race welcomed more foreign teams and foreign stars. In the three years prior, after decades of French dominance, Tour victories had been claimed in turn by Greg, an American; Stephen Roche, an Irishman; and Pedro Delgado, a Spaniard.

Now all of Europe awaited Delgado. As the reigning Tour champion, he would be last to start the opening time trial. But when his moment arrived, Delgado did not. He and his bicycle were conspicuously absent from the modest white trailer that served as a starting platform. Race officials paced, scowled, and shrugged. No *maillot jaune* had ever failed to appear at the start of a race.

Delgado's time trial began without him. Seconds ticked away in sickening beeps as camera crews raced up and down the street, hunting for the Spaniard. *"Deux minutes,"* an official cried. Finally he was spotted, a yellow blur pedaling through the parting crowd, leaping from his bicycle, and rolling it frantically up the ramp. *Allez allez*, the old French-men cried, a cheer—it loosely translates to *chop-chop!*—normally saved for after the race has started. Atop the platform at last, Delgado clambered onto his bicycle and wobbled down the ramp, two minutes and forty seconds behind schedule. He would finish the prologue dead last.

This was a Tour Delgado had been universally favored to win. Who else was there? Stephen Roche was back in 1989, and certainly a favorite, but his bad knee could flare up at any time. Andy Hampsten, the other great American cyclist, was an elite climber, but he had never finished the Tour higher than fourth. Atop this heap of also-rans sat Laurent Fignon, who had just capped one of cycling's most circuitous comebacks with his win at the Giro. Most prerace predictions listed Laurent and a few others, in various groupings, as likely contenders.

No one counted Greg.

Greg had barely entered the 1989 Tour. He and Kathy were broke. His house-of-cards ADR team had paid out only $12,000 of the $350,000 it owed him for the year. He had found the funds to ride the Tour at the last minute, circumventing his team to bring on an additional sponsor, a grocery-delivery business called Agrigel, two weeks before the race.

Yet, Greg was a former Tour champion, and he hadn't actually *lost* the Tour since his 1986 victory. He traveled to Luxembourg feeling almost as if he were defending his title. None of the purported contenders had failed to notice Greg's performance in the final time trial at the Giro a few weeks earlier. He'd played a little mind game with himself that day in Italy, riding the time trial as if he were challenging for the race lead, not wallowing in the middle of the pack. Six kilometers into the race, Greg had caught the rider who had started the course before him. At twenty kilometers, he caught another. He passed three more riders by the end.

But what did that really prove? Throughout the Giro, whenever the race had entered the mountains, Greg had sunk like a stone. He might have regained his time-trialing abilities, but, to all appearances, Greg was no longer a climber—and thus no longer a contender.

Many observers, particularly in Europe, saw the failure of Greg's vaunted comeback as final proof of his fundamental flaws as a cyclist:

his penchant for ice cream and cheeseburgers, his reckless forays onto the golf course, his insistence on including Kathy in his travels.

"The rules do not apply to him," one fellow cyclist had huffed.[1] Greg had flouted so many of cycling's traditions; now the cycling gods were punishing him.

"LeMond remains a long way from the champion of old," *Bicycling* magazine pronounced, shortly before the Tour. "Those who marveled at his extraordinary talent are still waiting, and the longer the wait, the less the hope."[2]

Greg harbored no illusions of victory in Paris: "No hopes, no expectations and no reserves of confidence like I'd had in 1986. All I knew was that my legs were better than they had been for a long time."[3]

Delgado's scatterbrained performance in the prologue—he later said he had simply lost track of the time—threw the Tour, and all the prerace predictions, into turmoil. The Spaniard might have been the most dangerous cyclist in the peloton, with his superior climbing skills and his potent team—yet suddenly Delgado was no longer the favorite. Journalists and fans began to scour the results of the brief prologue for clues to who might take his place.

They were all there, bunched atop the standings. Laurent, pedaling with the raw, diesel-engine power that had fueled his past Tour victories, had finished second that day, with a time of exactly ten minutes, behind a Dutch time-trial specialist named Erik Breukink. Greg had finished with the same time as Laurent. The standings "suggested two things," Laurent would note in his memoir. "Firstly, my form was perfect. Second, the man to beat would probably be LeMond."[4]

Laurent approached the 1989 contest with a new urgency. He was just twenty-eight; yet, it had to be acknowledged now that his peak was past. On the eve of this contest, Laurent had confided to Alain Gallopin, "1989 will be the last year I can win the Tour."[5]

Laurent had been preoccupied with Greg since the day of the revelatory Giro time trial. His coach and his *soigneur* had shared his concern. "I would say to Laurent, 'I'm worried about LeMond, because he's improving,'" Alain recalled. "Fignon would say, 'No, no, don't worry, he's too fat.' He would say he wasn't worried. But he said that because he was proud."[6]

Luxembourg City, July 2

After an inconsequential morning road race around Luxembourg City, the peloton regrouped for an afternoon team time trial.

Professional cycling is a paradox: an individual sport practiced by teams. No event drives that point home quite like a team time trial. On this day, each of the Tour favorites would stand or fall with his team. A cyclist with a weak team might lose seconds or minutes to his rivals; and weakness in the time trial presaged trouble in the mountains, where a contender might find himself without his team.

A year earlier, at the nadir of his career, Laurent Fignon had been dropped by his own team in a time trial. This year would be different. With its ride on July 2, Laurent's Super U would finally reveal itself as one of the great cycling teams of its era. This was no mere assemblage of stars, like the Renault squad that had featured Fignon, LeMond, and Hinault. Laurent's Super U squad was a proper team, a whole that exceeded the sum of its parts.

Cyrille Guimard had assembled the group with typical intuitive brilliance, as a perfect supporting cast for *le Grand Blond*. Now his men hurtled along the roadway in matching teardrop helmets and white disc wheels to complement their yellow, black, and white jerseys, with the giant red *U* on their backs, pedaling with mechanized precision, looking like a serpentine vision of cycling's future.

As the Super U cyclists neared the finish of the time trial, none of Laurent's teammates could quite match his pace. Their leader was back. "I could feel the power inside me, the power that was there on my best days," Laurent wrote. "I could simply pound the pedals, without worrying about the consequences."[7]

Laurent and his team finished the time trial with the fastest time by a margin of thirty-two seconds. Greg and his ADR team rode valiantly; yet, compared with Super U, ADR was widely dismissed as a rogues' gallery of *domestiques*, men with nary a prayer of victory at this Tour or any other. The most decorated rider of the bunch may have been Johan

Lammerts, a friend of Greg's from his Vie Claire days. No one but Greg was an elite climber—not that it mattered, for Greg himself seemed no longer able to climb. Yet the ADR men were credible time trialists, and they rode their hearts out on July 2, buoyed by Greg's surprise showing in the prologue.

Three of the nine ADR riders fell away from the group during a hilly section, unable to keep pace. That left the team weakened; six men could not ride as swiftly as nine. Still, at the end of the time trial, they stood only fifty-one seconds behind the winning time of Laurent's team, and had posted the fifth-best time among the twenty-two teams at the Tour. Greg's turnaround had invigorated them.

"We were all good riders," Lammerts recalled. "And we also believed in Greg, and for that reason, I think we gave our all."[8]

Laurent already regarded Greg as his chief rival in the racing to come. His remaining concerns about Pedro Delgado evaporated after the team time trial, at which Delgado and his demoralized team lost another four minutes to the leaders.

Greg wasn't thinking of rivals, because he was not thinking of victory. After two days of racing, he told the *New York Times* that his goal was simply "to do as well as I can," but he conceded he didn't know quite what that meant. "My goal would be top fifteen," he said at last. "Of course I'd like to be in the top five, top three, but I have to be realistic."[9]

Dinard, France, July 6

Finally, almost begrudgingly, Tour journalists began to include Greg's name among the men who might conceivably win the race. By July 5, a rest day after four race stages, Laurent sat in fourth place overall, Greg in fourteenth. None of the favorites ranked among the top three. The 1989 Tour had not yet delivered a stage so long or so difficult as to separate contenders from pretenders.

But the next day would bring a seventy-three-kilometer time trial through Brittany, starting at the coastal resort of Dinard and ending at the Bretagne capital of Rennes, a course long enough to shake the *domestiques* from the leader board. Greg went out for a practice run to familiarize himself with the twists and turns of the course, so that he might take them at a slightly higher speed the next day and gain a few seconds on his rivals.

Out on the road, Greg happened upon Roger Legeay, coach of the French team Z, whose sponsor, Roger Zannier, ran a chain of discount children's clothing stores. Zannier had stepped in for Peugeot when the venerable bicycle manufacturer ended its long tradition of cycling sponsorship, in 1987.

Peugeot had represented the old, xenophobic brand of cycling, favoring French riders at all costs. Z represented the new. Zannier was a businessman, and all he had asked in return for his $2 million annual investment was that the team deliver a Tour winner within three years. Three seasons later, no champion had emerged.

After some small talk, Roger Legeay said to Greg, "If you want, you can come to my team next year."[10] Greg was intrigued. Though another year remained on his contract with ADR, Greg was not getting paid, and all bets were off. As he rode up in the standings, Greg consoled himself with the thought that he would sign with the first team that approached him with a better offer. That team now appeared to be Z.

The night before the July 6 time trial, Greg suffered an attack of nerves, much like the angst that had descended on the eve of his world championship in 1983. Now, as then, Greg could not sleep because he knew he could win.

The next morning, leaders of the American 7-Eleven team approached officials with a piece of equipment that had never been used at the Tour. It was a pair of tri-bars, similar to the ones Ron Kiefel had steered to a stage victory in the Tour de Trump. The 7-Eleven team sought permission to use the bars. They noted that Olympic officials had allowed them at the 1988 games in Seoul. They even trotted out Eddy Merckx, the Babe Ruth of cycling. The Cannibal gave the bars his blessing. That clinched it: the bars were in.

The Americans had tested the bars in wind tunnels and were convinced they could gain a cyclist precious seconds in a time trial, alone against the wind. The Europeans had done their own tests and had come away unimpressed. Until someone used the bars to win a big race, their opinion was not likely to change.

Apart from the 7-Eleven riders, just one cyclist fitted a pair of tri-bars to his bicycle that day. Greg had glimpsed the tri-bars on the bicycle of Davis Phinney, a 7-Eleven rider, as Davis had whooshed past him at the Tour de Trump. Greg had beheld the receding figure and thought, *He looks more aerodynamic than me.*[11] Greg and his ADR coach, José de Cauwer, performed a simple test of their own before committing to the tri-bars. Greg set out for a warm-up ride alongside a teammate who rode with conventional bars. Watching the pair, De Cauwer noted that the tri-bars gave Greg's upper body the rounded shape of an egg, while his teammate plowed into the wind like an open parachute.

Riders started the time trial spaced a minute or two apart. Pedro Delgado, far down in the standings, set out early in the day, riding among *domestiques.* He seemed to pass one at every kilometer marker. Down but not yet out, the Spaniard posted the best time in the first half of the day, completing the course in one hour, thirty-eight minutes, and thirty-six seconds. He and the other early contestants enjoyed warm, sunny weather and a gentle coastal tailwind.

Later starters rode through a rainstorm into a headwind, slowed by slippery surfaces and by what the British term "heavy" air. The 7-Eleven riders lowered their bodies into a praying mantis position on their tri-bars. The Europeans fell back on more familiar tools: solid disc wheels, skintight uniforms, and teardrop helmets.

Chugging along the course like an ungainly freight train, Greg rocked gently back and forth on his bicycle, tucking his head down between his shoulder blades, raising it at intervals to glimpse the course ahead, looking not unlike a freestyle swimmer. He rode on such a high gear, turning his cranks at such a deceptively low cadence, that spectators might not have grasped the magnitude of his effort—until Greg passed the man who had started two minutes before him, and then the men who had started four, six, eight, and ten minutes earlier.

Greg pulled to the line with a time of one hour, thirty-eight minutes, and twelve seconds—twenty-four seconds faster than Delgado, two minutes faster than anyone else who had gone before him. He coasted to a stop. And for the first time in three years, a mob of reporters with cameras engulfed him.

Laurent set out twenty minutes after Greg in deteriorating weather, riding with two solid, white disc wheels and a matching white teardrop helmet—but no tri-bars. He exerted a massive effort against the rising wind, riding with the bravura of a *maillot jaune*, and he powered across the line in third place. His time was thirty-two seconds slower than Delgado's, fifty-six seconds slower than Greg's. The men would finish the day in the top three spots.

The victory put Greg in the *maillot jaune* for the first time since he had worn it on the podium in Paris, three years earlier. In overall time, he now led Laurent by five seconds. In the context of a 3,285-kilometer race, the margin was laughably small. Still, it was a lead.

Greg's comeback was complete. Never had he felt such elation—not in any of his prior victories, and certainly not after the soul-crushing duel with Hinault. He told an interviewer, "This is the most wonderful day of my life."[12]

The French public loved a comeback story—and now it had two. Greg's miraculous recovery was surely the more dramatic narrative, but Laurent's five-year journey through the cycling wilderness had played out on the covers of French cycling magazines, moving even Greg.

"Fignon has given me inspiration," he said after his time trial victory.[13] Both men had their supporters on the roads. French fans cheered mostly for Laurent, but the Belgians sided with Greg, as did most of the Dutch and German spectators and, of course, the Americans. In the press, Greg was the clear favorite.

The *Times* of London hailed Greg's performance as "a magnificent reply by the American to the many critics who had virtually written him off as a top cyclist."[14] Greg's tri-bars rated scant mention in most news reports of the day, and his rivals paid them little heed. Yet Greg knew they had made a difference. Together, the bars and Greg's superior form had delivered a victory that looked decisive, if not quite overwhelming. And perhaps that was a good thing. Had Greg annihilated the field, then every contender in the peloton might have gone out and purchased a pair of tri-bars.

Pau, France, July 10

One day after Greg donned the yellow jersey, the Union Cycliste Internationale released a fresh ranking of the world's top one hundred cyclists. Greg's name was not on it. Whatever hopes Greg now harbored for a high placing in Paris, the fact remained that he hadn't won a major race in three years. The Tour rolled on south without significant change in the standings, traveling from Rennes to the theme park at Futuroscope, then to Bordeaux, and finally to the foot of the Pyrenees, where the mountaintop battles would begin. Here, most observers expected Greg to falter, given his recent performances; surely his five-second lead would evaporate on the first climb like morning fog.

Stage 9, on July 10, took the peloton across four major peaks, including the Col de Marie-Blanque and the Col d'Aubisque, the latter an epic *hors catégorie* grind. Miguel Induráin, a tall young Spaniard riding on the Reynolds team with Delgado, broke away early and led the race across the final three peaks. Induráin was a capable rider, but he trailed Greg and Laurent by more than seven minutes in the standings, so their only concern was to limit his lead, which they did. Greg passed the day marking Laurent's wheel, conserving his energy and waiting to see how his body would react to the climbs.

In the final kilometers, Delgado attacked, opening a gap on the two leaders with surprising ease. Neither Greg nor Laurent chose to pursue; Delgado, too, was several minutes down on the leader board. Delgado finished the stage half a minute ahead of Greg and Laurent, who crossed the line with the same time. Greg retained the yellow jersey, while Delgado rocketed up in the standings.

Greg was infinitely relieved to have kept pace with his rivals on the first mountain stage. But Laurent was livid, outraged that Greg had spent most of the afternoon on his wheel, compelling Laurent to chase the Spaniards without help.

"He was barely willing to defend his jersey," Laurent huffed.[15] And therein lay Greg's sin. The *maillot jaune* was expected to lead, not to follow. French racing fans winced at the sight of the yellow jersey riding on the wheels of other men.

Greg found himself in a tactical predicament unbefitting the *maillot jaune.* The race leader customarily rode at the front of the peloton with an escort of teammates, "leading" only in a figurative sense. The actual business of leading the pack invariably fell to *domestiques*, who would line up at the front of the peloton in a spearhead formation, much like a flock of geese, with their leader tucked within the slipstream and doing half as much work. (In a crosswind, the spearhead would reorganize into a diagonal line.) But from the first Pyrenean climb, Greg found himself effectively alone, riding without his ADR teammates, who, however well-meaning, simply could not keep up.

In the press, Greg defended himself as best he could. "It's not for me to push," he said. "It's for Laurent."[16] After all, Greg was the one with the lead.

At two o'clock the next morning, Greg telephoned Kathy at their home in Belgium.

"You awake, honey?" he asked.

"Yes," she replied. "What are you doing awake?"

Greg was too excited to sleep. He wanted to tell Kathy that he was back. Greg had survived a day in the mountains, a feat that had been beyond him just one month earlier. That night, Kathy recalled, "We began to get greedy and actually think about the possibility of Greg winning the Tour."[17]

Now Kathy was too excited to sleep.

Cauterets, France, July 11

The second and final Pyrenean stage was short but steep, crossing four more peaks. The first was Col du Tourmalet, the highest paved pass in the mountain range. The Tourmalet formed the first link in a chain of three climbs, leading to the Col d'Aspin and the Col de Peyresourde. From there the peloton would climb to the ski resort at Superbagnères.

The pace up the Tourmalet was brutal, and for the first time at this Tour, Laurent found that he could not keep up. Gasping for breath, he struggled desperately to remain in contact with Greg. Laurent tried to hide his agony from the American, but then Greg looked back and saw the Parisian grab hold of a photographer's motorcycle, allowing its motor to tow him partway up the hill, a flagrant violation of Tour rules that should have disqualified him. Race officials sat in a car directly behind the motorcycle, stone-faced, and let the infraction pass. This was "incredible favoritism" toward a French competitor in a French race, recalled Andy Hampsten, who rode beside Greg that day.[18]

The moment exposed Laurent's weakness, and Greg's, too. Had Greg ridden with a strong team, he could have dashed away from Laurent with his teammates and left the Frenchman gasping, adding untold minutes to his lead. But Greg had no teammates on the Tourmalet, and he could not ride a hundred kilometers alone. So, he sat back and saved his energy. Laurent eventually recovered and returned to his side.

Laurent and Greg pedaled at an impasse for most of the day, marking each other as their rivals pulled away from them. Though Laurent rode with a stronger team, he too found himself without a teammate on the final climbs. The two men conferred, and Greg agreed to do some of the work—but not nearly enough for Laurent's tastes. Laurent grew increasingly agitated with Greg's conservative tempo. To him, it seemed that Greg was unable or unwilling to take the offensive. Laurent was too tired to launch his own attack. "But allowing LeMond to stay on my wheel all the way to the top would have driven me mad."[19]

Finally, a kilometer from the finish, Laurent accelerated fiercely and swept around the small group of riders that had contained both him and Greg, catching everyone by surprise. Greg lurched forward to catch him. It was a bluff. Greg was exhausted, but he didn't want Laurent to know it, so he expended his final reserves of energy to create the impression that he was in full control and that Laurent would never get away.

Greg reached Laurent's back wheel, and for a short stretch of roadway, the two cyclists rode together. But Greg was spent, and Laurent knew it. With two hundred meters to go, the Frenchman accelerated again. This time, instead of raising his own tempo apace, Greg slowed, and his bicycle began to wobble. He turned to look behind him, seeking aid that was not there. He looked helplessly down at his legs. In cycling parlance, Greg had cracked.

"The five seconds is going," Phil Liggett cried on British television. "So is the yellow jersey."[20]

Laurent powered forward, putting precious meters between himself and the man who held a five-second lead in the Tour de France. When Laurent crossed the line, he was twelve seconds ahead of Greg on the day and seven seconds ahead in the Tour.

In the postrace ceremony, Laurent donned the *maillot jaune* for the first time in five years; Greg's brief tenure was over. The day had produced enough drama to "fairly take your breath away," the *Guardian* observed.[21] The yellow jersey had changed hands; an improbable five-second lead had given way to an equally improbable seven-second lead. And Delgado, the Spaniard, had recovered so much lost time that he now stood in fourth place, a contender once more.

"I made LeMond explode," Laurent crowed to the press with a prize-fighter's bluster, sounding not unlike the Bernard Hinault of three or four years earlier. "I showed him I was the strongest. If he wants the yellow jersey, he'll have to walk over my body."[22]

Rather than fall back on the usual empty platitudes of victory, Laurent lashed out at his rival, calling Greg a "wheel-sucker"—a contemptuous term for a cyclist who exploits the wind resistance of another by riding on his wheel, refusing to do his share of the work. "Perhaps his team isn't up to the job," Laurent sniffed, "but the way he behaves is not acceptable for a *maillot jaune*."[23]

Up to now, Greg had openly admired Laurent, speaking (mostly) well of him to a skeptical press, defending him to other riders. He harbored fond memories of their time together on the Renault team; he hadn't forgotten the thoughtful card Laurent sent after the shooting. Laurent's torturous comeback had inspired his own. But Greg knew how swiftly Laurent's persona could shift from humility to arrogance, from candor to bluster. Success always seemed to go straight to his head.

The next morning, Greg walked up to Laurent and said, "Don't talk to me about not racing like a champion. I saw you hang on to the motorcycle, and if you consider that racing like a champion, I'd be happy to tell people about it." And he did—but not until after the Tour was over. The daily news cycle sat silent on the alleged infraction.[24] By the time Laurent compiled his memoirs, decades later, the motorcycle had slipped his mind.

Gap, France, July 16

Cyclists left the mountains and pedaled into the relative monotony of consecutive road stages: 158 kilometers from the mountain summit to Blagnac, a suburb of Toulouse; 242 kilometers to Montpellier, near the Mediterranean coast; and 179 kilometers to Marscille, the great port.

The race to Marseille fell on July 14, Bastille Day, a national holiday. Fittingly, the stage was claimed by a Frenchman, Vince Barteau, from Laurent's Super U team. Vince strayed from the patriotic script when he dedicated his victory to Greg, who had hired Vince to ride on his PDM team in the previous year, when Vince had feared his career was at its end. The gesture was not lost on French fans.

Vince had come to the 1989 Tour with divided loyalties. He rode tirelessly for Laurent; but on mornings when his teammate felt particularly strong, Vince would sneak into enemy camp and warn Greg, "Keep your head up today."[25]

On July 15, the peloton approached the Alps, riding 240 kilometers to the Alpine town of Gap. The Tour would then spend six days in the Alps, starting with a thirty-nine-kilometer mountain time trial from Gap to the ski resort of Orcières Merlette.

Laurent had now enjoyed five days with a seven-second lead. It was an absurdly narrow margin; yet Greg had found no way to reclaim even a single second on the flat stages.

But at this point Greg wasn't so sure he wanted the yellow jersey back just yet. The *maillot jaune* carried great weight. The cyclist in yellow was, on any given day, the most popular man in Europe, riding at the center of a vast cyclone of reporters and camera operators and race officials and fans—an exhausting role. On the road, the *maillot jaune* and his team bore the burden of more or less running each daily stage, riding at the front of the peloton, setting the pace and chasing down attacks. It was a big job—too big, frankly, for Greg's shabby team, which, by July 15, had shrunk from nine riders to five. One ADR cyclist had abandoned the race in the Pyrenees, another in Montpellier, and two others had been eliminated for falling too far behind in overall time. Super U,

Laurent's glorious team, remained largely intact, better equipped to handle the ebb and flow of the peloton.

Laurent and Greg had now traded the lead between them for more than a week. Still, many in the Tour entourage remained convinced that the rider in third place, Pedro Delgado, was the man to beat. In an *Irish Times* column, former Tour winner Stephen Roche wrote of Greg, "I cannot see him keeping up with the climbers in the Alps."[26] Roche predicted Delgado could easily seize the lead over the five Alpine stages. Greg seemed to agree. "For me," he told an interviewer, "the race is between Delgado and Fignon."[27]

The July 16 time trial was uphill all the way, with two stretches steep enough to garner a category-one rating. Greg again rode with his tri-bars; but on this course, the uphill grade, rather than the wind, was his principal foe. Tri-bars, solid wheels, and teardrop helmets might yield a faster ride on a flat surface, but they were dead weight on a hill.

Lesser riders, men with little chance to win the Tour, set out ahead of the race leaders and posted the three best times of the day, marks that neither Greg nor Laurent would match. Delgado, the superior climber, flew up the first big ascent, at one point gaining a full minute's advantage on Greg, who had started out some distance behind him.

Muscling up the mountainside, Greg was a painful sight, his body lurching back and forth, up and down on the frame, oblivious to style and grace as he fought to maintain his pedaling cadence on a high gear. He would climb out of his seat to pound the pedals, only to collapse back into the saddle, looking as if he were laboring in vain to find a comfortable position on his bicycle. Seasoned observers glimpsed Greg's ungainly form and surmised that both the mountain and the bicycle had gotten the better of him.

And then the grade eased, and Greg settled into a mechanized rhythm, stretching out on his tri-bars and motoring ahead. Here, the novel handlebars gave Greg the advantage over the Spanish climber, and Delgado's fifty-three-second lead began to dwindle. Greg crossed the line with a time of one hour, eleven minutes, and thirty-nine seconds. Delgado, who was supposed to devour the American on this mountainous course, had completed it just eight seconds faster.

Laurent was the last man to start the time trial. Out on the road, he failed to find his rhythm on either of the two punishing climbs. He pulled to the line in tenth place, forty-seven seconds slower than Greg, a result unbecoming the yellow jersey—which, at day's end, was no longer his.

"That is a marvelous ride by Greg LeMond today," announcer Phil Liggett told television viewers as the American crossed the line. "And now, if he can go well in the Alps, this could all go to Versailles and the final time trial."[28]

Gap, July 18

Since the shooting, Greg had struggled mightily with the vital business of recuperation. Finding his legs for the day's third or fourth mountain climb, regrouping after a brutal attack, absorbing the cumulative punishment of twenty-one consecutive marathons of cycling—those things had come easily before the accident. They had seemed impossible since.

For a cyclist forever struggling to catch his breath, the 1989 Tour seemed tailor-made. The course included two rest days, positioned at points on the calendar when Greg badly needed them. Most of the mountain stages traversed distances under 150 kilometers: brutal but brief. The entire course covered just 3,285 kilometers, four-fifths the distance Greg had pedaled to victory in 1986.

July 17 was a rest day, tucked thoughtfully between the mountain time trial and four looming Alpine stages. Greg spent the time with Kathy and his mother and father, all of whom had now joined him in Europe. Racing resumed the next day with Greg clad again in yellow. His first term in the *maillot jaune* had looked fleeting. This time, the threat Greg posed to his rivals seemed very real, and the jersey sat on his back like a target.

At such moments, a Tour leader with a strong team would summon his lieutenants to his side to control the race like traffic cops. But Greg barely had a team. Four other ADR riders remained, none of them climbers, all of them exhausted.

Laurent was operating at his petulant peak. Over the rest day, the press corps had awarded him the *Prix Citron*, the lemon prize, designating him the sourest cyclist in the peloton. Laurent was greeting journalists with customary flair, pushing and cursing his way through crowds, and conducting interviews through a crack in the team-car window.[29] Laurent seemed intent on amplifying the obvious contrast to Greg, the *good* sibling, who signed every autograph, answered every question, and smiled kindly into every camera, often lingering at the finish line until everyone else had left.

The French public seized any excuse to cheer Laurent, enamored of his comeback and indulgent of his ego; since the retirement of Hinault, three years earlier, *Monsieur Citron* was their only champion. But many in the press despised him, and when racing resumed, photographers refused to shoot him, leaving his image briefly absent from the sports pages.

Laurent now told reporters that while he might no longer be capable of winning the Tour, he would certainly do his best to help Greg lose it. It was not a particularly sporting thought, and it wasn't exactly true. In fact, Laurent and Cyrille Guimard had worked out a rough calculus for what sort of effort might be required if Laurent wished to regain the yellow jersey, which he most certainly did. Greg "was climbing less well than I was," Laurent recalled, "but was time-trialing more strongly. It was a simple equation, and it would be valid all the way to Paris."[30]

Four mountain stages remained: more than enough time and distance for Laurent to make up the paltry forty seconds that lay between him and the American—if Laurent was indeed the better climber. There remained one more time trial on the last day; but it was relatively short, and entirely flat, and no one following the race expected anyone to blow the field apart on that final ride into Paris.

The sixteenth stage covered two epic climbs, a category-one ascent up the Col de Vars near the middle of the route and, toward the end, an even steeper *hors catégorie* climb up the Col d'Izoard. When the stage began, attacks commenced almost immediately. Greg covered them all, pacing himself carefully to catch each rival, then settling back into his climbing pace, fully aware that no other ADR rider would be around to help him. By the top of the first climb, Greg sat among a group that contained Delgado and several other contenders—but not Laurent, who was beginning to slip back.

Laurent rejoined the group on the descent. On the second, steeper climb, Delgado attacked. Greg immediately gave chase, closing the gap easily and dragging several other riders along—and again leaving Laurent behind. Laurent fought back tenaciously, powering up the final climb alone and regaining much of the time he had lost. He crossed the line thirteen seconds behind the American, a gap that padded Greg's overall lead to fifty-three seconds. It was a paltry sum—yet neither man had led this Tour by more.

After two consecutive defeats by the American, brash, arrogant Laurent was gone; humble, self-deprecating Laurent had returned. "I just couldn't keep going in the climbs," he confessed, assessing the damage Greg had wrought. "Thirteen seconds is not much. But forty seconds plus thirteen is starting to add up."[31]

A few days earlier, when Laurent had worn the *maillot jaune*, a poll of team managers had favored the Frenchman as the likely winner in Paris. Now the same managers favored Greg. Indeed, much of the Tour caravan now dismissed Laurent as a contender in the five days of racing that remained. If the past few years were any guide, Laurent, like Greg, would fade in the mountains. Race commentators spoke as if this were now a race solely between LeMond and Delgado, a view Greg seemed to share. "He's the only one I've still got to worry about, I think," Greg had said at day's end.[32]

Briançon, France, July 19

The next morning, Laurent and Guimard "talked it all over, without holding anything back," Laurent recalled. They had to reverse the standings now, in the mountains, and put Laurent as far ahead of Greg as they could before the course flattened out and approached Paris. There, in the final time trial, Greg would regain the advantage. "Now," Laurent continued, "both LeMond and I vaguely understood that every second had to be contested, with no quarter given."[33] The Super U leaders crafted a plan. Laurent would attack near the end of that day's stage, at the foot of l'Alpe d'Huez, the most daunting climb in the Tour.

The race unfolded according to plan. Laurent spent much of the day riding just behind Greg, a position befitting his role as predator stalking prey. Then, on the first of the twenty-one hairpins of l'Alpe, Laurent attacked. Greg lurched forward to catch him. Laurent attacked again, and again Greg caught him. Laurent accelerated a third time, more viciously than before.

"Bent over his bike," Laurent remembered, Greg "ripped himself to bits to get back to me again."[34]

Tour spectators had seldom witnessed such a battle. Sadly, few would witness this one. Race cameras, hopelessly scattered along the route, captured only occasional moments of the spellbinding struggle between the Tour's most closely matched competitors in a generation.

The attacks had left both men reeling like boxers in the latter rounds of a fight. But Greg had to counter, lest Laurent attack him into utter exhaustion. He shifted into an enormous gear and powered up the slope, leaving Laurent behind. The Parisian could barely respond: "I managed to squirm up to him, but my legs were on fire."

Now Laurent, tapping some hidden reserve, attacked again, at full strength. A few seconds later, Greg was back at his side. The jousting ended in a stalemate. Both combatants had pushed beyond their limits. "Our lungs were hanging out," Laurent recalled, "and we watched each other, almost at a standstill, gasping like a pair of crazy young puppies."

There was still a mountain to climb. Both men fell into a steady pace and attempted to recover some semblance of rhythm. But Laurent's brutal attacks had taken a toll. Greg rode now like a wounded fighter, sitting lopsided on the saddle, head sagging, shoulders bouncing, swaying back and forth in an increasingly dire effort to keep pace with his foe.

Behind him, in the Super U team car, Cyrille Guimard could read Greg's body language and knew at once that he was spent. Guimard accelerated the team car, maneuvering to get up to his leader and issue instructions to attack.

Now, the battle between Greg and Laurent spread to a second front. Greg's coach, José de Cauwer, took evasive action with his car, swerving back and forth across the road to block Guimard from passing him and reaching his star rider. The cars collided, bumpers scraping, bits of metal falling off. Finally Guimard broke through and screeched up the mountain toward Laurent.

Six kilometers from the top, Guimard finally pulled up alongside Laurent. "Attack," he cried. "He's dying." His instinct was correct. There was just one problem. Laurent was dying too.

"I can't," Laurent panted. "I'm wasted." Guimard shrugged and retreated.

A kilometer passed, and then two, and Laurent recovered a modicum of strength. Guimard pulled up alongside Laurent again, looking even more agitated than before. "Attack him now," he screamed. "You've got to go now." Laurent gathered himself up and launched one final assault, accelerating away from Greg and a few other riders at the four-kilometer mark.

Delgado answered the Frenchman's acceleration, speeding away from the other contenders. Greg did not. He was utterly drained. Finally, in palpable agony, Greg pulled clear of the small pack and chugged up the mountainside, pedaling desperately to limit his losses.

When Laurent reached the two-kilometer mark, he had put fifty-two seconds between himself and Greg. One second more, and the *maillot jaune* would be his. Laurent redoubled his effort. As he crossed the finish line, Delgado swept past him. But the rousing cheer that greeted the two cyclists was for Laurent, whose heroics on the hairpins had not been missed by the French crowd. Thirty seconds passed, then a minute. Finally Greg appeared, dragging himself to the line a minute and nineteen seconds after Laurent. He had surrendered the *maillot jaune*.

Greg was heartbroken. When he saw Kathy, he told her, "Maybe I lost the Tour today."

Bourg d'Oisans, France, July 20

The closest Tour de France in a generation now somehow seemed closer still. The lead had changed hands three times between two men, passing from Greg to Laurent on July 11, back to Greg on July 16, then back to Laurent on July 19. Neither man had led by more than fifty-three seconds.

Now, after seventeen stages of racing, Laurent clung to a lead of twenty-six seconds. Many observers believed he would give it back to Greg in Paris, a few days later, at the final time trial, whose inclusion in the race route suddenly looked prescient. Yet this was, in fact, the third time Laurent had taken the yellow jersey at l'Alpe d'Huez. On both prior occasions, in 1983 and 1984, he had gone on to win the Tour.

Humble Laurent was gone; prickly, arrogant Laurent had returned. He sat beneath a tent at the foot of l'Alpe, reading an article in a French paper that recounted his exploits beneath the headline, "The Heights of Glory," signing autographs for fans, eyes never straying from the article. When a woman with a camera asked him to smile, Laurent replied, "Smile, smile. I'm just as cute when I don't smile."[35]

However, beneath the bluster, Laurent was anything but overconfident. He dared not take a twenty-six second lead into the final time trial, where he expected to lose a second to Greg for every kilometer they raced. On a twenty-five-kilometer course, that was dangerous arithmetic. Laurent knew he had one or two more chances to increase his lead, and he plotted an attack on the next stage, which featured a lengthy category-one climb to Saint-Nizier-de-Moucherotte toward the end of the route.

Three kilometers from the top of that climb, Laurent attacked, quickly opening a stretch of daylight between himself and the other contenders. Greg faced a difficult choice. This stage did not end at the summit, and Greg stood a good chance to regain lost time on the descent. But if Laurent built too great a lead, then he would hold it to the finish, and the Tour would surely be his.

Laurent had again chosen the perfect moment. Greg was exhausted. Riding without teammates, he had no one to pace him back to the Frenchman. He sat up, waiting for a response from Pedro Delgado, who was himself running out of time to vie for victory in Paris. The tactic worked. Delgado gave chase, and Greg fell in behind him. The gap began to close. But after a long turn leading, Delgado sat up and slowed, visibly annoyed that Greg would not contribute, challenging the American to take a turn at the front, if he could. Greg did not, because he could not.

Laurent reached the top of the mountain and careened into the descent toward another, shorter climb to the finish at the ski resort of Villard-de-Lans. Laurent was a superb descender, and his lead over Greg was growing, to thirty-five seconds, then fifty, as Laurent approached the final climb. Then, as Laurent neared the ski station, he plowed into a headwind, the mortal foe of a cyclist riding alone. Now the advantage flipped to Greg, who was sheltered behind four other riders. The Frenchman's lead began to dwindle.

Laurent crossed the line to rapturous applause from his French fans. "He knows that today, he's won the Tour de France," announcer Phil Liggett cried on British television. "I'm sure of that."[36]

In the headwind, Laurent's lead over Greg had shrunk to twenty-four seconds. But that was enough. Laurent now led the Tour by a total of fifty seconds over Greg and by two and a half minutes over Delgado.

Those who had projected Greg to win the Tour now favored Laurent. Yes, Greg would likely beat Laurent in the time trial that awaited them; he might recover as many as thirty seconds of his deficit to Laurent on the short ride into Paris. Laurent would have twenty more to spare.

"The race isn't over yet," Laurent pronounced—magnanimous in his moment of triumph.[37] On previous days in this Tour, Laurent had eviscerated Greg in the press. Now he sensed the battle was won, and he brimmed with praise for his vanquished foe.

"I know how much work you have to do to come back to the top level," he told the *New York Times*. "And I'm glad he's made it. I'm glad I've made it, too."[38]

Greg responded in kind. "It's nice to see him riding well again," he said. "I just wish he wasn't riding *this* well."[39] Hearing his own words, Greg burst into laughter, conceding that his chances for victory were now slim. Laurent's attack on the road to Villard-de-Lans had been a "vicious shot," the *Guardian* opined, "from which the American will surely not recover."[40]

Villard-de-Lans, France, July 21

The final Alpine stage included three climbs en route from Villard-de-Lans to the spa town of Aix-les-Bains. If either Greg or Laurent was going to attack, the place to do it was the final descent down the Col du Granier, a long and treacherous stretch that offered potential time gains to any rider reckless enough to cut the corners.

Out on the road, Greg and Laurent broke away from the peloton with three other men, all placed near the top of the leader board, each hoping for a chance to escape the others and move up in the standings. Greg looked the weakest, sitting at the rear of the group and occasionally yo-yoing off the back. Laurent, by contrast, veritably bounced up and down on his pedals, pulsing with energy. "I felt as if I had wings on my feet," he recalled.[41]

On the first of the three climbs, Laurent accelerated slightly and found himself opening a gap on the others. Was he mounting an attack? Cyrille Guimard steered up alongside him in the team car to ask. "I'm flying, Cyrille, that's all." Laurent replied.

"Then go for it!"

Laurent thought for a while, then replied: "I've got enough of a lead to win the Tour. I'm afraid I'll crack. It's a pointless risk." Guimard agreed, and Laurent eased up, allowing the other riders to catch him.

Near the top of the final climb, Greg attacked; Laurent surged forward and caught him. Greg attacked again, and again Laurent reeled him back. At the top of the mountain, Greg attacked again, hurtling down the mountainside at ninety-five kilometers per hour, slicing around turns and veering within inches of the roadside cliff as he labored to lose Laurent, who stuck tenaciously to his wheel. Neither rider wore a helmet.

The five leaders regrouped at the foot of the mountain. Greg's attacks had failed; he would gain no time today. As the finish approached, Greg swung around the group and into the lead, accelerating into a final sprint. Laurent leapt onto his wheel, but he could not catch the American. Greg raised his hands, pumped his fists, and swept across the line to victory—his second stage win at the Tour. Laurent crossed just behind him, awarded the same time.

As they coasted toward the crowd, Laurent reached over and placed his hand on Greg's back. Greg reached across and patted Laurent's yellow jersey. "Congratulations," Laurent said. This moment evoked another: the clasped hands of Greg and Bernard Hinault atop l'Alpe d'Huez, three years earlier. But that scene had been staged, and this one was real.

Laurent still held a fifty-second lead over Greg. Later that day, Laurent walked over and tapped Greg on the shoulder. "It's been a good fight," he said.[42]

Two more days of racing remained. But to Laurent, and to every journalist and spectator in France, the Tour was over.

EIGHT SECONDS

BECAUSE TOUR DE FRANCE STANDINGS are cumulative, the identity of the winner is usually revealed well before the final stage. The Tour is decided in the mountains, or in the time trials, where the holder of the *maillot jaune* amasses a lead of three minutes, or five, or ten, and carries it through the final days of inconsequential road racing into Paris.

Tour tradition dictates that racers do not vie for position in the overall standings on the last day, although they are certainly permitted to race for the stage itself, one final mad sprint along the Champs-Élysées to entertain the throngs. Century-old custom scripts the Tour's concluding stage as a leisurely roll into Paris, a race in name alone. Cyclists sip champagne, mug for the cameras, wear silly hats, and take in the scenery, accelerating only at the end for a chaotic dash to the line.

But this was France's bicentennial year, and July its bicentennial month, two hundred years since the storming of the Bastille. Tour organizers had wanted to stage something special. So, for the final day of racing, Stage 21, they had mapped out a short time trial, starting at the gilded palace of Versailles, symbol of the old monarchy, and proceeding along the bank of the Seine, past the Arc de Triomphe to the center of Paris. The final stage of this Tour was no mere processional. With every pedal stroke, riders stood to rise or fall in the standings. And with the cyclists in first and second place separated by a mere fifty seconds, the climactic time trial now looked like a stroke of genius.

On July 22, Laurent arrived at Gare de Lyon station and disembarked from the train for the final stage of the Tour, which would take place the next day. He stepped into a mob of reporters and photographers, pressing in and prodding him with questions. Laurent turned and barked at the cameras. He spat at one. That image—of the race leader, in his red T-shirt and white shorts, spitting at a Spanish camera crew—would be replayed over and over in the hours to come.

Laurent held the *maillot jaune* in a Tour he was heavily favored to win. Yet, as the contest drew to a close, he was frightened. For two days, the Frenchman had suffered in secret from an excruciating saddle sore—a boil just below the left buttock, at the precise spot where his body met the saddle of the bicycle. Ointments didn't help, and doping rules precluded pills, so Laurent had no choice but to tough it out. The pain had grown so severe that the cyclist could not produce urine for his daily drug test. "Just moving was a penance," he recalled.[1]

No one outside Laurent's inner circle knew of the injury. Observers chalked up his outburst on the train platform to Laurent being *Monsieur Citron*.

On the same train into Paris, Greg happened upon Vince Barteau. "Everybody on the train was so sure that Fignon had already won," Vince recalled—everybody except Greg.

The American looked at Vince and said, "I haven't lost yet."[2] And something in his eyes told Vince that Greg believed it.

To win the Tour, Greg would have to erase more than two seconds of Laurent's fifty-second advantage for every kilometer the two men traveled in the climactic time trial from Versailles into Paris, a distance of 24.5 kilometers. That night, reporters asked Paul Köchli, Greg's former coach, whether the American could do it. "It's not possible," Köchli replied. "One second a kilometer is possible. Two seconds a kilometer is impossible."[3]

An informal poll of riders and race officials, collected that day by the sports newspaper *L'Équipe*, gave the Tour to Laurent by a margin of fifteen to two. When Greg told Kathy he thought he could still win, she offered her emphatic agreement and her unconditional support, as she always did. Deep inside, though, she winced, thinking, *Oh, come on, don't even tell me that.*[4] She feared he was wrong, and she didn't know whether he could endure such a letdown. The night before the final stage, she lay in bed, sleepless, trying to think of another athlete who had suffered injuries as grievous as Greg's and had come back to the top of bicycling or, frankly, any sport. She could not.

Whatever his misgivings, Laurent still thought the race was his. "Greg believes he can win," Laurent informed journalists on the eve of the time trial. "But it is impossible. I am too strong in the mind and the legs."[5] It wasn't just talk. "I was convinced, deep inside," he acknowledged later, "that I could not lose." Laurent barely slept that night. In the morning, he climbed onto his bike for the customary warm-up session. A jolt of pain from the saddle sore immediately halted him. "I just couldn't turn the pedals," he recalled.[6]

Greg, by contrast, slept well. He awoke in his Versailles hotel room, refreshed but befuddled, uncertain where he was, or why, until the fog cleared and the gravity of the day dawned upon him. Dressed in his customary yellow T-shirt and a pair of blue shorts, he descended to the main floor to join his teammates at a long table for a gluttonous meal of cereal, pasta, bread, and eggs—thousands of calories of fuel for the effort to come.

After a leisurely ride with his ADR teammates to loosen the legs, Greg felt confident and strong. As the mechanic took his bicycle, Greg turned to Otto Jácome, his trainer, and said, "I feel so good today, I think I'm gonna win it."

Otto replied, "Of course you are going to win it." He thought Greg was simply talking about the time trial, rather than the Tour itself.[7]

A test run of the race route that morning left Greg unnerved. It was an easy course—too easy, mostly downhill in a tailwind. Riders would fly into Paris. No headwind would mean no suffering, and little chance for better riders to gain time on weaker ones. Worse, Greg would ride two minutes in front of Laurent, and that juxtaposition put him at a disadvantage. The Frenchman would be chasing him. Greg wondered now whether victory truly lay within his grasp.[8]

The real measure of a cyclist's progress in a time trial comes at the time checks, fixed points on the route that trigger stopwatch readings. The readings show the rider's elapsed time and compare it to the times of riders who have come before. The data are fed to coaches, who relay them to riders. Today this information is transmitted through a tiny earpiece, but in 1989, messages were shouted from open windows of moving cars.

That morning, Greg informed his incredulous coach that he did not want progress reports along the route. They would only distract him. His other stratagem was the odd-looking, U-shaped handlebar extensions. He figured the tri-bars might buy him a few extra seconds on the road.

Laurent had been spotted that morning with his own pair of tri-bars, testing them on his abortive warm-up ride. By race time, however, he would return to the traditional cow-horn bars favored by nearly every other cyclist in the peloton. Laurent and Cyrille Guimard decided that to adopt the bars on a whim would violate one of their cardinal rules: "We would only use new equipment if it had been tested properly before the event," the cyclist recalled.[9] The bars had not—at least, not by him.

By afternoon, the summer sun had burst through the clouds, and the temperature had surged into the eighties, with a gentle tailwind still blowing at the riders' backs.

Time trials typically deliver hours of monotony punctuated with a final burst of drama. On this Sunday, television commentators largely ignored the 136 men who rode out of the gate ahead of Greg and Laurent. Most of those riders raced without hope of rising or falling in the overall standings, because a minute or more separated them from each other in cumulative time. Pedro Delgado, the defending Tour champion, started the day two minutes and twenty-eight seconds behind Laurent, mired in third place and no doubt lamenting the two minutes and forty seconds he had lost by being late for the first time trial. The man in fifth place trailed the *maillot jaune* by more than eight minutes. The rider in tenth place stood nearly seventeen minutes behind. The man in fiftieth place stood almost ninety minutes back. Such is the damage inflicted over twenty stages of the Tour.

One rider who preceded both Greg and Laurent on the course was Phil Anderson, Greg's dear friend and sometime training partner. Like everyone else in the peloton, Phil wondered whether it was possible for Greg to reclaim fifty seconds from Laurent. The course seemed to provide an answer. "I hardly had to touch the pedals, because it was all downhill," he recalled, "To make up a minute in that distance, it's pretty bloody hard."[10] Phil left the course assuming Greg was doomed.

After another heavy meal, Greg checked out of his hotel and headed to the Palace of Versailles, where, outside the royal gates, a makeshift platform had been raised beneath a white canopy. He wove through the vast crowd that had gathered to witness the final showdown. He pressed toward a small warm-up loop behind the platform, where a few riders leisurely circled to loosen their muscles and focus their minds. When Greg spotted Laurent, he avoided the Frenchman's piercing gaze. Laurent sized up his opponent and decided the American looked relaxed. In fact, Greg was just as frightened as he.[11]

As he circled Greg in the shadow of the starting gate, Laurent could not completely hide his pain; his face looked drained. He tried to summon courage with these thoughts: *All that's left is the time trial. I've only got to do what I have to. I'll hurt like hell, but afterwards I'll forget it.*[12]

At 4:12 p.m., Laurent watched Greg accelerate down the ramp onto the Avenue de Paris. Two minutes later, Laurent followed him

It is in the first few kilometers of a time trial that riders discerns whether they are going to have a "big day," cycling parlance for a superior performance. Here they set a tempo that they mean to hold for the full course; they soon learn whether their bodies intend to cooperate.

Laurent sped through the Parisian suburb of Viroflay into Chaville. On the roadside, the dense throng at Versailles thinned into a single, patchy line of spectators. As Laurent reached the five-kilometer mark, Cyrille Guimard shouted the result of the first time check from the team car: "*Six secondes! Vous avez perdu six secondes!*"[13] His fifty-second lead had dwindled to forty-four. Absorbing those words, Laurent broke his rhythm, turned his head and gazed at his coach in disbelief. Then Laurent lowered his head and lifted his pace.

Two minutes up the road, José de Cauwer shouted the same statistic to Greg from the ADR team car. The coach had defied Greg's instructions, and Greg testily reminded him: no more updates. Nonetheless,

Greg couldn't stop his brain from processing the new data. He was gaining on Laurent, but only at a rate of one second per kilometer, not two.
He wasn't pedaling fast enough.

The course passed through the suburb of Sèvres to the west bank
of the Seine, where Greg reached a gentle incline. He rose from the
saddle, shifted his arms from the U-shaped handlebar extensions to
the traditional cow-horn bars, and bore down with the full weight of
his body, so as not to lose speed on the ascent. Pedaling at fifty-four
kilometers per hour, Greg flew across the Pont de Sèvres and carved
a hard right onto the Quai Georges Gorse, cutting the corner so close
that his shoulder nearly clipped a spectator. He rode now with the Seine
at his right.

Greg reached the 11.5-kilometer mark, another checkpoint. The
result flashed on television screens. Greg now had the fastest time on
the day, twelve minutes and eight seconds. He rode at a pace twenty
seconds faster than anyone who had come before. The only cycling fan
in Paris unaware of this development was Greg himself.

Two minutes and twenty-one seconds later, Laurent arrived at the
same checkpoint. Laurent had posted the third-fastest time, but he had
lost nearly half of his lead. His virtual advantage over Greg on the road
now stood at twenty-nine seconds. Greg was reclaiming nearly two seconds per kilometer, almost—but not quite—the margin he needed to
retake the lead. If their relative pace did not change, Laurent would still
win the Tour.

"Paul," Phil Liggett told his broadcasting partner, "we are looking
now at a Tour de France that will be decided by six or seven seconds. I
can't believe that as I say it."[14]

By the time Greg reached the fourteen-kilometer mark, passing the
Eiffel Tower, Laurent's lead had shrunk to twenty-six seconds. Greg was
still not gaining time fast enough to win. Yet, astute viewers now sensed
a pronounced difference between Greg's body and Laurent's as each
man wrestled with his bicycle on the long, flat straightaway. Laurent
rocked his shoulders back and forth, a sign that he was laboring to turn
the pedals. He had chosen a gear even larger than Greg's, which allowed
for greater speed but demanded greater effort. Laurent also seemed to

be listing slightly to the right, a futile effort to ease the weight on his saddle sore. Greg, by contrast, held the top half of his body almost still, signaling that he was not struggling to sustain his effort. As the live television camera switched from Laurent to Greg, observant fans noted a slight acceleration in the passing scenery.

Laurent's lead shrank to twenty-one seconds, and then to eighteen, and then to fifteen, where it stood as Greg passed the banner announcing the final four kilometers. Greg was still gaining time at two seconds per kilometer. With four kilometers remaining, he would have to ride faster still to pull back the remaining seconds.

Greg knew none of this. Neither did Laurent. As the numbers began to turn against the Parisian, Guimard stopped relaying the time gaps to his rider. Laurent knew that was a bad sign. He tried to ignore it; "the race took over everything." Laurent tried to lift his tempo. But he found, to his dismay, that he could go no faster. "I was asphyxiating."[15]

In the broadcasting booth, Phil Liggett told his British viewers, "We are going to say that the very last half mile of this year's Tour de France will decide who will wear the final yellow jersey. You cannot bring the race to a finer finish than that, and you could never script it in a hundred years."

The three-kilometer mark brought a gradual incline from the Place de la Concorde to the Arc de Triomphe along the Champs-Élysées. Greg attacked hard, as if Laurent were right behind him, knowing that the Frenchman might founder on the modest hill. He thought he heard a public-address announcer say he had gained between thirty-five and forty seconds on Laurent. It was his first real inkling of the chaos he was inflicting on the race. The crowd smelled an upset; American flags were popping up along the Paris sidewalks. Greg kept his head down and pedaled on.

Greg passed the Arc de Triomphe and made a final turn toward the finish, nearing the one-kilometer banner. He accelerated to sixty-five kilometers per hour as the course turned gently downhill. Laurent's lead had dwindled to ten seconds.

Now Greg could clearly see the cyclist in front of him, Pedro Delgado, who had started the course two minutes earlier. Delgado and his bicycle gave Greg a new target, a carrot to chase, a gap to close—a wonderful development for a cyclist riding alone in a time trial. Greg surged ahead, closing in on Delgado.

Greg had been gaining time on Laurent while riding uphill. Now Greg was descending, and Laurent would soon be climbing. Laurent's remaining lead began to melt away: ten seconds became eight, then six, then four.

Greg pedaled the final meters of the 1989 Tour de France. He crossed the finish line without a salute or fist pump and coasted his bicycle to a stop, head bowed, sunglasses slipping from his nose, looking like a man in defeat. Otto Jácome hurried to his side, handing him a towel and a bottle of Evian. "Greg, you were great," he shouted.

Kathy stood nearby, wearing a polka-dot dress and huddling with Greg's father. She waited with fingers pressed to her temples, as if working out the math of the race in her head, or perhaps laboring to hold back tears. She embraced Bob. Then the overhead scoreboard told her Greg had finished the course with a time of twenty-six minutes and fifty-seven seconds, the fastest ride of the day by a margin of more than half a minute. She screamed—"Greg!"—and clasped her hands to her mouth.

Greg had won the time trial, but Laurent still led the Tour. The Parisian had started the race two minutes after Greg. At the moment Greg crossed the line, Laurent sat two minutes and forty-eight seconds behind, with two more seconds to spare. If Laurent could only reach the line within the next two minutes and fifty seconds, the *maillot jaune* was his to keep.

In the broadcast booth, Paul Sherwen sputtered to his partner, "Phil, this is the most incredible thing I think I have ever seen in my life."

The final lap traversed cobblestones that set off vibrations of unspeakable agony in Laurent's body. He slowed into the final 180-degree turn just as his time reached 26:57, the moment when the race clock had stopped for Greg. Laurent was down to his final fifty seconds. A roar began to build among the scattered Americans in the massive crowd. Laurent rose from his saddle and broke into a desperate sprint, pedaling furiously onto the final straightaway, nearly colliding with the metal barriers at the roadside as his bicycle whipped from side to side. His French supporters stood in stunned suspense.

Over the previous three weeks of racing, neither Greg nor Laurent had enjoyed the full support of the French public; this was no replay of the 1986 contest, which had united all of France behind Bernard Hinault and his quest for a historic sixth Tour. Laurent wasn't as beloved as the Badger, and Greg's currency had risen sharply in the three years since his first victory. Yet, no Frenchman had won the Tour in four years, and the Parisian throngs had turned out on this sultry Sunday afternoon for a celebration. No one along the grand boulevard was quite prepared for the drama that now unfolded.

Greg caught a glimpse of Laurent on the horizon and reflexively averted his eyes. On British television, Phil Liggett beheld the *maillot jaune* in desperate flight and mused, "He could be losing the Tour de France by the blink of an eyelid on his own doorstep."

As Greg stood and watched the final moments of the Tour, he feared that *he* might lose the race by the blink of an eye on Laurent's doorstep. His own eyes darted up to the digital clock, then down to the yellow glimmer of the *maillot jaune*, then back up to the clock. A sickening thought seized his mind. *What if I lose the Tour by a single second?*[16]

A French media crew abruptly thrust a pair of white headphones onto Greg's head and attempted an interview. Greg closed his eyes and focused, trying to hear the feed on the headphones amid the din. It was no use. He frantically ripped the headphones off and trained his full attention on the race clock.

Laurent powered toward the line, trailed by an armada of motorbikes. He passed an array of Fiat banners. He could now see the finish, a block's length ahead. On the scoreboard above, the clock ticked forward: 27:45 . . . 27:46 . . . 27:47.

Time slowed and stretched in those final meters, as an entire nation counted down the last of *le Grand Blond*'s fifty seconds. Finally Laurent surged across the line. He fell from his bicycle and collapsed onto the pavement in a fetal crouch, his hands covering his face, his body utterly spent. The clock on the scoreboard had stopped. It read twenty-seven minutes and fifty-five seconds.

"He's lost the Tour de France," Phil Liggett screamed. "The crowd has realized it. Laurent Fignon has lost the Tour de France!"

After a journey of more than three thousand kilometers, Laurent had lost the race by the length of a football field.

Greg stood with head bowed, his hand sweeping his brow, looking as if he, too, had lost the Tour. Then he glimpsed the time on the scoreboard and stared in shock as he realized he had won. He sank to the ground, and then he bounded back up, pumping his fists. Otto, still at Greg's side, shouted, "You won it, Greg, you won it!"[17] Then Otto skipped off, dancing for joy, dragging Greg's red bicycle behind him.

Greg was dazed; the outcome of the race was so hard to process that it had plunged both victor and vanquished into a sort of shock. When Greg's head cleared, he rushed off to find Kathy, the one person in Paris with whom he wished to share the moment.

Across a security fence, Kathy was crying. The numbers on the scoreboard looked promising, but no one around her seemed quite sure how the race had ended. The suspense was unbearable. She finally turned to no one in particular and cried, "Did he win, or not?" Someone replied, "Yes!" Then she turned and shrieked "GREG!" and raced off toward the fence, which still separated her from her husband. Greg hobbled up to Kathy in his cycling shoes. They embraced across the metal links. "I can't believe it," Kathy gasped.

She really couldn't believe it. Kathy had thought Greg was going to lose. And only she knew how much this victory meant to him. Now they both heard the voice of Hinault, the five-time champion turned Voice of the Tour, announcing the results on the loudspeaker. She turned to Greg and shouted, "Eight seconds, Greg! You've got eight seconds less than Fignon!"

Johan Lammerts, Greg's faithful ADR teammate, watched the concluding moments of the Tour on a television in his hotel room, hoping his friend might win the stage and secure second place. When the final time flashed on the screen, he bolted upright and jumped up and down on the bed.

Some distance from Greg, in the middle of the crowded boulevard, Laurent lay on the pavement, gasping for air. He was, at that moment,

very nearly the only cyclist in France who did not know the outcome
of the Tour. "Well?" he cried, again and again, to the men fluttering
around him. No one dared answer. Finally, someone stepped forth from
the crowd, met his gaze, and said, "You've lost, Laurent."[18]

Laurent gathered himself into a seated position, seized a bottle of
mineral water from an outstretched hand, and drained it in long swigs.
He sat on the pavement at the center of a circle of older men, encased
within a larger circle of television cameras. One of the men held a towel
to Laurent's back, then cradled it against his neck. The men helped
Laurent to his feet. He felt numb, incoherent, his brain unable to process the facts it had been presented, as he hobbled forward aimlessly.
He recalled the moment in his memoir:

> I walk like a boxer who's concussed, in an improbable world of
> furious noise. The steps I take are robotic and aren't directed at
> anything. I've no idea where I am going and who is making me
> go there. I feel arms supporting me. Some shout. Some look hag-
> gard, groggy, wiped out. Others are celebrating. That's it, they're
> celebrating. It's easier to make out now, they are looking at me with
> a kind of happy hatred, as if it's a pleasure to see me lose. What's
> so good about it? I can't get a grip on it. I've lost. They've won. But
> who are they?[19]

Finally Laurent encountered a friendly face, that of Thierry Marie,
a teammate. Thierry threw himself into Laurent's arms, and both men
burst into tears. "I wailed like a child," Laurent wrote.[20] He hadn't cried
in public since his youth.

An American camera crew reached Greg for an interview. The interviewer asked him how this victory compared to his win over Hinault,
three years earlier.

"Nothing compares," Greg shouted. "Nothin', nothin', nothin',
nothin'."[21]

Kathy beamed at her husband.

In the days, months, and years to come, Laurent would tender several
excuses for his defeat that day in Paris. But when he greeted reporters

just after the race, he offered none. "I rode the hardest I could," he said. "Obviously, it wasn't good enough."[22]

Humble, plainspoken Laurent was back—this time for good. An hour later, at a postrace press conference, Laurent contemplated his loss with philosophical detachment. "Eight seconds—it's not the number that counts," he said. "Eight seconds, twenty, one minute. What does it change? I have still lost the Tour." Laurent told the assembled journalists to resist the urge to ascribe his defeat, however narrow, to a single cause. "I think there are a thousand places where I could have lost the Tour, and a thousand where Greg won it. Greg won the Tour fairly. He was obviously the strongest. I am certainly not angry with him. If anything, I am angry that I wasn't stronger than him."[23]

Almost lost amid the tragedy was the fact that Laurent had ridden the fastest time trial of his career. It wasn't so much that Laurent had lost the race as that Greg had won it. Greg had completed the course at an average speed better than fifty-four kilometers per hour. In the history of the Tour, no one had ridden a time trial faster.

At the winner's ceremony, Greg lifted five-year-old Geoffrey onto the podium, just as he had lifted a two-year-old Geoffrey three years earlier. Father and son wore matching pink caps. Race officials handed Greg a crisp new *maillot jaune.* He pulled it over his yellow-and-white ADR jersey, carefully replacing the pink cap when he had finished. He exchanged the obligatory kisses with the ceremonial French model and hoisted the winner's bouquet over his head.

Then Greg posed for pictures with the men he had defeated, Laurent to his right, Pedro Delgado to his left. Laurent looked stricken. Greg turned to him and whispered, "You won the Giro, Laurent," recalling his triumph in Italy just a month prior.

Laurent smiled wanly and replied, "I don't give a damn about the Giro."[24]

The fifty-five musicians of the band of the Eighth Regiment of the French Signal Corps had prepared "La Marseillaise." Now, on the flustered conductor's cue, they lurched instead into an awkward rendition of "The Star-Spangled Banner."

As he stood atop the podium, Greg thought back over the previous
months, to the time when he had lain in his bed and cried, thinking
his cycling career was over. He thought of the races he had finished but
could not win, and the races he had started but could not finish, and
the amateur cyclist on the back roads of California whose pace he could
not match. He remembered his first labored steps across the floor of his
hospital room, the hours of surgery, the blood dripping from the colander that was his body. He remembered lying in the dirt at his uncle's
ranch, thinking he would never see his family again. And then his mind
returned to the present, to the simple fact of his victory, and he felt a joy
such as he had never felt before.[25]

THE SEQUEL

A FEW HOURS AFTER the podium ceremony in Paris, Kathy LeMond sat alone along a deserted Champs-Élysées, exhausted, pregnant, and broke. A car pulled up. Inside sat François Lambert, owner of ADR, Greg's team. He asked Kathy what she was doing. Kathy explained: Greg had been swept away in a crush of admirers, and everyone else had left. The wife of the Tour de France champion was stranded, lacking the funds to take a taxi back to her hotel. Mortified, Lambert peeled off a 500-franc note from his billfold and handed it to Kathy. He realized, then, that it was the first money he had paid the LeMonds all summer.[1]

Kathy would not want for cab fare again. Within forty-eight hours of his second Tour victory, Greg was fielding invitations to race in twenty-six celebratory criterium races, at $10,000 to $15,000 apiece. Back at the LeMond home in Belgium, Bob was negotiating the last of twenty sponsorship deals for Team LeMond, whose fortunes had reversed literally overnight.

Greg and Kathy decamped to Deauville, a beach resort in Normandy, to escape their many pursuers, only to be awakened by the room telephone at one the next morning. It was Bob. He told Greg that François Lambert, the ADR owner, had just arrived at the front door with José de Cauwer, the team coach. Once admitted to the dwelling, Lambert had marched over to a table and emptied a gunnysack full of money. The cash totaled $175,000, the portion of Greg's annual salary that the team should have paid him half a year earlier.

"What if it's drug money?" Bob asked.

"I don't care," Greg replied. "It's my money."[2]

* * *

Laurent Fignon spent the final days of July in private mourning. His narrow defeat by *l'Américain* in Paris had redefined his career—and not for the better. Now Laurent would be forever remembered not as a man who had won the Tour twice, but as a man who had lost it once, by the narrowest margin in history.

"French people had cried that day," recalled Alain Gallopin, Laurent's best friend and trainer.[3] So had Laurent. And he awoke the next day to a strange new reality. Suddenly he was beloved. French people had cried for *him*. They loved him now, the way they had loved Raymond Poulidor, the Eternal Second. Fan letters began pouring in, twenty a day.

Laurent didn't care about being popular. He cared about the Tour. Finally, two days after its conclusion, he telephoned Alain. He was ready to talk.

"Listen to me, Alain," he said. "I was second in the Tour. You hear me? Second. I did not win. It was LeMond who won. The others can tell me anything they want, that I was the moral victor, that LeMond had equipment that I did not have, that eight seconds is nothing, a whole bunch of crap. But you, Alain, you will tell me no stories. I came in second, that's all." And then he hung up. They would never speak of that Tour again.[4]

Laurent now studiously avoided the Champs-Élysées. He caught himself, at random moments, measuring bits of his life in eight-second segments: *one, two, three, four, five, six, seven, eight*. Walking along a sidewalk, watching a passing sports car, climbing a flight of stairs, reading a paragraph in a Stephen King book: you couldn't do much in eight seconds. How, then, could eight seconds have transformed Laurent's life so completely?

At week's end, the Union Cycliste Internationale released new world rankings, and Laurent sat at the top. His second-place finish at the Tour, coupled with his win at the Giro and other feats, had generated enough points in the arcane ranking system to elevate him to number one, surely a moment of cruel irony for the sullen Parisian.

Greg's own ranking had leapt from 146 to 18, reflecting the points reaped in his Tour victory, though neither number quite suited a reigning Tour champion. In truth, the ranking was obsolete. And perhaps Greg was the first Tour champion to grasp the new reality of late-century professional cycling. For Greg's generation and the ones to follow, the Tour would be very nearly all that mattered. Fame and fortune, contract dollars, and sponsorship deals—they all hinged on success at *le Tour.* That one race delivered more publicity, more celebrity, more *money,* to the cyclist who won it than all the other races combined. Perhaps Greg saw this simple fact more clearly than his European peers because he lived half his life in the United States, where the Tour was the only cycling event most people had ever heard of.

Within a week of his second Tour victory, Greg was courted by nine professional cycling teams. The man who had reaped cycling's first million-dollar contract over three years was now rumored to be worth upward of a million dollars a year, more than anyone had yet been paid to ride a bicycle. That three-year, million-dollar contract in 1984 had made Greg perhaps the first professional bicycle racer in the modern era to realize his full market value. His contract had transformed the industry, and by 1989 some of Greg's rivals earned more than he did.

Now at least three teams were willing to pay him $1.5 million a year, twice the highest salary paid to any cyclist in 1989. Of those suitors, Greg chose Z, the team of Roger Legeay, the one coach who had shared Greg's conviction that he would return to the top. The coach and his new captain agreed on the details the night before the world championship road race.

There was, in fact, one race on the cycling calendar beside the Tour that held Greg's attention. By 1989, Greg had won the world championship race once and finished second twice, the most dominant performance by any cyclist in that decade. The 1989 edition was set for August 27 in Chambéry, the historic capital of Savoy in southeastern France. The race spanned twenty-one laps around a twelve-kilometer course, rolling past vineyards, sunflower fields, and a lake, crossing three sharp climbs before a final, twisting descent to the finish. Greg trained hard, spending two weeks in the Alps, riding six hours a day.

But race morning found him inexplicably tired; such were the vagaries of a one-day contest.

All of Europe awaited a rematch between Greg and Laurent. Greg now led a comparatively weak American national team, while Laurent commanded a strong French squad on his home turf, essentially a rerun of the David and Goliath contest between Greg's ADR team and Laurent's Super U two months earlier.

Racing commenced beneath a gentle sun. Several laps in, as the weather deteriorated, word spread that Greg was yo-yoing off the rear of the peloton, looking spent. He was having a bad day, and after nineteen of the twenty-one laps, he considered dropping out. Then he nearly crashed. Rather than defeat him, the mishap "brought my adrenaline up," he recalled.[5] He felt suddenly awake. And now he held a modest advantage over his peers. In his hours of torpor, Greg had ridden conservatively, saving his energy. Now he worked his way toward the front of the pack.

As the final lap began, Greg rode within a small group that contained Laurent and most of the other contenders. When they reached the final climb, Laurent attacked, accelerating away up the left side of the road. The race appeared to be his—until Greg appeared on the road behind him, closing the gap and settling in directly behind the Frenchman, who was not yet aware of his presence. Voilà! Here was the battle the fans had come to see.

Greg swept around Laurent and attacked, flying past him up the mountainside. At first Laurent was too stunned to react. After a moment's hesitation, he tore off in pursuit of the American. Greg crossed the summit first and clung to a meager lead as they hurtled down the other side.

"Laurent Fignon's worst nightmare has come back to life," a commentator announced on ESPN.[6]

Laurent caught Greg on the descent. After a few tentative jabs, the Frenchman latched onto the American's wheel, a tactical position that might allow him to surge past Greg at the finish. Greg had sat on Laurent's wheel through much of the 1989 Tour; now Laurent would return the favor. Greg responded with an angry flip of his hand, calling out the Frenchman for riding in his wake.

It felt like a reprise of the battle between the two champions that had played out along the hairpins of l'Alpe d'Huez several weeks earlier. But this time other riders pedaled close behind. As Greg and Laurent sparred, their pursuers were closing in fast. The two rivals finally set aside their differences and sprinted off toward the finish, which now sat two kilometers away, accelerating just in time to keep pace with the men who had caught them.

The cyclists rode together for a time, testing one another with half-hearted attacks, each man marking the others. With half a kilometer to go, Laurent and Greg simultaneously launched one final sprint, Laurent on the right, Greg on the left. Irish sprinter Sean Kelly and a few others fell in behind them.

Both men knew they stood little chance of beating the Irishman in a head-to-head sprint, so they accelerated early, hoping to dull Kelly's speed. Greg pulled into the lead, and he never lost it. Laurent faded, his energy spent. With a few meters to go, Kelly surrendered, slumping his shoulders in defeat with the certainty of a veteran sprinter, though he trailed Greg by no more than the length of a bicycle wheel. Greg punched the sky in victory. Laurent, bested by the American again, coasted to the line in sixth place.

"I was ready to quit," Greg laughed when it was over. "And it worked out. Everything seems to be working out right now."[7] Greg had won the race with a long, sustained burst of speed, overcoming the long odds of a mass sprint by riding all the sprinters into exhaustion. The technique was classic Fignon. And Greg had used it to beat him.

"When I attacked on the last climb up the Montagnole Hill, who chased and caught me? LeMond," Laurent recounted sardonically. "When I attacked again later, who counterattacked? LeMond. When I tried to get away with a kilometer to go, who came after me? LeMond. This has been LeMond's year, and he's really become my bête noire."[8]

In September, Greg announced his new contract with team Z, worth $5.7 million over three years. Greg would now earn almost $2 million a year.

His ascent would continue. On September 27, Greg paid a second visit to the White House, now occupied by George H. W. Bush. This time

Kathy and the boys did not attend. They were home, preparing for the third LeMond child, Simone, due in October.

One might assume Greg's second victory would garner less attention than the first. Yet, American mass media, however ignorant of professional cycling, immediately grasped the significance of Greg's comeback. No one could recall an athlete who had returned to the top of such a demanding sport after such a terrible injury. Five and a half million people had watched Greg's final time trial at the 1989 Tour on American television, a record for the sport.

Greg signed television and book deals. He appeared with Johnny Carson on the *Tonight Show*. He played video games with the Rolling Stones backstage at the Minneapolis Metrodome. He bought an $84,000 Mercedes convertible. He delivered fast food on his bicycle in a commercial for Taco Bell. All those happy distractions kept Greg from his training regimen through the winter, when his telephone rang so incessantly that he changed the number once a month. When he returned to Europe in late January to start the season with his new team, Greg was out of shape and overweight.

"The most difficult part of the winter is saying no to people," Greg explained to a *USA Today* reporter, one of many to whom he had said yes.[9]

Greg's 1990 cycling season began with no more promise than the two that had preceded it. In February, he dropped out of the Spanish Ruta del Sol before the first climb. He finished ninety-seventh at Paris–Nice and abandoned the Critérium International.

"I feel very, very tired," he told a reporter.[10]

Cycling fans expected great deeds from the *maillot jaune* and from the world champion; Greg was both. Some greeted his lackluster performance with unbridled hostility, spitting at him from the roadside and hissing that he dishonored the world champion's rainbow jersey that sat on his shoulders.

At the end of March, Greg fled to Minnesota, complaining of a mystery virus, later diagnosed as mononucleosis. Z team officials announced he would take off most of April. The stricken cyclist finally surfaced in Washington, D.C., a few weeks later for a one-day criterium around the nation's capital. It was part of a three-race series, whose organizers had paid him $200,000 just to show up. With sixteen laps to go, he abandoned the race. Greg proceeded to the Tour de Trump, the marquee American cycling event of that era, and finished in seventy-eighth place. At the Giro d'Italia, he rolled in nearly three hours behind the leaders.

Thus, as July approached, the highest-paid man in professional cycling, defender of the *maillot jaune*, was not regarded as the clear favorite to win the 1990 Tour de France. The American "has had illness and misfortune perch on his shoulder like a malevolent sprite," the *Guardian* observed.[11]

The race again seemed wide open; the peloton had lacked a proper *patron* since the retirement of Hinault, four years earlier. Spaniard Pedro Delgado, still regarded as the world's finest climber, was the consensus choice to win, along with the usual honor roll of past Tour winners and near-winners, including Greg, Laurent, and Irishman Stephen Roche.

Paul Köchli, Greg's former coach, was one of the few who knew better. He had seen Greg at the Tour de Suisse. After his disastrous spring and early summer, Greg had finally found his legs in Switzerland in June, riding among the leaders and finishing a respectable tenth. "For me," Köchli told the *New York Times*, "he's the main favorite."[12]

Laurent had won neither the Tour nor the world championship; yet he had ridden through the fall of 1989 and the spring of 1990 with a consistency Greg could not match. He had finished the 1989 season by winning the Grand Prix des Nations, the unofficial men's world time-trial championship. His effort on that September day poignantly evoked Greg's ride in the final time trial of the Tour. Greg had ridden the fastest time trial in Tour history. Now, two months later, Laurent set a new speed record for the Grand Prix course. He might have lost the Tour, but he had not lost his Gallic pride. That evening, proud *soigneur* Alain Gallopin told Laurent, "When you are in form, you can do anything, you know."[13]

Laurent entered the 1990 season riding with a new sponsor, as the home-improvement retailer Castorama stepped in for the departing

Super U. He also sported a new jersey, whose design suggested a pair of bright blue overalls.

In March 1990, Laurent and his overalls pedaled to victory in the Critérium International, the unofficial men's national championship of France. But as spring faded into summer, Laurent's season began to unravel. As usual, his problems seemed more psychological than physical. Poor results at the Tour of Flanders and Paris–Roubaix sapped his confidence, and by the time he returned to the Giro d'Italia in May as defending champion, he pedaled within a pall of gloom.

A crash in Italy completed Laurent's demoralization. He went down in a dark tunnel and clambered back onto his bicycle with a dislocated pelvis. Four days later, in a thick fog, he abandoned the Giro. The pelvis injury hadn't fully healed by the time he entered the Tour.

The 1990 Tour began with a swift, six-kilometer time-trial prologue on June 30 at the Futuroscope theme park. Greg finished second, four seconds behind time-trial specialist Thierry Marie. Oddly, no other former Tour champion placed near the top. Laurent settled for fifteenth place.

Two days later, on the first stage of proper racing, four men blew the Tour apart.

In the opening minutes of a 139-kilometer road stage, four riders stole away from the peloton. Three were strong climbers, and all were vying for bonus sprint points atop a modest summit. They crossed it, sprinted for points, and eased up. Then they noticed that the peloton was not giving chase. So the four cyclists raised their pace. Their lead grew to two minutes, then four, then eight. In the final kilometers, the full peloton broke into a desperate chase, but it was too late. The breakaway crossed the line more than ten minutes ahead. Steve Bauer, Greg's Canadian friend and the best-placed rider in the group, donned the *maillot jaune*.

Laurent had entered the Tour as "a tired man, physically and mentally," he recalled.[14] He lagged behind the leaders, riding among the *domestiques* in the rear of the peloton, a place where bad things happened. Tour contenders rode at the front of the peloton partly to avoid all the pileups and meltdowns behind them.

In Stage 3, Laurent went down on a rain-soaked turn, bruising a calf muscle. In Stage 4, he and his teammates became trapped behind a crash that split the peloton in two; at day's end, Laurent had lost forty-four precious seconds to Greg and the other contenders.

"Any chance of winning the Tour was now a distant illusion," he wrote in his memoir.[15]

On the next stage, the longest of the Tour, Laurent dismounted his bicycle at a feed station and unpinned the number from his back. He climbed into his team car and held a newspaper over his face, so the hated photographers could not capture the moment. Then he hailed a passing helicopter, whose presence he had presumably arranged in advance.

"It has been his only uplifting experience since the race began," one reporter observed drily.[16]

A year earlier, Laurent had predicted to Alain Gallopin that the 1989 contest would be his last chance to win the Tour; now, through his own actions, the premonition seemed to be coming true.

"I'm sorry for him," Greg said of the departed Frenchman, "even if he has not been very kind to me lately."[17]

The 1990 Tour had become a war of attrition. The four cyclists from the breakaway held a ten-minute advantage. It was up to Greg and the others to chip away at their lead.

The race reached the Alps on July 10. Now Greg faced a choice. He was still a contender to win the Tour; yet one of his teammates, Ronan Pensec, had joined in the four-man breakaway and sat within seconds of the race lead. Greg could either attack those men, including Pensec, or back off and ride in the service of his teammate. Greg chose duty over glory, riding as an overqualified lieutenant to his French comrade—to the utter delight of the French, who at last had someone to cheer. On the final, eight-kilometer ascent up Mont Blanc, the highest mountain in the Alps, Greg and his team set a fierce pace, leading Pensec away from his rivals to take the *maillot jaune*. Greg remained nearly ten minutes off the lead.

The next day brought Stage 11, perhaps the most difficult of that year's Tour, with a cumulative five thousand meters of climbing. On the descent of the first climb, the dreaded Col de la Madeleine, the peloton slowed to collect food bags for lunch. Greg, holding his bicycle with one hand, hit a pothole and went down, somehow bringing an elderly woman with him. He leapt up to aid the woman, asking, "Are you okay?" For the moment, he cared more about her welfare than the outcome of the Tour. Her husband did not.

"Go on, get out of here," the husband cried. "Don't worry about her."[18]

Greg had fallen on his left hand. When he examined it, he saw that his middle finger was dislocated. He straightened it and pushed it back in its socket with the dispassion of someone adjusting his cap, and then he remounted his bicycle.

Another crucial stage loomed the next day. The Tour's second time trial covered only 33.5 kilometers, but it was nearly all uphill, ending at the ski resort at Villard-de-Lans. One by one, the beneficiaries of the Stage 1 breakaway were succumbing to exhaustion. Steve Bauer had lost the yellow jersey two days earlier. Today, on Stage 12, Ronan Pensec would fall. His strength sapped in the Alps, Pensec finished the time trial in forty-ninth place.

The *maillot jaune* now passed to Claudio Chiappucci, the last of the four escapees, a relatively unsung Italian rider who had somehow managed to finish the time trial just a few seconds behind Greg.

Racing resumed after a rest day, and few observers expected any surprises on a short but hilly Stage 13. But Greg and his Z team had a plan. On the idle day, Otto Jácome provided counsel: "Tell Pensec to attack Chiappucci," he said. "In the hills, he will not have anybody to help him, and he will be chasing Pensec, and you will have the opportunity to attack him."[19]

It was a calculated bluff. Chiappucci would ride now to defend his yellow jersey. If he thought Pensec was threatening to retake it, Chiappucci might feel compelled to chase, exhausting his own energy and creating an opening for Greg. With Pensec out of the *maillot jaune*, Greg's leadership of the Z team was restored. He was free to ride his own race.

At the start of Stage 13, the Z team dispatched Pensec on an early breakaway. As Otto had predicted, Chiappucci took the bait, setting off to recapture Pensec. Just as Chiappucci was about to catch Pensec, Greg launched a furious counterattack, flying past the spent Italian.

The attacks had torn the field apart. Chiappucci limped home nearly five minutes after Greg. Finally, Greg sat within striking distance of the race lead. He now trailed Chiappucci by two and a half minutes. Greg had not won a stage, and he remained in third place. Yet he brimmed with confidence. "I'm looking to make this a much harder race," he told the *New York Times*.[20]

Race pundits assumed Chiappucci would soon surrender his yellow jersey. On the first day in the Pyrenees, the Italian surprised everyone by launching an attack. At the foot of the imposing Col du Tourmalet, Chiappucci led by two minutes. Unless Greg acted quickly, Chiappucci would build an unbreakable lead. Greg thus attacked on the steepest portion of the Tourmalet, the highest pass in the Pyenees, breaking clear of the pack, followed by the two great Spanish climbers, Delgado and Induráin. At the summit, Greg had drawn to within a minute of Chiappucci on the road. Greg crested the mountain and hurtled down the other side with utter abandon, taking untold risks. He caught Chiappucci at the foot of the final climb to the ski resort at Luz Ardiden.

With seven kilometers left to climb, Greg attacked again, riding up the mountainside in a grinding sprint. After two kilometers of this savagery, he had gained a minute on Chiappucci. By the last kilometer, he stood more than two minutes ahead.

At the finish, Greg pushed through the crowd to find Kathy. They hugged and kissed, and Greg breathlessly asked if she knew where his rivals sat on the road behind him. Chiappucci was staging a heroic rally, sprinting to the line and clinging to his *maillot jaune* by a mere five seconds over Greg. Delgado was nearly four minutes back.

All of France now assumed Greg would win the 1990 Tour. Yet Greg remained the incurable worrier, reminding anyone who would listen that a lot could happen before Paris. He seemed, if anything, more nervous about his chances for victory now than in 1989, when his odds were indeed slim, and more fearful of some mishap than in 1986, when the

Tour director himself had fretted for Greg's safety. When Greg dared to speak of eventual victory, he would reach up to the headboard of his hotel bed and rap on the wood.[21]

The next day, Greg's superstitions seemed to be confirmed. As he crested the Col de Marie-Blanque, riding at the front of the pack, he suffered a flat tire. He was alone, without a team car or a teammate. Greg looked left and right, searching the road for anyone who might lend him a tire, and saw no one. He thought, *What a stupid way to lose the Tour.*[22] He waited for what seemed an eternity—it was actually less than a minute—for a spare wheel, which proved defective, and then a spare bicycle.

At such moments, cycling chivalry prescribed a cessation of hostilities. Even with the race in the balance—especially then—a cyclist did not exploit the mechanical misfortune of a rival. Yet just when Greg's tire went flat, Chiappucci attacked. By the time Greg remounted, he had lost more than a minute to Chiappucci, the one cyclist who could still beat him to Paris.

Here karma came into play. A week earlier, Greg had shelved his own ambitions to play dutiful teammate to Pensec, the Frenchman who then wore the *maillot jaune.* His selfless act had endeared him to all of France, a nation held in thrall by a glimpse of an actual Frenchman riding in yellow. Now Greg's formidable French team massed to return the favor.

Two teammates sat some distance behind Greg on the roadway. They sprinted up to meet their leader, and together the three cyclists stormed off after Chiappucci. Two other Z riders sat ahead of Greg in a breakaway. They slowed to wait for him. Soon, Greg rode within a five-man armada, tearing up the roadway in blue-and-yellow jerseys splashed with comic-book graphics.

Greg was seething. He and his teammates hurtled down the descent at a hundred kilometers per hour, taking spine-chilling risks as they shaved seconds from the Italian's ill-gotten gap. Twenty-one kilometers later, Greg and his teammates finally reeled Chiappucci in.

Four stages of racing remained, but three were flat contests that would not alter the standings. Thus Chiappucci brought his slender advantage into Stage 20, a 45.5-kilometer time trial, nearly twice the length of the legendary showdown between Greg and Laurent a year earlier. Greg, still regarded as the world's best time trialist, would have an hour on the road to recover five seconds from the Italian. "If I lose," he told the *New York Times*, "I'm going to have a very, very bad day, and he's going to have the best day of his life."[23]

But Greg's victory was hardly assured. By the final days of the Tour, he was slowed by a steady accumulation of minor maladies: a swollen left foot, dating to the very first day of the contest; a painful saddle sore, acquired in the first week; a throbbing finger, dislocated on Stage 11; and a stiff back, strained when he had thrown his bicycle wheel in frustration after the puncture on Stage 17. The saddle sore, in particular, would have surely resonated for Greg's Parisian rival, had Laurent remained in the race.

On July 21, the peloton gathered at Lac de Vassivière in the Limousin region of central France. To win the Tour, Chiappucci had to preserve at least a shred of his five-second lead. The Italian started three minutes after the American. Five kilometers in, Chiappucci had already surrendered two seconds to Greg. A few kilometers later, he had lost the lead and the Tour. At the end, Chiappucci stood two minutes and twenty-one seconds behind Greg, the new race leader, who had finished the time trial in a respectable fifth place.

The 1990 Tour ended in traditional fashion with a ceremonial ride into Paris, rather than the climactic time trial of the previous year. When the peloton finally reached the city center and Greg glimpsed the Champs-Élysées, he nearly cried, overcome with relief that his defense of the *maillot jaune* was nearing an end. After eight ceremonial laps, Greg crossed the line for the last time. He lifted his arms in a victory salute, though he rode in the middle of the pack.

Greg now joined an exceedingly short list of men who had won the Tour three times: Philippe Thys, a Belgian, in the century's second decade, and Louison Bobet, a Frenchman, in the postwar 1950s. Three others sat ahead of them, with five Tour victories each: Anquetil, Merckx, and Hinault.

The French public cheered Greg all along the royal boulevard, and Kathy beamed from the sidelines, holding three-year-old Scott in her arms. Cycling purists grumbled, though, that Greg had won this third Tour without claiming a single stage. He had prevailed with tactics and consistency, not with bold breakaways or dominant time trials. For Greg, every day of the 1990 Tour had been a good day; each of his rivals had suffered bad ones.

As Greg cleaned up for the victory ceremony, he turned to his *soigneur* with a thoughtful smile and said, "This Tour was not so exciting, eh, Otto? Not like last year."[24]

THE DECLINE

GREG'S THIRD TOUR DE FRANCE victory did little to quell his critics, a Gallic chorus populated chiefly by aging cycling fans and former champions. To them, Greg earned too much and accomplished too little.

In the summer of 1990, *Forbes* magazine ranked Greg twenty-seventh among the world's thirty wealthiest athletes, with an estimated annual income of $4.2 million in salary and endorsements. Greg was, after all, the dominant athlete in his sport. Yet, within days of his latest Tour triumph, Greg was again missing races. This time the purported malady was a saddle sore, the same one that had vexed Greg in the final days of the Tour. Greg would take most of a month off the bicycle to allow the wound to heal, forsaking nearly $100,000 in criterium fees, but he recovered in time for the world championship road race in September. However, that race, staged in Japan, was a bust for Greg. An unsung Belgian stole victory in a surprise breakaway.

Hoping to evade the publicity binge of the previous winter, Greg returned home and stayed there, leaving his country estate only to escort Kathy and their children to Disneyland and to ski in Colorado. After a customary winter layoff, Greg remounted his bike, pedaling alongside the family's new motor home the fifteen hundred miles from San José, California, south to Cabo San Lucas, Mexico, at the tip of the Baja California peninsula. A small entourage accompanied him, including trainer Otto Jácome and teammate Johan Lammerts, both of whom presumably joined Greg on the arid journey out of pure friendship. They had planned to cover 125 miles a day, but Greg had been off his bicycle, and his form proved so poor that the daily target was quickly halved. Greg struggled whenever the road began to rise.[1]

Throughout the spring and into the summer of 1991, Greg drifted in and out of the peloton, drawing fresh rebukes from the cycling traditionalists who felt his pitiful form mocked the great races. He abandoned the Milan-San Remo in March. Three months later, when he dropped from contention at the Giro d'Italia in the Apennine mountains, the Italian sports newspaper *La Gazzetta dello Sport* fumed that Greg had collapsed "like a piece of antique furniture, eaten by worms."[2]

Then, in the final days before the Tour, Greg staged another miraculous recovery. He entered the ten-day Tour de Suisse and felt reborn, though he finished outside the top ten. In late-June training rides, Greg flew down the road behind Otto and his motorbike, holding a steady speed of eighty-five kilometers an hour; a year earlier he had managed only eighty. He approached the Tour feeling better than in either of the two previous editions, which he had won. As the race neared, Greg told Kathy, with uncharacteristic hubris, "I'm going to win the Tour breathing through my nose."[3] His extended family journeyed to France en masse to watch him—enough LeMonds and Morrises to fill ten hotel rooms in every host town.

The Greg LeMond of 1991 was widely viewed as the strongest man in the peloton, at least in the context of the Tour. Yet, oddly enough, Greg was no longer regarded as master of any single discipline in cycling. A week before the start of the 1991 contest, Greg turned thirty, an age that professional cyclists generally acknowledged was the beginning of the end. The average Tour victor was twenty-eight, and few winners were past thirty. Greg hadn't won a single Tour stage since 1989—not in a time trial, not in the mountains, and certainly not in a sprint.

"Greg is not the best at anything, except winning the Tour," one team manager observed on the eve of the 1991 contest.[4] Others smelled blood.

"He's had a good run," said Claudio Chiappucci, the young Italian whom Greg had edged the previous summer. "It's someone else's turn."[5]

And then the Tour began, and at the end of the first stage Greg wore the *maillot jaune*. In the fashion typical of his late career, Greg slipped atop the leader board by finishing third in the five-kilometer opening prologue and placing well in a bunch sprint the next day, winning neither event but riding just well enough in each to secure the overall lead.

Greg lost the yellow jersey in the days of inconsequential racing that followed, but he remained at the head of a group of likely contenders. In the Tour's first real contest, a seventy-three-kilometer time trial on Stage 8, Greg reclaimed the race lead, finishing well ahead of all his rivals save one: Spanish cyclist Miguel Induráin, the Big Mig, powerful lieutenant to Pedro Delgado. The effort left Induráin in fourth place, suddenly a threat. Greg still worried about various other riders, including the Dutch time-trial specialist Erik Breukink, who now stood in second place, and Gianni Bugno, the young Italian in seventh. But he had beaten those men before. Oddly absent from his thoughts was Induráin, who had now bested Greg in four consecutive time-trial stages at the Tour. In fact, hardly anyone rated the Spaniard a serious challenger after his poor overall finishes in prior Tours.[6]

The rivalry with Breukink, who rode for PDM, would last exactly three more days. On July 16, as the Tour entered its eleventh stage, the Dutchman abruptly withdrew from the race—along with his nine-man team, the first such mass exodus in the history of the race. The entire squad had fallen ill. Team officials blamed food or drink. Yet all of the peloton ate more or less the same food, and no one else was sick. Hoteliers who had hosted the stricken riders howled in indignation.

His Dutch adversary swept aside, Greg now beheld a clear path to victory. But he still had to outflank the rest of the peloton, which suddenly seemed to be riding just a hair faster than it had ever ridden before.

Maurice Garin won the inaugural Tour de France in 1903 at an average speed of 25.7 kilometers per hour. In the decades that followed, the Tour gradually lifted its pace, to 30 kilometers per hour in the 1930s, and to 35 kilometers per hour by 1960. Laurent Fignon won his two Tours at average speeds of about 36 kilometers per hour. Greg won his first, in 1986, at 37 kilometers per hour.

By the time of Greg's return from injury, the peloton's pace had risen again. He won the 1989 Tour at an average speed of 37.5 kilometers per hour. In 1990, he logged an average hourly rate of 38.3 kilometers. Based purely on relative speeds, the Greg of 1990 would have easily beaten the Greg of 1986. Yet, the Greg of 1990 failed to win a single stage in that year's Tour, seizing ultimate victory seemingly by wits alone against rivals who often rode faster than he. In 1991, the peloton lifted its pace again, logging an average speed of 38.7 kilometers per hour. Greg was flying, but so were his rivals. And Greg was growing weary.

On the first mountain stage of the 1991 Tour, Greg found himself suddenly in trouble. Riding within a group that contained all the favorites, he ran out of water. At such moments, a teammate is typically dispatched back to the team car to collect supplies and deliver them forward. But no one else from Greg's Z team had managed to keep up, and Greg didn't dare risk dropping back to collect water for himself. So he rode on, pushing himself further into dehydration with every pedal stroke.

Greg finished the day with roughly the same time as all the other contenders, although he surrendered his *maillot jaune* to Frenchman Luc Leblanc, who had joined a bold breakaway. That night, Greg paid for his effort with fever and aches. And the next day would bring a brutal reckoning

The Tour's most difficult stage, on July 19, took the cyclists 232 kilometers across five mountain passes, including the *hors catégorie* Aubisque and Tourmalet. Half a kilometer from the top of the Tourmalet, the third climb of the day, Greg slipped off the back of a group containing several of his rivals. At the summit, he sat seventeen seconds behind them, and the other contenders sensed the race had reached its climactic moment.

Greg descended with abandon, flying down the mountainside to regain contact with the group. But when he reached it, Miguel Induráin was gone. The Spaniard had launched an attack on the descent. Though he still rode as Pedro Delgado's lieutenant, Induráin stood well ahead of his team leader in the standings, and on this day he would prove himself the stronger man. Cycling was, in the end, a Darwinian endeavor.

Greg pressed forward in desperate pursuit. He realized now that the Tour might be decided in the next few kilometers.[7] By the foot of the following climb, Induráin had built a one-minute lead. Greg could still see him up the road ahead. But as the race wound up the slope of the Col d'Aspin, the Spaniard powered forward and padded his lead with alarming ease. Greg rocked and swayed atop his bicycle, riding clumsily, as he always did when he climbed; but this time, his efforts bore no fruit. He could not keep up.

Induráin, now minutes ahead of the American, pedaled with a smooth and seemingly effortless rhythm, as if he were out on a weekend ride. Claudio Chiappucci, the Italian who had mocked Greg at the race's start, broke away from the others and flew up to join the Spaniard.

Television commentators and their cameras found Greg midway up the Aspin and assumed they were watching the men in front. Soon they realized they were not. "And this is not the leading group," broadcaster Phil Liggett gasped, watching as three lesser riders swept around Greg, passing him so quickly that it appeared Greg was standing still.[8] A short distance later, as Greg wobbled violently on his bicycle in search of elusive momentum, his rear wheel clipped the front bumper of a team car, and Greg fell pathetically to the pavement. He scampered onto his bicycle and accelerated back to the group, which had gone on without him.

Greg labored in palpable agony, falling behind all of his peers, until finally he rode alone, sapped of energy and pedaling listlessly forward. At twenty kilometers to go, he was joined by a teammate, dispatched by Greg's manager to limit his losses; there was now no question of erasing them. The two Z cyclists rode the final kilometers together, the teammate slowing to a pace that his depleted leader could sustain to the finish.

Greg limped across the line more than seven minutes behind Induráin, who now led the Tour. "He was stronger than me," Greg conceded at day's end.[9] And then it dawned on the cycling press that the Spaniard might be unbeatable. He was already the strongest man in the time trials, and now he had proven strongest in the mountains, the arena where he had faltered before. There was nothing more to prove.

Greg now sat in fifth place in the Tour. He trailed Induráin by more than five minutes, a gap that suddenly looked insurmountable. Swirling rumors suggested that Greg was ill, that he was not sleeping, that his feet had swelled, that he was about to drop out of the race. Greg slipped into near-seclusion, dodging reporters and pleading for privacy. The curious were directed to a 900 number—surely a first for the Tour—to pay $1 a minute for prerecorded observations on Greg's progress.[10]

American journalists, flown to France to record Greg's historic fourth Tour victory, did their best to preserve a facade of suspense, reminding readers that Greg had trailed by even more time in 1990 and had rallied to win. Three days later, as the Tour reached the Alps, Greg rewarded their faith. Seemingly recovered, he launched a solo attack near the end of a hilly stage in hundred degree heat, finishing in second place and gaining nearly half a minute on the riders ahead of him in the standings. But his momentum was fleeting. The next day, Induráin struck back, attacking on the slope of l'Alpe d'Huez and adding two more minutes to his lead. Greg could not respond. He now trailed Induráin by more than six minutes.

"I can't win this race," Greg conceded to a reporter in his hotel room that night. "Induráin's too strong."[11]

Further indignity would follow. On the final mountain stage, Greg limped to the finish in fifty-ninth place, nearly eight minutes behind the leaders, pedaling "with a curious, wide-eyed, vacant gaze on his face," as one observer recalled.[12] He fell to eighth place in the standings, fourteen minutes behind Induráin. Never had he looked so vulnerable.

"I've learned how to accept defeat," Greg told a reporter. "That has been my best accomplishment this year."[13]

In the closing days of the Tour, Greg recovered some of his old spark. And on the final day of racing, Greg offered a parting gift to Paris racing fans: a solo breakaway onto the Champs-Élysées, where he transformed the customary champagne-and-pictures victory lap into a mad dash around the grand boulevard. He held off the peloton for thirty kilometers, to the shrieking delight of spectators, who hadn't seen *l'Américain* ride with such abandon since the last time he rode into Paris alone, on the final day of the 1989 Tour. Such was the respect still afforded him by the peloton that Induráin's entire Banesto team assembled in time-trial formation at the front of the pack to chase Greg down. The French sports paper *L'Équipe* dubbed him *Père Courage*: Father Courage.

Greg finished the Tour in seventh place, thirteen minutes behind Induráin, the winner; Gianni Bugno placed second, Claudio Chiappucci third. In the five prior Tours Greg had entered, he had never finished lower than third. "Seventh, third or second," he sighed, "I don't know that it makes much difference."[14]

For as long as anyone could remember, Greg had treated every other race as a training ride for the Tour. Now, having lost the Tour, his priorities seemed to shift.

In the previous year, Greg and Kathy had retreated from the shores of Lake Minnetonka to a remote, forested forty-acre compound in horse country to the north, the better to raise their family in peace. Their million-dollar, neo-Georgian mansion encompassed nearly twelve thousand square feet, space now filled with Russian Impressionist oil paintings, antique Scandinavian furniture, century-old Persian rugs, and a Pac-Man game; Greg had become an avid collector of antiquities. A Mercedes sat in one heated garage, a motor home in another. To complete the cordon of protection, Greg sometimes screened incoming telephone calls by answering them in a high-pitched, faux-British accent. He and Kathy savored their time together with their family.

It was emblematic of his diminished career hopes that Greg entered the Tour DuPont in spring 1992 riding to win. The DuPont chemical conglomerate now lent its name to the premier American stage race, having supplanted Donald Trump as its sponsor. In years past, Greg would have treated the DuPont as a low-stakes warm-up for the Tour. He was five pounds overweight, with a touch of gray at the temples to counterbalance the glow of eternal youth that suffused his face. On May 7, in Delaware, Greg won the brief, three-mile prologue. It was his first victory in a stage of any bicycle race in three years.

By the final day of racing, Greg led the DuPont by thirteen hundredths of a second, the closest battle anyone could remember—closer even than the great Tour de France showdown of three years earlier. Greg won the race in a dramatic time-trial ride through Washington,

D.C., his celebrity drawing one hundred thousand spectators out to the streets. Perhaps the crowds sensed they would get few more chances to see the great champion ride to victory. In fact, Greg would never win a professional bicycle race again.

Apart from that laurel, Greg's 1992 cycling season unfolded in now-familiar fashion. He finished fifty-eighth in the weeklong Tour Méditer-ranéen in February and eighty-first at Paris–Nice in March but improved to eleventh at the eight-day Critérium du Dauphiné Libéré in June and to fourth at the Tour de Suisse.

Greg turned 31 just before the start of the 1992 Tour. Of all the Tour winners in the three prior decades, only one had been older. After his struggles of the prior year, he entered the Tour in the comfortable position of dark horse, the same role he'd played in the run-up to the 1989 race. Then Greg was a mid-career cyclist staging an unprecedented comeback. Now he was a journeyman, clearly fit but oddly diminished.

"I think that, after Hinault, I am still the best Tour de France rider of this generation," Greg said at the start of the 1992 race. "But this year, I have to admit I'm toward the end of my career."[15]

If the future belonged to anyone, it was Induráin. After conquering the 1991 Tour with surprising ease, the Spaniard had swept to victory with equal facility in the 1992 Giro d'Italia. He had dominated the peloton for less than a year—yet he had already established a formula that suggested many victories to come. A world class time trialist who had learned to climb, Induráin would contain his rivals in the mountains and obliterate them in the race against the clock. That was how Jacques Anquetil had won the Tour—and Anquetil, nicknamed *Monsieur Chrono*, had won five.

Even before the 1992 Tour began, Greg's three-year sponsor, clothier Roger Zannier, announced that he would not renew Greg's $5.7 million contract when it lapsed at year's end. Greg was no longer worth the money. The American arrived at the Tour already complaining of exhaustion, the malady that would define the final act of his career. A one-day journey from Greg's seasonal home in Belgium to the Tour's start in northeastern Spain had somehow stretched to two days, his progress impeded by a wave of labor strikes.

The opening prologue went to Induráin. Greg finished a meager fifteenth, a result that presaged an easy repeat victory for the Spaniard. Sensing his own vulnerability, Greg attacked wherever he could. On the sixth stage, a rough-and-tumble journey across steep hills and cobblestones in the rain, Greg powered a four-man breakaway that threatened to turn the Tour on its ear. Joined by erstwhile rival Chiappucci and two other strong riders, Greg escaped in the final twenty kilometers of the course, a move so daring, given the rain, that the peloton balked. Greg threw Induráin on the defensive, finishing more than a minute ahead of the Spaniard and lifting himself into contention.

The 1992 Tour would visit seven different nations—starting in Spain and proceeding through France, Belgium, the Netherlands, Germany, Luxembourg, and Italy—and largely skirt the legendary mountain peaks. It was a design that left Induráin two clear opportunities to claim the lead: a pair of lengthy time trials. The first arrived in Stage 9.

Induráin started the sixty-five-kilometer stage sitting in twelfth place in the standings; Greg was tenth, Laurent fifteenth, and the *maillot jaune* sat on the shoulders of a little-known Frenchman, Pascal Lino. By the twenty-third kilometer of his time-trial ride, the Spaniard held the fastest time of the day by a margin of more than a minute. At the midpoint, he led by nearly two minutes. Near the end of the course, he caught and passed Laurent Fignon, who had started six minutes before him. The Parisian had thought he was riding well; he was stunned. That night, as he enjoyed a massage from Alain Gallopin, Laurent announced, "My career is finished."[16]

No one in the peloton could remember such a dominating ride. Induráin had finished the time trial in just under eighty minutes, a full three minutes faster than the second-place rider, a teammate on his Banesto squad. Greg had finished four minutes behind Induráin. Like Laurent, Greg had thought he was riding well.

However badly the new decade was unfolding for Greg, it was going worse for Laurent.

Unlike Greg, Laurent had entered the 1991 and 1992 cycling seasons without false hope. While Greg labored to convince himself he was the same athlete who had won the Tour three times, Laurent pedaled forward with new humility, convinced, he recalled, "that I was no longer the cyclist I had been in 1983, and that it was now time to stop kidding myself."[17]

While Greg had not yet seriously mulled a life beyond cycling, Laurent's potential future already lay within his grasp. He was co-owner of his cycling team, Castorama, along with Cyrille Guimard. As the 1991 season dawned, Laurent told Guimard he envisioned easing out of the role of team leader and into that of manager.

There was just one problem: the team already had a manager, and Guimard was not keen to share his power. And thus was sown the seed that would poison a decade-long friendship. Guimard promptly undermined Laurent's authority among the Castorama cyclists by favoring another cyclist, Luc Leblanc, recently hired as co-leader. Now Laurent would see how he liked sharing his own power.

As the season progressed, Guimard began to implement race strategy without telling Laurent, leaving him out of the loop—something he had never done before. One night, in the race hotel, the simmering feud exploded into a cursing fight. "For the first time in our life together," Laurent recalled, "we didn't like each other."[18]

The next month, at the brutal Paris–Roubaix contest, Guimard ordered Laurent to ride at the head of the pack, not for any strategic reason but simply to put a Castorama jersey in front of the television cameras. Another violent argument ensued; the two partners stopped speaking.

Laurent's relationship with his coach hit the shoals at a delicate moment in his marriage: His relationship with Nathalie was "a furnace of tension," an atmosphere that rivaled his workplace rapport with Guimard. "My whole environment seemed to be falling apart," Laurent recalled in his memoir.[19]

The nadir arrived a short time later. Guimard demanded that Laurent withdraw from the 1991 Tour, on the pretext that the cyclist was disrupting team unity. Laurent refused, and he told the team's sponsor that he would have no further dealings with Guimard.

Laurent finished the 1991 Tour in sixth place, just ahead of Greg. He arrived in Paris in the same state of bewilderment as the American, "because, paradoxically, I didn't feel short of form or mentally out of the race." Like Greg, Laurent was riding well—yet everyone else seemed to be riding better.[20]

For the coming season, Laurent would need a new team. He sat back for a time and waited for the phone to ring, assuming that his name and record would attract a flood of offers. But none came. One morning, he resolved to quit cycling. Then he changed his mind and began calling teams himself. He finally settled on an Italian squad sponsored by Gatorade, the sports drink company. Laurent's annual salary would slip from $900,000 to $650,000, and he would no longer ride as team leader. Instead, he would pedal in support of Gianni Bugno, winner of the 1990 Giro and runner-up in the 1991 Tour. His new team's green jersey gave Laurent the look of a rolling Gatorade bottle.

In the 1992 cycling season, the great battles would be waged between Induráin, Bugno, Chiappucci, and one or two others. Yet for Laurent, the enemy was Greg. The two cyclists shared a competitive impulse that set them apart.

Laurent drew strength from rivalry. In 1984, his rival was Bernard Hinault. In 1989 and beyond, it was Greg. One had only to read Laurent's caustic quotes in the press to discern how narrowly he viewed the Tour. For him, it was a contest between two men. Discussing the rivalry in 1992, Laurent observed, "Revenge would be only in the Tour de France, because that's the race I lost to him."[21] Greg, by contrast, raced against himself, against his demons, against the course—but not against other cyclists. Men such as Fignon and Hinault and Chiappucci would enter his thoughts, even dominate them, when they threatened his place in the standings, but they were ephemeral adversaries. The rivalry never lasted beyond the race itself.

Thus, as Laurent recovered from the shame of being caught and passed by Induráin in that revelatory time trial on the ninth stage of the 1992 Tour de France, his thoughts dwelt not on catching the Spaniard but on punishing the American.

Induráin's performance had lifted him into second place in the Tour, three minutes ahead of Bugno, Laurent's captain; it might as well have been three hours, given the Italian's hopes of ever regaining the time.

Yet Laurent approached his teammates two days later and proposed a bold attack in the mountains. Laurent argued that the team might yet secure a podium place for Bugno, who sat now in sixth place and still stood a good chance to finish second or third behind Induráin. But Laurent's real target was Greg, the man in fifth place, just ahead of Bugno and three minutes behind Induráin.

Laurent's teammates did not share his passion for breaking Greg LeMond. When the stage began, they hung back; Laurent was livid. He pressed on alone, riding what amounted to a hundred-kilometer time trial across the Vosges mountain range, pedaling against the entire peloton. Summoning a vestige of his legendary power, he held on till the finish, sweeping across the line twelve seconds ahead of his nearest pursuer.

This was Laurent's finest performance since the 1989 Tour, and his ninth career stage win in the great race—more than any other cyclist of his generation. Ironically, Laurent's exploits did little to impede Greg, who actually moved up from fifth place to fourth in the chaos Laurent had wrought.

Though Laurent had been unable to break Greg, the peloton soon would. The 1992 Tour would be the fastest on record, the eventual winner posting an average speed of 39.5 kilometers per hour, a pace Greg could not sustain. By the time the contest reached a string of three consecutive mountain stages that was generally regarded as the most demanding stretch in the race, Greg announced that he was spent.

"I don't understand what's happening," he told a reporter. "I'm exhausted. It's incredible; I feel I've drained all my reserves after a week."[22]

On the second of the three torturous stages, Greg finished fifty minutes after the leaders—not just beaten but utterly humiliated, falling so far behind that he was almost disqualified from the race. Greg arrived so late that spectators were filing past him down the mountainside to their cars and hotels as he approached the line. Dismounting his bicycle, Greg was surrounded by reporters. He found energy he had previously lacked and raced toward his hotel room, with the reporters in tow. They caught him at the elevators.

"Once you're bad, you're bad," he offered. "I've never felt this bad in the Tour. That's all I can say."[23]

Greg was now so far out of contention that there was no question of victory, nor even a top-ten finish. Would Greg abandon the race?

"This is the Tour de France," he replied. "I will never drop out of the Tour."[24]

The next day, on a 186-kilometer stage through the mountains, Greg limped up the first of three brutal climbs, the Col du Galibier. At the top, he already lagged half an hour behind the leaders. He stopped at a food station, climbed off his bicycle, and abandoned the race.

"My legs are gone," he said.[25] The next day's editions of *L'Équipe* called him *Monsieur Tout-LeMond*: Mr. Average.[26]

Greg returned to Minnesota to ponder what had gone wrong. Blood tests revealed nothing. He wondered whether he had trained too hard or entered too many races. Deep inside, though, Greg knew better. He was still performing near his peak. There was nothing fundamentally wrong with him—not in the 1992 Tour, nor in 1991. He had shown flashes of brilliance in both races. He had flown through the time trials. In the previous decade, Greg's regular pace had been fast enough to win. Now other men were riding faster.

A month after the Tour, an interviewer asked Greg what to make of Induráin, the fastest cyclist of them all. Induráin had won the 1992 Tour by a comfortable margin of four minutes and thirty-five seconds over Italian rival Chiappucci. (Laurent, after his mountaintop heroics, had faded to twenty-third place.) In his final time trial, Induráin had averaged 52.35 kilometers an hour over a course of sixty-four kilometers. Since the advent of the Tour, no cyclist had covered a time trial of that length at such speed.

Greg, too, had broken records with his victorious time trial at the 1989 Tour. But Greg was a phenomenon, a man who had threatened to win the Tour the first time he entered it. And Induráin? *Miguelón* had dropped out of the first two Tours he entered. On the third try, he had finished among the water carriers in ninety-seventh place. In three subsequent tries, he hadn't managed to place higher than tenth. Now, the Big Mig looked unbeatable. How could Greg, or anyone, explain the transformation?

"I haven't seen anything like it in the history of cycling," Greg replied. "[But] you see new things in sports all the time."[27]

Two years earlier, in February 1990, Kathy LeMond had been awakened one night by a telephone call. As she reached for the receiver, she felt panic course through her body. Midnight telephone calls seldom brought good news. She answered the phone. The caller was alternately screaming and crying. Kathy yelled at Greg to wake him. It gradually dawned on her whose voice it was: Annalisa Draaijer, wife of Johannes Draaijer, an old teammate of Greg's from PDM.

"He's dead," she cried. "He is cold. He is cold. I am so afraid. Oh my God. Oh my God."[28]

Annalisa had awakened in their apartment in the Netherlands to find that her husband's heart had stopped. She had attempted CPR, but she could not revive him. She had summoned an ambulance. Kathy stayed on the phone with her until it arrived.

Draaijer had been the second Dutch cyclist to die an untimely death in a span of six months. The first, Bert Oosterbosch, had suffered a fatal heart attack at thirty-two. Now, Draaijer had died at twenty-six of a heart blockage. Professional cyclists did not simply drop dead. Whispers soon spread through the peloton that both men had perished after experimenting with a new and potentially revolutionary drug called EPO.

Erythropoietin is a natural hormone secreted by the kidneys to regulate production of red blood cells, the vessels that deliver oxygen to the body. A synthetic form, recombinant erythropoietin, appeared in the mid-1980s. It was a breakthrough in the treatment of anemia, a malady brought on by a deficit of red blood cells.

By the close of the decade, the cycling community had begun to eye EPO as a potential wonder drug. Throughout the 1980s, cyclists had experimented with blood doping—injecting blood before big races to boost their red blood cell count. Blood doping was a dangerous and complex procedure that involved the drawing, storage, and reinfusion of the cyclist's own blood. By comparison, EPO looked safe. For cyclists, it mimicked the effects of altitude training, an age-old regimen of riding in mountainous, oxygen-thin settings to encourage the body to produce red blood cells. More red blood cells meant more oxygen. More oxygen meant a cyclist could ride farther at peak exertion, suffer less, and recover more quickly. In a three-week, ultra-endurance contest such as the Tour de France, a cyclist who took EPO could sustain a level of energy and endurance well beyond what the body could support on its own.

Professional cycling had never seen such a drug. Yet EPO was dangerous. As the drug produced more red blood cells, the blood thickened, and sometimes it clotted. By the early 1990s, riders had weighed the advantages of EPO against its perils, and some teams began to seek out doctors who could help them minimize the risks. Between 1991 and 1994, EPO gradually suffused the peloton.

From the first Tour de France in 1903 through Greg's triumphal performances in 1989 and 1990, doping had been endemic, and many Tours had been won by men who had taken drugs. Yet, in none of those victories had dope itself been deemed the decisive factor.

"Back then, there was no drug, whatever it might have been, that could turn a donkey into a thoroughbred," Laurent recalled. "Never. From [Italian legend Fausto] Coppi to Hinault, passing through the eras of Anquetil and Merckx, there was no magic that could dose up lesser riders to compete on equal terms with the greats. Exceptional human beings, like their extraordinary exploits, were authentic."[29]

Cyclists quickly recognized that EPO could boost their oxygen capacity—and thus, their performance—by perhaps 10 percent. Armed with that advantage, a cyclist who took EPO could nearly always beat a rival who was clean. An average cyclist could metamorphose into a champion.

Laurent had heard rumors about cycling's new drug, and about its casualties. The peloton buzzed with speculation that EPO had somehow figured in the shocking withdrawal of the entire PDM team from the 1991 Tour. In time, Laurent began to see EPO all around him. He noticed "guys I barely knew coming more often to the head of the pack and setting a crazy pace, way beyond what you would expect." Peers from other teams "improved without training any more than before, sometimes while doing less. It was blatant. I wasn't fooled."[30]

So thick was the veil of secrecy around "preparation" in professional cycling that Laurent never really spoke with anyone about EPO until the close of the 1992 season, when a teammate approached him with an offer.

"Laurent," he said, "you know that there is a super preparation product out there at present; perhaps we could have a look and see what we can do with you."[31]

Laurent politely declined. Blood doping was illegal—not that it mattered, because regulators had no way to test for EPO. Laurent knew the risks, and as a cyclist in the autumn of his career, he didn't see the point.

Kathy's midnight telephone call from Annalisa Draaijer at the start of the 1990 season had provided Greg's introduction to EPO. Johannes had gone to bed that night complaining of lethargy and had died in his sleep. The next day, a PDM team official had instructed the widow to "gather every vial and pill you can find and put them in a bag."[32] Annalisa later told the German magazine *Der Spiegel* that her husband had taken EPO.[33] His death provided a powerful cautionary tale for Greg, who would remember the midnight call for years to come.

At a few pivotal moments in his career, Greg had taken a public stance against doping—a position few of his colleagues would dare to adopt. He had chastised French cyclist Pascal Simon for allegedly doping to victory at the 1983 Dauphiné Libéré. He had called out his old PDM team a year after leaving it, telling a journalist in 1909 that its leaders had pressured him to dope. His comments violated the omertà—code of silence—that concealed doping. PDM officials had brushed off Greg's accusations with mafioso swagger. "He should watch what he says," a team spokesman had warned.[34]

The decision not to use EPO was perhaps simpler for Greg than for Laurent. Laurent had at least dabbled in dope during his career; Greg had not. In Greg's adolescence, cycling had delivered him from the psychic pain of sexual abuse. Now, as an adult, Greg clung to cycling in much the same way he clung to Kathy. Both represented something pure in Greg's tainted life. Greg's cycling feats informed his identity. Greg was a champion, an honest champion. He had won his races fair and square, not by cheating, and certainly not by doping. The pride he drew from victory offset some of the guilt he bore as a survivor of abuse. Greg never doped—in part because the shame of a failed drug test was something his wounded psyche might not endure.[35]

Through the formative years of Greg's cycling career, Bob LeMond had served as the consummate sports dad. He trained with his son, drove him to races, even raced alongside him, all while investing generously in the best equipment and providing handsomely for Greg and the rest of his family. When Greg's career took off, Bob evolved into the sport's most assertive manager, single-handedly transforming the cycling profession by demanding that Greg be paid a salary to match the top earners in professional sports back home. French cycling executives howled at Bob's bare-knuckle tactics, skills he had honed in building his real-estate business. But Bob got results, and Greg got Tour de France victories.

Bob had built his own career, and Greg's, on a foundation of hard work and boundless self-assurance. The latter trait, perhaps Bob's greatest strength, would seed disaster at LeMond Enterprises. Bob's abundant confidence had made Greg a millionaire; yet, on occasion, Bob would overplay his hand.

When Bob's methods worked, they often yielded deals that were lucrative but fleeting. "The list is long," *Bicycling* magazine observed in 1993. "Remember Greg's Taco Bell TV commercials? His cycling brochure inside Chex cereal boxes? The ads for almonds, gym equipment, duffel bags? Then there were the cycling products: Huffy bikes, Brancale shoes, Time pedals, Carnac shoes, Avocet cycle-computers, Oakley sunglasses, Puma clothing, Scott handlebars, Look shoes. . . ."[36] All had come and gone. Greg's decline as a cyclist was one reason; his father's management style was another.

"There isn't a person in this business they haven't crossed," said Michael Aisner, the former head of the Coors Classic stage race.[37] Yet Aisner and other critics acknowledged that Bob did it all for his son.

After the painful reorganization of Team LeMond in 1987, the LeMonds had continued to dabble in bicycle design. Greg's multimillion-dollar contract with the Z cycling team, negotiated largely by Bob, propped up the family business by putting the team on LeMond bicycles.

At the close of the 1980s, professional cyclists were exploring alternatives to the traditional steel frame. Frames built of aluminum or titanium were often lighter than the five-pound steel triangles that had supported the bodies of Anquetil and Merckx. But aluminum frames, stiff and unresponsive, made for a jarring ride, while titanium frames felt a bit *too* flexible.

By the 1991 season, Greg and his Z team were experimenting with titanium frames and with another, truly radical material, carbon fiber. Carbon fibers suspended in pliable epoxy resin could yield a frame lighter than any made of metal. Greg favored carbon frames, but the rest of his team did not. Carbon bicycles of that era had a significant flaw: joints were connected with aluminum lugs. Aluminum and carbon were incompatible, and the bikes were prone to break. Bicycle makers hadn't yet discovered a way to fashion reliable lugs of compatible carbon.

In the winter of 1991, Greg learned of a bicycle craftsman in San Francisco who seemed to have solved that problem. Craig Calfee, a former bicycle messenger, had found a way to use carbon, rather than aluminum, to join the pieces of his carbon frames. He manipulated the fibers until he had a frame that delivered the same ride as the finest steel. The finished product weighed three pounds.

One day in early 1991, a Frenchman entered Craig's shop. His name was Jean-Pierre Pascal. When he beheld Craig's carbon frames, Jean-Pierre exclaimed, "You need to send one of these bikes to Bob LeMond."[38] Jean-Pierre told Craig he ran an American outpost of a European pedal manufacturer, and he said Greg was a client. Craig didn't believe him. But then a fax arrived from Greg, sketching out the dimensions of a bicycle frame. Craig built the frame in four days. He sent it to Bob. Bob sent it to Europe, where Greg tested it. Greg telephoned Craig and asked how quickly he could build eighteen more.

In a cinematic moment, Craig flew to France and met with Greg atop the Col d'Èze. Greg had just tested one of Craig's carbon-fiber frames on the final stage of the Paris–Nice race. He arrived at the summit

wearing a broad grin; the bicycle had performed beautifully. Now Greg
wanted to test the frame on a descent. Carbon bikes tended to wobble
at speed, not a desirable trait. Craig pictured the frame cracking and
depositing Greg's broken body on the mountainside.

The frame held. From the bottom of the *col*, Greg pedaled up to
Craig and shook his hand. "Craig," he said, "this is the most amazing
bike I've ever ridden."[39]

Bob paid Craig $25,000 for custom molds and set up Greg LeMond
Bicycles near his business office in Reno. He imported Pat Blades, Greg's
brother-in-law, to run the factory. Greg's mother kept the books. Jean-
Pierre Pascal handled sales.

Friends in the cycling community had warned Craig that to deal with
Bob LeMond was to engage in a war of attrition. Greg's father would
encourage endless rounds of negotiations, racking up legal fees on both
sides. Then, once Bob sensed the other party was worn down, he would
change the terms of the deal.

Bob had offered Craig a $24,000 licensing fee for his frame design
and 5 percent of each frame sold. The lawyers negotiated for months.
Then, shortly before the contract was to be signed, Bob telephoned
Craig, who recounted the following conversation:

"I've been talking to my investors," Bob told Craig, "and they don't
want to do the $24,000."

"Oh, that's funny," Craig replied. "I was going to call you this morning and tell you it's going to be $25,000, because I just got a bill from
my lawyer."

"But . . . I'm saying it's zero," Bob said.

"And I'm saying it's actually a thousand bucks more than before. Or
Greg will have to find somebody else's carbon bikes to ride."[40]

Bob was stunned. The former bicycle messenger had outflanked him.
He relented.

In late 1991, a Japanese investor pledged $3 million to the new busi-
ness. A year later, nearly one million dollars had been spent, and Greg
LeMond Bicycles had produced roughly 250 bicycles, well short of
the thousands the team had envisioned. Even more troubling, the
frames that did roll off the line developed an alarming defect: parts

were falling off. Craig had cautioned the LeMonds that a glue used to hold gear-shift levers and water bottles in place "wasn't 100 percent," but they hadn't acted on his warning. Customers began to return the bikes.

Craig sensed Greg's father was in over his head. "Bob was trying to manage a business that he had little experience managing," he recalled.[41] Pat Blades, the man who had shot Greg five years earlier, had no background in either carbon fiber or bicycle design. Yet now he ran a carbon-fiber bicycle factory. Craig was retained as a consultant but rarely consulted.

Jean-Pierre Pascal struggled to find common ground with Greg's father and brother-in-law. Finally, Jean-Pierre telephoned Greg. He told him that the company was in debt, and that his father was largely to blame. He warned Greg that the Japanese money would never arrive. He accused Bob of squandering company funds. "Greg, your dad is not being straight with you," he said.[42]

And so, three days before Thanksgiving in 1992, Greg traveled to Reno to fire his father. In the end, he didn't have to. In the middle of the meeting Greg had called with a family attorney, Bob stood up and said, "I quit. I'll see you," and walked out the door.[43]

Greg and Kathy quickly concluded Bob had not mishandled company funds. Yet his father was deeply hurt by the accusation. Bob maintained his son hadn't given him enough money to run the business. Greg had assigned Bob an initial budget of only $200,000, Bob recalled; "I couldn't do it with that."[44]

Greg LeMond Bicycles was quietly shut down. The remnants of the company were eventually sold to the established bicycle maker Trek. Craig and Jean-Pierre moved on. When the dust had settled, Greg and Bob were no longer speaking.

Bob had effectively shuttered his real-estate business in 1987 to run his son's cycling career full-time. Now he exited Team LeMond and resumed selling real estate. Bertha sided with her husband; she was angrier than Bob at the way Greg had treated him. Kathy sided with her husband. Greg and Bob, the men at the center of the feud, would not talk for four years.

For Greg, the silence was agony. "I wanted my dad to know that I loved him," he recalled, years later, his voice breaking with emotion. "I just wanted him as my dad."[45]

The ugliness of that winter left Greg unprepared, again, for the start of a new cycling season. Greg returned to Europe in February 1993, riding for the same team but under a new sponsor, the French insurer GAN. His new contract would pay $1.3 million over two years, less than half his previous salary. Given his diminished currency, Greg grudgingly accepted the terms.

Greg retreated to Belgium in March for a month of training rides behind Otto Jácome's Vespa. Soon he was again hitting eighty kilometers per hour. "And that was as good as he's ever done," Otto apprised a visiting journalist.[46] But then Greg fell into a familiar pattern: entering races and abandoning them. He withdrew from the Paris–Roubaix cobblestone classic in April and the Route du Sud stage race in June.

EPO was now an unavoidable topic. The riders of Greg's GAN team sought a meeting with their coach, Roger Legeay. The subject was doping, although that word was never uttered. Someone from a rival team had shared vital intel with one of Greg's teammates, pulling back the curtain on the regimen of "preparation" that now fueled the peloton. Team doctors were mixing a cocktail of EPO, testosterone, and human growth hormone to effectively erase the cumulative toll of a three-week bicycle race. Without artificial aids, most cyclists suffered a steady drain of testosterone and red blood cells over the course of a Grand Tour; by mid-race, their powers of endurance and recuperation might be reduced by half. A modern doping program could restore the cyclist to the peak of his powers—and beyond.

"You guys have no chance," the rival had told Greg's teammate.[47]

The teammate, Frenchman Philippe Casado, confronted Legeay. "This is what's going on," he told his coach, according to Greg. "Either you provide the same, or you lay off." Casado felt it unfair of Legeay to demand performance from his riders while they pedaled at a disadvantage.[48] Legeay refused. The GAN team raced clean, like other French teams. The French cycling establishment saw itself as the standard-bearer for *la vie claire*. By decade's end, that stance would exact a grievous cost in lost victories and unfulfilled promise.

Casado left the team for another. Two winters later, just shy of his thirty-first birthday, he dropped dead on a rugby field.[49]

Greg chose to remain on the GAN team, convinced he could race clean and compete. And he did—for a time. Then Greg entered the three-week Giro d'Italia, where he was afflicted with another spell of chronic fatigue, plus a nasty bout of hay fever.

No matter how hard Greg trained, no matter how fast he pedaled, he could no longer keep pace with the peloton. There seemed no point in entering the Tour. Greg withdrew from the race roster, citing a depressed immune system. He returned to Minnesota for more tests.

Greg had just turned thirty-two. Even his most optimistic fans now assumed his best years lay behind him. Greg remained convinced the problem was not age. Yet, for the first time in his career, he began to lower his expectations. Perhaps his future lay not in Grand Tours but in single-day contests. Greg began to speak buoyantly of his prospects in the Olympic bicycle road race, scheduled for Atlanta in the summer of 1996, when Greg would be thirty-five.

Still seeking a medical explanation for his maladies, Greg consulted with one doctor after another. Finally he saw a sports doctor who was well acquainted with the peloton.

"Greg, there's nothing wrong with you," the doctor said, according to Greg. He gave Greg the name of a prominent European colleague, a name synonymous with doping. "You need to contact him," the doctor explained, "because if you're not on EPO, you don't have a chance."[50]

By the time he entered the 1993 Tour, Laurent Fignon had long since abandoned hope of victory. Yet, like Greg, Laurent now found himself struggling simply to keep up. The humiliation began with the seven-kilometer opening prologue, in which the Parisian finished sixty-seventh, forty-three seconds behind the Tour's reigning Superman, Miguel Induráin, who would ride on to his third consecutive Tour victory in Paris.

Induráin wasn't the only one riding at a fever pace. The entire peloton pedaled faster than ever. Stage 6 of this Tour would go down as the fastest single road stage in race history, completed at an average speed of 49.4 kilometers per hour. Perhaps it was that ride Laurent recounted, years later, in his memoir:

"One day, when the peloton was a very long way from the finish and an early break of no importance had escaped, the whole group suddenly accelerated. In a few minutes, the whole peloton was riding at 50 kph in single file." Curiosity drew him to the front, where he found a French *domestique* leading the chase. "He looked as if he was barely trying," Laurent recalled, "but he was riding at more than 50 kph on his own, his hands on the top of the bars in a three-quarters headwind."

Laurent asked, "Do you know how fast you're going?"

The other rider just shrugged. "Pah. They said to ride, so I'm riding."

The next stage unfolded at the same insane speed, and the next. To Laurent, "Nothing seemed 'normal' anymore."[51]

The final blow fell in the Alps. On Stage 10, a day of three epic climbs, Laurent launched an attack. He sat low in the standings, so he posed no threat, and no one chased. Laurent thought he might cap his career with one more glorious victory.

Laurent was climbing with much of his former power. And then he looked back and beheld an alarming sight: "I saw a vast group of riders come up to me. There were at least thirty. Or forty. Not one of them seemed to be pushing it." Some were Laurent's peers, men he had beaten with ease a decade earlier. Yet the pack glided effortlessly past him. Laurent could not keep up. "[This] was something that went beyond mere humiliation. It was a death blow."[52]

The next day, Laurent mounted his bicycle and rode up the Col de la Bonette, the highest pass in the Tour, in last place. Laurent rested his hands atop the handlebars and pedaled easily, breathing deeply as he savored his final moments in the Tour de France. He pressed gently on the pedals, took in the scenery, allowed his mind to wander back across the dozen years of his cycling career. "The col was all mine, and I didn't want anyone to intrude."[53]

When he reached the valley below, Laurent climbed off his bicycle.

* * *

In 1994, for the first time in his career, Greg entered the Tour de France with no illusion of victory. Roger Legeay, his *directeur sportif*, now openly referred to Greg as a super-*équipier*: a glorified *domestique*.

Before, Greg had struggled in the mountains; now he struggled on hills. He lost nine minutes in the first five stages of racing and dropped to 145th place. By Stage 6, from Cherbourg to the Bretagne capital of Rennes, Greg had had enough. After 183 kilometers, he pedaled to a stop. No team car materialized, so Greg climbed inside the "broom wagon," the van that trailed the peloton to pick up stray *domestiques* the race had left behind. He unpinned the number from his jersey. Greg, like Laurent, would never ride another Tour.

Greg returned to Minnesota and redoubled his efforts to identify the problem with his body. He still did not consider that his own under-achievement and the peloton's overachievement might be linked.

Tests revealed dramatic fluctuations in Greg's aerobic metabolism. Before the Tour, Greg's heart and lungs had generated prodigious quan-tities of oxygen. After the Tour, Greg's cardiopulmonary fitness was depleted to the level of a recreational cyclist. His capacity to consume oxygen for energy had plummeted in that span from six liters per min-ute to four. Greg could no longer recover from the exertions of profes-sional cycling.

To examine his cells up close, doctors ordered a muscle biopsy. Anesthesia might have tainted the results, so doctors strapped Greg down and sliced seven slivers of muscle from his thigh, carving him up, he said, "like sashimi."[54] Tests on those samples revealed the cause of Greg's lethargy: mitochondrial myopathy, a disease of the mito-chondria, the tiny cellular energy factories. Mitochondrial myopathies could trigger a range of symptoms, from muscle weakness to seizures and dementia. In Greg's case, the principal symptom appeared to be intolerance for exercise. The affliction would appear only when he pushed his body to its peak; at those moments, his mitochondria would shut down.

Mitochondrial myopathy generally struck the very young or the very ill. Greg was an elite athlete. What made him different? Doctors hypothesized a reason: lead poisoning. Among elite athletes, only Greg had three dozen shotgun pellets in his body.

"No one as healthy as Greg has had problems like this," pronounced Dr. Rochelle Taube, of Minneapolis. "He is a case study of one."[55]

The diagnosis fit the facts; yet, it ignored an inconvenient truth. Laurent, the one other cyclist of Greg's generation who might be termed an equal, had struggled just as much as Greg in the final years of his career. And Laurent was not sick.

Greg flew to Los Angeles and called a press conference. There, on December 3, flanked by Kathy and his doctors, Greg announced his retirement.

"Eighteen years ago, when I began racing, I never dreamed I'd be standing up here today," he said. "I've been amazed at the growth of this sport, and the coverage it's received. I'm proud of the role I've played, and I feel lucky.

"So, I'm not complaining about anything. And I'm still young. Old to be a bike rider, perhaps, but young for life."[56]

THE TEXAN

THE DAY AFTER Greg withdrew from his final Tour de France in 1994, the telephone rang at the LeMond home in Belgium. Kathy answered.

"Hi, this is Lance."

"Lance who?"

"Lance Armstrong."[1]

Lance Armstrong was a young cyclist on the Motorola team, a unit descended from the pioneering American 7-Eleven team and led by Greg's friend Andy Hampsten. Greg had met Lance, had raced with him, had followed his career, and had seen him touted as the next Greg LeMond.

Kathy probably assumed Lance was calling to pay his respects. He was not.

"I want to rent your house," he said.

Lance was little more than a rookie, and Greg was a legend. For Lance to telephone Greg at the twilight of his career to offer congratulation, even consolation, might have warmed the hearts of the weary LeMonds. For him to call with designs on their house was impetuous, if not insulting.

"What do you mean?" Kathy asked, trying to process the request.

"Well, Greg's cooked," Lance said bluntly, according to Kathy. "He's finished. I want to rent your house."

"Well, it's not for rent," Kathy said frostily, and the call was over.

Lance Edward Gunderson was born on September 18, 1971, in the suburbs of Dallas. His mother worked at Kentucky Fried Chicken. His father delivered newspapers. Lance was named for Lance Rentzel, a star of the Dallas Cowboys football team.

Like Bob LeMond, Linda Mooneyham had married young—on her seventeenth birthday. She dropped out of high school to have her baby. She tried to make things work with her son's biological father, but they split before Lance turned two. Linda swiftly remarried. Terry Keith Armstrong was a salesman at a meat company. A product of military school, Terry would discipline his adopted son with a wooden paddle from his college fraternity.

Terry Armstrong coached Lance's peewee football team as if his life depended on it. At bedtime, Terry would read Lance an old Vince Lombardi speech about what it took to be Number One. In time, Lance's competitive fire would burn brighter than his stepfather's.

Like Greg, Lance turned to individual sports. In Lance's case, the reason was that he could not stand it when his teammates failed. His first real passion was the triathlon, an event that showcased both endurance and versatility. At thirteen, Lance purchased his first road bike, a Mercier from France. He began to crisscross Texas, entering triathlons and frequently winning them. By fifteen, Lance was training several hours a day, logging a weekly quota of thirty miles on foot, six miles in the pool, and three hundred miles on his bicycle.

Lance rode in his first proper bicycle race in the summer of 1986, at age fourteen, entering a track event at an industrial park in Plano and easily winning it. By 1987, Lance had reached his full height of five feet ten inches and a weight of 150 pounds, and he began to challenge top adult triathletes. He was earning $1,000 a month, enough for Linda Armstrong to end her second marriage, which hadn't panned out much better than the first.

"In ten years, I will be the best," Lance apprised the *Dallas Morning News* at fifteen. Confidence was a strong suit.[2]

Lance would win consecutive national triathlon championships in 1989 and 1990, at ages eighteen and nineteen. But by the close of the decade, he had resolved to concentrate his considerable talents on cycling. Triathlons were generally decided in the final leg, the run, and that was Lance's weakest discipline.

In 1989, coaches of the American national cycling team invited Lance
to the tryouts in Colorado Springs, the same venue where Greg had so
impressed coach Eddie B. more than a decade earlier. Lance made the
team and traveled to Moscow that summer at seventeen for the junior
world championship road race, where he turned in an odd but inspiring
performance. Early in the race, Lance surged into the lead, outpacing
the world's best junior cyclists until the final kilometer, when he was
caught and passed.

Lance was no LeMond; at this stage in his own life, Greg had *won* the
junior world championship. Still, Eddie B. was intrigued. The coach met
with Lance and Linda Armstrong. Lance asked whether cycling might
yield the same bounty in fame and fortune as triathlons. Eddie told
Lance that Greg had achieved both. Lance left the meeting with a new
goal. He would be the next Greg LeMond.

At the start of the 1990 season, Lance joined Eddie's team, which
was sponsored by the Subaru motor company and by the San Francisco
investment firm Montgomery Securities. Lance would earn $12,000 a
year, the same salary allotted to Greg when he had joined Cyrille Guimard's Renault team a decade earlier.

Lance possessed the raw talent to become an elite athlete—if not, perhaps, a superstar. His VO_2 rating, scientific shorthand for an athlete's ability to consume oxygen, had been measured at 79.5, a figure that put him
roughly on par with Andy Hampsten, leader of the 7-Eleven cycling team.

Whatever Lance's limitations, he had yet to encounter them. Young
Lance, like young Greg, had won most of the athletic contests he had
entered, albeit on a provincial stage. Now, riding with the Subaru-
Montgomery team, Lance seemed to think he could outride everyone.
What's more, he appeared incapable of competing on a team unless he
was its leader. He resisted the role of *domestique*. Greg, for all his potential, had taken naturally to the role of helper, and his loyal service to
the likes of Fignon and Hinault was the stuff of cycling lore. But Lance
could not bring himself to serve; it was not in his DNA. Instead, he
would flout Eddie's instructions and take off alone. Most of the time, the
peloton would eventually overtake him. Once in a while, Lance would
hold on to win.

The Texan's performance at the 1990 amateur world championship road race, staged in Japan, perfectly illustrated both the best and
worst in him. Near the start of the race, Lance launched a solo escape.
He held off the peloton, but eventually a handful of cyclists bridged
the gap to join him. The breakaway endured to the finish. But by that
time Lance was exhausted, and ten other riders sprinted past him to
the line.

It was one of the best showings by any American at the international
level since Greg's ascent. But Lance had ridden the race without any of
Greg's savvy. Lance had no sense of tactics; if anything, his approach
mirrored that of a young Laurent Fignon, who knew only how to attack.
Lance's coaches came to regard him as the nation's best amateur cyclist.
Some began to eye him as the next LeMond, a title that had been
ascribed to a succession of young cyclists over the previous decade. It
was a kiss of death. One by one, these to-be heirs would falter and fade.
The next LeMond had yet to emerge, and the label made Lance uncomfortable, even if he privately nursed that very ambition.

"I'm not the next Greg LeMond," he told the *New York Times*. "I'm the
first me."[3]

In 1992, Lance jumped to the new Motorola team, the only American cycling organization with the pedigree to compete in Europe.
That August he entered his first professional bicycle race, the Clásica
de San Sebastián, a top-drawer, single-day summer contest held in
Spain. Here, finally, Lance discovered the limit of his native gifts. He
finished last. Now Lance understood that many in the professional
peloton pedaled faster than he, and that nearly everyone pedaled
smarter.

Lance returned to Austin, the hilly Texas capital that was now his
home, and rode five hundred miles a week to train for the 1993 season.
He had never worked so hard for anything.

The next summer, Lance finished second at the Tour DuPont, the
same prestigious American stage race Greg had conquered a year earlier. This feat alone proved Lance now had the form to challenge Andy
Hampsten for leadership of the Motorola team. He also commanded the

celebrity to dethrone Greg as the focal point of stateside cycling events. At some imperceptible point along the route of the twelve-day contest, one journalist observed, "the public changed sides."[4] Lance Armstrong was the new star of American cycling.

A victory at another high-profile race in Pittsburgh put Lance in contention for a million-dollar prize known as the Thrift Drug Triple Crown, offered to any cyclist who could sweep three consecutive contests in different states. Here Lance revealed a newfound sense of tactics—and a preternatural understanding of cycling culture. He had a team-mate approach the captain of a rival team with a proposition: if the two teams would work together to help Lance win the Triple Crown, Lance would pay the other team a share of his winnings.[5]

The rival team eased off. Lance won the second race, and the third. The million-dollar purse was his. At the prize ceremony Lance declared, "Everybody won today."[6] Some months later, at a hotel in Italy, the rival team collected its cut: 50 million lire, a sum worth roughly $30,000, wrapped in a panettone box.[7]

Lance now earned $500,000 a year. Yet, for all his rising fame, he remained a *domestique* on the Motorola team, whose leader, Andy Hamp-sten, had finished the 1992 Tour in fourth place. Lance would soon turn the Motorola team on its ear.

In July 1993, Lance entered his first Tour de France—the Tour that would be Laurent Fignon's last, held without a struggling Greg LeMond. In the second week of racing, Lance shocked the peloton by winning the final sprint in a road stage—and becoming, at twenty-one, the youngest American to claim a stage victory at the Tour. Coaches pulled Lance from the race before it entered the mountains, as he was not a climber. At five feet ten inches and 165 pounds, he carried too much weight to fly up Alpine slopes like Andy, the team's best climber, who was twenty-five pounds lighter. Lance had the raw power to muscle over short, steep hills, but on an actual mountain he would sink like a stone.

Lance was emerging instead as an exceedingly talented one-day racer, capable of riding at a high, sustained speed over a hundred miles of racing and then winning the race with a burst of awesome power. He decamped to Italy to begin training for the 1993 world championship road race in Oslo, Norway.

The 258-kilometer contest found Lance at a moment in his career when he had learned enough about cycling tactics to remain within the peloton for most of the race, saving his energy and biding his time. Yet Lance was still cocky enough to stage a solo breakaway in the final lap, several kilometers before most others would have dared.

The best cyclists in the world bore down on him in a driving rain. Somehow Lance managed to hold his lead, and by the time he rounded the final turns, everyone else was racing for second. In the last kilometer, Lance had the luxury to sit up in the saddle, blowing kisses and waving to the crowd, pausing repeatedly to look back over his shoulder in disbelief for pursuers who weren't there. And just like that, Lance was his nation's second modern-day world champion of men's professional cycling. At the finish, he and his young mother broke down in tears.

As Lance posed with his medal, television commentator Phil Liggett mused, "And could it be we're watching the man who will replace the great Greg LeMond in the years ahead?"[8]

Lance and Linda proceeded together to the postrace ceremony with Norway's King Harald. When a guard stopped Linda at a checkpoint, Lance snapped, "I don't check my mother at the door."[9]

No one understood the significance of the day better than he. "My life has changed forever," Lance said.[10] The Texan's brash victory lap and his cheek toward the Norwegian king cemented his reputation with the European press. On that day, at age twenty-one, Lance became the most hated superstar of cycling since Laurent Fignon.

"He has the ill temper of an irascible, capricious, occasionally surly champion," *La Gazzetta dello Sport* opined. "He is a Texan who walks with his shoulders thrust forward, and who has a high regard for himself."[11]

World championship in hand, Lance began to grumble about the caliber of hotel rooms and meals afforded his team and to behave as if he, rather than Andy Hampsten, were its leader. Success was going to his head. Linda Armstrong traveled to Minnesota and sought an audience with Greg and Kathy LeMond. Greg had been about the same age as

Lance when he'd won his first professional world championship. Over coffee, Linda asked Greg and Kathy how to negotiate a cycling contract. According to the LeMonds, she also asked how to curb her son's runaway ego: "How do I get Lance to be less self-centered and actually care about other people during all this?"[12]

An awkward silence ensued. Greg and Kathy didn't know quite how to respond. In the end, they offered what counsel they could, telling Linda to keep her son close and to choose his business partners with care. What more could they say? Greg and Lance were fundamentally different. Greg was a sweet-natured people pleaser, averse to conflict; Lance seemed to thrive on it. Greg had met and paired off with the love of his life while still in his teens; Lance seemed to change girlfriends as often as he swapped bicycles.

The next three years would affirm Lance's position as a world-class cyclist. Their passage would also suggest to some that the 1993 world championship ride might have marked the zenith of his career. While Lance won big races in 1994, 1995, and 1996, none matched the triumph in Oslo. In 1994, Lance finished second at Liège–Bastogne–Liège, perhaps the most grueling one-day event in cycling. In 1995, he won the Tour DuPont and captured another stage at the Tour. In 1996, he conquered both the DuPont and La Flèche Wallonne, the great, single-day Belgian classic. Lance now earned an estimated $850,000 a year, the highest pay afforded any cyclist on the Motorola team, which he now led. He had fulfilled his promise as a first-rate competitor in a single discipline of cycling, the one-day classic. By the close of the 1996 season, Lance had risen to seventh in the world cycling rankings. Apart from Andy Hampsten, Lance was surely the finest American cyclist since Greg.

But Lance was not Greg. He wilted in the mountains. He competed, but did not dominate, in time trials. He lacked, in short, the two skills necessary to win Grand Tours. He carried too much muscle to climb, and his cardiopulmonary engine didn't generate quite enough horsepower to carry that weight up a mountainside or to beat the race against the clock. Lance would drop out of the Tour de France in 1993, 1994, and 1996. In 1995, he would limp to the finish in thirty-sixth place.

At the end of the 1996 season, Lance began to suffer crippling head-aches and blurred vision, and one day he coughed up blood, symptoms that would have sent most sufferers sprinting to a doctor. But Lance never got sick, so he brushed it off, along with a mysterious new pain in his right testicle—until the pain grew so severe he could no longer sit on his bicycle.

Doctors diagnosed a virulent form of testicular cancer, which had spread to his brain. Lance was told his chance for survival hovered somewhere below 50 percent. He was twenty-five.

Three days before the start of the 1998 Tour de France, French officers stopped a car driven by a *soigneur* to the top-ranked Festina cycling team. Inside they found a veritable rolling apothecary: 234 doses of synthetic EPO, 80 vials of human growth hormone, and 160 testosterone capsules, among other items. Under questioning, the *soigneur* confessed: his team ran a systematic doping program. Tour director Jean-Marie Leblanc expelled Festina from the Tour. Several other teams resigned in protest, thinning the peloton by half before the finish in Paris. *Le Tour* had never known such scandal.

EPO was everywhere. By general consensus, it had arrived around the start of the Induráin epoch. The Big Mig had won his Tours at average speeds of thirty-eight and thirty-nine kilometers per hour, which was roughly analogous to hitting fifty and sixty home runs in consecutive seasons in baseball, although Induráin never failed a drug test and was never formally accused of doping. For those in the know, the defining moment in the EPO era had come on April 20, 1994, when riders from Italy's Gewiss cycling team finished first, second, and third in La Flèche Wallonne, the Belgian classic. The three had escaped the peloton seventy kilometers from the finish and, despite a frantic chase, had held on to win. The victory seemed to defy physics. Three men simply did not hold off an entire peloton in full flight over such a distance.

The next day, the team's doctor, Michele Ferrari, spoke with *L'Équipe*. Asked whether the riders had taken EPO, he noted that the drug could be purchased without a prescription in Switzerland, "and if a rider does, that doesn't scandalize me." Asked if he thought the drug dangerous, Ferrari replied, "EPO is not dangerous; it's the abuse that is. It's also dangerous to drink ten liters of orange juice."[13]

Ferrari would shortly ascend to a sort of high priesthood of "preparation," charging hefty fees to script medical programs for top professional cyclists. Bicycling officials still had no way to test for EPO, which occurred naturally in the human body. But they knew its effects: EPO flooded the system with red blood cells. In 1997, officials enacted a new rule that barred riders from competing if the share of red blood cells in their bodies exceeded 50 percent, a figure well above normal.

That rule, plus the inherent dangers of EPO, prompted cycling teams to organize their doping efforts under team "doctors," many of them glorified drug runners. The Festina affair, as it came to be known, illustrated that injections, transfusions, and pills had moved to the very center of the sport.

For comment, the sports press naturally turned to cycling's Mr. Clean.

Upon his retirement, at age thirty-three, Greg LeMond stood as the unrivaled and unblemished icon of professional cycling in the United States. Greg had eased into the life of a restless country squire, skiing in Vail, bicycling at fundraisers, and investing in a string of Bruegger's Bagels stores, while the Trek bicycle company revived and expanded his LeMond brand. Bored and thirsting for competition, he had dabbled in auto racing, until that sport proved too costly, and his victories too few.

When journalists tracked him down for comment on the Festina affair, Greg was in Europe, chaperoning a group of cyclotourists willing to pay $12,000 apiece to pedal parts of the Tour route with a former champion.

"This is probably good for cycling," Greg said of the doping revelations. "It's a wake-up call."[14]

Greg was very nearly the only star of cycling willing to speak out against dope. Active cyclists honored the sport's code of silence from fear of reprisal on the road; accuse a fellow cyclist of doping, and he just might push you off a cliff. Most retired cyclists stayed quiet because they themselves had doped. That Greg had raced clean made him almost unique among professional cyclists of any stature. His disapprobation of the Festina scandal was natural; it was also news. Most of the peloton responded to the arrests of numerous riders and staff by portraying the police as villains and the cyclists as victims.

Toward the end of the 1998 Tour, Greg spotted two American cycling executives on the patio of a top-flight restaurant in France. One was Thom Weisel, a San Francisco investor who backed the top American cycling team, sponsored now by the U.S. Postal Service. The other was a Postal Service publicist.

"Listen," Greg told them, "I am really sorry that you have to see this mess this year. The sport obviously has a lot of work to do, but it is cleaning up."

According to Greg, Weisel shot back, "I think this is bullshit. Riders should be able to take whatever they want." (Weisel denied saying this.)

Greg returned to his table, but he had lost his appetite.[15]

The Postal team had a new hire in 1998, a cyclist who was attempting a comeback oddly reminiscent of Greg's.

Lance Armstrong, given up for dead by the European cycling establishment, had recovered from brain surgery and chemotherapy and was back on a bicycle. Lance's first, tentative half-mile outing around his Austin neighborhood on a mountain bike in the fall of 1996 had echoed Greg's wobbly procession down the street of his gated California community on a fat-tired ten-speed, nearly a decade earlier.

The Texan had been overwhelmed by the outpouring of support during his fight against cancer, including a two-page letter from the king of American cycling, Greg LeMond. "If you ever need to talk to somebody," Greg had written, "I'm here."[16]

No team had wanted him. But Lance had immediately grasped the publicity value of his recovery from cancer, a disease whose survivors numbered more than fifteen million in the United States alone. Even before he rejoined the peloton in early 1998, Lance approached New York publishers with a pitch for a book. He wanted a minimum advance of $150,000. The publishers balked; Lance was all but unknown outside cycling.[17]

Undeterred, Lance launched a foundation under his not-quite-familiar name to raise money for cancer research.

In the fall of 1997, Lance began negotiations to join the Postal Service team. Its leaders harbored considerable reservations—not so much because of the cancer, but because Lance had amply demonstrated in his precancer career that he was not a team player. In the end, the cancer changed their minds. The new Lance appeared to be a changed person: humble, mature, a man reborn. He even looked ready to settle down with his girlfriend du jour, a public-relations executive named Kristin.

Lance's first comeback race, in February 1998, was the Ruta del Sol, the same venue where Greg's teammates had pushed him to the finish in the depths of his own comeback, ten years earlier. Lance finished in fifteenth place, a good result even for a healthy rider.

But the next month, Lance faltered, abandoning the eight-day Paris–Nice stage race. His comeback had stalled. Lance considered retirement. He had already beaten cancer. He could return to Austin and run his foundation. Lance's mother and an inner circle of friends persuaded him to ride one more race.

Both Lance and Greg raced to exorcise demons. Greg's was the shame and guilt of abuse. Lance's was rage—boiling anger at the father who had abandoned him, at the stepfather who had beaten him, at the coaches who had indentured him to other men, and now at the teams that thought him finished.

Anger powered Lance to victory at his next European race, the Tour de Luxembourg in June 1998, and then to a fourth-place finish at the Spanish Vuelta in September. The latter performance marked a minor miracle for Lance: for the first time in his career, he found that he could compete with the climbers in the mountains. He rode now with superior savvy, conserving his energy and attacking when the moment was right.

Lance's managers considered his success in the Vuelta. He had entered the race fresh, not after consecutive months of daily exertions within the peloton. Quite by accident, Lance had found a new strategy for survival in the Grand Tours. Still, all the tactics in the world couldn't fully explain the Texan's newfound climbing skills. The peloton rumor mill hummed with intrigue.

Following the 1998 season, Lance traveled to Minneapolis to visit the parents of Kristin, his new wife. Shortly after Christmas, they invited Greg and Kathy over for dinner. Greg and Lance hardly knew each other; yet the two men now had much in common.

The women hit it off immediately. Kristin asked Kathy what she could expect while accompanying her husband around Europe, far from home and kin. Greg and Lance chatted amicably about cycling—until this exchange, recounted by Greg:

"What do you hope to do this next year?" Greg asked.

Lance offered, "I hope to win the Tour."

Greg was startled. "Well, that's a really good goal," he said. "So, what other ambitions do you have?"

Lance replied, "I want to win four Tours."

The remark seemed scripted to offend. Greg had, after all, won only three Tours.

Greg offered polite encouragement: "That's good. That's great!" He felt certain, though, that Lance lacked the physiology to win the Tour. Greg believed a cyclist with a VO_2 rating of 79.5 would never conquer the Tour, a conviction that Lance's prior record seemed to bear out. On the drive home, Greg turned to Kathy and said, "I feel bad for him, because he's delusional."[18]

Lance completed his comeback on the eve of American Independence Day, stunning the cycling world by winning the brief time-trial prologue to the 1999 Tour de France. Injuries and drug suspensions had driven several favorites from the peloton. Still, Lance's performance seemed to prove the Texan had somehow mastered the art of time trialing.

A week later, Lance pedaled to victory in a much longer time trial, beating his nearest rival by almost a minute over a course of nearly sixty kilometers. Now he led the Tour by more than two minutes. American journalists mobilized to cover an unfolding comeback story like no other.

Greg followed the narrative with unique empathy. Lance's comeback reminded him of his own. There was just one sour note. Two months before the Tour, another story had reached Greg's ears. It was one of those gossipy, third-hand accounts heard all too often in cycling circles. According to this one, Lance had crowed to a fellow cyclist that he approached his comeback Tour with a mysterious advantage. Lance had something no one else had, and it was undetectable.[19]

Greg laughed it off. He believed in Lance. Yet, as he watched the Tour progress, Greg could scarcely believe how thoroughly Lance had transformed. Tour commentators marveled at how the stricken Texan had rebuilt his body after cancer; these stories would feed the burgeoning Lance Armstrong mythos. Before cancer, Lance had sported a sprinter's build: massive thighs supporting a chiseled torso, too heavy for climbing mountains but perfectly proportioned for explosive sprints. Cancer had stripped those muscles away. Lance had turned that misfortune to his advantage, reconstructing the muscles that mattered to a cyclist and ignoring the rest. The effort left him with sleek but powerful thighs beneath a visibly slimmer torso. Lance had lost power, the analysts said, but he had also lost weight. He returned to the peloton with a faster cadence, turning the pedals more quickly on a lower gear, a strategy that theoretically allowed him to climb mountains with newfound ease.

But those mountains were yet to come, and Lance had never shown much promise as a climber. Greg journeyed to the start of the first mountain stage, boarded the Postal team bus and found the *maillot jaune*.

"Man, you are just flying up there. Unbelievable," Greg said. "I am so happy for you."

"Thanks," Lance replied.

Greg offered encouragement: "I've got to tell you, your capability of doing that time trial, that'll translate directly into climbing. Don't let anybody tell you that you're a time trialist and not a climber. If you can time-trial like that, you can win the Tour."

"I know," Lance replied coolly.[20]

Greg left the bus feeling sheepish. Clearly Lance did not need his encouragement.

The next day's course featured five major climbs and ended at the resort of Sestriere, across the border in Italy. On the final climb, Lance rose from his saddle and began to sprint, turning the pedals so quickly, and with so little visible effort, that a casual observer might have assumed the cameras were slanted upward rather than the road. He won the stage easily, finishing half a minute ahead of his nearest rival and building an overall lead of six minutes, which he would not relinquish.

On television, announcer Phil Liggett intoned, "He's American, his name is Lance Armstrong, and it's a long time since we've seen a performance like this."[21]

Greg watched the climb on a screen at a nearby hotel, surrounded by shrieking tourists. Only one man remained silent. He was a mechanic who had worked on the disgraced Festina team. According to Greg, the man tapped him on the shoulder, gestured to the soaring Texan, and muttered, "*sur le jus.*" *On the juice.*

"What?" Greg replied.

"*Sur le jus.*"

"How do you know?"

"Look at his eyes," the mechanic said. "His breathing. There's no suffering."[22]

Greg tried to cast the mechanic's words from his mind. He sincerely believed the sport had cleaned up after the Festina affair. Some cyclists continued to dope, but American cyclists mostly raced clean. Surely Lance and his team—hosted, as it was, by a federal agency—were not *sur le jus.*

By the next day, Lance Armstrong was a global celebrity. Journalists, cancer survivors, and millions of ordinary people seized on his comeback story, which was almost without parallel in the history of elite sports. For many Americans, it was entirely without parallel; the story of Greg LeMond had never quite saturated the nation's popular culture, and now, a decade later, it was fading fast.

A few days later, the *New York Times* and the *Austin American-Statesman* published separate articles that broached a distressing theory: perhaps Lance was doping. Perplexingly, the articles relied almost entirely on comments from Lance himself and from his agent. The articles noted an outbreak of "innuendo" in the European news media, a campaign of whispers suggesting Lance was not winning the Tour on water alone. They quoted Lance in response to his critics, telling the *Times*, "Sweat is the secret of my success." Yet, the stories cited no direct quote from any accuser.[23]

In fact, most of the European cycling press was celebrating Lance and his comeback right along with their American peers. Lance and his entourage seemed to have planted the stories themselves. Greg remained a believer. Speaking in Lance's defense, he told a British interviewer, "I know it's possible to win the Tour without taking anything."[24]

A few days later, the cause of Lance's concern came to light. The French newspaper *Le Monde* reported that a drug test from the first day of the Tour had found trace amounts of corticosteroids in Lance's urine. The governing body of professional cycling, the Union Cycliste Internationale, leapt to the Texan's defense, stating that the steroid had come from a skin ointment Lance had used, with a prescription.

Le Monde pressed its case. Lance had not declared the ointment on his doping form, a certificate cyclists filed at the start of the Tour. A reporter challenged Lance on that point at a news conference. In reply, the cyclist asked, "Monsieur *Le Monde*, are you calling me a liar or a doper?"[25]

Lance dismissed *Le Monde*, perhaps Europe's most esteemed newspaper, as "the gutter press."[26] These were bold words from the mouth of an athlete who had risen to the top of his sport only that month.

Tour organizers had dearly hoped the Festina affair would cleanse the peloton of its most blatant dopers. Perhaps, they prayed, the pace of the race would finally slow, and the whispers of scandal would subside. Alas, the 1999 Tour would go down as the fastest on record. For the first time in a century of racing, the average speed topped forty kilometers per hour.

But all that was forgotten by the time of the Postal Service victory party, staged within the elegant Musée d'Orsay in Paris. A bowl of apples provided centerpieces for each table, a conscious effort to seed the Lance legend. As he had pedaled up the Sestriere en route to his breakthrough mountaintop victory, Lance had exulted into the team radio, "How do you like them fuckin' apples?"[27]

Lance concluded the season with a new contract that delivered up to $2.5 million a year in salary and potential bonuses. His Tour victory allowed the Postal team to sign more than twenty new sponsors. Lance's personal sponsor, Nike, flew him to New York on a chartered jet. He appeared on the morning news shows and sat for interviews with David Letterman and Larry King. He rang the opening bell at the New York Stock Exchange. He met with President Bill Clinton in the Oval Office, and with Vice President Al Gore in the Roosevelt Room. He taped commercials for Nike, American General Insurance, and, naturally, the Postal Service.

A publisher now offered $400,000 for the rights to Lance's memoir. A producer pledged $500,000 for a TV movie deal. Lance signed endorsement deals worth more than $7.5 million with more than a dozen companies. His likeness would soon appear on a Wheaties box. His speaking fee soared to $100,000. By year's end, Lance had attained a level of celebrity approaching that of basketball star Michael Jordan, who had retired a year earlier as the best-known athlete in the world.

"In the beginning, we had this brand of brash Texan, interesting European sport, a phenomenon," Lance's agent told an interviewer. "Then you layered in 'cancer survivor,' which broadened and deepened the brand. But even in 1998, there was very little corporate interest in Lance. And then he won the Tour de France in 1999, and the brand was complete. You layered in 'family man,' 'hero,' 'comeback of the century,' all these things. And then everybody wanted him."[28]

Lance's arrival reordered the American bicycle industry. Sales of road bikes had soared after Greg's first Tour victory in 1986 but flattened after his retirement, and then they had very nearly gone extinct. The new craze was mountain bicycles, with fatter tires and endless gear options; at the moment of Lance's ascent, mountain bikes commanded 95 percent of the market. Then the trend began to reverse. Road bikes rebounded, and a new generation of mostly affluent, male cyclists took to the roads on status-symbol road machines. Jaded pros called them MAMiLs: middle-aged men in Lycra.

Lance easily won a second Tour in 2000. This time he defeated the finest competition in Europe, completing the race six minutes ahead of his nearest rival, German steam engine Jan Ullrich. As with Laurent Fignon's triumphal Tour in 1984, Lance's second victory seemed to affirm that the first had been no fluke.

Yet doubters remained.

Greg traveled to Provence that July for a reunion of the Z cycling team that had conquered the Tour a decade earlier. Over dinner, a venerated mechanic named Julien de Vriese regaled Greg and Kathy with tales of Lance and his Postal team. According to the LeMonds, de Vriese described what he had seen just two months earlier at the team's training camp in the Pyrenees. The camp operated like a hospital, he said, a constant blur of injections and pills: "When they weren't on their bikes, they were on IVs." He also spoke of a $500,000 payment to cycling officials—a transaction possibly involving Nike, a prominent sponsor—to smooth over Lance's positive drug test at the 1999 Tour. "This isn't cycling anymore," the mechanic lamented.[29] De Vriese would later deny saying those things, and Nike officials would deny any role in a payoff. The conversation left Greg deeply concerned for his sport.

In the fall, news leaked that French prosecutors were investigating a tip about the Postal team's medical program. French reporters had trailed team doctors and filmed them dumping medical waste at a rest stop far from their hotel. The journalists recovered syringes, bloody bandages, and packaging for a drug called Actovegin, a blood-doping product made from calf's blood. The drug was not banned; but French doping laws, stricter than those of international cycling, made it a crime to use performance-enhancing drugs, even legal ones.

American news media mostly ignored the story. Lance announced he would withdraw from the following year's Tour if the persecution continued, even as he mocked the investigators and dismissed the seized drug as "Activ-o-something."[30] The following April, according to the LeMonds, Julien de Vriese told Greg that Lance's team had effectively killed the probe by claiming, falsely, that the calf's-blood drug had been used to treat the mechanic's diabetes. De Vriese would later deny saying this.

Greg was becoming convinced that Lance and his Postal Service team were cheats. He thought back to another rumor he'd recently heard and dismissed, suggesting that Lance had admitted to doping when questioned by cancer doctors before the surgery that saved his life. Now, Greg wondered: *Had Lance doped throughout his career? Had dope given him cancer?*[31]

Ever so gradually, Greg began to leaven his public comments with subtle doubts about Lance and his team. In November 2000, at a charity auction in New York, Greg opined, "The entire doping situation needs to be resolved soon for the good of the sport. It's time for everyone to come clean."[32]

The Festina scandal had nearly detonated the 1998 Tour. Tests during the 1999 season found nearly half of professional cyclists had excess iron in their blood, a red flag for EPO. The Tours of 1998, 1999, and 2000 would be the three fastest on record, all with average speeds exceeding 39.5 kilometers per hour. The peloton now seemed to traverse mountains and flats at roughly equal speeds.

In the spring of 2001, a group of sports doctors invited Greg to speak at a symposium in San Antonio, seventy-five miles from Team Lance headquarters in Austin. Greg spoke about his disdain for the "doctors" employed by professional cycling teams, whom he regarded as glorified pushers. Greg became focused on the speaker who preceded him, Ed Coyle, director of the Human Performance Laboratory at the University of Texas. Coyle held a doctorate in animal physiology. He was there to explain the Lance Armstrong miracle.

Cancer had somehow transformed Lance from a successful cyclist into the greatest athlete of his generation. There were two competing theories to fit that fact. The first, embraced unequivocally by most American fans and journalists, invoked nature and nurture in equal parts. Lance was a genetic prodigy, born with a supersized heart that fueled a once-in-a-generation VO_2 engine, among sundry other gifts. ("His thigh bones are unusually long," a *New Yorker* profile noted, as if contemplating an excavated dinosaur.)[33] And Lance was a uniquely industrious competitor. He trained harder than his rivals. In spring, he led his team up and down mountains to be crossed that summer in the

Tour. Those rides were "a trade secret, something no other team does," the *Texas Monthly* explained, describing the very ritual that had drawn the Renault cycling team to the Alpine commune of Briançon fifteen winters earlier.[34]

The second theory, favored by the Texan's critics and by many cycling fans in Europe, was dope. By 2001, reporters at *L'Équipe* were convinced EPO had pervaded more than 90 percent of the peloton in the previous decade. If Tour de France contenders doped in such numbers, then surely a clean competitor stood no chance. Of Lance, one British cycling writer observed, "If he isn't a doper, he must stand almost alone in his sport."[35]

Coyle had studied Lance's physiology over a seven-year span, before and after cancer. He had measured Lance's VO_2 capacity periodically over those years and found it had fluctuated between 66 and 81. At the time of the first Tour victory, in 1999, Lance's VO_2 reading was a comparatively modest 71.5. Thus, Lance's oxygen consumption couldn't explain his vast improvement. Then there was the matter of Lance's weight. The comeback narrative suggested post-cancer Lance was a lighter man; ten or fifteen fewer pounds could transform a cyclist's climbing skills. But some of the weight data Coyle had collected showed Lance heavier after cancer than before.[36]

Coyle had to find additional reasons for Lance's miraculous transformation. He theorized that, in the comeback years, Lance had greatly improved the efficiency of his leg muscles in converting oxygen into power. Perhaps, he mused, relentless training had left the Texan with a greater quotient of slow-twitch muscle fibers, helpful in endurance contests, at the expense of fast-twitch muscle, useful for short bursts of power.

Greg had studied cycling physiology; to him, Coyle's theories didn't wash. Greg believed Lance possessed the physical gifts of a middling Tour de France rider; in his view, for Lance to win the race without some artificial aid was not possible.

In the summer of 2001, the Outdoor Life Network offered live coverage of the Tour in the United States for the first time. Stateside viewers watched French fans boo Lance in real time as he pedaled to his third consecutive victory, a feat that surely proved him, finally, the equal of Greg. The European cycling press awarded him the *Prix Citron*, the same honor they had bestowed upon Laurent Fignon a dozen years earlier, for his sour temperament. Lance was now the first Tour cyclist to employ his own bodyguard. Much of Europe saw the Texan as a villain, and he did not disappoint.

"If they thought I was unaccommodating before," Lance snapped, "wait till they see me in the future."[37]

In Europe, the Lance three-peat would be overshadowed by breaking news. On the Tour's first weekend, newspapers reported that Lance was a client of Michele Ferrari, the most notorious sports doctor in Europe. Ferrari was due to stand trial on doping charges.

The story was broken by David Walsh, an investigative journalist in Britain. Walsh said Lance and his teammates had adopted a blood-boosting program six years earlier, in 1995, an effort centered on EPO. An unnamed teammate told him Lance "was a key spokesperson when EPO was the topic."[38]

Front-page news on the continent, the story drew mostly dismissive coverage back home. A *New York Times* account was typical. Beneath the headline, "Accused, Armstrong Defends His Honor," the U.S. newspaper of record essentially handed Lance the keyboard. The 865-word article quoted only him. "At the end of this bike race, if I'm lucky enough to win again," Lance said, "all the stuff that gets written—all the innuendo, all the speculation, all the critics, all the people who don't want anything good for cycling—it doesn't matter. It doesn't matter to my family, my friends or my team."

He added, "It's purifying to me that I've been honest."[39]

Greg and Kathy knew enough about journalism—and spoke enough French—to surmise that American journalists were censoring their coverage of Lance; anything that ran counter to the legend was ignored. Kathy confronted Samuel Abt, author of the *Times* story and unofficial dean of the tiny school of American cycling journalism. Why, she asked him, wasn't the *Times* covering Lance the way the European papers did?

According to Kathy, Abt sniffed about a "higher standard" at the *Times*; then he provided a more credible answer: "If you write negatively about Lance, you lose all access." If Abt lost access to the United States' superstar cyclist, he might lose his beat.[40]

The country's non-reaction to the Lance Armstrong doping story mystified cycling writers in Europe. But at least one American reader took note. Greg dispatched an e-mail to Walsh. "Great work, David," Greg wrote. "You're on the right track."[41]

Walsh responded by telephoning Greg for comment. Greg chose his words carefully, finally settling on an ambivalent quote that cycling fans could take how they wished. "If Lance is clean, it is the greatest comeback in the history of sports," he said. "If he isn't, it would be the greatest fraud."[42]

Two weeks passed. Greg traveled to London on business. Then he returned to Minneapolis, where he met Kathy at the airport and climbed into the family station wagon. As if on cue, Greg's cell phone rang. He turned to Kathy and mouthed the words, "It's Lance."[43]

According to the LeMonds, the following conversation ensued:

"Greg, I thought we were friends," Lance opened.

"*I* thought we were friends," Greg replied.

"Why did you say what you said?"

"About Ferrari? Well, I have a problem with Ferrari. I'm disappointed you are seeing someone like Ferrari. I have a personal issue with Ferrari and doctors like him. I feel my career was cut short. I saw a teammate die. I saw the devastation of innocent riders losing their careers. I don't like what has become of our sport."

"Oh, come on, now," Lance replied. "You're telling me you've never done EPO?"

The question caught Greg off guard. No one had ever publicly accused Greg of doping. Few riders had privately suspected Greg of doping. Surely Lance knew that. Why, Greg asked, did Lance think he had used EPO?

"Well, your comeback in '89 was so spectacular. Mine was a miracle. Yours was a miracle. You couldn't have been as strong as you were in '89 without EPO."

Lance began to rattle off names of performance-enhancing drugs; some of them Greg had never heard before. Surely, Lance pressed, Greg had taken these drugs. Greg grew indignant. As much as Lance protested the endless comparisons, he seemed transfixed by the parallels between his own life and Greg's. Greg had won a world championship; Lance had won a world championship. Greg had nearly died; so had Lance. Greg had married a woman from the Upper Midwest and settled in Minneapolis. Lance had married a woman from Minneapolis. Lance had even hired Julien de Vriese, Greg's former mechanic. Lance seemed to view Greg as both a role model and a sort of father figure.

But Greg had not doped. And that, in Greg's mind, was where the similarities ended.

"Listen, Lance," he said, "before EPO was ever in cycling, I won the Tour de France."

Greg reminded Lance of the disparities between their VO_2 measures. Greg's had reached 93. Lance's topped out in the low 80s. In Greg's mind, the two men might as well have come from different planets.

"Tell me one person who said I did EPO," Greg said.

"Everyone knows it," Lance replied.

"Are you threatening me?"

"If you want to throw stones," Lance said, "I will throw stones."

THE FEUD

THE AMERICAN CYCLING INDUSTRY of 2001 was a small world, the professional cycling community smaller still. Lance Armstrong and Greg LeMond were very nearly its only celebrities; between them, the two men had more or less cornered the market in sponsorships and licensing deals.

For many years, Greg's face had adorned seemingly every ad in every cycling magazine in the United States. Then Greg had faded, and Lance had arrived. By the time of their 2001 showdown, Lance was the most powerful man in American cycling. Greg was about to learn the full reach of his power.

Within days of the phone conversation outside the airport, Greg began to field calls from the masters of the tiny cycling universe: Thom Weisel, the San Francisco investor who backed Lance's cycling team; Terry Lee, CEO of the Bell Helmets company, and John Burke, president of Trek, the largest U.S. bicycle maker.[1] Greg even heard from some of his closest friends. From every caller, the message was the same: Greg shouldn't be saying those things about Lance. His comments weren't doing him any good. This would not end well.

The Trek bicycle company sponsored both Lance and Greg, and Trek sold more than ten thousand bicycles a year under the LeMond name. Burke told Greg that Lance wanted him to retract his statement to David Walsh. If Greg refused, then he and Trek bikes might not have a future. Negotiations stretched on for days; Greg finally told his attorney to take care of it. Lance's agent wrote the retraction and submitted it to *USA Today*.

It read, in part, "I believe Lance to be a great champion and I do not believe, in any way, that he has ever used any performance-enhancing substances. I believe his performances are the result of the same hard work, dedication and focus that were mine ten years ago."[2]

Greg read it in the paper and wept.[3]

Having identified Greg as a threat, Team Lance set about discrediting him, seeding rumors in the cycling community that Greg was an emotionally unstable alcoholic who felt threatened by Lance's ascent. One reporter telephoned to ask Greg if he had a heroin problem.

Greg might have thought the humiliating retraction marked rock bottom. The next two years would be worse. Greg took to smoking and drinking heavily. He fell into a deep depression. He slept at odd hours and suffered bouts of insomnia, which sometimes drove him into the kitchen at midnight to cook and consume an entire batch of chocolate pudding. He began to personify the caricature drawn up by Lance and his publicists. He took to tape-recording important telephone conversations. The parade of calls after Greg's showdown with Lance had left him feeling betrayed by all of his business contacts and most of his friends; the entire cycling world seemed to have sided with Lance. The talking points emanating from Austin suggested that by coming after Lance, Greg had attacked the entire population of cancer survivors. Such talk reached the schools of Minnesota, where Greg's children now endured taunts.

The LeMond family started to unravel. Geoffrey, Greg's older son, was battling depression himself and going in and out of treatment facilities. Geoffrey had never quite recovered from the trauma of seeing his father's gunshot wounds.

In February 2002, when Geoffrey showed up late to his own eighteenth birthday party, father and son had it out. By evening's end, another two generations of LeMond men had stopped speaking.

Greg's abuser was a constant companion during those months, haunting his thoughts. One night, drunk to the edge of unconsciousness, Greg resolved to tell Kathy about Ron. He couldn't do it. He hemmed and hawed and finally mumbled, "I'll tell you on my death bed," before passing out.[4]

Six weeks later, Greg fled to Arizona with another woman. He had become convinced that he had to lose everything—"my wife, my kids, my house, every cent I had"—to find himself.[5] Oddly enough, his strategy worked. Finally, fearing that Kathy was going to leave him, Greg flew home, broke down in sobs, and revealed his darkest secret. Afterward, he and Kathy felt closer than ever.

But while Kathy responded to Greg's confessions with love, empathy, and support, Greg's parents did not.

Bob and Bertha LeMond hadn't spoken much with their son in a decade. Greg and Bob had finally resumed occasional contact at the end of the 1990s, but the rapport between Bertha and Greg remained chilly. Now both parents recoiled at Greg's questions. It was "a shame-based reaction," Greg recalled.[6] The cycle of estrangement rolled on.

Greg's worst years were Lance's best. In 2002, Lance won a fourth consecutive Tour, surpassing Greg's American record. *Sports Illustrated* named him sportsman of the year. President George W. Bush appointed the fellow Texan to his cancer advisory panel. When the Tour organization hosted a ceremonial gathering that fall to honor past champions and to mark the one hundredth anniversary of the race, Greg was invited—and then systematically marginalized, as organizers worked to steer him clear of Lance.

In 2003, Lance won a fifth Tour, equaling the record set by Anquetil and matched by Merckx and Induráin.

"I used to think Lance was the next Greg LeMond," an American cycling fan told the *Boston Globe*. "It turns out LeMond was the first Lance."[7]

Amid rumors of philandering, Lance and Kristin Armstrong divorced. Lance began dating rock star Sheryl Crow. They appeared together on the *Oprah Winfrey Show* to plug Lance's cancer foundation and to tout its new line of yellow Livestrong bracelets. Nearly a million of them sold in a single day.

Greg was now convinced Lance was doping; most of the American public was just as sure he was clean. Greg had better sources. American fans relied on the American media, which responded to the steady drumbeat of doping allegations from Europe by alternately ignoring them, burying them inside the sports section, or dismissing them as baseless innuendo from a jealous continent.

Lance and his sponsors openly mocked their European accusers. One Nike ad from the era showed Lance taking a blood test in front of reporters. In a voiceover, Lance edgily intoned, "Everybody wants to know what I'm on. What am I on? I'm on my bike, busting my ass, six hours a day. What are you on?"[8]

As the 2004 Tour approached, Lance was again the favorite. Observers spoke of a record-breaking sixth victory with an air of inevitability.

A few weeks before the race began, the European press heralded the release of a new book, *L.A. Confidentiel*, whose subtitle promised to reveal *Les Secrets de Lance Armstrong*. *L.A. Confidentiel* delivered a published account of a long-rumored hospital-room scene, a revelation that had first been passed to the authors as a tip from Greg. The authors alleged that, in a conversation with doctors following cancer surgery in 1996, Lance had casually admitted to taking EPO and human growth hormone, among other forbidden pharmaceutical fruits. The book also asserted that Lance had covered up his first failed drug test, in 1999, by procuring a backdated prescription. A onetime Postal Service team masseuse described using makeup to cover telltale bruises on the Texan's arm.

The authors were David Walsh, of Britain's *Sunday Times*, and Pierre Ballester, a former reporter at *L'Équipe*. In terms of pedigree, the partnership was somewhat akin to a *New York Times* reporter collaborating with an alumnus of *Sports Illustrated*. Yet the U.S. legacy media resisted presenting the findings as news, and English-language publishers wouldn't touch the book, which appeared only in French. At a press conference shortly before the start of the Tour, Lance tendered a literary rebuttal to Walsh: "I think extraordinary accusations must be followed up with extraordinary proof."[9] His comments were clearly directed at his American audience; for European fans, doping in cycling was the essence of ordinary.

The book set off act two of the simmering feud between Lance and Greg. Inside, readers found a full transcript of the airport conversation

and an account of the subsequent pressure on Greg to recant his criti-
cisms of Lance. The authors acknowledged Greg as a source. Greg, still
humiliated by the groveling apology of three years earlier, came out
swinging. He told *Le Monde*, "Lance is ready to do anything to keep his
secret. . . . I don't know how he can continue to convince everybody of
his innocence."[10]

The Texan's defenders struck back. A columnist from Lance's hometown paper, the *Austin American-Statesman*, wrote of Greg, "The sniping
smacks of little more than bitter jealousy of a man who is flirting with
remaking history." The comments perfectly distilled the talking points
Lance and his team had circulated to counter Greg's attacks.

"You got proof, LeMond?" the columnist sneered. "Present it. Otherwise, go cycle up a mountain."[11]

Lawyers for the Trek bicycle company dispatched a letter to Greg,
warning that his comments breached his contract. By hurting Lance,
he hurt Trek, which sponsored both men.

Greg was now a cycling pariah. Sponsors vanished into the mist. Dealers at trade shows avoided his gaze. At the same time, Greg was becoming a magnet to others who dared speak out against Lance. After the
publication of *L.A. Confidentiel*, Greg received an e-mail from Emma
O'Reilly, the masseuse and star of Ballester and Walsh's book. When
they subsequently spoke, Emma told Greg that Julien de Vriese, Lance's
mechanic, had ferried drugs in a hollowed-out shoe heel. Meanwhile,
Kathy became friends with Betsy Andreu, the wife of Frankie Andreu,
Lance's former teammate. The Andreus had provided Walsh eyewitness
accounts of Lance's hospital admissions. Betsy recounted to Kathy the
night in 2001 when Lance had first heard Greg's "greatest fraud" remark
and vowed, "I am going to fuck him over."[12]

One of the more striking facets of the ongoing quarrel between the
two cycling icons was that, even after three years, almost no one had
come to Greg's defense. The task of rehabilitating his public image
finally fell to Andy Hampsten, the *other* great American cyclist—and one
of a few cycling stars from the recent past who had never been accused
of doping. Toward the end of the 2004 Tour, Andy posted an open letter
to *VeloNews*, a popular American cycling journal.

"Greg has put himself into personal and business difficulties by speaking out," Andy wrote, addressing the sponsors whom Lance had pressured to drop Greg. "Voluntarily placing himself in this position shows me honesty and bravery far beyond what most of us could muster." Andy urged his peers to resist the judgment that Greg was "simply jealous of being eclipsed as the dominant American cyclist," taking aim at Lance and his talking points.[13]

That summer Lance won his sixth consecutive Tour de France. Anquetil and Merckx had won only five. Now, for better or worse, Lance stood alone.

The Texan's campaign to exile Greg from the American cycling industry had proven remarkably effective. But Greg was a seasoned litigator, and he had deep pockets of his own. In February 2005, after a protracted legal battle, a jury awarded Greg $3.5 million from the coffers of Protective Technologies, a New York firm that had tried to back out of a licensing deal to sell a LeMond line of helmets, seat covers, and locks in Target stores.

In July 2005, Lance won his seventh Tour. He had already announced that the race would be his last. To many European cycling fans, his quest to extend his record disrespected the proud tradition of professional cycling. Many of those fans assumed, of course, that Lance was doping. Across the Atlantic, the attitude was predictably different. To American fans, it seemed fitting that an American athlete should sweep into a foreign sport and dominate it like no one before.

At the close of the 2005 Tour, Lance gave a speech. Race officials did not ordinarily hand the microphone to the *maillot jaune* at the finish. Then again, this was no ordinary Tour. Lance delivered a message equal parts inspirational, patronizing, and bitter. "Finally," he concluded, "the last thing I'll say for the people who don't believe in cycling, the cynics and the skeptics: I'm sorry for you. I'm sorry you can't dream big, and I'm sorry you don't believe in miracles."[14]

They didn't. A few weeks later, the French sports paper *L'Équipe* published an investigative report that alleged Lance had tested positive for EPO on six urine samples collected during his very first Tour victory, in

1999. A French laboratory had subjected the old samples to a new test, unavailable half a decade earlier. The findings ran beneath the head-line *Le Mensonge Armstrong*: The Armstrong Lie.

Here was the first seemingly irrefutable evidence that Lance had doped. Jean-Marie Leblanc, the head of a Tour organization that had always defended the cyclist, finally broke rank. "He owes an explana-tion to us, to everyone who followed the Tour," he said. "What *L'Équipe* revealed shows me that I was fooled, and we were all fooled."[15]

Lance dismissed the report, from Europe's lead sports newspaper, as "tabloid journalism."[16] He taunted his accusers on *Saturday Night Live*. Yet, the report was damning, and a few American journalists finally began to publicly question the Lance legend.

"It's true Armstrong has never failed a drug test," opined T. J. Quinn of the *New York Daily News*. "Neither has Barry Bonds. Neither have Jason Giambi, Mark McGwire or Jose Canseco, the great East Ger-man runners of the 1970s or 80s, or Keith Richards. 'I've never failed a drug test' ranks with 'We came to play' among all-time meaningless sports declarations." Quinn drew particular attention to the alarms raised by Greg, which he likened to "Hank Aaron calling Bonds a cheat."[17]

In 2004 and 2005, a fresh round of litigation would deepen the fis-sure between Lance and Greg. An insurance firm called SCA Promo-tions owed Lance a $5 million bonus for his record-breaking sixth Tour victory. Lance's cycling team had taken out a policy from the insurer to cover the bonus, if Lance managed to earn it.

By 2005, the insurer was now convinced that Lance hadn't truly *earned* the bonus, even if he had won six Tours. The firm set out to document Lance's 1996 hospital admission. Lawyers deposed Betsy and Frankie Andreu, who gave their accounts. They also sought a third witness, a longtime friend of Lance's named Stephanie McIlvain. But she denied that Lance had discussed dope with his doctors.

Kathy testified about the fateful phone call from Lance outside the airport. Greg countered the unhelpful testimony from Stephanie McIlvain. Greg had tape-recorded a half-hour telephone conversation with McIlvain in 2004. Lawyers for the insurance firm played it at the hearing.

Greg knew of the hospital-room admission, and he knew McIlvain had heard it. In their conversation, he had asked whether she would tell the truth if the matter came to court.

"If I was subpoenaed, I would," she replied. "'Cause I'm not going to lie. You know, I was in that room. I heard it."[18]

By the end of the hearing, the insurance company had a strong case that Lance had doped. Yet, after all the effort, the firm opted to settle rather than risk a verdict. Lawyers predicted the arbiters would rule in Lance's favor as long as he retained his Tour titles. In the eyes of cycling's governing body, Lance was still a champion.

In May 2006, police busted a Spanish sports doctor named Eufemiano Fuentes. Inside his apartment they found blood plasma belonging to a who's who of the peloton. Operación Puerto, as the investigation was called, opened up the biggest cycling scandal since Festina, bringing down nearly every star of professional cycling, save the one who mattered most. Lance's timely retirement now looked positively prophetic. The scandal left the field wide open for the 2006 Tour, the first to be staged without him since 1998.

The new favorite was Floyd Landis, an American cyclist from Pennsylvania's Mennonite country who had served as an elite lieutenant to Lance. Floyd was the real deal: a superior all-around rider, gifted at climbing, descending, and time trialing. His VO_2 score had been measured at 90, nearly as high as Greg's.

The 2006 Tour delivered an epic battle of also-rans, with Landis seizing a slender lead after two weeks of racing. The American's deteriorating right hip, which would require surgery after the race, only heightened the drama. On Stage 16, a mountain haul that featured four brutal climbs, Landis cracked, running out of fuel and plummeting to eleventh place, seemingly out of contention.

The very next day, Floyd attacked, alone, on the first of five peaks. Observers groaned. The American could never hold off the peloton over five mountaintops. Yet, somehow, he did. By day's end, Floyd had ridden himself to within seconds of the race lead. He went on to win the Tour by less than a minute, easily the most gripping finish since the arrival of Lance.

Three days later, Floyd learned he had failed a drug test. On the day of his bold suicide attack, his urine had betrayed excess testosterone. Now, the man in the *maillot jaune* risked disqualification from the Tour, an indignity without precedent in a century of racing.

Reporters reflexively turned to Greg for comment. "I hope, for the sport's sake, that Floyd has the courage to come clean on everything," he said. "He needs to say everything about the sport, what's happened in the past, what's happening right now."[19]

According to Greg, Floyd telephoned him a short while later and asked, "Why are you speaking out like this?"[20]

Greg told Floyd it was time to face facts. Yes, Floyd could lie, and he could fight. "You might get away with it," Greg said, "but if you have any conscience, it's going to kill you in the end. If you come clean, you could be the one person that saves the sport."

Greg proceeded to tell Floyd the story of sexual abuse he had hidden from the world for most of his life. He told Floyd how the secret had eaten away at him, and he described the cathartic release of finally telling the truth. He urged Floyd to do the same.

Floyd protested: "Greg, if I come clean, I would destroy all of my friends and hurt so many people."

Greg replied, "Floyd, I'm fifteen years older than you. Do you think your friends in cycling are your friends? They're just acquaintances. You think your whole life is cycling, but it's just a small part of it. There is so much more beyond that."

Floyd listened politely to Greg's advice. Then, he ignored it, marching off into a hopeless battle against the doping authorities.

From Floyd's Mennonite upbringing, Greg had inferred that he would respond differently to his own moral crisis than Lance had to his. He was wrong. When Greg injudiciously shared their conversation, Floyd responded by posting a public threat to Greg on a cycling website.

"If he ever opens his mouth again and the word Floyd comes out," Landis wrote, "I will tell you all some things that you will wish you didn't know."[21]

In the preceding years, Greg had shared his story of abuse with his wife, his parents, and a few others. Now he had shared it with a desperate man.

That fall, for the first time, American journalists began to feed the growing body of investigative evidence against Lance. Reporters from the *New York Times* found two teammates from the 1999 Tour willing to admit using EPO. One was Frankie Andreu, whose prior testimony about Lance's hospital-room admission had fractured their friendship. The other spoke on condition of anonymity. Both cyclists claimed they had never seen Lance dope. Still, it was a start.

Lance dismissed the report as "distorted sensationalism," invoking terms not commonly associated with his nation's newspaper of record.[22]

Greg had waited seven years for someone, anyone, to come clean. Of Frankie's confession, he said, "It takes a lot of courage for him to go against the grain and go against a lot of people who want to help keep this buried."[23]

Indeed, Pat McQuaid, president of the governing body Union Cycliste Internationale, sniffed that Frankie's confession would have "no effect at all" on Lance's legacy.[24]

In the spring of 2007, Floyd took his battle against the U.S. Anti-Doping Agency into arbitration. Doping authorities called on Greg to testify about the telephone conversation with Floyd. Greg agreed, though he feared the repercussions.

On the evening before his appearance, Greg and Kathy drove to a hotel near Pepperdine University in Malibu, the neutral site chosen for the hearing. En route, Greg's cell phone rang.

Greg recounted the following conversation:

"Hi Greg," the caller said. "This is your uncle."[25]

"My uncle?" Greg replied, confused.

"This is your uncle. Do you remember me?"

"Who is this?"

"This is your uncle, and I'm going to be there tomorrow, and we can talk about how we used to hide the weenie."

"Who the fuck is this?" Greg exploded, as the line went dead.

The call left him shaking. Kathy sat with Greg and his lawyer in the hotel lobby until one o'clock in the morning. Greg called the police, but he was too addled to complete the report. It quickly became clear the "uncle" was not Ron. The log on Greg's Blackberry revealed the call had come from Floyd's business manager.

The next day, in a hearing room at Pepperdine, Greg recounted the conversation with Floyd, including the abuse, and the subsequent call from his manager, who was sitting behind Floyd in that very room. An attorney for Floyd turned to the manager and declared, "You're fired."[26] By day's end, his phone call and Greg's abuse were international news.

Throughout the summer of 2007, as mediators weighed his case, Floyd would crisscross the nation, raising money for his legal defense fund and hawking copies of his best-selling memoir, *Positively False* Floyd's response to the doping allegations, like Lance's, was uniquely American. European cyclists accused of doping generally professed their innocence and took their lumps. They didn't write books, hire publicists, harangue accusers, and lodge protracted appeals.

A few days after the hearing, Greg took another unexpected call, this time from his father. Greg and his parents hadn't really spoken since the smaller revelation of his sexual abuse within his family four years earlier. Now Bob was calling to tell Greg that his mother was dying. Afflicted with liver disease and suffering horribly, Bertha had resisted burdening her son, but Bob thought it was time. He summoned Greg to the hospital at Stanford University, where Bertha had lain comatose for days. When Greg arrived at her bedside and took her hand, she suddenly opened her eyes and looked straight into his. Greg said goodbye. A few days later Bertha died. Her passing would finally rekindle Greg's relationship with his father.

Greg emerged from the Floyd Landis saga a stronger man. He purchased a $20,000 German police dog to protect his family and his home.

Thus armed, he set out to tie up some loose ends. He was motivated, in part, by a new appreciation for his own mortality. Doctors had discovered that the quotient of lead in Greg's bloodstream had quadrupled in just a few years. Released by the shotgun pellets that lay within Greg's body, the lead put him at risk for a heart attack or stroke. The time bomb had finally detonated.

But had those pellets poisoned Greg's cycling career? The Festina and Puerto scandals cast the peloton in a new light. It now seemed clear that EPO and blood doping had indeed transformed the cycling sport, just as Laurent—and to a lesser degree Greg—had sensed in his twilight years. A new term entered the cycling vocabulary: *passive doping.* It denoted the theory that clean riders, such as Greg, could irreparably damage their bodies by laboring to keep up with dopers. Had EPO contributed to Greg's physiological collapse?

Greg was finally ready to face his demons. He hired a private investigator to find Ron.

Greg had lived in perpetual fear that Ron would reappear in his life and threaten to tell the world what he and Greg had done, for Greg had told almost no one. He would ask himself, *What if all these people knew this had happened to me?* At such times, fear, shame, and panic clouded Greg's rational mind.[27]

The detective found Ron in minutes, still apparently living and working in Nevada. Kathy telephoned his workplace, only to learn that Ron had abruptly fled to Italy.

In the spring of 2008, Greg filed a lawsuit against Trek, alleging that the firm had intentionally allowed the LeMond brand to languish. After rescuing Greg LeMond Bicycles from insolvency in 1995, Trek had built the brand into a $15 million a year business. Over time, the partnership had yielded more than $100 million for Trek, of which $5 million had gone to Greg. But sales had flattened in recent years, while other road-bicycle brands continued to grow. Trek blamed the slump on Greg. Greg blamed it on Trek, and some of his data were damning. Between 2001 and 2007, for example, sales of LeMond bicycles in France—where Greg was a national hero—had totaled just $10,393.

The dispute was really about Lance. The bicycle maker argued that Greg had harmed its business by "publicly disparaging an important Trek-endorsed athlete."[28]

Greg replied that he felt a duty to speak out about the scourge of doping in professional cycling. He noted that the Trek company hadn't minded his anti-doping stance until the spotlight fell on Lance. The lawsuit appeared to cast Trek, a family-owned Wisconsin firm, in the odd role of defending doping culture in cycling.

Lance came across as a vengeful bully. Greg produced a tape recording of a phone call with John Burke, the Trek CEO, wherein Burke acknowledged that Lance was leaning on him. Greg's lawyers argued that "the nature of Mr. Armstrong's pressure constituted extortion."[29]

The industry circled its wagons. The trade journal *Bicycle Retailer and Industry News* trotted out a parade of bicycle salesmen to complain about Greg. One store owner observed, "It's really hard to sell bikes when the spokesperson for the line is engaged in a continuous barrage of negative statements about bike racing."[30]

The lawsuit would drag on for two years, finally ending in an out-of-court settlement, a messy finish to a fifteen-year partnership. The terms were confidential, but Trek announced it would donate $200,000 to 1in6.org, a little-known charity for male survivors of sexual abuse. Greg had joined the group as a founding board member, becoming the public face of a discomfiting topic.

In the fall of 2008, Lance announced a triumphal return to professional cycling. He would enter the 2009 Tour with the unheralded Astana team, based in Kazakhstan.

His brand burned brighter than ever. The Lance Armstrong Foundation now employed seventy-five people and was raising a new head-quarters in Austin, where city planners were laying a Lance Armstrong Bikeway. Lance partied with actors Matthew McConaughey and Jake Gyllenhaal, dated actresses Ashley Olsen and Kate Hudson (having parted ways with Sheryl Crow), and traveled in a personal jet. Lance's website could mobilize a Livestrong army of millions at the drop of a press release.

By this time, most of Lance's American fans knew of the doping allegations, and most of them didn't care. A new Nike ad, released to coincide with Lance's return, interspersed scenes of the champion pedaling with images of cancer patients in hospitals. Over the montage, Lance toyed with his accusers: "The critics say I'm arrogant, a doper, washed-up, a fraud, that I couldn't let it go. They can say whatever they want. I'm not back on my bike for them."[31]

At 11:12 a.m. on June 11, 2009, Lance greeted his millions of Twitter followers with a most unexpected tweet: "Sending out my best to Laurent Fignon who was recently dx w/ cancer. A friend, a great man, and a cycling legend. Livestrong Laurent!!"[32]

And thus did the cycling world learn that an enigmatic legend of French cycling was fighting for his life.

THE LAST BREATH

RETIRED AT THIRTY-THREE: the prospect did not suit Laurent any more than it did Greg. Both men had been hyperactive boys, and both had channeled the excess energy into their cycling careers. Now those careers were over, and neither man could sit still for long.

Laurent had arranged one final victory lap, a largely ceremonial ride in the Grand Prix de Plouay in August of 1993. He told the cycling press that he owed it to his fans, betraying an arrogance that was, one writer remarked, "almost touching in its naïveté."[1] Perhaps none of the fans had come for a last glimpse of the cyclist now ranked 201st in the world. But within the peloton, *le Grand Blond* still mattered. Laurent pedaled to the front of the pack, and someone pronounced, "Look, everyone, make sure you see this: This is the last time you will see Laurent Fignon on a bike."[2]

He retired at the moment he became convinced he could no longer compete. He told Alain Gallopin, his longtime trainer, "It is not possible for me to win the Tour any more. And, honestly, when that is not possible, I don't care about anything else."[3]

Laurent was at peace. Yet, one morning in early 1994, he realized with alarm that a new cycling season had begun, and that his peers were now in training. Sitting on his sofa, he would recall in his memoir, "A sort of terror gripped me. An insidious fear that gnawed at my stomach and ran up and down my spine. I stood up, swaying in a gust of anguish . . ."[4]

Rather than surrender to panic, Laurent ordered his thoughts and took quick stock of his life. Money? Laurent had retired with roughly 2 million francs in the bank, a modest fortune in mid-'90s currency, and with a few properties to his name. Pastimes? Laurent was staying active mostly by playing golf. He would soon accept an invitation to commentate on cycling races for Eurosport, the pan-European sports network.

Laurent might have sought a job as a *directeur sportif* and managed a cycling team. But no one approached him; he was, after all, a former winner of the *Prix Citron*. Instead, Laurent carved out a new identity as a race organizer. In 1996, he launched the Île-de-France Cyclotourist Trophy, a series of four recreational rides scattered around France, with a grand finale outside Paris. He booked historic *châteaux* for each stage and hired chefs to cater the meals. Joined by Alain, Laurent assembled tables, unclogged toilets, and even erected crash barriers along the course, often laboring past midnight. Attendance rose from a few hundred in the first year to a thousand in the second and third.

But Laurent struggled to turn a profit. And when things went awry, all of France would revert to its native mistrust of the arrogant Parisian. One race day, Laurent's caterer arrived three hours late, forcing him to reimburse a thousand outraged cyclotourists. The next day, a local paper published a photo of a cyclist urinating on the walls of Versailles, with a headline that translated to "Fignon: Never Again."[5]

At the close of the millennium, Laurent scaled up his ambitions. He bid for ownership of Paris–Nice, the Race to the Sun, an eight-day stage race run in March and steeped in French cycling history. The event had been owned by the Leulliot family for nearly half a century, but now they were selling. Laurent prevailed, beating out a competing offer from the organization that ran the Tour de France. His winning bid surpassed 4 million francs, much of it borrowed.

Almost immediately, Laurent found himself under duress. Ownership of the race put him at odds with the Société du Tour de France, making the organizer of cycling's biggest race into a competitor. Paris–Nice had faded in luster during the 1990s; the best cyclists now flocked to Italy for the rival Tirreno–Adriatico race. Laurent sought to woo them back with a compelling course. He proved a formidable organizer and staged exciting contests in 2000 and 2001, even persuading television broadcasters to boost their coverage tenfold. But he found himself forever haggling with towns on the route, whose councils and mayors had to be convinced to host the race. Often he found that Tour de France organizers had gotten there first, instructing local officials to turn Laurent away if they wished to ever host a stage of *le Tour*.

After two years, in 2002, Laurent reluctantly sold Paris–Nice to his Tour de France rivals, losing 2 million francs in the transaction. That setback would plunge Laurent into perhaps the darkest chapter of his life to date. Along with most of his money, the Paris–Nice adventure had sapped his motivation. And the sale came as his marriage to Nathalie, mostly harmonious for the past two decades, was finally unraveling; they would separate well before their 2006 divorce. Laurent took to playing golf every day, sometimes twice a day. He confessed to Alain that he felt empty inside.

Laurent would salvage just one memento from his abortive career as race organizer: a budding romance. Valérie Bordes was born in 1969 and raised in Nevers, along the Loire in central France. As a student, with her chestnut hair, sculpted cheekbones, and luminous blue eyes, she easily found work as a Tour de France hostess; she once presented the winner's bouquet and a kiss on the cheek to Spanish champion Miguel Induráin. Valérie progressed from tossing promotional goodies at spectators to transporting cyclists for the Peugeot organization. Eventually, someone introduced her to Laurent, telling the cyclist, "Check out her eyes."[6] He offered her a job as his assistant. She declined his first dinner invitation but accepted the second. Their first date, and first kiss, fell on August 31, 1997, the night of Princess Diana's car crash.

Over dinner, Laurent told Valérie how his head had swelled after his first Tour victory, fourteen years earlier. At night's end, she felt he had revealed little of himself. She realized later that he seldom revealed more. Valérie came to accept Laurent's reserve, the quality that left even dear friends feeling they barely knew him. She learned to tolerate his wandering eye, even directing his attention to attractive women on Paris sidewalks. Laurent told her he loved spring, because that was when women began to undress. She accepted those impulses because Laurent no longer seemed to act on them.

"The only infidelity he could manage," she recalled, "was to spend the day at the other end of France on a golf course, his passion, or to devour a book."[7]

Valérie had never known Laurent as a bicycle racer, but she soon became acquainted with the competitive fire that had driven him. He played Scrabble as if to the death. Once, out on a weekend bicycle ride, while Laurent awaited his girlfriend on a hill, he watched in agony as a recreational cyclist pedaled past him. When she arrived, Laurent placed his right hand under her bicycle seat and summoned his ferocious power to drive both bicycles forward, up and over the hill and past the astonished challenger.

Valérie quickly surmised a fundamental truth of Laurent's personality. His aloofness, which the French public and cycling press attributed to haughty arrogance, was really nothing more than crippling shyness. Deep down, Laurent was anything but arrogant. He viewed his considerable career accomplishments with an essential humility. He regarded his own legend with a dismissiveness that bordered on sacrilege.

In a rare interview around that time, Laurent commented on his legendary ride against Greg in 1989: "It was an interesting Tour, as Tours go. I was disappointed at the time, sure, but over time the disappointment has disappeared. There are more serious things in the world."[8]

After that eight-second defeat, Laurent had sulked in his apartment, weeping at his misfortune, vowing never to ride his bicycle again. Now, more than a decade later, he regarded the episode as a chapter of his life that was finished. He routinely ignored invitations to gather with other cycling old-timers to ride in exhibition races, to eat and drink at celebratory banquets, or to hold court in hospitality tents, reliving past glories. When fans recognized him on the street, Laurent often told them they were mistaken, and he did it without malice.

Yet the old scars remained. When Valérie took Laurent to Nevers to meet her cycling-mad grandfather, the elderly host attempted to break the ice by asking, "Do you have any news from Greg LeMond?"[9] Valérie beheld her grandfather with horror. To ask Laurent about Greg, she recalled, was like "talking about rope to a hanged man."

"No," Laurent spat back. "No news. I have nothing to do with Greg LeMond."

The visit was brought to a speedy conclusion. A few days later, Laurent telephoned the stricken grandfather to apologize.

In darker moments, Laurent still regarded Greg as the man who had more or less ruined professional cycling. Greg had been the first Tour champion to prize that race at the expense of all others. That bias was a product of Greg's heritage; he came from a country that knew no other bicycle race. Yet his philosophy had quickly suffused the peloton. Miguel Induráin, the dominant cyclist of the early 1990s, steadily narrowed his ambitions once he had conquered the Tour. By focusing single-mindedly on that race, he became the first man to win five Tours in succession. Lance Armstrong and Jan Ullrich, the dominant cyclists of the early 2000s, took that philosophy to its logical conclusion, all but ignoring the balance of the racing calendar.

Many French fans viewed the situation from the reverse perspective. They saw Laurent, along with the great Hinault, as the last Tour champions to show real passion for the full cycling season. Through his victories at Milan–San Remo, Flèche Wallonne, and other races virtually unknown outside the continent, and through his work with the Paris–Nice contest, Laurent had amply illustrated his affection for his sport.

Much as the French had despised Laurent in his first, insouciant ride to Tour victory, that 1983 contest had set off perhaps the most exciting span in the modern history of professional cycling, culminating in Laurent's own tragic defeat in Paris six summers later.

One day in July 2007, Greg stopped by to visit Laurent at the broadcasting booth of France 2, the public television channel that now employed Laurent as a Tour commentator. Talk naturally turned to 1989, and soon the two men were compelled by the hosts to sit and watch videotaped highlights of the mythic race. The pair sat in silence as the tape rolled, each studiously avoiding the other's gaze. When the reel reached the moment of Greg's victory on the Champs-Élysées, the American grimaced and lowered his eyes, no doubt wincing at Laurent's distress in revisiting that scene. Laurent forced a pained smile.

When the tape was finally over, the two former combatants smiled at each other in palpable relief. They parted warmly.

In the latter half of the 2000s, Laurent occupied himself with a new pet project, the Centre Laurent Fignon, an entertainment complex with a luxury hotel and gourmet restaurant, set at the foot of the legendary Col du Tourmalet in the Pyrenees. There Laurent conceived a series of training camps and cycling courses across panoramic mountain passes.

In May 2008, Laurent and Valérie wed in a ceremony staged on the grounds of the Centre Fignon. The groom wore a white suit, the bride a pistachio gown. They spoke of a honeymoon in Polynesia, but a year later the trip had not materialized. Laurent had become absorbed in his work at the center and was preparing a memoir.

Laurent's reunions with Greg became an annual ritual. They met in 2008 for a bicycle ride and lunch. They dined again in 2009, and talk turned to the waning days of their cycling careers. Greg asked his old adversary, "What was it like, the last couple years?" Laurent replied, "I was always tired. I would go from race to race without training," he said, because racing left him too weary to train. It dawned on Greg that the two men had suffered the same fate, ground down by a peloton that drew its power from dope.[10]

Laurent spent the spring of 2009 promoting his book, which was to be published under the wistful title *We Were Young and Carefree*. He returned one evening from a round of interviews complaining of a stiff neck. The pain persisted. Finally, Laurent guided Valérie's hand to a spot on the right side of his neck, where she felt a pair of hard, marble-sized balls rolling beneath the skin.

Valérie urged Laurent to see a doctor. He balked, but a few weeks later he relented. A series of simple tests revealed nothing, but a friend advised Laurent to seek a biopsy. A sample was collected. The doctor telephoned Laurent in his car some hours later to deliver the findings. When Laurent concluded the conversation, he put his hand on his wife's leg.

"Well, I have cancer," he said. "Don't worry. It can be cured."[11]

The doctors had found cancer cells in Laurent's lymph nodes. They did not yet know the cancer's source, although they suspected one of the organs of his digestive system. The cancer had spread, and they could not effectively treat it until they learned where it had taken seed. Laurent was forty-eight.

He entered chemotherapy in late May, reassuring Valérie with confident bluster that she did not share. "The lymph nodes? We'll remove them," he told her. "The chemo? A few sessions will suffice."[12]

Chemotherapy would continue through July, when Laurent was scheduled to give commentary on the Tour for both radio and television. Laurent revealed the illness to his contacts at the networks but swore them to secrecy; he wanted to tell the public in his own time, on his own terms. Lance Armstrong preempted that plan.

Lance and Laurent had met just once, but it had been a memorable moment for both men. In 1996, Lance was in Paris to announce a hiatus in his cycling career as he fought his own battle with cancer. Lance was bald and gaunt, and no cycling team would have him.

"And get this," Laurent divulged in his memoir. "The evening after that press conference, before he was due to catch the next morning's plane back to the U.S., he was on his own at his hotel in Roissy. Everyone had simply dropped him."[13] Nathalie invited him over for dinner. Lance was touched. He opened up to the French champion about his fears of dying. He charmed Nathalie, complimenting her on a meal "so good," he quipped, "it feels like my hair is growing back."[14] Laurent wondered whether he was seeing the Texan for the last time.

The two men had not seen each other in the intervening years. But Lance was staging his 2009 comeback on the Astana cycling team under the tutelage of Alain Gallopin, Laurent's dearest friend, who was now Astana's *directeur sportif.* No doubt Lance learned of Laurent's cancer from Alain. Still, his June 11 tweet announcing Laurent's illness to the world caught the Fignons unprepared.

With the European media now clamoring for a statement, Laurent granted an interview to Europe 1, the broadcaster that would shortly employ him as a commentator.

"They've detected cancer in my digestive tract," he told the interviewer, "but it's not clear exactly where. It is bad news." Doctors thought the disease might have originated in the pancreas. Pancreatic cancer was nearly always fatal. "Therefore," Laurent finished, "I do not know how long I have to live."[15]

Laurent's name was now in the news for both the cancer and his memoir, particularly the passages that portrayed a peloton suffused with dope. At a time when seemingly every star of cycling stood accused of doping, and almost no one was owning up, such revelations were big news. Laurent's peers indulged his confessions because he was dying. Talk now inevitably turned to whether Laurent's doping had *caused* his cancer. It was the same question that had hung like a pall over Lance and his achievements for a decade. Doctors assured Laurent there was no proven link between either amphetamines or corticosteroids and cancer of the digestive system. But Laurent was careful to note that they could not rule it out.

Laurent's battle with cancer endeared him to the French public, adding a new dimension of poignancy to their tragic hero. The Frenchman who once could not muster the support of his own nation at the Tour was now universally loved.

Rather than embrace his public, Laurent retreated ever further into a tight circle of friends: Alain Gallopin; Vince Barteau, his freewheeling former teammate; and, of course, his young wife. When Valérie asked why he had so few friends, Laurent would reply that such was the lot of a champion. "When you are the leader," he would say, "you have few friends; you do not fraternize with your teammates; the others treat you with restraint; you are alone."[16]

Laurent's closest friends would show up at his door unannounced. Had they telephoned first, Laurent would have told them what he told the rest of the world: he was tired and preferred to be left alone.

Valérie had seen Laurent cry exactly three times: once while watching a reality television show, once during the French national anthem at a rugby final, and once at their wedding. Now he cried about his cancer in their Paris home, and it unnerved her. But Laurent fought bravely, enduring torturous tests without complaint, even briefly embracing an anticancer diet heavy in antioxidants and fruits—a considerable step for a man who had always fastidiously avoided fruits and vegetables. Alas, he reverted to his old ways two months later.

By the time Laurent began his on-camera work at the 2009 Tour, a second cycle of cancer treatment had taken a toll. His golden hair was falling out, his appetite depleted. Laurent could have easily begged off his Tour duties, but he had given his word. Chemotherapy was scheduled in cities along the race route.

Already Laurent had a reputation for prickly commentary; in previous editions of the Tour, he had openly criticized riders and teams when he questioned their race strategy—and he was usually right. The ravages of cancer had left him grumpier still. One viewer wrote in with the observation, "Illness has not rendered you generous or kind."[17] But many fans found something inspiring in Laurent's candor. It showed courage.

The work, and the letters, lifted Laurent's spirits immeasurably. Throughout the three weeks of racing, broadcasters had made little note of Laurent's affliction—until the last day of the Tour, when the program host finally acknowledged the thought on everyone's mind.

"I will not individually thank everyone who participated in this Tour de France," he told viewers.[18] "The only one I would like to name is the person right next to me, Laurent Fignon. I would like to thank him for being here, for having the courage to join us, and to tell him that I am counting on seeing him again next year, Laurent. To tell him, for myself, that as long as I am here"—emotion swelled in his voice as he turned to Laurent to complete the sentence—"you will be with us."

Laurent offered polite thanks. A colleague added a few words. A long, awkward silence followed. Laurent was never one to break an awkward silence.

"Listen," he finally offered. "If I can say a word of thanks in my turn: When I learned I had this disease, I called to tell you about it, and immediately you said to me, 'Laurent, we will do as you wish.' And it obviously touched me, and it obviously helped me, and I was very happy, and . . . and . . ."

Laurent broke down then, collapsing onto the commentary desk, burying his face in his hands. As his body sank from the frame, the camera cut to a serene shot of the peloton pedaling around a traffic circle, while the microphone recorded a champion's sobs.

The treatments shrank Laurent's lymph nodes, buoying his confidence. But then they swelled again, and as the months ticked by, a precise diagnosis continued to elude his doctors. Laurent gradually lost the strength to tie his shoes. One evening, after absorbing another round of bad news from the doctors, Laurent and Valérie ate a joyless dinner on wooden stools in their kitchen. When they had finished, Laurent rose, walked around the table, and lifted his wife down from her stool, wrapping her in his arms as she began to cry.

"My darling," he told her, "if I have to die, then so be it; that's life. You will be sad for a while, and then you will go back to your life. I would do the same for you."[19] In the moment, his words sounded cold. Only later would Valérie realize that her husband was setting her free.

That winter Valérie reached out to Alain, who was working with Lance Armstrong. Lance had met with Laurent briefly after the cancer diagnosis. The cancer survivor had urged the cancer patient to pursue novel treatments with gusto. Lance himself had been saved by an experimental treatment.

"If the doctors offer you something," Lance had said, "do it with conviction."[20] Lance had offered to put Laurent in touch with the best specialists in the United States. Laurent had politely declined. Now, working behind her husband's back, Valérie accepted the Texan's offer.

It was Laurent himself, by his wife's account, who finally guessed at the source of his cancer. One day, surveying the result of the latest scan, Laurent beheld an image of his lung and glimpsed a spot. He asked his doctor what it was. "Nothing special," the doctor replied. A few days later, doctors called to inform him he was suffering from lung cancer. Laurent was improbably happy. Now his cancer could be properly treated. Survival rates for lung cancer surpassed those for pancreatic cancer.

A costly and exhausting journey to the Memorial Sloan Kettering Cancer Center in New York confirmed the diagnosis. Valérie, hoping to make the most of the trip, posed a question to the New York doctors that she had never asked before:

"What is the stage of the disease, doctor?"

"Four," he replied.

"And how many stages are there?"

"Four."[21]

Laurent returned to the Tour in 2010, summoning the energy to comment on all twenty-one stages despite his pain. A tumor pressing on a vocal cord reduced his voice to a trebly rasp. But Laurent held nothing back, lashing out at the race leader, Andy Schleck, of Luxembourg, when Schleck drifted back to the team car to collect supplies: that was the job of a *domestique*. When a colleague asked Laurent if he hadn't been a bit harsh, Laurent replied, "It's okay. A month from now, I might be dead."[22]

The morning after his final Tour broadcast, Laurent awoke in searing pain, unable to speak or walk. Doctors found that fluid had filled his lungs. Laurent's condition ebbed and flowed in the days that followed. On August 12, friends and family gathered to celebrate his fiftieth birthday in his hospital room. That evening, he sent Valérie a text message of thanks. "I love you," he wrote, "and do not worry, we will overcome all this." He signed the note, "Lolo who loves you."[23]

It was now a matter of days. Old friends came by to pay their respects. Vince Barteau brought a smile briefly to his lips by inspecting Laurent's T-shirt and asking, in mock surprise, "Isn't that my shirt?"[24] It was a remark Laurent had often made to Vincent, who had a habit of borrowing shirts.

Laurent Fignon died at half past noon on August 31, 2010, after drawing one long, last breath into his cavernous lungs. Tributes poured in. France hadn't lost a racer of his stature since the passing of the great Anquetil in 1987, at fifty-three, of stomach cancer.

"Just woke to the news that Laurent Fignon has passed on," Lance Armstrong wrote on Twitter. "He was a dear friend and a legendary cyclist. We will miss you, Laurent. RIP LF."[25]

Greg paid his respects in an interview on the news channel France 24. "He had a very, very big talent, much more than anyone recognized,"

Greg said. "We were teammates, competitors, but also friends. He was a great person, one of the few that I find was really true to himself. He didn't have an ego. He really knew himself."[26]

Most of the obituaries opened and closed with memories of the 1989 Tour. Just as he had predicted, Laurent would be remembered not for the many races he had won, but for one he had lost.

AMENDS

LANCE ARMSTRONG sealed his second comeback by finishing the 2009 Tour de France in third place. His American fans were crushed. Still, Lance was thirty-seven years old, ancient for a professional cyclist, and he had taken three years off.

French cycling fans loved a comeback. Yet the more jaded among them found something unseemly in Lance's return. If he had indeed doped, and if he had ridden to seven Tour victories without getting caught, then his exit had been perfect. A vainglorious comeback tempted fate.

In spring of 2010, former Tour de France champion Floyd Landis dispatched a mass e-mail to cycling officials in the United States and Europe. Four years earlier, Greg had spilled his secret to Floyd. Now, Floyd would reveal his own. Floyd admitted that he had doped for most of his professional career. He also accused his U.S. Postal Service teammates of doping—including Lance. In eleven years of doping allegations against Lance, Floyd was the first cyclist to name him, the first to violate the sacred omertà.

"I want to clear my conscience," Floyd told the sports network ESPN. "I don't want to be part of the problem anymore."[1] Unfortunately, Floyd had spent four years and $2 million on a campaign to convince the public he was clean. That made him an easy target for voices of the cycling establishment, who greeted his confession with hostility born of fear.

"I feel sorry for the guy, because I don't accept anything he says as true," said Pat McQuaid, president of the Union Cycliste Internationale, the organization ostensibly charged with policing professional cycling.[2]

"It's his word versus ours," said Lance, addressing himself in the majestic plural. "We like our word."[3]

But Floyd had an ally. Pleased that Floyd was finally following his advice, Greg chose to forget the little stunt that had outed him as a survivor of sexual abuse and rode to the embattled cyclist's defense. "It is clear to me that Floyd has paid a heavy price," Greg said in a statement, "and I support Floyd in his attempt to free himself from his past."[4] Greg lent Floyd two of his own lawyers to help in the fight against Lance, who was now a common enemy.

Floyd's e-mail triggered an investigation by the federal Food and Drug Administration. Doping wasn't a crime, so prosecutors set about building a case that Lance and his team had defrauded their sponsors by using drugs. The feds contacted Lance's former teammates and many of the characters who had testified in previous hearings. For the first time, Lance's old teammates faced federal prosecutors who wore badges and trotted out words like "perjury." Word soon leaked that Floyd would not be the only one to name names.

Agents contacted Greg and Kathy, who were overjoyed. "We've been waiting ten years for this," Kathy said.[5]

Prosecutors took particular interest in the cassette tape of Greg's 2004 conversation with Stephanie McIlvain, Lance's friend. On the tape, Stephanie cast Lance as the evil Oz of American cycling, holding an entire community in an icy grip of intimidation and fear, a talent that might explain how he had managed his public image so well for so long. "For someone to have that much influence on people is scary," she had told Greg.[6]

Lance had dismissed every past investigator as a kangaroo court. He had written off reporters from the *New York Times* and the *Wall Street Journal* as tabloid hacks. Now, he took aim at an agency of his own government, warning, "I'm not going to participate in any kind of witch hunt."[7]

In the summer of 2010, Lance rode in his final Tour. Mobbed by reporters with doping questions at every stop, the Texan went into virtual hiding, dispatching a press agent to play tape-recorded comments from Lance after each stage. It was a new twist on Greg's 900 number of two decades earlier.

In mid-race, Greg predicted to a French newspaper that the federal investigation of Lance spelled "the beginning of the end." Lance went on French television with a response, urging Greg to "tell the truth about 1989," implying Greg himself had doped.[8] Lance was finally going public with the threat he had tendered to Greg nine years earlier. Yet the fact that Lance had never acted on it suggested even he didn't really believe it.

Lance rolled into Paris in twenty-third place, more than half an hour behind the leaders. That disappointment prompted Lance's second, and presumably final, retirement from the peloton. The federal doping investigation could now proceed without further distraction. By the time Lance hung up his bicycle, word had leaked that several old teammates had spoken against him. Even Sheryl Crow would weigh in, testifying in 2011 that she had watched Lance receive transfused blood in Belgium.

In May 2011, the investigative news program *60 Minutes* aired a blockbuster confession nearly as consequential as Floyd's. This one featured another of Lance's former protégés, Tyler Hamilton. A soft spoken New Englander, Tyler had pedaled for the Postal squad since its inception. He was a superb climber and time trialist, which made him a contender at the Tour. After escorting Lance to three wins, Tyler decamped to other teams and became a celebrated symbol of grit. In 2002, he rode to second place in the Italian Giro with a broken shoulder, enduring such pain that he ground his teeth to the nubs. In 2003, he rode to fourth place in the Tour, this time with a broken collarbone.

Then Tyler pedaled into a hailstorm of scandal. First he failed a drug test at the 2004 Olympics in Athens, where he had captured a gold medal in the individual time trial. He failed another test later that year at the Spanish Vuelta, in which he had won a stage. Tyler escaped the first sanction on a laboratory error. The second one stuck: someone else's blood had been found in his veins. He waged a million-dollar legal battle, positing a bizarre defense. Tyler claimed to have had a vanishing twin, who had died in utero, leaving foreign cells in his body. The appeal failed, and Tyler was banned from cycling for two years. He returned to the peloton, only to be ensnared in Operación Puerto, the epic 2006 doping scandal, for taking EPO. Rumors followed wherever he pedaled. Tyler's team finally dropped him. Like Floyd, he was a cyclist scorned.

Now, Tyler told the *60 Minutes* interviewer that both he and Lance had doped. Lance and his lawyers denounced Tyler as a "confessed liar in search of a book deal"—which was true.[9] Hein Verbruggen, the former president of cycling's governing organization, all but begged the public to believe Lance, saying the Texan had "never, never, never" doped.[10] Yet, two of Lance's most talented former teammates had now turned against him.

The omertà was broken.

The case against Lance appeared to be hurtling forward—until, in February 2012, it abruptly halted. Prosecutors announced, without explanation, that they had closed the investigation and would file no charges, dropping the anticlimactic bombshell on a Friday before the Super Bowl. Press coverage gave little hint of a reason; cycling insiders speculated Lance had somehow leveraged his considerable influence inside the Beltway to shut it down.

Greg and Kathy were crushed. They took small consolation in the day's other news. An obscure, nongovernmental nonprofit, the United States Anti-Doping Agency, would carry on the fight. The Anti-Doping Agency had gotten Floyd Landis banned from cycling for two years after the 2006 Tour; now the panel was pursuing Lance. But the agency had no authority to put him in prison or to assess a seven-figure civil penalty. With Lance retired from cycling, the *New York Times* predicted that any sanctions it imposed would be "primarily symbolic."[11]

Lance continued to cruise around the planet in his Gulfstream jet, vacationing in France, bicycling in Hawaii, and revisiting the athletic pursuit that had been his first real calling, the triathlon. The criminal inquiry was over. Yet, in the court of public opinion, the mood toward Lance had shifted. A few years earlier, American columnists had joined the Texan in mocking his accusers, and reporters had printed news stories that read like press releases from Team Lance. Now Lance faced skeptical reporters from big papers asking tough questions, and columnists were straying from the script.

In *USA Today*, Christine Brennan reminded readers of the $32 million the Postal Service had spent on Lance and his team: "That's a federal agency sponsoring an American who remains a role model for millions. If some of that agency's money was spent on drugs and deceit, as so many cyclists have said, isn't it time we found out?"[12]

Months passed in ominous silence. Then, on June 12, 2012, the Anti-Doping Agency announced its findings. The agency named Lance, along with four of his cycling "doctors" and his coach, in a far-reaching doping conspiracy, stretching from the dawn of his post-cancer comeback in 1998 through the conclusion of his career and beyond. The six stood accused of "false statements to the media, false statements and false testimony given under oath and in legal proceedings, and attempts to intimidate, discredit, silence and retaliate against witnesses."[13] At least ten of Lance's former teammates and coworkers had testified against him.

The agency could not put Lance in prison—but within the world of elite sports it held considerable sway. Suddenly, Lance faced the loss of all seven Tour de France titles, the very source of his fame.

Lance remained defiant. "These charges are baseless," he said, "motivated by spite and paid for by promises of anonymity and immunity."[14] On the ascendant platform of Twitter, he posted the hashtag #unconstitutional.

The Texan and his high powered lawyers set to work attacking the small agency and dismantling its case. But the task proved unexpectedly tricky. To prevail against Lance, the Anti-Doping Agency had only to convince two members of a three-person panel that a preponderance of evidence supported its findings. Lance's lawyers filed a federal lawsuit that challenged the panel's very existence. Lance's cancer foundation lobbied Congress to revoke its federal funding. Nothing worked.

Finally, on August 23, Lance announced that he would not fight the charges against him. "There comes a point in every man's life when he has to say, 'Enough is enough,'" he said, still waxing defiant. "For me, that time is now."[15] Lance and his handlers had underestimated their opponent. Upon his surrender, the agency proceeded to strip Lance of every award he had won in fourteen years of competition, including his Tour victories.

And just like that, Lance Armstrong was no longer a Tour de France champion.

Greg was at home in Minnesota when the news flashed across his television screen. He had thought the truth would never come out. Now it had, and Greg and Kathy felt no joy, only profound relief that their battle was over. In an interview with David Walsh, the journalist to whom Greg had given the "greatest fraud" quote, Greg searched his brain until he found something nice to say about Lance, something conciliatory: "He has got a very powerful network of people that have done a lot of amazing stuff on his behalf."[16]

A professional cyclist did not attack an opponent who had crashed to earth.

On October 10, the Anti-Doping Agency forwarded its case against Lance to the Union Cycliste Internationale. Perhaps because this group had defended Lance so fiercely, the agency simultaneously posted essentially the entire case online. Now hundreds of thousands of ordinary cycling fans could peruse records of payments to doping doctors and confessions from old teammates. Social media lit up with observations.

For a few days, it looked as if Lance might survive the scandal after all. The Anti-Doping Agency had stripped him of his Tour titles, but cycling's governing board had to ratify the decision to make it stick. And, despite the mountain of evidence now circulating on the Internet, most of Lance's sponsors vowed to stand behind him.

There was one more blow to be struck, and it would come from Kathy LeMond.

On October 16, a small knot of chanting protesters formed outside the campus of Nike in Beaverton, Oregon, pressuring Nike to drop Lance as a client. They were outraged by the story, told by Kathy years earlier in a deposition, that Nike might have played some part in an alleged $500,000 payment to the Union Cycliste Internationale to cover up Lance's positive drug test in the 1999 Tour. (Nike denied it.)

The Anti-Doping Agency's data dump had put Kathy's testimony online. It was old news to the cycling community but new to most of the mainstream press, which quickly posted stories asking whether Nike had participated in a doping conspiracy. Nike dropped Lance the next day.

Nike had been Lance's core sponsor. As it turned out, the company's unflagging allegiance had supported a house of cards. By day's end, Lance had lost $75 million in endorsements, and he had stepped down as chairman of his cancer foundation.

As bad as Kathy's testimony looked for Nike, it looked worse for cycling's governing organization. On October 22, after more than a decade of defending Lance, the Union Cycliste Internationale stripped him of his titles.

"Lance Armstrong has no place in cycling," said Pat McQuaid, its president.[17]

The governing group acknowledged accepting more than $100,000 in donations from Lance and his team, though it denied the $500,000 payoff alleged by the LeMonds.

The Lance legend would not have survived as long as it had without the support of his sponsors and the governors of professional cycling. Now he had lost both, and the rest of the empire soon crumbled. Tufts University revoked an honorary degree. Several Lance Armstrong gymnasiums quietly changed their names. *Sports Illustrated*, which had named Lance Sportsman of the Year in 2002, named him "Anti-Sportsman" of 2012. The Tour de France organization erased his name from its record books.

Apart from the sycophants, perhaps the group most complicit in sustaining the Texan's myth had been the American news media. Lance and his handlers had proven alarmingly adept at managing and manipulating press coverage at home for a decade, even while journalists eviscerated him in England and France. Part of the problem was that the United States lacked a cycling press. Few publications employed full-time cycling writers, and reporters who did file stories on Lance and the Tour often knew little of the sport.

Samuel Abt of the *New York Times*, perhaps the nation's best-known cycling writer, offered a sort of apology for thirteen years of mostly flattering coverage. "I reported what I knew"—which, he conceded, "was admittedly not much."

Abt's column included a telling anecdote. He recalled a moment, near the end of Lance's career, when Lance confronted him on a train, demanding to know whether America's preeminent cycling writer was "digging up dirt" against him. Plenty of journalists were—in Europe. "I don't know anything about this," Abt replied. Then the journalist assured his subject, "Whoever it is, I won't help."[18]

In January, word spread that Lance was finally ready to talk. He had agreed to tape an interview with Oprah Winfrey. Greg and Kathy feared Oprah would allow Lance to co-opt the interview, as he so often did. So Kathy sent Oprah a message on Twitter: "I hope you get educated before the interview. I know people that can help you."[19]

Kathy did not expect a reply. But then a producer called. Kathy told of her own experience with Lance, and she referred the producer to other cycling insiders.

In the resulting interview, broadcast over two days, Lance admitted that he had doped, that he had bullied, and that he had lied. "I viewed this situation as one big lie," he said, "that I repeated a lot of times." Still, Lance would not admit that he had cheated. To cheat, he reasoned, was to exploit an unfair advantage. Most of the top cyclists doped. "I viewed it as a level playing field," he said.[20]

Lance had made a round of phone calls before the interview, tendering apologies to some of those he had wronged, perhaps so that he could tell Oprah he had made amends. One of those calls went to the LeMond home. This time, the LeMonds did not pick up the phone.

Lance had lost his legacy on October 22, 2012, a Monday. By the end of that week, Greg was reclaiming his.

On October 25, three days after the ruling by the Union Cycliste Internationale, Greg posted a letter to his Facebook page calling on the group's leader, Pat McQuaid, to step down. "I have never seen such abuse of power in cycling's history," he wrote.[21]

Critics charged that McQuaid and his predecessor, Hein Verbruggen, had brought cycling to its knees, standing by as the sport and its signature race were reduced to punch lines in late-night television monologues. Much of the blame seemingly lay with Verbruggen, the UCI head from 1991 to 2005. He had watched blood doping suffuse the peloton for half a decade before finally, in 1997, imposing a 50 percent limit on the share of red cells in the blood, a mandate that tacitly encouraged cyclists to continue doping right up to the new limit. The Festina scandal had played out under Verbruggen's watch. Verbruggen allegedly had helped conceal Lance's plan for a backdated prescription in 1999, which might have brought him down before he won his first Tour. For the next thirteen years, he and McQuaid had defended Lance against every accuser with the passion of worshipful parents, even as their union accepted donations from Lance and his team. Now, there were asterisks, rather than winners, in the record books for seven consecutive editions of cycling's flagship event.

If the embattled cycling leaders thought Lance's exit from the sport after the 2005 Tour would restore order, they were mistaken. Lance, his team, and their backroom deals had imposed a cruel order on the Tour. Now that order was gone. The first Tour without Lance, in 2006, had devolved into farce when Floyd Landis's victory began to unravel a few days after his arrival in Paris. The next year, a slender Dane named Michael Rasmussen was fired from his team over missed drug tests while wearing the *maillot jaune*. One day Rasmussen was leading the Tour; the next day he was gone. Sycophantic television commentators barely mentioned his name again; it was almost as if he had never existed. The winner of the 2010 Tour, Spaniard Alberto Contador, would lose his title over a failed drug test. As those events unfolded, cycling fans found it ever harder to take their beloved race seriously. The doping revelations against Lance, Landis, and Contador were not unlike the allegations mounting against baseball superstars Barry Bonds, Roger Clemens, and Alex Rodriguez. But the toll on cycling seemed far worse; no doping scandal had changed the outcome of a World Series.

In the days and weeks after Lance's downfall, a band of journalists, bloggers, doping critics, and former cyclists united under the banner Change Cycling Now, launching a campaign against McQuaid and recruiting a reluctant Greg to stand in as temporary head of the Union Cycliste Internationale if no one else could be found. McQuaid clung tenaciously to his job, only to be ousted the following year in an orderly election, defeated by a man who, unlike Greg, actually wanted the job: Brian Cookson, the former head of British cycling.

Over much of the previous decade, Greg had avoided the public eye. By 2009, when *Bicycling* magazine had published a piece titled "What-ever Happened to Greg LeMond?" it seemed Greg's own community had forgotten him. Now, bit by bit, he began to emerge triumphantly from cycling's wilderness.

In the summer of 2013, at Kathy's urging, Greg took his family to France to attend the Tour de France as a celebrity, rather than an out-cast. With the Armstrong controversy swept away, Kathy thought a trip to the Tour might actually be fun, and the LeMonds surely deserved some.

Greg had blamed Jean-Marie Leblanc, the longtime Tour director, for his ostracism from the one-hundredth anniversary ceremonies in 2002. Greg hadn't publicly returned to the Tour until 2007, when Leblanc had retired and Christian Prudhomme, another former sports journalist, had been installed in his place. Greg had described that visit as "an absolute blast";[22] yet he had still felt uneasy at the Tour and vaguely unwelcome. Now, revisiting the great race in 2013, Greg had an epiphany: whatever his currency in the United States, he remained a top-drawer celebrity in Europe. When someone spotted him atop l'Alpe d'Huez, the vast crowd began to chant his name.

In an October 2013 appearance on CNN's *Anderson Cooper 360*, billed as his first in-depth interview since the Armstrong affair, Greg finally found a large and receptive audience for his theories on what Lance would have accomplished in cycling without performance aids. "If he was clean, [if] everybody was clean," Greg told Cooper, "he was top-thirty at best." Greg said Lance belonged in jail.[23]

Greg spent that fall rebuilding his brand and his bicycle business. In September, at the annual sales convention known as Interbike, store owners and suppliers welcomed him like a long-lost friend. Greg intro-duced a new series of limited-edition road bicycles commemorating his three Tour de France wins, the first to bear the LeMond brand since his split with Trek five years earlier.

By the summer of 2014, hundreds of articles, blog posts, and websites had dutifully noted that Greg was now, once again, the only American to have won the Tour de France. Yet Lance Armstrong still cast a long shadow. Even in disgrace the Texan commanded a Twitter following of nearly four million.

If there was a moment when the allegiance of the cycling community shifted irrevocably back to Greg, perhaps it was the July 2014 publication of an open letter to Greg from Mark McKinnon, a famed political adviser and former board member of Lance's Livestrong charity.

"Lance won't say it," McKinnon opened, "but I will. I apologize."

McKinnon had spent ten years on the foundation board. "Through all those years," he wrote, "I was complicit in pushing the myth. And all I really knew about you was what I heard through Lance, Inc. I don't have to tell you it was not flattering." Only after Lance's downfall had McKinnon done his own research. "And now we know that while others were artificially enhancing their strength, you refused," he wrote. "In fact, take away the doping, the hunting accident, and the race you gave up for Hinault, you probably would have won more Tours than any rider ever, legally or illegally. . . . For years your bright light was darkened by a blizzard of lies, cheating and innuendo. And despite all this, from all the objective accounts that I've now read about you, unlike Lance, you are honest, humble and kind."[24]

In Europe, Greg's brand had never faltered. At the close of the 2000s, while Lance and his comeback distracted most of the cycling press, Scottish journalist Richard Moore had set out to retell the story of Greg's epic battle against the great Hinault. His book, *Slaying the Badger*, had been published in England in 2011, and in the United States the following year, captivating the cycling world. Then, in the summer of 2014, the American sports network ESPN aired a documentary adapted from the book. The film went into heavy rotation, retelling Greg's story to a wide swath of the American public.

On the ESPN broadcast, legions of American viewers who had not glimpsed Greg since his crowning Tour victory, a quarter century earlier, beheld a changed man. A receding crown of gray hair topped a haggard face, and deep lines framed his sunny smile and piercing blue eyes.

Greg's body carried fifty more pounds than in his racing days, and it sat encased within a back brace; a midwinter accident on icy Minnesota roads had fractured a vertebra. Yet those eyes still exuded a powerful magnetism.

That year, Greg accepted an invitation from the continental network Eurosport to provide live commentary on the Tour, just as Laurent Fignon had done in the previous decade. That coverage, along with a new monthly program titled *LeMond of Cycling* (a play on Greg's surname, which resembles the French words for "the world"), would air in more than fifty countries—although not, oddly, in the United States.

Greg was growing into his role as the conscience of professional cycling. In the spring of 2015, he opened a new front in the battle against doping.

Whispers of "mechanical doping" had started in 2010, when television cameras caught Swiss time-trial specialist Fabian Cancellara sweeping past his rivals on a steep grade at the Tour of Flanders in Belgium. He accelerated as if propelled by a rocket, never rising from his saddle or exerting much visible effort. The scene, replayed endlessly on YouTube, looked like a computer-generated trick from a Hollywood superhero movie. Three years later, in 2013, British cyclist Chris Froome raised fresh suspicions by winning the Tour de France on a bicycle that seemed at times to pedal itself. Astute fans posted videotaped footage of bicycles with rear wheels that spun on hypnotically as their owners lay sprawled on the pavement after a crash.

Cycling officials began to check bicycles for concealed motors, tiny machines that might add fifty or one hundred watts to the three hundred or four hundred watts the cyclist could generate alone. "I believe it's been used in racing," Greg told a reporter. "I believe it's been used sometimes in the Grand Tours."[25] Both Cancellara and Froome denied mechanical doping, and Froome joined Greg in urging cycling officials to perform more rigorous checks.

The controversy cast Greg in the customary role of whistle-blower, and a new character, Brian Cookson, as the defensive head of the embattled cycling union. Cookson said cycling officials had tested for hidden motors and found none. Greg insisted the tests didn't go far enough.

Frustrated at the tepid response, Greg had a bicycle built around a concealed motor and demonstrated it on l'Alpe d'Huez. A video of the
demonstration went viral.

Several months later, in January 2016, Greg's warnings proved
prescient. Cycling officials found a motor concealed within a bicycle
belonging to Femke Van den Driessche, a nineteen-year-old competitor
from Belgium. In a bike check at a race, cycling officials had discovered
a motor and a battery tucked inside the Belgian's seat tube, and a Blue-
tooth switch fitted beneath her handlebar tape. She was banned from
the sport for six years. Television's late-night hosts feasted on another
absurd cycling scandal.

Greg stepped up his rhetoric against the Union Cycliste Internationale. In one interview, he cited a report that the governing group had
tested no more than two dozen bicycles for concealed motors at the
prior year's Tour. "If that is true," he said, "it's criminal."[26] Greg proposed a few simple fixes that, if costly and tedious, would surely catch
the cheats. He urged officials to ban cyclists from changing bikes in
mid-race, a popular practice in the years since his retirement. Race
bicycles, he said, should be tagged before an event, sequestered after,
and tested one by one. The tests, he said, should employ thermal imag-
ing, a scan to detect heat emanating from a motor, and X-rays.

Cycling leaders vowed they would test many more bicycles in the
future, using their technology of choice, a scanner that detected the
magnetic resistance generated by a motor. Greg questioned whether it
would work.

Back in Minnesota, the new LeMond bicycle business was turning a
profit. Greg's LeMond Revolution stationary bicycle, priced at $400 to
$1,400, was yielding seven-figure annual sales and the bulk of the com-
pany's revenues. By 2015, a limited run of 300 commemorative Tour de
France road bikes, priced at $6,500 to $10,000, was selling out, along
with the new Washoe road bicycle, named for the windswept valley
where Greg's cycling career had taken flight.[27] All three of Greg's children were back in Minnesota, and two worked for their father in an
office near the Minneapolis ballpark.

In August 2016, Greg announced an ambitious new plan for his family business. LeMond Bicycles would become LeMond Composites, partnering with a federal agency to revolutionize the role of carbon fiber in American industry.

In the quarter century since Greg's early experiments with carbon-fiber bicycles, carbon had eclipsed steel and aluminum as the material of choice at the high end of the cycling market. Carbon frames offered an unrivaled combination of strength (high) and weight (low). But carbon was costly. While researching carbon suppliers, Greg had found a team at the Oak Ridge National Laboratory, a research arm of the U.S. Department of Energy, with a new production process that reportedly lowered costs by more than half. Now, the team would work for Greg. LeMond Composites opened in October 2016, as the LeMonds christened a sixty-five-thousand-square-foot factory in an industrial park outside Knoxville, Tennessee, home to the Oak Ridge lab. Greg's company was projected to raise $125 million, create 242 jobs over five years, and deliver sixteen to twenty million pounds of carbon fiber annually by 2018.

"This is an opportunity to change the world," Greg said.[28]

A few months later, the project appeared to implode. In December, Greg fired Connie Jackson, the CEO of LeMond Composites and leader of the team with the breakthrough technology. Jackson sued Greg, alleging, among other things, that she and her husband were owed nearly half a million dollars, and that Greg had used company funds to send his family to the 2016 Tour de France. Greg sued Jackson, alleging that she had failed to share the proprietary technology at the heart of the new company. The future of LeMond Composites looked grim—until April, when the parties settled out of court. The terms were largely confidential, but a new partnership with Deakin University in Australia, announced in June 2017, suggested Greg had found a new source for low-cost carbon. LeMond Composites rolled on.

That summer the LeMonds put their forty-acre Minnesota estate up for sale, including the 11,550-square-foot Georgian mansion at its center, priced at just under $5 million. After thirty years in Minnesota, Greg and Kathy would now spend much of their time in the Great Smoky

Mountains of Tennessee, and the family business might soon take them around the world.

In January 2017, Greg appeared in a *60 Minutes* story on mechanical doping, another step back toward the public life he and Kathy had once savored. Greg and Kathy had been working secretly with French police at the Tour. The segment reported that roughly a dozen cyclists had used motors in the 2015 edition of the race. Perhaps the more shocking revelation, though, concerned Team Sky, the British juggernaut whose cyclists would win the Tours of 2012, 2013, 2015, 2016, and 2017. French authorities told *60 Minutes* they had weighed every bicycle in the peloton before a key time-trial stage in 2015 and had found one team, Sky, with heavier bicycles than the others. The weight discrepancy was eight hundred grams—the approximate weight of a concealed motor. Team officials denied mechanical doping; viewers were left to ponder why else a team might field heavier bicycles. "Cycling weight is everything," Greg told *60 Minutes*. "If your bike weighs a kilo more, you would never race on it."[29]

Team Sky was the new face of professional cycling. After a century without a Tour winner, Britain suddenly had two: Bradley Wiggins in 2012, and Chris Froome in 2013, 2015, 2016, and 2017. Both were lithe climbers, positively gaunt by comparison to the fleshy cyclists of Greg's day, men capable of winning both mountain stages and time trials.

In an interview during the 2016 Tour, a reporter with the French sports paper *L'Équipe* had asked Greg about Froome's now-infamous attack on the slopes of Mont Ventoux in 2013. The Brit had pedaled away from his rivals, opening a yawning gap while riding on a relatively small gear with little apparent effort. Greg told the reporter, "You can't open a gap on small gears."[30] By attacking Froome and Team Sky, Greg was taking on a cycling dynasty and its preeminent cyclist, not to mention Cookson, the UCI director and former head of British cycling. Yet for Greg, all of this was familiar terrain.

August 13, 2016, dawned cloudy and cool in La Crescent, Minnesota, weather disappointing for a summer Saturday but fortuitous for a

bicycle ride. At seven a.m., a cheerful Greg and Kathy arrived at Veterans Park to join a sleepy entourage of recreational cyclists, dressed in
bright Lycra and unloading custom carbon bicycles from sport-utility
vehicles. As the couple emerged into the parking lot, a polite knot of
cyclists formed around them. Kathy stepped forward to greet the riders one by one, planting kisses on unsuspecting cheeks; she had just
returned from France and had not yet reacclimated to American habits. Greg clutched a pair of Gatorade bottles upside down and smiled
radiantly as he joined one conversation, then another and another. The
circle grew larger, populated mostly by middle-aged men, all wide-eyed
and reverential as they eased in to meet him. Half an hour later, Greg
had barely touched his sleek black bicycle.

Greg was there, as a celebrity guest, for the Apple Blossom Bike Tour,
a charity ride to raise money to end polio, and LizFest, a festival to
honor the memory of Elizabeth Holman-Melde, a woman of twenty-five
who had died of lung cancer four years earlier. Elizabeth's father had
gone to high school with Kathy. The events lay across the river from La
Crosse, Wisconsin, Kathy's hometown.

This was a rare chance for Greg's adoring fans to see him; he and
Kathy popped up here and there around the globe, but few of their
appearances were foretold. This one was, and it drew cyclists from several hundred miles away.

"I'm so glad to meet you, Greg," one middle-aged man gushed.
"You're my hero."

Another walked up and announced, "I've got a yellow jersey from the
Champs-Élysées; I'm wondering if you'd sign it."

A woman approached Greg, sobbing. Her husband had so wanted to
meet him before he died. She had written the LeMonds a letter. Greg
and Kathy remembered it, and her, immediately. Each hugged her in
turn.

Greg signed a procession of T-shirts and helmets and LeMond bicycle
frames and posters, chatting amicably with an orderly procession of
fans, oblivious to the passing minutes. Finally, Greg glimpsed a pack of
cyclists setting out on the course and broke away from his conversation.

"Whoa, whoa, whoa!" he exclaimed. "We've gotta go!" He set out on his LeMond bicycle, with a picture of his granddaughter's face pasted on its handlebar stem. He pedaled alone. Most of the cyclists who had come to see him were already half a mile up the road.

Greg had intended to ride the full course of sixty-seven miles, but he and a small group of elated fans got lost along the way. They completed about fifty miles before returning to the park. Greg was flushed and drenched in sweat.

"It's not the bicycle," he laughed, "it's the legs." He dismounted his bicycle and padded across the lawn in his socks, looking for water. He found two bottles, drained them in succession and settled into a chair next to a crate of apples to greet his followers.

Greg and Kathy had been up since dawn. They would return for LizFest and remain at Veterans Park until ten that night, eating and drinking and talking with old friends and former classmates and complete strangers who wanted a glimpse of their idol. According to the day's schedule, this was lunchtime, Greg's only chance to rest. Kathy stood patiently by, gazing lovingly at her husband, the benevolent savior of American cycling, as he held court with his fans. She knew he would not leave until he had spoken to every last one.

Greg peered out at the gaggle of cyclists—men, women, and children clutching shiny helmets and rolled-up posters and freshly pressed T-shirts that told the world they had ridden with Greg LeMond.

Smiling, Greg beckoned: "You want me to sign some of this?"

AUTHOR'S NOTE

I GREW UP in a home where bicycle racing, rather than baseball, framed the summer months. My father, Pierre, was an immigrant from bicycle-mad Belgium who had pedaled nearly three thousand miles across the United States at age eleven, accompanied by his father and younger brother. He raced bicycles throughout his high school and college years. Now, thirty years later, bicycle wheels hung from suspended broomsticks in our basement and bicycle frames dangled from hooks in the garage. I owned my first fixed-gear track bike at six. I owned a spoke wrench at twelve. Though we lived just a mile from Wrigley Field, home of the Chicago Cubs, our preferred spectator sport lay twenty-five miles away, at the Ed Rudolph Velodrome in Northbrook, Illinois. There, on Thursday nights, we would file into the grandstands for an evening of bicycle races.

I never entered a bicycle race; I lacked the reckless, daredevil spirit I recognized in the racers, who jostled and bumped like bulls at Pamplona and regularly sustained gruesome injuries. Instead, I threw myself into a routine of recreational cycling, pedaling back and forth across the North Side of Chicago on summer days and taking long weekend rides into the suburbs with my father. I loved the hypnotic rhythm, the bucolic scenery, and the rush of accomplishment that came after a long ride.

My teenage years coincided with the ascent of bicycle racing as a televised sport in the United States. In 1982, my father and I watched network coverage of the first Great American Bicycle Race, an organized and sanctioned event held across the same insane distance my father had traversed at eleven; needless to say, we sat transfixed. The next year, we watched the first extensive network coverage of the Tour de France, pared and packaged into breathless, synthesizer-drenched weekly segments on CBS. Laurent Fignon, the remote Frenchman they called *le Professeur*, became my hero, gliding to victory with his mop of straw-colored hair, granny glasses, and John McEnroe headband. A year later, I cruelly abandoned Fignon and embraced a new hero, Greg LeMond, the first American to contend for victory at *le Tour*. With his golden hair, blue eyes, and bronzed skin, LeMond looked as if he'd ridden right off the set of *Breaking Away*, a film that had both celebrated and excoriated European cycling, still fresh in my memory. In 1984, we watched LeMond fall to Fignon. In 1985, we watched LeMond challenge the great Hinault, and we cheered the Badger to his historic fifth Tour victory even as we cursed the cruel team politics that required LeMond to race for second place. In 1986, we watched in awe as LeMond slew the Badger, claiming our nation's first Tour victory and denying Hinault—and France—a record-breaking sixth title.

The next spring, we read that LeMond had been injured, not in a bicycle race but a hunting accident. It didn't sound serious, and we were surprised to note his absence not just from that year's Tour but from the next one as well. Not until the summer of 1989, when a wave of news features announced LeMond's triumphal return, did we realize how near death he had come.

That summer at the Tour, LeMond faced off against a rejuvenated Fignon. The diminished champions waged a battle so fierce that weekly television capsules could not keep up. We turned to the newspapers, devouring the daily installments in the *Chicago Tribune* as LeMond and Fignon traded savage blows and a slender lead. On the Tour's final weekend, we returned to our television and watched the final moments of the race in stunned disbelief. A videotape of that decisive stage became a treasured artifact that we trotted out when friends stopped by, in the vain hope that they would savor it as much as we had.

I left Chicago in 1990 to start my career as a journalist. My interest in professional cycling gradually waned, along with the careers of LeMond and Fignon. The 1990s were a fallow period for American cycling, and I mostly ignored the Tour—until 1999, when Lance Armstrong wrote the first chapter of his own comeback. Now American racing fans could watch the Tour unfold in real time on cable television and follow exhaustive daily coverage online.

I rooted for Lance, and I bought his memoir for my father, but my unease grew with his every Tour victory. He dominated the race as completely as Miguel Induráin, the Big Mig, who had won the Tour in consecutive years from 1991 to 1995. But Induráin was Spanish, and Armstrong was American; the Texan's dominance seemed more oppressive somehow. By the time Armstrong mopped up his unprecedented sixth and seventh victories, I could barely watch.

I set out to write this book in the fall of 2015. Walking around my neighborhood one day, I realized with a jolt that the 1989 Tour de France was the perfect topic for a book: a great, forgotten story. The parade of events that had erased the story from the nation's collective memory became the book's final act. LeMond's amazing comeback and three historic Tour victories had been eclipsed by Armstrong's even-better comeback and *seven* historic Tour victories. I knew the uncanny parallels between Armstrong's comeback and LeMond's. I wanted to recount the 1989 Tour—not merely LeMond's finest hour, but the greatest Tour ever staged and one of the most stirring sports narratives of my lifetime. Even in France there was little debate on that point. Perhaps after writing the book I could finally persuade old friends to watch that grainy videotape of the final time trial into Paris.

In assembling my manuscript, I relied on hundreds of newspaper articles published across forty years in the United States, England, Ireland, and Canada; teetering stacks of cycling magazines from the United States, England, Belgium, and France; and numerous books from both continents. A few sources merit special mention: *Greg LeMond's Complete Book of Bicycling*, cowritten with Kent Gordis, for details of LeMond's childhood and his amateur and professional career through his first Tour victory in 1986; Sam Abt's *LeMond: The Incredible Comeback of an American Hero*, with its exhaustive interviews of LeMond through the 1989 comeback; Richard Moore's excellent *Slaying the Badger*, and the subsequent ESPN documentary, for their meticulous reconstruction of the 1985 and 1986 Tours; Bill and Carol McGann's *The Story of the Tour de France*, which I consulted repeatedly for Tour stage dates, lengths, and results; Matt Rendell's *Blazing Saddles*, my favorite retelling of the Tour's "cruel and unusual" history; and two books, *From Lance to Landis* by David Walsh and *Wheelmen* by Reed Albergotti and Vanessa O'Connell, for unvarnished accounts of the Armstrong era.

For the life and times of Laurent Fignon, I relied heavily on his memoir, *We Were Young and Carefree*. For his final years, I consulted *Laurent*, the memoir of his widow, Valérie. Among many newspapers and magazines, I returned most frequently to the *New York Times*, *Washington Post*, *Chicago Tribune*, and *Los Angeles Times*; to the British *Times*, *Sunday Times*, and *Guardian*; and to the magazines *Sports Illustrated*, *Winning: Bicycle Racing Illustrated*, *Bicycling*, and *Vélo*. I must also single out Irish journalist Paul Kimmage, whose 2007 interviews with Greg and Kathy LeMond told me as much as any book.

Above all, I relied on my own interviews. I spent many hours with Greg and Kathy LeMond in visits to Minnesota, Wisconsin, and Tennessee. I spoke repeatedly to Greg's father, Bob; to his sisters, Kathy and Karen; and to his in-laws, Mary and Sacia Morris. For the chapters on Greg's childhood and amateur years, I interviewed boyhood friends and fellow cyclists, including Frank Kratzer, Cliff Young, Roland Della Santa, George Mount, Kent Gordis, Jeff Bradley, Ron Kiefel, and Greg Demgen, and Greg's first real coach, Eddie Borysewicz. For Greg's professional career and first Tour victory, I spoke to Greg's friends, teammates, and competitors including Phil Anderson, Andy Hampsten, Stephen Roche, Steve Bauer, Jock Boyer, Noël Dejonckheere, and Vince Barteau, and to his coaches, Maurice Le Guilloux and the great Cyrille Guimard. For the shooting, comeback, and eventual decline, I tapped those sources and others, including Greg's doctor, Sandy Beal; his dear friend and *soigneur*, Otto Jácome; Dr. Mark Hom, Greg's diehard fan and cowriter; Nathan Jenkins and Ron Stanko, lawyers who represented the LeMonds; Team LeMond colleagues Jeff Sanchez, Craig Calfee, and Jean-Pierre Pascal; coach Roger Legeay; and teammate Johan Lammerts.

Two key sources for the Armstrong era, Lance himself and former teammate Floyd Landis, politely declined interview requests. In their absence, I relied on voluminous published reports and court documents, on the fine documentary *Stop at Nothing*, and on Greg's numerous accounts of the era in radio interviews, podcasts, and print. I interviewed Greg's oldest son, Geoffrey, and revisited old LeMond friends including Greg Demgen and Frank Kratzer. I consulted Lance's memoir, *It's Not about the Bike.* I spoke or corresponded with Edward Coyle, a physiologist who studied Armstrong; Dan Zeman, a physiologist who studied LeMond; Mark McKinnon, a former Livestrong board member; Thom Weisel, Armstrong's longtime financial backer; and Ben McCarthy, a LeMond company spokesman.

For the crucial chapters on Fignon, I translated numerous books and articles from the original French; in the end, most of them proved poor substitutes for Fignon's candid and revealing memoir. I interviewed childhood friend Rosario Scolaro and lifelong friend Vince Barteau. I returned again and again to Alain Gallopin, Laurent's closest friend and longtime *soigneur.* Laurent's first wife, Nathalie, and widow, Valérie, helped immensely with framing the cyclist's life outside the peloton.

Whenever I paused in the manuscript to quote a character, I searched for the best, most articulate, and evocative comment available, even if it came from someone else's notebook. Some of the observations collected in Moore's *Badger* book or Abt's *LeMond,* for example, simply could not be topped. When recounting events twenty or thirty years past, I generally favored comments reported the next day, or the next month, over interviews conducted two or three decades on. When quoting material translated by British writers, I made a few light edits to de-Anglicize the text; thus, "mates" became "friends."

This book is not about doping. Yet dope has been part of professional cycling since its inception. I have come to view doping in cycling much as I regard it in baseball. I divide each sport, and its competitors, into two distinct eras: the years before doping influenced results, and the years after. I'm no expert on baseball, but I don't sense much concern among statisticians about the feats of hitters and pitchers in the eras of Mike Schmidt and Reggie Jackson. As for cycling, I am inclined to agree with most of the retired riders I interviewed, who believe doping began to affect results in the Tour and other contests in the early 1990s. EPO, cycling's wonder drug, seems to have permeated the peloton by 1993.

Greg LeMond is often described as the last great Tour de France champion of the "clean" era. I have read most of the articles written about him, and I have found no credible allegation that he doped from any source, named or unnamed. Lance Armstrong famously questioned LeMond's record-breaking performance in the final time trial of the 1989 Tour, implying that LeMond could not have accomplished it without artificial aids. But that is conjecture.

I interviewed dozens of men who competed with LeMond, and at one point or another, I asked most of them whether they thought he had raced clean. One cyclist did not. His evidence against LeMond, like Armstrong's, was the breathless time trial that opens this book. He would not allow me to name him.

Most of the riders I interviewed still regard Lance Armstrong as an extraordinary cyclist. So do I.

My father died in 2004, weeks before Armstrong won his sixth Tour. In our final conversation, Pop asked me to look after his bicycles. I did, and I have kept his beloved Schwinn Paramount in good working order. I can't say I'm riding it much these days, and I have long since forgotten how to operate a spoke wrench. Then again, I've been busy with the book.

I want to thank all of my interviewees for their time, their help, and their support. Thanks to Beth Biersdorf in Minnesota for arranging the crucial first meeting with the LeMonds. Very special thanks to Phil Anderson and Anne Newell in Australia, Andy Hampsten in Colorado, Alain Gallopin in France, Dr. Sandy Beal in Oregon, Otto Jácome in Mexico, Dr. Mary Morris in Wisconsin, Roland Della Santa, Bob LeMond, Kathy LeMond McGee, Karen LeMond Melarkey, and Cliff Young in Reno, Dan Zeman in Minnesota, and Greg and Kathy LeMond, all of whom spoke to me several times over many months. Thank you to Deborah Grosvenor, an agent who changes lives, including mine; to George Gibson and Jamison Stoltz, my superb editors at Grove Atlantic; to

Catherine Favier-Kelly, my translator; to Mark Linnen, a Washington cyclist and one-man Library of Congress on obscure LeMond sources; to my mother, Betty, and late stepfather, Jon, who read and helped shape the manuscript; and to Sophie, my beautiful wife, who happens to be one of the best editors on earth.

PHOTO CREDITS

Page 1: Major Taylor, George Van Norman via *Wikimedia Commons*; Frank Kramer via *Wikimedia Commons*.

Page 2: All images courtesy of Greg LeMond.

Page 3: Greg LeMond in Della Santa jersey, courtesy of Greg LeMond; Eddie Borysewicz, courtesy of Eddie Borysewicz; Greg and Kathy on bicycle, courtesy of Greg LeMond; Greg and family, courtesy of Mary Morris.

Page 4: All images, © Offside Sports Photography Ltd.

Page 5: Cycling team, © Offside Sports Photography Ltd; 1984 Tour de France, © Graham Watson.

Page 6: All images, © Offside Sports Photography Ltd.

Page 7: 1986 Tour de France, © Cor Vos; LeMond's victory, © Offside Sports Photography Ltd.

Page 8: Victory dinner, © Offside Sports Photography Ltd; Giro d'Italia, © Cor Vos.

Page 9: Greg in hospital, © Offside Sports Photography Ltd; X-ray, courtesy of Greg LeMond.

Page 10: 1989 Tour de France Map © Martin Lubikowski, ML Design, London; 1989 Tour de France, © Offside Sports Photography Ltd.

Page 11: All images, © Offside Sports Photography Ltd.

Page 12: Greg's victory, © Offside Sports Photography Ltd; Laurent's defeat, © Offside Sports Photography Ltd; Greg and Kathy, © Getty Images.

Page 13: 1989 victory podium, © Offside Sports Photography Ltd; 1989 World Championship, © Graham Watson.

Page 14: All images, © Offside Sports Photography Ltd.

Page 15: Greg and Lance Armstrong, © Offside Sports Photography Ltd; 100th Tour de France anniversary, © Cor Vos.

Page 16: Greg and Kathy, © Getty Images; Greg signs jersey, courtesy of Daniel de Visé.

NOTES

Prologue

1. "My Edited Video," YouTube video that incorporates ABC and Channel 4 broadcasts of 1989 Tour de France, posted by "yesroh," October 1, 2011, https://www.youtube.com/watch?v=eJ8xXmfNUXk, accessed May 17, 2017.
2. Samuel Abt, *LeMond: The Incredible Comeback of an American Hero* (New York: Random House, 1990), 190.
3. "My Edited Video," ABC and Channel 4 broadcast of 1989 Tour de France, Stage 21.
4. Laurent Fignon, *We Were Young and Carefree*, trans. William Fotheringham (London: Yellow Jersey Press, 2010), 18.
5. "My Edited Video," ABC and Channel 4 broadcast of 1989 Tour de France, Stage 21.

The Gift

1. Bob LeMond, author interview, January 20, 2016.
2. Bob LeMond, author interview, January 26, 2016.
3. Kathy LeMond McGee, author interview, September 8, 2016.
4. "Zephyr," *twainquotes.com*, http://www.twainquotes.com/Zephyr.html, accessed May 17, 2017; from Mark Twain, *Roughing It* (Hartford: American Publishing Company, 1872).
5. Abt, *LeMond*, 16.
6. Abt, *LeMond*, 16.
7. Frank Kratzer, author interview, February 4, 2016.
8. Bob Ottum, "Climbing Clear Up to the Heights," *Sports Illustrated*, September 3, 1984, https://www.si.com/vault/1984/09/03/620227/climbing-clear-up-to-the-heights.
9. The LeMonds have never disclosed Ron's surname in a published interview. It is withheld here for that reason.
10. Greg LeMond, author interview, October 10, 2017.
11. Abt, *LeMond*, 17.
12. Richard Moore, *Slaying the Badger: Greg LeMond, Bernard Hinault, and the Greatest Tour de France* (Boulder, Colorado: VeloPress, 2012), 56.
13. Greg LeMond and Kent Gordis, *Greg LeMond's Complete Book of Bicycling* (New York: G. P. Putnam's Sons, 1987), 18.
14. "Must Hear: Greg LeMond Speaks Out in Wide-Ranging Interview on Irish Radio," *VeloNews.com*, October 6, 2012. Greg LeMond, 2012 podcast interview

by Ger Gilroy, as quoted by VeloNews.com. Accessed May 17, 2017., http://www.velonews.com/2012/10/news/must-hear-greg-lemond-speaks-out-in-wide-ranging-interview-on-irish-radio_256161.

15. Young recalled meeting LeMond several months earlier, in summer 1975.
16. Roland Della Santa, author interview, January 20, 2016.
17. Della Santa interview, January 20, 2016.
18. LeMond and Gordis, *Complete Book of Bicycling*, 19.
19. Della Santa interview, January 20, 2016.
20. Cliff Young, e-mail message to author, February 25, 2017.
21. Young e-mail.

The Wheelmen

1. David Slack, "Who Else Is Here for the Punishment?" *Island Life* blog, August 20, 2008, https://publicaddress.net/islandlife/who-else-is-here-for-the-punishment/, accessed September 4, 2017.

LeMonster

1. Roland Della Santa, author interview, February 3, 2016.
2. Marco Fanelli, "Still a Fan, Greg," *Marco Off the Mark* blog, September 27, 2008, http://marcofanelli.blogspot.com/2008/09/still-fan-greg.html, accessed September 4, 2017.
3. Kent Gordis, author interview, September 18, 2015.
4. Kent K. Gordis, "Who's the Turkey in the Yellow Jersey?" in *Greg LeMond: The Official Story*, supplement to *VeloNews*, April 1995.
5. Karen LeMond Melarkey, author interview, October 13, 2016.
6. Kathy LeMond McGee, author interview, March 22, 2016.
7. LeMond and Gordis, *Complete Book of Bicycling*, 21.
8. Jay Goldberg, "It's All in the Diet for Young Cyclist LeMond," *Nevada State Journal*, July 15, 1976.
9. Noël Dejonckheere, author interview, June 2, 2016.
10. Kratzer interview.
11. Kratzer interview.
12. Kratzer interview.
13. Roland Della Santa, author interview, April 12, 2016.
14. Geoff Drake with Jim Ochowicz, *Team 7-Eleven: How an Unsung Band of American Cyclists Took on the World—and Won* (Boulder, Colorado: VeloPress, 2011), 156.
15. Eddie Borysewicz, author interview, October 24, 2016.
16. Borysewicz interview, October 24, 2016.
17. Greg Demgen, e-mail message to author, February 18, 2016.

The Pilgrimage

1. Paul Kimmage, "The Natural," *2r*, March 20, 2013, https://www.facebook.com/2Rmag/posts/396440210453708, accessed May 18, 2017.

2. Greg LeMond, author interview, April 23, 2016.
3. Abt, *LeMond*, 22.
4. Kathy LeMond, author interview, April 22, 2016.
5. Kathy LeMond interview, April 22, 2016.
6. Kathy LeMond interview, April 22, 2016.
7. Demgen eventually recovered from the romantic blow and remained close with both LeMonds.
8. Kathy LeMond, author interview, August 13, 2016.
9. Kathy LeMond interview, August 13, 2016.
10. Greg LeMond interview, April 23, 2016.
11. Ed Pavelka, "America's World Junior Champion," in *Bicycle Racing in the Modern Era: Twenty-Five Years of Cycling Journalism from the Editors of VeloNews* (Boulder, Colorado: VeloPress, 1997), 182.
12. Kathy LeMond interview, April 22, 2016.
13. Bob LeMond interview, January 26, 2016.
14. Kathy LeMond interview, April 22, 2016.
15. Moore, *Badger*, 62.
16. Jeff Bradley, author interview, February 17, 2016.
17. Samuel Abt, "American Cyclist Moves Up," *New York Times*, September 29, 1982.
18. Abt, "Moves Up."
19. LeMond and Gordis, *Complete Book of Bicycling*, 26.
20. Greg LeMond, interview by Bill McGann, "Greg LeMond: Professional Cycling's Talented Revolutionary," *BikeRaceInfo*, February 24, 2007, http://www.bikeraceinfo.com/oralhistory/lemond.html.
21. Kathy LeMond interview, April 22, 2016.
22. Abt, *LeMond*, 33.
23. Abt, *LeMond*, 77.
24. Kathy LeMond interview, April 22, 2016.
25. Dejonckheere interview.
26. Greg LeMond interview, April 23, 2016.
27. Jean Marie Leblanc, "Hinault: Hello America!" *Vélo*, December 1980.
28. Leblanc, "Hello America."
29. Kratzer interview.
30. Kratzer interview.

Le Parisien

1. Fignon, *Carefree*, 25.
2. Fignon, *Carefree*, 26.
3. Fignon, *Carefree*, 27.
4. Fignon, *Carefree*, 27.
5. Fignon, *Carefree*, 25.
6. Fignon, *Carefree*, 28–29.
7. Fignon, *Carefree*, 40.
8. Jean-Paul Ollivier, *Laurent Fignon* (Grenoble: Éditions Glénat, 2001), 13.
9. Fignon, *Carefree*, 30.
10. Rosario Scolaro, e-mail message to author, May 23, 2016.

11. Fignon, *Carefree*, 31.
12. Fignon, *Carefree*, 33.
13. Scolaro e-mail.
14. Fignon, *Carefree*, 35.
15. Scolaro e-mail.
16. Scolaro e-mail.
17. Fignon, *Carefree*, 38.
18. Fignon, *Carefree*, 41.
19. Fignon, *Carefree*, 42.
20. Fignon, *Carefree*, 42.
21. Fignon, *Carefree*, 44.
22. Alain Gallopin, author interview, May 4, 2016.
23. Fignon, *Carefree*, 40.
24. Gallopin interview, May 4, 2016.
25. Fignon, *Carefree*, 45.
26. Fignon, *Carefree*, 45.
27. Fignon, *Carefree*, 46.
28. Cyrille Guimard, author interview, May 24, 2016.
29. Fignon, *Carefree*, 47.

L'Américain

1. Kathy LeMond interview, April 22, 2016.
2. Kathy LeMond interview, April 22, 2016.
3. Kathy LeMond interview, April 22, 2016.
4. Abt, *LeMond*, 37.
5. Henri Quiqueré, "Deux Americains a Paris," *Miroir du Cyclisme*, February–March 1981.
6. LeMond and Gordis, *Complete Book of Bicycling*, 28.
7. John Dower (dir.), "Slaying the Badger," *30 for 30*, ESPN, volume 2, episode 19, aired July 22, 2014.
8. Kathy LeMond interview, August 13, 2017.
9. "The Three Wives," *Winning: Bicycle Racing Illustrated*, August 1986.
10. Barry McDermott, "Goldilocks 1, Bears 0," *Sports Illustrated*, July 13, 1981.
11. Claude Parmentier, "Greg LeMond a L'Ouest du Nouveau," *Sprint International*, May 1982.
12. "World Cycling Championships Road Race Goodwood 1982," YouTube video of Channel 4 broadcast of 1982 cycling world championship road race, posted by Jason Stack, October 27, 2010, https://www.youtube.com/watch?v=jjZnpXZ9MP4, accessed May 19, 2017.
13. Kathy LeMond, author interview, April 23, 2016.
14. Abt, "American Cyclist Moves Up."
15. Henri Quiqueré, "Greg LeMond une Etoile est Nee," *Miroir du Cyclisme*, October–November 1982.
16. Quiqueré, "Etoile."

17. Phil Anderson, author interview, May 25, 2016.
18. LeMond and Gordis, *Complete Book of Bicycling*, 30.
19. Abt, *LeMond*, 91–92.
20. Robert Silva, "Greg LeMond Fait ses Classes," *Vélo*, October 1982.
21. Quiqueré, "Etoile."
22. Guimard interview.
23. Vince Barteau, author interview, May 25, 2016.
24. Barteau interview.
25. Paul Kimmage, "The Agony and the Ecstacy," *2r*, April 5, 2013, https://www .facebook.com/2Rmag/posts/534227359949423, accessed May 19, 2017.
26. LeMond and Gordis, *Complete Book of Bicycling*, 31.
27. Matt Rendell, *Blazing Saddles: The Cruel and Unusual History of the Tour de France* (Boulder, Colorado: VeloPress, 2008), 63.
28. Rendell, *Saddles*, 122.
29. Rendell, *Saddles*, 138.
30. Rendell, *Saddles*, 144.
31. Simon Van Zuylen-Wood, "Free Lance Armstrong! Not All Dopers Are Created Equal," *New Republic*, June 22, 2012, https://newrepublic.com/article/104236 /free-lance-armstrong-not-all-dopers-are-created-equal.
32. "Simpson: Martyr, Example, Warning," *CyclingNews*, July 20, 2007, http://www .cyclingnews.com/features/simpson-martyr-example-warning/.
33. This exchange, taken from Kimmage's "Agony" article, implies Jock Boyer doped. Jock maintains he did not. In any case, Jock retired before the EPO era.
34. Pierre Chany, "Greg LeMond le Pionnier," *Vélo*, September 1983.
35. Abt, *LeMond*, 47.
36. Moore, *Badger*, 57.
37. Anderson interview, May 25, 2016.
38. Moore, *Badger*, 95.
39. John Wilcockson, "Inside Cycling with John Wilcockson: Greg LeMond's First Rainbow Jersey," *VeloNews*, October 1, 2005, http://www.velonews .com/2005/10/news/inside-cycling-with-john-wilcockson-greg-lemonds-first -rainbow-jersey_8987.
40. Abt, *LeMond*, 48.
41. Dave Chauner, "A Star is Born," *Winning: Bicycle Racing Illustrated*, November 1983.
42. Wilcockson, "Rainbow."
43. Moore, *Badger*, 98.

Le Tour

1. Rendell, *Saddles*, 19.
2. Rendell, *Saddles*, 38.
3. Rendell, *Saddles*, 90.
4. Rendell, *Saddles*, 102.
5. Trip Gabriel, "Tour de Force," *Rolling Stone*, October 9, 1986.

Le Grand Blond

1. Fignon, *Carefree*, 54.
2. Michael Barry, "How It Feels to Train for the Tour de France," *Esquire*, June 30, 2014, http://www.esquire.co.uk/culture/news/a6305/how-it-feels-to-train-for -the-tour-de-france/.
3. Fignon, *Carefree*, 66–67.
4. Fignon, *Carefree*, 56.
5. Fignon, *Carefree*, 72.
6. Fignon, *Carefree*, 72.
7. Fignon, *Carefree*, 77.
8. Fignon, *Carefree*, 73.
9. Fignon, *Carefree*, 82–83.
10. Fignon, *Carefree*, 86.
11. Barteau interview.
12. Fignon, *Carefree*, 89.
13. Fignon, *Carefree*, 92.
14. Fignon, *Carefree*, 93.
15. Fignon, *Carefree*, 94.
16. Fignon, *Carefree*, 95.
17. Fignon, *Carefree*, 96.
18. Fignon, *Carefree*, 97.
19. Fignon, *Carefree*, 98.
20. John Wilcockson, "Kelly's Performance Has Them All Talking During Tour Halt," *Times* (London), July 20, 1983.
21. Fignon, *Carefree*, 99.
22. Fignon, *Carefree*, 99.
23. "Kelly's Dream Fades on Alpine Way," *Irish Times*, July 21, 1983.
24. Fignon, *Carefree*, 100.
25. Samuel Abt, "French Novice, 22, Is Winner of Tour," *New York Times*, July 25, 1983.
26. Samuel Abt, *Off to the Races: 25 Years of Cycling Journalism* (Boulder, Colorado: VeloPress, 2002), 27.
27. John Wilcockson, "A Victory for Caution," *Sunday Times* (London), July 24, 1983.
28. Fignon, *Carefree*, 105.
29. Fignon, *Carefree*, 61.
30. Fignon, *Carefree*, 62–63.
31. Fignon, *Carefree*, 106.
32. Nathalie de Barallon, e-mail message to author, February 10, 2016.
33. De Barallon e-mail.
34. Fignon, *Carefree*, 106.
35. Fignon, *Carefree*, 107–8.
36. Alain Gallopin, author interview, January 26, 2016.
37. Samuel Abt, *A Season in Turmoil: Lance Armstrong Replaces Greg LeMond as U.S. Cycling's Superstar* (Boulder, Colorado: VeloPress, 1995), 16.
38. Moore, *Badger*, 91.
39. Fignon, *Carefree*, 113.

40. Fignon, *Carefree*, 111.
41. Fignon, *Carefree*, 112.
42. Greg LeMond interview, October 10, 2017.
43. This episode derives from Fignon's memoir, where it occupies a full chapter.
44. Fignon, *Carefree*, 122–23.
45. Fignon, *Carefree*, 125.
46. Robert McG. Thomas Jr., "Scouting; Ahead of Himself," *New York Times*, May 19, 1984.
47. Samuel Abt, "U.S. Cyclist Riding Hard for the Tour," *New York Times*, June 27, 1984.
48. Fignon, *Carefree*, 133.
49. Fignon, *Carefree*, 135.
50. Moore, *Badger*, 126.
51. A. W. Benjamin, "An American in Paris," *Bicycling*, November–December 1984.
52. Samuel Abt, "Tour Moves to Alps as Fignon Excels," *New York Times*, July 16, 1984.
53. Fignon, *Carefree*, 130.
54. Fignon, *Carefree*, 137.
55. Fignon, *Carefree*, 137.
56. John Wilcockson, "Colombian Stages First Win," *Times* (London), July 17, 1984.
57. Fignon, *Carefree*, 139.
58. "Fignon's Tour de Force," *Winning: Bicycle Racing Illustrated*, October 1984 (author unknown).
59. Ottum, "Climbing Clear."
60. Fignon, *Carefree*, 140.

The Deal

1. This conversation is reconstructed from several sources, including Greg LeMond and Daniel Friebe, "The Greatest Tour of All," Part 3, *BikeRadar* blog, September 2, 2000, http://www.bikeradar.com/us/blog/article/part-2-the -greatest-tour-of-all-by-greg-lemond-22650/, accessed September 4, 2017; and Paul Kimmage's "The Natural."
2. Maurice Le Guilloux, author interview, August 8, 2016.
3. Abt, *LeMond*, 86.
4. *Vélo*, October 1984.
5. Abt, *LeMond*, 84.
6. Moore, *Badger*, 114.
7. LeMond and Friebe, "Greatest," Part 3.
8. Fignon, *Carefree*, 142–43.
9. Samuel Abt, "Hinault Winner Again," *New York Times*, July 22, 1985.
10. Owen Mulholland, "Greg LeMond, Bernard Hinault and the 1985 Tour de France," *BikeRaceInfo*, http://www.bikeraceinfo.com/riderhistories/Lemond-Hinault1985-Tour.html.
11. Mulholland, "1985 Tour."
12. Moore, *Badger*, 145.
13. Le Guilloux interview.

14. Samuel Abt, "Victory within Reach of Weary Hinault," *New York Times*, July 18, 1985.
15. This scene is based on author interviews with LeMond, Roche, and Le Guilloux, and accounts by John Wilcockson in *VeloNews* (John Wilcockson, "Inside Cycling with John Wilcockson: The Real Story behind Hinault v. LeMond in '85," *VeloNews*, http://www.velonews.com/2005/12/news/inside-cycling-with -john-wilcockson-the-real-story-behind-hinault-v-lemond-in-85_9232) and Richard Moore in his *Badger* book.
16. "1985 Tour De France Part 8 of 9," YouTube video of CBS television coverage of 1985 Tour, posted by "GoliathAngel," October 5, 2010. https://www.youtube .com/watch?v=xrSltZ2xPVo, accessed May 21, 2017.
17. Abt, "Weary Hinault."
18. CBS coverage, 1985 Tour.
19. Moore, *Badger*, 154.
20. Greg LeMond with John Wilcockson, "Greg LeMond's Tour Diary," *Winning: Bicycle Racing Illustrated*, October 1985.
21. Le Guilloux interview.
22. Jean-Jacques Simmler, "La Vérité sur L'Opération Fignon," *Vélo*, June 1985.
23. "A Race Apart," *Winning: Bicycle Racing Illustrated*, October 1984 (author unknown).
24. Samuel Abt, "Fignon Retains Tour Title," *New York Times*, July 23, 1984.
25. Fignon, *Carefree*, 145.
26. Fignon, *Carefree*, 148.
27. Fignon, *Carefree*, 149–50.
28. Fignon, *Carefree*, 150.
29. Fignon, *Carefree*, 153–54.
30. Fignon, *Carefree*, 155.

The Betrayal

1. Moore, *Badger*, 163.
2. Abt, *LeMond*, 84.
3. E. M. Swift, "Now It's on to the Mountains: The Americans Were Doing Right Well, So Far, in the Tour de France," *Sports Illustrated*, July 21, 1986.
4. Andy Hampsten, author interview, January 11, 2016.
5. The headline, Hinault's "strongest rider" remark, and Mitterand's call all were reported by Moore in *Badger*, 181.
6. Fignon, *Carefree*, 155.
7. Philippe Bouvet, "Laurent Fignon: 'Maintenant, ça ne Dépend Plus que de Moi . . .'" *Vélo*, February 1986.
8. Fignon, *Carefree*, 159.
9. Fignon, *Carefree*, 160.
10. Fignon, *Carefree*, 161.
11. Samuel Abt, "Fignon Testing Form in Return to Tour," *New York Times*, July 5, 1986.
12. Fignon, *Carefree*, 162.
13. Moore, *Badger*, 1.
14. Paul Kimmage, *Rough Ride* (London: Yellow Jersey Press, 2007 edition), 81.

15. Moore, *Badger*, 202.
16. Moore, *Badger*, 204.
17. Moore, *Badger*, 205.
18. Moore, *Badger*, 206.
19. "1986 Tour de France, stage 13," YouTube video of Channel 4 broadcast of 1986 Tour de France, Stage 13, posted by Christopher Smith, October 9, 2006, https://www.youtube.com/watch?v=je1v0E_e7QQ, accessed May 23, 2017.
20. Moore, *Badger*, 214.
21. Moore, *Badger*, 222.
22. Moore, *Badger*, 225.
23. Brian Moynahan and John Wilcockson, "Cycling: The Tour—Bonjour Mr. America," *Sunday Times* (London), July 27, 1986.
24. E. M. Swift, "An American Takes Paris: Pushed to the Limit by Bernard Hinault, Greg LeMond (in Yellow) Rode to a Historic Win in the Tour de France," *Sports Illustrated*, August 4, 1986.
25. "Col du Granon - Tour de France 1986 Stage 17," YouTube video of Channel 4 broadcast of 1986 Tour de France, Stage 17, posted by "Matteomjb," January 18, 2016, https://www.youtube.com/watch?v=f0YDIb9Ts04, accessed May 23, 2017.
26. Samuel Abt, "LeMond Surges into Lead in Alps Stage," *New York Times*, July 21, 1986.
27. Abt, "LeMond Surges."
28. Dower, "Badger."
29. Kimmage, "The Natural."
30. Jered Gruber, "LeMond's 21 Turns," *Peloton*, undated, http://pelotonmagazine.com/travel-culture/lemonds-21-turns/.
31. Dower, "Badger."
32. Michael Dobbs, "Sacrebleu! An American Leads in Bicycling's Tour," *Washington Post*, July 22, 1986.
33. Moore, *Badger*, 252.
34. Dower, "Badger."
35. Kimmage, "The Natural."
36. Le Guilloux interview.
37. "1986 Tour de France Stage 20 Part 2," YouTube video of CBS television coverage of 1986 Tour, Stage 20, posted by "yesroh," August 2, 2011, https://www.youtube.com/watch?v=rwT_bprdW6M, accessed May 23, 2017.
38. Dower, "Badger."
39. Gifford, "LeMond vs. World."

Twenty Minutes

1. "A Cheering Crowd, Estimated at 10,000 People, Lined the . . ." United Press International, Aug. 8, 1986.
2. Angus Phillips, "LeMond: Road is Unending," *Washington Post*, September 5, 1986.
3. Jeff Sanchez, author interview, January 31, 2016.
4. Sanchez interview, January 31, 2016.

5. Abt, *LeMond*, 116.
6. Author interview with source who shared this conversation on condition of anonymity, 2016.
7. Quoted material from the shooting through LeMond's arrival at the hospital comes from Abt's *LeMond* book and from an October 10, 2017, author interview with LeMond.
8. In an author interview on October 10, 2017, LeMond recalled this conversation taking place at the ranch. In Abt's *LeMond* book, it occurs later, at the hospital.
9. Leonard Witt, "Countdown to Victory," *Star Tribune*, June 25, 1989.
10. "Greg LeMond, Pro Cyclist," *Fearless*, Outdoor Life Network, season 1, episode 3, aired October 12, 2004.
11. Kathy LeMond interview, August 13, 2016.
12. Kathy LeMond interview, August 13, 2016.
13. Abt, *LeMond*, 114.
14. "Cyclist LeMond Stable After Hunting Accident," *Washington Post*, April 21, 1987.
15. Jeff Sanchez, author interview, January 20, 2016.
16. Mary Morris, author interview, August 14, 2016.
17. Abt, *LeMond*, 115.
18. Mary Morris interview.
19. Mary Morris interview.
20. Mary Morris interview.
21. "LeMond Leaves Hospital," United Press International, April 27, 1987.
22. "Lemond Leaves," UPI.
23. Sacia Morris, author interview, August 14, 2016.
24. David Walsh, "LeMond's Bid to Be the Best," *Bicycling*, August 1987.
25. Rich Carlson, "After the Shooting," *Winning: Bicycle Racing Illustrated*, July 1987.
26. Dr. Sandra Beal, author interview, January 27, 2017.
27. Sacia Morris interview.
28. Sacia Morris interview.
29. Robert Zeller, "Hunting Mishap Takes Toll: LeMond's Future Shot Full of Holes," *Globe and Mail* (Toronto), June 13, 1987.
30. Phil Hersh, "LeMond feels '100 Percent,' Accelerates Comeback," *Chicago Tribune*, June 23, 1987.
31. Samuel Abt, "LeMond Starts on Road to '88," *New York Times*, October 14, 1987.
32. Fignon, *Carefree*, 164.
33. Fignon, *Carefree*, 166.
34. Fignon, *Carefree*, 168.
35. Alain Gallopin, author interview, September 19, 2016.
36. Fignon, *Carefree*, 171.
37. Fignon, *Carefree*, 175.
38. Fignon, *Carefree*, 178.
39. Fignon, *Carefree*, 180–81.
40. Fignon, *Carefree*, 181.
41. Greg LeMond interview, April 23, 2016.
42. "Tour de France Champion Greg LeMond, Whose 1987 Season . . ." United Press International, July 22, 1987.

43. Jeff Sanchez, author interview, August 31, 2016.
44. Sanchez interview, August 31, 2016.

The Comeback

1. Greg LeMond interview, April 23, 2016.
2. Andrew Washburn, "Repeating: Greg LeMond Back on His Bike after Shooting," Associated Press, October 3, 1987.
3. Greg LeMond interview, April 23, 2016.
4. Washburn, "Repeating."
5. Otto Jácome, author interview, September 20, 2016.
6. Tim Blumenthal, "All the Right Moves," *Winning: Bicycle Racing Illustrated,* June 1988.
7. Fignon, *Carefree,* 182–83.
8. Gallopin interview, September 19, 2016.
9. Jef Vertommen, "A Frenchman's Resurrection," *Winning: Bicycle Racing Illustrated,* June 1988.
10. Fignon, *Carefree,* 185.
11. Fignon, *Carefree,* 188.
12. Fignon, *Carefree,* 189–90.
13. Fignon, *Carefree,* 195.
14. "Report: Seven out of Eight PDM Riders Doped at 1988 Tour de France," *Cycling News,* January 23, 2013.
15. Jácome interview, September 20, 2016.
16. Phil Hersh, "LeMond Making a Healthy Comeback in Cycling," *Chicago Tribune,* April 6, 1989.
17. This passage is based on several sources, including Richard Moore's book *Étape: 20 Great Stages from the Modern Tour de France* (Boulder, Colorado: VeloPress, 2014), which, on p. 298, quotes Greg LeMond as saying, "My dad was driving me crazy and I wanted to end it, but I didn't know how to tell him."
18. Kimmage, "Agony."
19. Abt, *LeMond,* 159.
20. Jácome interview, September 20, 2016.
21. Fignon, *Carefree,* 204.
22. Fignon, *Carefree,* 206.
23. This conversation is taken from the Kimmage "Agony" article.
24. Jácome interview, September 20, 2016.
25. Fignon, *Carefree,* 208.
26. Fignon, *Carefree,* 209.

The Battle

1. David Walsh, "LeMond's Bid."
2. David Walsh, "A Tour of Honor," *Bicycling,* July 1989.
3. Greg LeMond and Daniel Friebe, "The Greatest Tour of All," Part 2, *BikeRadar* blog, August 2, 2009, http://www.bikeradar.com/us/blog/article/part-2-the-greatest-tour-of-all-by-greg-lemond-22650/, accessed September 4, 2017.

4. Fignon, *Carefree*, 5–6.
5. Fignon, *Carefree*, 226.
6. Gallopin interview, September 19, 2016.
7. Fignon, *Carefree*, 6.
8. Johan Lammerts, author interview, October 25, 2016.
9. Samuel Abt, "Cycling; LeMond Faces a Major Test," *New York Times*, July 6, 1989.
10. Roger Legeay, author interview, November 23, 2016.
11. LeMond and Friebe, "Greatest," Part 2.
12. Abt, *LeMond*, 176.
13. John Wilcockson, "LeMond Finds an Answer to His Critics," *Times* (London), July 7, 1989.
14. Wilcockson, "Answer."
15. Fignon, *Carefree*, 8.
16. "LeMond Keeps Lead in Tour," *New York Times*, July 11, 1989.
17. E. M. Swift, "Le Grand LeMond," *Sports Illustrated*, December 25, 1989.
18. Andy Hampsten, author interview, November 29, 2016.
19. Fignon, *Carefree*, 9.
20. "1989 Tour de France Stage 10," YouTube video of Channel 4 coverage of 1989 Tour de France, Stage 10, posted by "yesroh," September 16, 2011, https://www.youtube.com/watch?v=s90meplN3h0, accessed May 25, 2017.
21. Stephen Bierley, "Millar's Peak of Perfection," *Guardian* (London), July 12, 1989.
22. Franz Lidz, "Vive LeMond!" *Sports Illustrated*, July 31, 1989.
23. Fignon, *Carefree*, 9.
24. A search of news dispatches found no mention of the motorcycle incident until the December 25 Swift article "Le Grand LeMond," which recounted Greg's remonstrance.
25. Swift, "Le Grand."
26. Stephen Roche, "Delgado Is the Man They All Have to Beat," *Irish Times*, July 13, 1989.
27. "1989 Tour de France - Stage 10 to Superbagneres," YouTube video of ABC television coverage of 1989 Tour, Stage 10, posted by "socalrider909," July 1, 2010, https://www.youtube.com/watch?v=sV_3zOlyU30, accessed May 25, 2017.
28. "1989 Tour de France Stage 15," YouTube video of Channel 4 coverage of 1989 Tour de France, Stage 15, posted by "yesroh," September 23, 2011, https://www.youtube.com/watch?v=3XpT6JpkBiI, accessed May 25, 2017.
29. Noel Truyers, "Looking Ahead," *Winning: Bicycle Racing Illustrated*, June 1990.
30. Fignon, *Carefree*, 10.
31. "Uphill Racer: Greg LeMond Uses the Slopes to Stretch His Lead over Fignon in Tour de France," *Los Angeles Times*, July 18, 1989.
32. Samuel Abt, "On a Cruel Climb in the Alps, LeMond Rises to the Challenge," *New York Times*, July 19, 1989.
33. Fignon, *Carefree*, 11.
34. The battle at l'Alpe d'Huez was reconstructed primarily from these sources: Fignon's memoir, Swift's "Le Grand LeMond," an author interview with LeMond teammate Johan Lammerts, and television footage.
35. Abt, *LeMond*, 184.

36. "1989 Tour de France Stage 18," YouTube video of Channel 4 coverage of the 1989 Tour de France, Stage 18, posted by "yesroh," September 26, 2011, https://www .youtube.com/watch?v=CU_FjlXNccE, accessed May 25, 2017.
37. Samuel Abt, "Fignon Widens Lead in Tour," *New York Times*, July 21, 1989.
38. Abt, "Fignon Widens."
39. Abt, *LeMond*, 183.
40. Stephen Bierley, "Fignon Turns the Screw," *Guardian* (London), July 21, 1989.
41. This observation and the ensuing conversation are taken from p. 14 of Fignon's memoir, *Carefree*.
42. Fignon, *Carefree*, 15.

Eight Seconds

1. Fignon, *Carefree*, 15.
2. Barteau interview.
3. Abt, *LeMond*, 187.
4. "Greg LeMond," *Fearless*.
5. Moore, *Étape*, 306.
6. Fignon, *Carefree*, 17.
7. Jácome interview, September 20, 2016.
8. Greg recounted his unease in an interview with ABC television at the finish: "1989 Tour de France Final Time Trial - LONG VERSION - Greg Lemond - Laurent Fignon," ABC broadcast, posted by "socalrider909," January 23, 2011, https://www.youtube.com/watch?v=rWyfb3I17Leg, accessed September 25, 2017.
9. Fignon, *Carefree*, 21.
10. Phil Anderson, author interview, August 26, 2015.
11. Matt Fitzgerald, "Book Excerpt: 'How Bad Do You Want It?'" *VeloNews*, October 7, 2015, http://www.velonews.com/2015/10/news/road/book-excerpt-how-bad -do-you-want-it_387255.
12. Fignon, *Carefree*, 17.
13. Fitzgerald, "'How Bad.'"
14. Except where noted, all quoted material from the final time trial is taken from "My Edited Video," broadcasts of 1989 Tour de France.
15. Fignon, *Carefree*, 18.
16. LeMond recounted this fear to reporters from *Sports Illustrated* and *New York Times*.
17. Abt, *LeMond*, 192.
18. Fignon, *Carefree*, 18.
19. Fignon, *Carefree*, 19.
20. Fignon, *Carefree*, 19.
21. "My Edited Video," ABC and Channel 4 broadcast of 1989 Tour de France, Stage 21.
22. Abt, *LeMond*, 193.
23. Rupert Guinness, "Scant Silver Linings for Fignon," *Winning: Bicycle Racing Illustrated*, October 1989.
24. Fignon, *Carefree*, 19.
25. Abt, *LeMond*, 194.

The Sequel

1. LeMond and Friebe, "Greatest," Part 3.
2. LeMond and Friebe, "Greatest," Part 3.
3. Gallopin interview, January 26, 2016.
4. Valérie Fignon, *Laurent* (Paris: Grasset, 2013), Kindle edition.
5. Greg LeMond, author interview, August 13, 2016.
6. "1989 World Championship Road Race," YouTube video of ESPN broadcast of 1989 cycling world championships, posted by "yesroh," October 5, 2011, https://www.youtube.com/watch?v=BXSeWVUalBk, accessed May 26, 2017.
7. "1989 World Championship," ESPN broadcast.
8. Abt, *LeMond*, 196.
9. James Raia, "LeMond Eager to Get Rolling," *USA Today*, January 22, 1990.
10. "LeMond Quits Fifth Race of Season," United Press International, March 28, 1990.
11. Stephen Bierley, "Cycling: Tour de France—The Maillot is Yellow, the Men are Lions," *Guardian* (London), June 30, 1990.
12. Samuel Abt, "LeMond Riding on Confidence," *New York Times*, June 30, 1990.
13. Fignon, *Carefree*, 216.
14. Fignon, *Carefree*, 225.
15. Fignon, *Carefree*, 225.
16. Alan Fraser, "France Outraged by Fignon's Surrender," *Independent* (London), July 5, 1990.
17. "Fignon Could Not Have Won Tour—LeMond," *Los Angeles Times*, July 5, 1990.
18. Rich Carlson, "Born to Ride the Tour," *Winning: Bicycling Illustrated*, October 1990.
19. Otto Jácome, author interview, February 8, 2016.
20. Samuel Abt, "LeMond Breaks Free to Close Gap," *New York Times*, July 15, 1990.
21. Carlson, "Born to Ride."
22. John Wilcockson, Phil Liggett, and Rupert Guinness, *The Cycling Year: A Record of the 1990 Cycle Racing Season* (Boulder, Colorado: VeloNewsBooks, 1990), 96.
23. Samuel Abt, "Rallying in the Pyrenees, Team Repays LeMond," *New York Times*, July 19, 1990.
24. Guy Andrews, *Greg LeMond: Yellow Jersey Racer* (Boulder, Colorado: VeloPress, 2016), 254.

The Decline

1. "LeMond: Gone Surfin'," *Cycling Weekly*, March 2, 1991.
2. Phil Hersh, "Tour of Italy Paved with Troubles for LeMond," *Chicago Tribune*, June 7, 1991.
3. Matt Walsh, "A Meeting of Minds," *Cycle Sport* (date unknown, posted June 2012 to http://www.calfeedesign.com/wp-content/uploads/2012/06/Cycle-Sport-Feature-Calfee-Design-and-Greg-Lemond.pdf, accessed September 4, 2017).
4. Debbie Becker, "LeMond: Let the Good Times Roll," *USA Today*, July 2, 1991.
5. Sandra Bailey, "Is LeMond Still the One to Watch? Oui!" *Washington Post*, July 6, 1991.

6. LeMond made little or no mention of Induráin in dozens of interviews around this time.

7. Recounting the stage in the *New York Times*, Samuel Abt wrote that the entire lead group of cyclists "knew they were in the battle that would probably decide the entire race." ("LeMond Falters, Dropping to 5th: Induráin in Lead of Tour," July 20, 1991.)

8. "tour de france 1991 channel 4 stage 13," YouTube video of Channel 4 broadcast of 1991 Tour de France, Stage 13, posted by "crazzyhourse," March 29, 2012, https://www.youtube.com/watch?v=yvhNDNDuj88, accessed May 26, 2017.

9. Elliott Almond, "LeMond Falls Back to Fifth," *Los Angeles Times*, July 20, 1991.

10. Sandra Bailey, "LeMond Is Poised to Climb," *Washington Post*, July 23, 1991; Samuel Abt, "A Fine Day for Argentin of Italy," *New York Times*, July 22, 1991. In author interviews, Bob and Greg LeMond denied employing a 900 number.

11. Samuel Abt, "Cycling; As Leader Climbs Well, LeMond Loses Hope," *New York Times*, July 24, 1991.

12. Frank Lawlor, "LeMond Runs Out of Hope," *Philadelphia Inquirer*, July 25, 1991.

13. Steven G. Brunner, "LeMond: Too Little, Too Late," *Los Angeles Times*, July 26, 1991.

14. Sandra Bailey, "For LeMond, Tour Has Come Full Cycle," *Washington Post*, July 28, 1991.

15. Phil Hersh, "LeMond Hoping to Take Another Tour," *Chicago Tribune*, July 2, 1992.

16. Alain Gallopin, author interview, January 5, 2017.

17. Fignon, *Carefree*, 227.

18. Fignon, *Carefree*, 229.

19. Fignon, *Carefree*, 230.

20. Fignon, *Carefree*, 236.

21. Frank Litsky, "These Days, Fignon Is Simply Charming," *New York Times*, May 14, 1992.

22 Debbie Becker, "LeMond Exhausting Chances," *USA Today*, July 17, 1992.

23. Steven G. Brunner, "LeMond Can't Explain Bad Day," *Los Angeles Times*, July 19, 1992.

24. Brunner, "Bad Day."

25. Steven G. Brunner, "LeMond Exits Tour as Hampsten Soars," *Austin American-Statesman*, July 20, 1992.

26. Alexander Wolff, "Basking in Glory," *Sports Illustrated*, August 3, 1992.

27. Elliott Almond, "Not Done at 31: LeMond Might Be Tired, but That Doesn't Mean He's Quitting," *Los Angeles Times*, August 29, 1992.

28. Kimmage, "Agony."

29. Fignon, *Carefree*, 254.

30. Fignon, *Carefree*, 253.

31. Fignon, *Carefree*, 252.

32. Paul Kimmage, "She Knows—This Is What Death Sounds Like," *Irish Independent*, August 24, 2014, http://www.independent.ie/sport/other-sports/cycling/paul-kimmage-she-knows-this-is-what-death-sounds-like-30531503.html.

33. "Schlamm in den Adern," *Der Spiegel*, June 10, 1991.

34. Randy Harvey, "Drug Use Said to Concern LeMond: Attorney Claims Dutch Team Wanted Cyclist to Try Testosterone," *Los Angeles Times*, July 25, 1989.

35. In 2007, Kathy LeMond told journalist Paul Kimmage, "I think Greg was carrying such a load of shame that . . . he couldn't have survived a positive drug test."
36. Scott Martin, "The Lowdown on LeMond," *Bicycling*, June 1993.
37. Martin, "Lowdown."
38. Craig Calfee, author interview, November 15, 2016.
39. Matt Walsh, "Meeting of Minds."
40. This exchange was recounted by Calfee. Bob LeMond said he did not recall it.
41. Calfee interview.
42. Jean-Pierre Pascal, author interview, November 16, 2016.
43. Bob LeMond, author interview, May 12, 2017.
44. Bob LeMond interview, May 12, 2017.
45. Greg LeMond interview, October 10, 2017.
46. Samuel Abt, "LeMond's Slow Climb toward the Tour de France," *New York Times*, April 12, 1993.
47. Alex Holmes (dir.), *Stop at Nothing: The Lance Armstrong Story*, ABC Commercial, Passion Pictures, 2014.
48. Greg LeMond, interview by Bob Babbitt and Paul Huddle, *The Competitors Radio Show*, podcast, August 1, 2006.
49. LeMond told this story many times, though details varied from one telling to the next. LeMond said he deeply admired Legeay for his stance. Legeay, in an interview for this book, said he did not recall taking it.
50. Kimmage, "Cycle."
51. Fignon, *Carefree*, 257.
52. Fignon, *Carefree*, 258.
53. Fignon, *Carefree*, 259.
54. Alexander Wolff and Richard O'Brien, "Scorecard," *Sports Illustrated*, December 12, 1994.
55. Nolan Zavoral, "Full Cycle," *Star Tribune*, December 4, 1994.
56. Geoff Drake, "Goodbye, Greg: America's Greatest Cyclist Ends a Stunning Career," *Bicycling*, February 1995.

The Texan

1. The LeMonds recounted this conversation in Reed Albergotti's and Vanessa O'Connell's book *Wheelmen: Lance Armstrong, the Tour de France, and the Greatest Sports Conspiracy Ever* (New York: Dutton, 2013), pp. 68–69, and in a 2012 interview with Irish broadcaster Pat Kenny on the Raidió Teilifís Éireann network.
2. Phil Hersh, "American Cycling Champion Has the World at His Feat," *Chicago Tribune*, September 5, 1993.
3. Frank Litsky, "Cycling; Armstrong May Not Win, but Watch This Space," *New York Times*, May 13, 1991.
4. Abt, *Season in Turmoil*, 60.
5. The Albergotti and O'Connell book *Wheelmen* posits Lance as sole author of this negotiation. However, Juliet Macur, in her book *Cycle of Lies: The Fall of Lance Armstrong* (New York: Harper, 2014), suggests "several riders" on his team devised the plan.

6. Macur, *Cycle of Lies*, 45.

7. This alleged episode has been recounted in dozens of books and articles, with the payoff generally valued at $100,000. The lower figure here is based on historic exchange rates.

8. Holmes, *Stop at Nothing*.

9. Lance Armstrong with Sally Jenkins, *It's Not about the Bike: My Journey Back to Life* (New York: G. P. Putnam's Sons, 2000), 62.

10. Hersh, "Feat."

11. Hersh, "Feat."

12. Macur, *Cycle of Lies*, 77.

13. David Walsh, *From Lance to Landis: Inside the American Doping Conspiracy at the Tour de France* (New York: Ballantine Books, 2007), 52.

14. Samuel Abt, "LeMond Considers Drug Issue a Wake-Up Call," *International Herald Tribune*, July 30, 1998.

15. The conversation is taken from Albergotti and O'Connell, *Wheelmen*, 103; LeMond confirmed it in an author interview on October 10, 2017. Weisel's response is from an author interview on September 7, 2017.

16. Greg LeMond interview, October 10, 2017.

17. Albergotti and O'Connell, *Wheelmen*, 89.

18. Greg LeMond interview, October 10, 2017.

19. Greg LeMond interview, October 10, 2017.

20. Albergotti and O'Connell, *Wheelmen*, 116.

21. "Lance Armstrong Sestriere 1999," Outdoor Life Network coverage, posted by "Epic Cycling," April 23, 2016, https://www.youtube.com/watch?v=B6hM9ejMiAk, accessed September 25, 2017.

22. Holmes, *Stop at Nothing*.

23. Samuel Abt, "Cycling; Questions on Doping Shadow Armstrong," *New York Times*, July 16, 1999. As evidence of a smear campaign against Lance, the *Times* story offered a single, ambiguous headline translated from a Belgian newspaper: "Armstrong Puts a Bomb under the Tour."

24. Andrew Longmore, "Cycling: Interview – Greg LeMond: Defender of the Clean Machine," *Independent on Sunday* (London), July 18, 1999.

25. Robin Nicholl, "Cycling: Tour de France—Armstrong Versus Le Monde," *Independent on Sunday* (London), July 25, 1999.

26. David Walsh, *Lance to Landis*, 134.

27. Armstrong and Jenkins, *Bike*, 239.

28. Michael Hall, "Lance Armstrong Has Something to Get Off His Chest," *Texas Monthly*, July 2001.

29. Kathy LeMond deposition, October 20, 2005, Lance Armstrong and Tailwind Sports, Inc. v. SCA Promotions, Inc. and Hamman Insurance Services, Inc., arbitration proceeding, 298th District Court, Dallas County, Texas.

30. "IOC: Actovegin Covered by Blood Doping Ban," December 14, 2000, Cyclingnews.com, http://autobus.cyclingnews.com/results/2000/dec00/dec14news.shtml.

31. For a more thorough account of Greg's change of mind, see the chapters "LeMond Feels the Heat" in David Walsh, *Lance to Landis*, and "Hematocrits and Hypocrites" in Albergotti and O'Connell, *Wheelmen*.

32. Sal Ruibal, "LeMond: Time to 'Come Clean,'" *USA Today*, November 17, 2000.
33. Michael Specter, "The Long Ride," *New Yorker*, July 15, 2002.
34. Hall, "Chest."
35. Hall, "Chest."
36. In defense of the "lighter Lance" theory, Coyle notes that most of his weight data were collected in the off-season and did not reflect the pounds Lance shed before the start of each Tour.
37. Samuel Abt, "An American without Tears Tweaks the Tour," *New York Times*, July 31, 2001.
38. Samuel Abt, "Cycling; Suggestions of Doping Still Dog Armstrong," *New York Times*, July 9, 2001.
39. Samuel Abt, "Accused, Armstrong Defends His Honor," *New York Times*, July 16, 2001.
40. Kathy LeMond deposition.
41. Albergotti and O'Connell, *Wheelmen*, 144.
42. David Walsh, "Paradise Lost on Tour," *Sunday Times* (London), July 29, 2001.
43. The quoted conversation appeared in David Walsh's *Lance to Landis* book. Paraphrased material comes from that source and others, including the *Stop at Nothing* documentary. Armstrong portrayed the call very differently. He denied threatening LeMond; indeed, he said it was he who endured verbal abuse from the Minnesotan, who was inebriated.

The Feud

1. Weisel said in an interview that did he not remember making the call.
2. Don Cronin, "LeMond Backs off Armstrong Quotes," *USA Today*, August 15, 2001.
3. Kimmage, "Cycle."
4. Kimmage, "Cycle."
5. Kimmage, "Cycle."
6. Bill Gifford, "Greg LeMond vs. The World," *Men's Journal*, July 2008.
7. Tom Haines, "French Tour Fans Cry: Vive la Lance!" *Boston Globe*, July 29, 2002.
8. "Lance Armstrong Nike Commercial," YouTube video of Nike television commercial featuring Lance Armstrong, posted by "jchau," December 9, 2005, https://www.youtube.com/watch?v=MIl5RxhLZ5U, accessed June 12, 2017.
9. Sal Ruibal, "Doping Stealing Tour Spotlight," *USA Today*, July 2, 2004.
10. William Fotheringham, "Armstrong Wars with LeMond and LeMonde," *Guardian* (London), July 16, 2004.
11. Kirk Bohls, "Lance Sticks to His Guns: No Needle in the Haystack," *Austin American-Statesman*, July 16, 2004.
12. Holmes, *Stop at Nothing*.
13. Andy Hampsten, "Open Letter from Andy Hampsten," *VeloNews*, July 24, 2004, shared by its author via e-mail message on December 14, 2016.
14. "Lance Armstrong Paris," YouTube video of 2005 Tour de France, podium presentation, posted by "silversea9," February 10, 2011, https://www.youtube.com/watch?v=cNfV4XxKXrA, accessed June 13, 2017.
15. David Walsh, *Lance to Landis*, 235.

16. Samuel Abt, "Armstrong Fends off New Drug Accusations," *New York Times*, August 23, 2005.

17. T. J. Quinn, "Getting Picky on Lance," *New York Daily News*, July 31, 2005.

18. David Walsh, *Lance to Landis*, 266.

19. Juliet Macur, "Tour Champ Is Suspended after Testing Positive," *New York Times*, July 28, 2006.

20. Greg LeMond recounted this conversation in the Kimmage "Cycle of Abuse" interview.

21. Mark Zeigler, "A Bizarre Turn," *San Diego Union-Tribune*, May 18, 2007.

22. Juliet Macur, "Armstrong Defends Himself as Official Raises Questions," *New York Times*, September 14, 2006.

23. Macur, "Questions."

24. Juliet Macur, "Armstrong Not among Those Praising Cyclist Who Used EPO," *New York Times*, September 13, 2006.

25. Greg LeMond recounted this conversation in the Kimmage "Cycle of Abuse" article.

26. Gifford, "LeMond vs. World."

27. Greg LeMond interview, October 10, 2017.

28. Steve Frothingham, "Trek Announces an End to Deal with Greg LeMond," *VeloNews*, April 8, 2008, http://www.velonews.com/2008/04/news/trek -announces-an-end-to-deal-with-greg-lemond_74387.

29. Nathaniel Vinton, "The Tour de Feud," *New York Daily News*, May 4, 2008.

30. Megan Tompkins, "LeMond Dealers Unfazed by Trek Lawsuit," *Bicycle Retailer and Industry News*, May 1, 2008.

31. "'Driven' Nike / Lance Armstrong Commercial :60," YouTube video of Nike television commercial featuring Lance Armstrong, posted by Grant Owens, July 2, 2009, https://www.youtube.com/watch?v=Gw1ExWtx5tc, accessed June 13, 2017.

32. "Former Tour de France Victor Fignon has Cancer," *USA Today*, June 12, 2009.

The Last Breath

1. Samuel Abt, "Fignon: French Cycling's Angry Young Man Coasts to the End of His Bumpy Road," Samuel Abt, *The New York Times*, September 29, 1993.

2. Fignon, *Carefree*, 263.

3. Gallopin interview, January 5, 2017.

4. Fignon, *Carefree*, 264.

5. Valérie Fignon, *Laurent*, 187.

6. Valérie Fignon, *Laurent*, 21.

7. Valérie Fignon, *Laurent*, 31.

8. Edward Pickering, "Laurent Fignon: My Way or the Fairway," *Cycling Weekly*, August 31, 2010, http://www.cyclingweekly.com/news/latest-news/laurent -fignon-my-way-or-the-fairway-57955.

9. Valérie Fignon, *Laurent*, 31.

10. Greg LeMond interview, October 10, 2017.

11. Valérie Fignon, *Laurent*, 40.

12. Valérie Fignon, *Laurent*, 49.

13. Fignon, *Carefree*, 282.
14. Nathalie de Barallon, e-mail message to author, September 20, 2017.
15. Daniel Simms, "Laurent Fignon Treated for 'Advanced' Cancer," *Cycling News*, http://www.cyclingnews.com/news/laurent-fignon-treated-for-advanced-cancer/.
16. Valérie Fignon, *Laurent*, 70.
17. Valérie Fignon, *Laurent*, 115.
18. "Notre ami Fignon craque en Direct," YouTube video of France 2 television coverage of the 2009 Tour de France, Stage 21, posted by Patrick Pagnier, July 28, 2009, https://www.youtube.com/watch?v=B5j7NV2hPCE, accessed June 13, 2017.
19. Valérie Fignon, *Laurent*, 260.
20. Valérie Fignon, *Laurent*, 145.
21. Valérie Fignon, *Laurent*, 174.
22. Jean-François Quenet, "The Legacy of Laurent Fignon," *Ride Cycling Review*, June 24, 2011, http://www.ridemedia.com.au/past-issue/the-legacy-of-laurent-fignon-ride-50/.
23. Valérie Fignon, *Laurent*, 207.
24. Valérie Fignon, *Laurent*, 237.
25. Lance Armstrong [@lancearmstrong], Twitter post, August 31, 2010, 7:05 a.m., https://twitter.com/lancearmstrong/status/22618786611, accessed September 4, 2017.
26. Stephen Farrand, "LeMond Remembers Fignon," *Cyclingnews.com*, http://www.cyclingnews.com/news/lemond-remembers-fignon/.

Amends

1. Bonnie D. Ford, "Landis Admits Doping, Accuses Lance," *ESPN.com*, May 19, 2010, updated May 21, http://www.espn.com/olympics/cycling/news/story?id=5203604.
2. Juliet Macur and Michael S. Schmidt, "Landis Admits Doping, Accuses Top U.S. Cyclists," *New York Times*, May 21, 2010.
3. Ford, "Landis Admits Doping."
4. Nathaniel Vinton, "LeMond Races to Landis' Defense," *New York Daily News*, May 21, 2010.
5. Juliet Macur, "Armstrong Foe Subpoenaed in Cycling Probe," *New York Times*, July 16, 2010.
6. Juliet Macur, "Recording May Play Role in Armstrong Inquiry," *New York Times*, September 16, 2010.
7. Brendan Gallagher, "Tour de France 2010: Lance Armstrong Ready to Co-operate over Doping Fraud Allegations," *Telegraph* (London), July 15, 2010.
8. Both LeMond's quote and Armstrong's are from Sal Ruibal, "Hills Get Steeper, Words Get Harsher," *USA Today*, July 19, 2010.
9. Eddie Pells, "'60 Minutes' Report: Armstrong Encouraged Doping," *USA Today*, May 23, 2011.
10. "Verbruggen Says Armstrong 'Never, Never, Never' Doped," *Cycling News*, May 24, 2011, http://www.cyclingnews.com/news/verbruggen-says-armstrong-never-never-never-doped/.

11. Ian Austen, "Inquiry on Lance Armstrong Ends with No Charges," *New York Times*, February 3, 2012.
12. Christine Brennan, "Armstrong Isn't Passing Smell Test," *USA Today*, May 26, 2011.
13. Matthew Beaudin, "USADA Letter Paints Dark Picture of Armstrong Era," *VeloNews,* June 13, 2012, http://www.velonews.com/2012/06/news/usada-letter-paints-dark-picture-of-armstrong-era_223925.
14. Juliet Macur, "Armstrong Faces New Doping Charges," *New York Times*, June 14, 2012.
15. Juliet Macur, "Armstrong Ends Fight against Doping Charges," *New York Times*, August 24, 2012.
16. David Walsh, "Off Yer Bike!" *Sunday Times* (London), August 26, 2012.
17. "Lance Armstrong Has No Place in Cycling," *Cycling News*, October 22, 2012, http://www.cyclingnews.com/news/mcquaid-lance-armstrong-has-no-place-in-cycling/.
18. Samuel Abt, "Rip Lance Time," *New York Times*, August 27, 2012.
19. Kathy LeMond [@KathyLeMond], Twitter post, January 8, 2013, 4:49 p.m., https://twitter.com/kathylemond/status/288809810265260033, accessed September 4, 2017.
20. "Lance Armstrong & Oprah Winfrey: Interview Transcript," *BBC.com*, January 18, 2013, http://www.bbc.com/sport/cycling/21065539.
21. Greg LeMond, Facebook post, October 25, 2012, https://www.facebook.com/greglemond/posts/10151127372613494, accessed September 4, 2017.
22. Oliver Gill, "Interview: How Greg LeMond Re-Found His Place at the Tour de France," *Road Cycling UK*, July 22, 2016, https://roadcyclinguk.com/racing/interview-greg-lemond-re-found-place-tour-de-france.html.
23. Brent Schrotenboer, "LeMond Slams Lance, Says Actions Criminal," *USA Today*, October 22, 2013.
24. Mark McKinnon, "I Pushed the Lance Armstrong Lie: An Open Letter to Greg LeMond," *Daily Beast*, July 31, 2014, http://www.thedailybeast com/i-pushed-the-lance-armstrong-lie-an-open-letter-to-greg-lemond.
25. Tour de France roundup, Associated Press, July 22, 2015.
26. Tom Cary, "Greg LeMond Criticises UCA over 'Half-Hearted' Mechanical Doping Tests," *Telegraph* (London), July 3, 2016.
27. Figures taken from John Rosengren, "Greg LeMond's Next Ride," *MinnPost*, May 8, 2015, https://www.minnpost.com/twin-cities-business /2015/05/greg-lemonds-next-ride.
28. Mike Blackerby, "LeMond Composites Marks Opening in Oak Ridge," *Knoxville News Sentinel*, October 12, 2016.
29. "Enhancing the Bike," *60 Minutes*, CBS News, broadcast January 29, 2017.
30. "Greg LeMond: Miracles in Cycling Still Don't Exist," *Cycling News*, July 20, 2016, http://www.cyclingnews.com/news/greg-lemond-miracles-in-cycling-still-dont-exist/. Because the quote was translated from French, this author has edited it for clarity.

INDEX